A PROGRAMMING
LOGIC

A PROGRAMMING LOGIC

WITH AN INTRODUCTION
TO THE PL/CV VERIFIER

ROBERT L. CONSTABLE
Cornell University

MICHAEL J. O'DONNELL
Purdue University

CONTRIBUTIONS BY
SCOTT D. JOHNSON

WINTHROP PUBLISHERS, INC.
Cambridge, Massachusetts

189447

LIBRARY OF CONGRESS CATALOGING IN PUBLICATION DATA

Constable, Robert L
  A programming logic.

  Bibliography: p. 370.
  Includes index.
  1. PL/CV (Computer program language) 2. Computer
programs--testing. 3. Logic, Symbolic and mathematical.
I. O'Donnell, Michael J, 1952-   joint author II. Title.
QA76.73.P252C66   001.6'42   78-10650
ISBN 0-87626-726-6

To our families

Cover design by Harold Pattek

CONTENTS

PREFACE

Herein you will find a rigorous logical system in which
to formalize a style of reasoning about computer programs.
The logic is a foundation for understanding programs as
thoroughly as you understand algebraic equations. It is
also a language for communicating arguments to a computer
for mechanical verification.

No compellingly definitive style of reasoning about
programs has yet been presented, but the Floyd-Hoare style
logic of intermixed commands and assertions, which we
formalize here, has already influenced programming in two
important ways. The complexity of proof rules for procedures in the presence of aliasing amongst parameters and
global variables has led to programming styles which eschew
aliasing, and to recent programming languages which forbid
it. And the technique of associating invariants with loops
has been accepted in some circles as the natural informal
way to understand iteration.

This logic has been useful to students who want to understand the mathematical principles that underlie the construction and analysis of programs. Edsger Dijkstra's calculus of programs in *A Discipline of Programming* serves the
same purpose but goes beyond conventional programming languages and treats as well the methodology of programming
(which we do not).

The language used to communicate arguments to the computer is PL/CV. It is a formal logic built on the Cornell
programming language PL/CS. PL/CV is described in detail
in the Appendix. The logic of the main text of the monograph is not specific to any existing programming language,

and is not described in every detail needed for communicating with machines. This allows a certain informality and generality conducive to explaining the principles that apply to a completely formal logic for the core of any modern procedural language such as Algol 60, Algol 68, Pascal, FORTRAN 77 or PL/I. We do not exploit this informality to propose, as Dijkstra does, ideas for a new programming language. We instead concentrate on the novel concepts arising from the formal logic.

By basing PL/CV on the highly reliable PL/C and PL/CS compilers, thoroughly tested in an instructional environment, we can isolate those practical issues specific to our style of programming verification. We chose a PL/I based core language for PL/CV rather than Pascal because we could work closely with the language implementors. The PL/CS subset was formulated at Cornell to meet a variety of educational objectives compatible with ours. Professor Richard Conway, who led the PL/CS design and implementation groups has described the language in his book *A Primer on Disciplined Programming*.

Content of the work

This text presents some of the results of a project begun in 1975 at Cornell University. Our goal was to develop a logic for reasoning about programs which is at once intuitive and formal, and to implement an automatic proof checker for the logic. The logic should have a relation to traditional formal systems analagous to the relation between Algol and Turing Machines. We believe that the resulting logic is sufficient to teach the principles of reasoning to beginning programmers, who may then apply these principles informally in their later work. We also hope that this logic may serve as the basis for mechanically aided verification of practical programs.

We are now writing about a version of the logic, PL/CV2, over a year old in design. It can express succinctly the class of arguments we began to analyze, but it is rather cumbersome in dealing with certain array arguments which the newest versions of the logic will express easily. Nevertheless, the system even as described here

could be used to help guarantee the correctness of extremely critical programs. As more effort is put into the
enrichment of the logic, less effort will be needed for the
proofs of correctness and eventually even moderately critical programs will be verified in the system.

Use of the monograph

To the average reader, this monograph and the logic it
describes will not be valuable because it helps him or her
verify an extremely critical program (most programmers
never even write such programs let alone verify them). But
it will demonstrate exactly what it means to specify a formal logic of programs. As a consequence the reader can
learn formal logic in a context especially interesting to
computer scientists, and he or she can see one way to lay
the foundations for highly sophisticated intelligent computer assistance in the writing and documentation of everyday programs.

We assume that readers will know programming in high
level procedural languages such as Algol, Pascal or PL/I.
We assume acquaintance with mathematical proofs. The monograph is not a leisurely textbook, it is a relatively terse
introduction to the simple parts of a vast and complex new
subject. It could be used as a supplemental book for various computer science and mathematics courses at either intermediate or advanced levels (such as discrete structures,
advanced programming, logic and algorithms, formal logic or
theory of computing).

The monograph can also be used in an advanced course
in program verification. There are a number of new ideas
in it which can be compared to other approaches and ex-
plored further. For example, the programming logic does
not fit the classical pattern of partial or total correctness because commands themselves are treated like statements; the predicate calculus is based on a block structured constructive natural deduction system (arguments are
rapidly checked for correctness by a proof checking algorithm which recognizes certain immediately obvious inferences); number theory is axiomatized with essentially only
three high level rules, etc. The text cites the extensive
bibliography to relate our ideas to others.

ACKNOWLEDGMENTS

The PL/CV logic was implemented with Scott D. Johnson as chief programmer, Tat-Hung Chan doing arithmetic and Dean B. Krafft doing the assertion table. These superb assistants contributed in innumerable other ways to the completion of the verifier and the monograph. Professor Robert (Corky) Cartwright was a valuable consultant in our implementation effort.

Professor Richard Conway and the PL/C group implemented the underlying programming language, PL/CS. Jim Donahue contributed valuably to discussions with the PL/C group. Professor Conway also provided us with encouragement and resources as well as very friendly reception for our work at Winthrop Publishers.

We received valuable criticism of early drafts of this monograph from Ed Clarke, Carol and John Constable, Steve Fortune, David Gries, Carl Hauser, Niel Immerman, Gary Levin, and John Privitera.

The staff of the Computer Science Department at Cornell, Diane Duke, Linda Rask and Debbie Ray helped move the manuscript along for over a year of typing. Debi Fields typed the first draft and Marie Olton typed the final copy (with Amanda on her lap at the end). The staff at Winthrop Publishers, especially Deborah Lott, aided this effort considerably, and Mike Meehan made all our dealings with Winthrop a pleasure.

The research for PL/CV was supported in part by the National Science Foundation research grants DCR-74-14701, MCS-76-14293, MCS-77-08198, and MCS-76-22360.

Ithaca, New York   Robert L. Constable
Lafayette, Indiana   Michael J. O'Donnell

May 1978

1

INTRODUCTION

General context

There is a certain satisfaction in computing because progress is so visible. In 1978 we can compute a thousand times faster than we could in 1968, and we do it with smaller and cheaper equipment. Today programming languages are sophisticated mathematical systems that allow the user to define his own data types and process them recursively in parallel. We can solve problems with algorithms which are asymptotically better than any known before. We plan to build systems requiring years of programming resulting in million line programs processing billions of bits of data. These are significant intellectual and engineering achievements.

This visible progress depends on an invisible current of theoretical knowledge which determines its course. As the tangible products of computer science become more complex and more vital, the need for the intangible results of theory to control the course of progress becomes more important. These needs have in fact been discussed since the beginning of computer development (see [Goldstine and von Neuman 48, McCarthy 63]). They have been continually important in computing theory (see [Kleene 52, Turing 39, deBakker and Scott 69, Manna 74]). But the computing community has only recently become aware of the practical and immediate need for new approaches to understanding, controlling and guaranteeing the behavior of large computing systems. Such articulate spokesmen as E. Dijkstra and C.A.R. Hoare are largely responsible for the clarity of the current situation and for the focus of recent theoretical work (see [Dahl, Dijkstra, Hoare 72, Dijkstra 76]).

We are now well aware that the first step toward controlling complex computation is to describe them in terms that *people* can clearly understand. In general, the more we need to be certain about our ideas, the more completely and clearly we explain them to others, the more we seek a listener skeptical of our arguments. A programmer may be tempted to think that by writing a program he has carefully explained his ideas to himself and to the computer, and therefore when the computer answers as he expects, he concludes it has agreed to the argument. But the computer with its language processor is not a reliable critic. It does not understand programs; it executes them. Therefore if we expect to guarantee the performance of algorithms, we must write them so that people comprehend them.

To learn to understand programs, we need a language in which to talk about them. In designing this language we must decide what notations are convenient, exactly what these notations mean, and how to reason correctly and compellingly within the language. These three decisions form the traditional parts of logic: syntax, semantics, and proof theory. The resulting language should be natural and intuitive, since it is intended for human comprehension. But we would also like the language and its proof techniques to be entirely formal, so that we may study it mathematically and process it automatically. Only automatic processing will allow humans to cope with the numerous repetitions and boring details that occur in reasoning about programs.

The problem of designing and processing languages that are at once intuitive and formal has been faced before, in the designing and interpreting (or compiling) of programming languages. The present task of producing a language for reasoning about programs is very similar in flavor, if not in detail, to the more traditional task of producing programming languages.

The development of higher level programming languages entailed clear economic gain with respect to programmer productivity and reliability. It is entirely possible that significant gains of this type will follow from the design of formalisms for reasoning about programs. Regardless of economic incentive, the intellectual challenge of the problem is significant. Mathematicians, logicians and computer scientists have long pondered the relationship between programs and proofs. In studying how to formalize reasoning about programs, there may be discoveries about this relationship which have an impact on pure mathematics and logic, especially on its constructive aspects. These discoveries will surely also have an impact on our view of the programming process and on our methods of teaching programming.

Central issues

Given the importance of the problem of understanding complex computations and given our commitment to investigating it, what are the central questions and issues? Consider first the conceptual questions of how to prove statements about programs. The concept of mathematical proof has evolved over the centuries, advancing from ancient principles of rhetoric to the twentieth century's formal proofs, but there is no general consensus of what kinds of proof are appropriate to programming. Should proofs be expressed in the programming language itself so that a program is also a proof, or should the program be translated into a conventional mathematical language? Should the proof be presented separately from the program or written directly into the program text? Should proofs be checked by machine or are they to be certified by humans? Will programming proofs be a minor variant of some existing form of proof or will they involve some bold new idea?

On the engineering side of the problem of program analysis we are faced with another set of questions. Will it be possible for a mechanical theorem prover to provide a proof of program correctness when given the program and certain assertions about it? Should we expect the programmer to supply most of the proof and have it checked by machine? Can we develop useful programming languages in which the programs act as proofs? We explore the consequences of one set of plausible answers to those questions.

Goals and contributions

In this monograph, we concentrate on one aspect of describing programs, namely a formalism for proving program correctness. Our main characters are *asserted programs*. These are programs containing assertions about intermediate states in a computation. The assertions and commands together may be used to prove that the program satisfies a certain input-output specification. We take the liberty of calling the set of well-formed asserted programs a *programming language*, and we use the word program to refer to asserted programs as well as programs in the usual sense. The language of programs without assertions is called the *command language*.

The programming language is only one part of a more general language of programs in which it is possible to describe the process of program development, to relate different programs and to reason about program properties which cannot be described by input-output specifications. However, the programming language of this monograph is adequate for the special reasoning involved in the verification of a large number of programs, especially the type commonly treated in the literature.

The design of our programming language was determined by a few simple criteria which we discuss here. The command language was taken to be the core of a standard Algol-like procedural language. It is adequate for elementary programming instruction, yet it uses only commands for which simple forms of reasoning can be found (see [Hoare, Wirth 73]).

The implemented system takes as its command language a disciplined subset of PL/C, called PL/CV. This language is described in detail in [Conway, Constable 76, Constable, Donahue 75, Conway, 78]. However, a similar subset of Algol 60, Pascal, or Algol 68 would serve just as well. In this report, we use an Algol 68-like syntax to write the commands. In the Appendix the PL/CV version is given in detail.

The deductive part of the programming language is based on the first order predicate calculus, the basic formal language of mathematical logic. Most formal systems of proof found in logic texts are designed for ease of expressing and proving metatheorems about their soundness, completeness, and deductive power. Just as in computing theory textbooks most formal models of computation, such as Turing machines, are chosen for their ease in expressing metatheorems about computability, enumerability and unsolvability. This is usually achieved at the expense of readability, writability and understandability of formal proofs and formal algorithms. Our goal here is to present a rigorous and sound formal system, sufficient for proving important properties of textbook programs, which is as readable, writable and understandable as possible. This system should be to ordinary formal proofs as Algol is to Turing machines. Several characteristics of the new system follow directly from this goal.

Since programs are often long and highly structured, a

proof concerning a program P should contain exactly one copy
of P. To minimize eye travel and page turning, additional
text should appear with the program in the position at which
it is most relevant. We choose, therefore, to write proofs
as asserted programs.

New notation adds to difficulties in comprehension.
So our assertions are expressed in the familiar first order
predicate calculus instead of in the relational calculus of
[deBakker, Scott 69, Park 69, deBakker, deRoever 73].
Moreover, we avoid a special notation such as Hoare's primitive $\{P\}A\{Q\}$ [Hoare 69] preferring the more common notion of
asserting a formula P in the context of an argument which
may involve commands. New objects, such as a special element, say $\bot$, to denote an undefined value (as in [Scott 70,
Milner 72]) may also increase confusion for a naive user.
So we give a semantics based only on traditional domains
such as integers and strings and the total functions on
these domains or subsets of them.

A formal system is most understandable when it closely
mimics informal methods. We adapt the Natural Deduction
System (for the predicate calculus) from [Gentzen 35,
Prawitz 65] with a new presentation of number and string
theory for arguments not involving executable statements.
For executable statements, we imitate the naive reasoning
used by many beginning programmers, who run a finger along
the program text and describe the state of the computation
at each point. This imitation produces proof rules similar
to those of [Floyd 67, Hoare 69, 71, Hoare, Wirth 73].

Since computations are usually considered worthless unless they terminate, we abandon the partial correctness notion of Floyd and Hoare, who assume termination but never
prove it. Instead, the appearance of an executable statement in a proof entails an assertion that the statement
halts. So executable statements, as well as predicate calculus assertions, must be justified by proof rules. When
necessary, the partial correctness notion may be recaptured
by making additional assumptions. We succeed by this approach in treating recursive functions, which were never
handled satisfactorily in terms of partial correctness.

The formal system sketched above is simple enough to be
used by undergraduates, yet rich enough to be a vehicle for
studying many of the interesting questions concerning computational reasoning. Hopefully, it may also enlighten the
problem of designing powerful yet understandable programming

languages by clarifying the ways in which we think about such languages.

The (asserted) programming language presented here is only a beginning. The present rules of inference are very simple, so they are easy to understand and well suited for instructing new programmers. In this regard they are similar to the instruction sets of early languages such as FORTRAN. We envision adding numerous sophisticated rules to make the language more concise. However, we do not imagine a general purpose theorem prover as part of the system, either in its abstract form or its implemented form. We feel that a general theorem prover decreases the intelligibility of the logic and lessens our control over the structure of the asserted program.[†] One of the main methodological tenets of our system, and one of its important novelties, is that a program and a proof of its correctness are developed and presented together. The assertions relate the commands and the commands add constructive expressiveness to the assertions.[††] The proof text serves as mechanically checkable documentation for the program. This relationship would be obscured by a general theorem prover.

We hope that the implemented system will be a valuable tool in experiments both with the utility of these new languages of asserted programs and with their value in programming instruction (as well as in general instruction on the mathematical aspects of programming.) Perhaps such a system will also be interesting to logicians because it allows a great deal of expressiveness beyond usual first order predicate calculi.

Outline

Chapter II presents a novel treatment of the predicate

[†] It should be noted that the very high level proof rules we envision for the system bring us quite close to the use of theorem provers restricted to quantifier free formulas as in [Wegbreit 76].

[††] This implies in particular that unlike the system of [Igarashi, London, Luckham 75] we do not translate command text into traditional mathematical language.

calculus in which arguments rather than formulas are the main syntactic objects. Arguments correspond rather closely to programs, this is particularly true of the constructive block structured arguments we feature. The (classical) semantics given to arguments extends very smoothly to programs. This chapter is self-contained. An excellent advanced treatment of the subject is [Prawitz 65], a good elementary treatment is [Anderson, Johnstone 62]. The most relevant related research appears in [de Bruijn 70, Weyhrauch 77]. An account of PL/CV automatic inference occurs in [Krafft 78].

Chapter III presents axiomatic number·theory building upon ring axioms and induction to formulate three high level rules. We treat constructive proofs explicitly to exhibit the computational content of number theory. The closest account in the literature is [Kleene 52]. A detailed account of the implementation of PL/CV arithmetic appears in [Chan 78]. This chapter also presents a tentative attempt to organize PL/I string theory. The only relevant literature we know of is [Corcoran, Frank, Maloney 74].

Chapter IV is the heart of the monograph. In it we extend the logic to include arguments with commands. First assignment and conditionals are added and analyzed, then iteration and finally gotos. The positional semantics of Chapter II is extended to give a completely mathematical semantics for programs. It should be compared with the denotational semantics of Scott and Strachey (see [Stoy 77, Milne, Strachey 76]).

The natural deduction style proof system is extended to commands. In the case of iterative commands, such as the while statement, these rules require proofs of termination before the command can be introduced in an argument. The while elimination rule is similar to Hoare's original "while axiom". Our rules should be compared to those in [Floyd 67, Hoare 69, Hoare, Wirth 73, Dijkstra 76]. There is substantial literature concerning proof rules for elementary commands and verification of elementary programs. We make relevant comparisons and citations to the literature in this chapter (including the exercises). Good general sources are [Manna 74, Manna, Waldinger 77, 77a, 77b, Igarashi, London, Luckham 75].

Chapter V begins with an analysis of substitution for variables in arguments with commands, showing how to treat the assignment operator and the procedure call as variable

binding operators. This concept is used to explain the restrictions on substitution of actual parameters for formal
parameters in the procedure call rule. The chapter also
contains a simple rule for proving the termination of mutually recursive procedures and a procedure call rule much
like Hoare's original in [Hoare 71]. It is interesting to
compare our rules to the well known Scott induction used in
[Milner 72].

Chapter VI extends the methods of Chapter V to recursive functions. It is noteworthy that our approach leads
to a remarkably simple function rule where the methods of
partial correctness are fraught with error (see [Clint,
Hoare 72, Ashcroft, Clint, Hoare 76]). The most important
issue of Chapter VI is the treatment of partial functions
in the logic, especially in the predicate calculus. We discuss at length alternative approaches. One approach is
developed fully in the monograph, the other is treated in
PL/CV. The methods of Scott provide another alternative.
The reader should examine this alternative carefully, for
example in [Milner 72, Cartwright 76].

Chapter VII gives an account of adding arrays to the
logic. They are treated in the monograph as finite functions. A similar account appears in [Dijkstra 76]. PL/CV
takes a different approach which permits more flexibility
and allows certain array deductions to be done automatically. There are two long examples in this chapter culmi-
nating in a proof of the recursive sorting algorithm quicksort.

The Appendix is an excerpt from the PL/CV user's manual. The PL/CV syntax is quite different than that in the
main text. But the underlying logic is the same except
that the Appendix follows an essentially different approach
to arrays and functions (an approach discussed in Chapter
VI). Moreover, arrays are included in the manual right
from the beginning so that rules are presented only once
with all necessary provisos specified. Of course, all matters of detail needed when communicating with a machine are
explicit; thus the Appendix may be consulted to resolve matters left ambiguous or incomplete in the main text.

Most exercises are routine, intended to illustrate main
concepts. But there are exercises which explore very
briefly new topics and exercises which summarize alternative
approaches and cite the relevant literature. There are a
few exercises which would challenge a good graduate student

to explore the system more deeply.   These are marked with
an asterisk.

One of the unfortunate consequences of separating the
programming language and logic used in the monograph from
PL/CV is that none of the many formal proofs presented in
the monograph has been checked by the mechanical proof
checker.   This means that the likelihood of error in the
long examples is very high.   We hope you will tolerate
these errors by understanding the limited purpose served
by these examples.

Availability of PL/CV

The PL/CV system is available to the public.   It is
distributed by the PL/CS project at Cornell University.
For information contact:

> PLC Group
> Computer Science Department
> Cornell University
> Ithaca, New York   14853

2

THE PREDICATE CALCULUS

2.1   INTRODUCTION

The logic of programs is based on the first order predicate calculus. Invented in the twentieth century to formalize mathematics, this calculus was the first major step beyond Aristotelian logic. It is at the center of modern mathematical logic and versions of it have been extensively studied for seventy years. On this foundation we build our programming logics.

For the programmer the first step to understanding the predicate calculus may be to view it as an extension of the usual class of boolean expressions (say of Algol) obtained by adding the logical operators "there is an x" ($\exists x$) and "for all x" ($\forall x$). By choosing the right basic predicates, say those for set theory, the whole of mathematics can be expressed in the calculus. Indeed, most of our natural language reasoning can be represented in the calculus.

The term "first order predicate calculus" covers a wide variety of formal systems, many of them catalogued in [Church 56]. The calculus can be *pure*, having no interpreted predicate or function constants, or *applied*. It can be *single sorted* or *many sorted*. It can be constructive or classical. It can allow defined functions or not. The version we present is quite rich. Most logic textbooks present the classical pure single sorted predicate calculus with equality. We present a classical many sorted applied predicate calculus with equality and definitions in which a constructive subsystem is distinguished. Moreover, the central syntactic category in most accounts is the *sentence* or *formula*. In this account the main entity is the *argument*.

2.2 INFORMAL ARGUMENT

The style of this logical system was conceived principally to offer natural expression of our reasoning. To discover the common methods of reasoning, one could examine numerous informal arguments and extract patterns. This was done for mathematical arguments by Gerhard Gentzen in his 1935 paper "Investigations into Logical Deduction" [Szabo 69]. Gentzen's formulation of logic was called a *Natural Deduction System*.

Many systems of formal logic define a proof as a sequence of assertions, each of which is either an axiom or follows from previous assertions by some rule of inference. Informal proofs have a richer structure, involving arguments within arguments and the use of temporary assumptions and locally defined names.[†] In informal reasoning, an argument may be appreciated as comprehensible and even valid without being accepted as a complete proof. So we define an *argument* as a syntactically reasonable discourse, a *valid argument* as an argument which is semantically true, and a *proof* as an argument in which each assertion is justified by a proof rule. With these considerations in mind, we modified the system of Dag Prawitz's monograph *Natural Deduction*.

2.3 THE SYNTAX OF ARGUMENTS

Predicate Calculus Assertions

Predicate calculus assertions (formulas) may be defined by the following context-free grammar with some type restrictions given later. The abbreviation $\{a_1,\ldots,a_n\}^+$ denotes all

---

[†]In his book, *Natural Deduction*, Prawitz uses a tree notation to formalize such proofs. We use a more readable notation based on block structured programming languages. The Polish logician Jaskowski in 1929 defined such systems based on work of Lukasiewicz in 1926. Our system is remarkably similar to Jaskowski's, though we arrived at it from programming language considerations without knowing of Jaskowski's 1929 work (see [Prawitz 65], p. 98-99). There are several textbooks of logic based on natural deduction, for example [Quine 61], [Anderson and Johnstone 62].

finite nonempty sequences of a_i's while $\{a_1,\ldots,a_n\}*$ includes the empty sequence as well. So $\{a_1,\ldots,a_n\}* =$
$\{a_1,\ldots,a_n\}^+ \cup \{\Lambda\}$ where Λ denotes the empty string. The
abbreviation $\{a_1,\ldots,a_n \ \S \ b\}^+$ denotes all finite nonempty
sequences of a_i's separated by b's. Thus $\{0,1\S;\}^+$ includes
sequences such as 0;0, 0;1, 1;1, 1;0;1, ... Square brackets, [ ], indicate an optional phrase and curly brackets,
{ }, enclose a set of alternatives. Undefined symbols such
as "variable" have intuitive meanings. The grammar given
here is ambiguous, but precedence rules will disambiguate it.
The order of precedence is among <=>, =>, ∨, &. The unary
operators, ∀, ∃, ¬ have lower precedence. Thus
A => ∀x . A(x) <=> B & ¬C∨D is equivalent to
(A => ∀x . A(x)) <=> (B&¬C)∨D. The PL/CV grammar of the
Appendix is unambiguous and can be used to supply productions
left out of this grammar.

$$
\begin{aligned}
\text{exp} \ \rightarrow \ &\text{variable}\\
&\text{constant}\\
&\text{exp infix-operator exp}\\
&\text{function-symbol (\{exp \ \S,\}}^+\text{)}\\
&\text{(exp)}
\end{aligned}
$$

$$
\begin{aligned}
\text{bexp} \ \rightarrow \ &\textit{true} \ | \ \textit{false}\\
&\text{exp infix-relation exp}\\
&\text{predicate-symbol (\{exp \ \S,\}}^+\text{)}\\
&\text{bexp \& ... \& bexp}\\
&\text{bexp ∨ ... ∨ bexp}\\
&\text{bexp <=> ... <=> bexp}\\
&\text{bexp => bexp}\\
&\text{¬ bexp}\\
&\text{(bexp)}
\end{aligned}
$$

$$
\begin{aligned}
\text{assertion} \ \rightarrow \ &\text{bexp}\\
&\text{quantifier . assertion}\\
&\text{assertion \& ... \& assertion}\\
&\text{assertion ∨ ... ∨ assertion}\\
&\text{assertion <=> ... <=> assertion}\\
&\text{assertion => assertion}\\
&\text{¬ assertion}\\
&\text{(assertion)}
\end{aligned}
$$

$$
\begin{aligned}
\text{quantifier} \ \rightarrow \ &\exists \ \text{variable-list } [\textit{where} \text{ assertion}]\\
&\forall \ \text{variable-list } [\textit{where} \text{ assertion}]
\end{aligned}
$$

variable-list → {simple-type idlist}$^+$

idlist → {variable §,}$^+$

simple-type → type names will be given later, they include *integer, string, boolean.*

Intuitively, a predicate calculus assertion is the formal
equivalent of an English-declarative sentence.
    Variable names in assertions serve two different pur-
poses. For instance, in the assertion x > 0, x is the name
of some object which is alleged to be greater than zero.
But, in the assertion Ɐ *integer* x . x*x ≥ 0, x is merely a
place holder for an arbitrary object of type *integer*. In
x > 0, x is said to be *free*; in Ɐ *integer* x . x*x ≥ 0, x is
bound.

Definition: An occurrence of a variable x in a quantifier
 Ɐ type...x... or Ǝ type...x... is a *binding occurence* of x.
An occurrence of x within P or Q in an assertion of one of
the forms Ɐ type...x... . P, Ɐ type...x... *where* Q . P, Ǝ
type...x... . P, Ǝ type...x... *where* Q . P, is a *bound* occurrence of x. Any other occurrence of x in an assertion is
a *free* occurrence of x.

Note that an occurrence of x may be free in a subassertion,
but bound in a larger assertion. For instance, x is free in
x > 0 but bound in Ǝ *integer* x .(x*x = 16 & x > 0). Recog-
nizing the difference between bound and free occurrences of
variables is essential to understanding the meanings of assertions and to reasoning correctly with them.
    In describing ways of reasoning with assertions, the
notion of syntactic substitution is also important. Intuitively, we may have an assertion P which says something about
an object named x (i.e., x occurs free in P), and we may
wish to say the same thing about another object named by
some expression t. To do this, we simply replace free occurrences of x in P by t.

Definition: P(t/x) is the assertion obtained by simultaneously replacing every free occurrence of x in P by t.
$P(t_1/x_1...t_n/x_n)$ is the assertion obtained by *simultaneously*
replacing every free occurrence of every x_i by the corresponding t_i. $P(t_1/x_1)...(t_n/x_n)$ is the assertion obtained

13

by replacing all free occurrences of x_1 in P by t_1, then replacing all free occurrences of x_2 in $P(t_1/x_1)$ by t_2, ..., then replacing all free occurrences of x_n in $P(t_1/x_1)...(t_{n-1}/x_{n-1})$ by t_n. All the forms of substitution above may also be applied to expressions.

For the formal notion of substitution above to capture the intuition of saying the same thing about t which P said about x, the expression t must mean the same thing when substituted into P as it does by itself. Here is an example where the intuition fails:

> P is $\forall$ *integer* y . x < y*y
> t is y + 100
> P(t/x) is $\forall$ *integer* y . y + 100 < y*y

The problem is that an occurrence of y in t became accidentally bound in P(t/x). When such accidental binding takes place, syntactic substitution often produces nonsense, and should not be performed.

Definition: t is free for x in P iff no occurrence of a variable in t becomes bound in P(t/x).

In the future, we will *always* insist that t is free for x before substituting t for x.

An argument is a sequence of assertions and arguments. To delimit arguments within arguments, we use the brackets *proof...qed*. The phrase *assume* P at the beginning of an argument indicates that the assertion P will be assumed within the argument. Phrases starting with *arbitrary* or *choose* at the beginning of an argument indicate that certain variables will be used as temporary names.

The following productions complete the grammar for arguments in the pure predicate calculus.

> proof-group $\rightarrow$ [label:] *proof* qualifier; argument; *qed*
> argument $\rightarrow$ [label:] assertion
> proof-group
> {argument §;}$^+$
> qualifier $\rightarrow$ [label:] *assume* assertion [*arbitrary* variable-list]

14

[label:] *choose* variable-list *where* assertion

[label:] *arbitrary* variable-list [*where* assertion]

The idea of free and bound occurrences of variables may be extended to arguments.

Definition: An occurrence of a variable symbol x of the form *arbitrary* type...x... or *choose* type...x... is a *binding* occurrence of x. A binding occurrence of x in an assertion is also *binding* in an argument containing the assertion.

An occurrence of a variable symbol x in any assertion within a subargument of the form *proof arbitrary* type...x... *qed* or *proof choose* type...x...*qed* is a *bound* occurrence of x. A bound occurrence of x in an assertion is also *bound* in an argument containing the assertion.

Any other occurrence of x in an argument is a *free* occurrence.

Example:

∀ *integer* x .((∃ *integer* y . y*y < x) => x > 0) is a true assertion. An informal argument for this assertion is:

> Let x be an arbitrary integer.
>> Assume that ∃ *integer* y . y*y < x.
>> Choose such a y.
>> y*y ≥ 0, so x > 0.

Therefore, ∀ *integer* x .((∃ *integer* y . y*y < x) => x > 0). Such an informal argument may be formalized as:

proof arbitrary integer x;
  proof assume ∃ *integer* y . y*y < x;
    proof choose integer y *where* y*y < x;
      y*y ≥ 0;
      x > 0
      qed
    qed
  qed;
∀ *integer* x . ((∃ *integer* y . y*y < x) => x > 0).

This is a valid argument (i.e., semantically true as well as syntactically meaningful) for integers.

A Programming Logic

Type Restrictions

To each constant, infix-operator, function-symbol, infix-relation and predicate-symbol in a language is associated a *type description* denoting the range of values of the symbol. The type description of a constant symbol is a simple-type symbol, the same sort of description that appears after $\forall$ or $\exists$ (e.g., *integer, string, boolean*, etc.). Other type descriptions are of the following forms, where $atype_1$, ...,$atype_n$,$btype$ are simple-type symbols:

symbol	type description
infix-operator	$atype_1 \times atype_2 \to btype$
function-symbol	$atype_1 \times \ldots \times atype_n \to btype$
infix-relation-symbol	$atype_1 \times atype_2 \to boolean$
predicate-symbol	$atype_1 \times \ldots \times atype_n$

Later we will introduce symbols like = which have different types in different occurrences. Type symbols are not directly associated to variables, but the type of any bound variable occurrence can be determined from its context. To determine the type of a bound occurrence of x, find the smallest subassertion or subargument containing that occurrence which starts with a binding occurrence of x. The simple-type symbol just to the left of the binding occurrence is the type for the bound occurrence of x. For instance the type of x in $\forall$ *integer* x $\cdot$ (x*x > 0) is *integer* and the type of x in

> *proof arbitrary string* x *where* x > 'a'
> ⋮

is *string*. A free occurrence of x in an argument may be assigned any simple type symbol provided that every free occurrence of the same variable has the same type description (some assignments may lead to syntactically incorrect statements as described below).

Type descriptions extend to expressions in the natural way. If f is of type $atype_1 \times \ldots \times atype_n \to btype$ and $t_1, \ldots, t_n$ are of types $atype_1, \ldots, atype_n$ respectively, then $f(t_1, \ldots, t_n)$ is of type $btype$. An expression, assertion or argument given by the grammar of this section is

16

syntactically correct if every subexpression is assigned a type by the rule above, and in every subassertion of the form $R(t_1,...,t_n)$ where R is of type $atype_1 \times ... \times atype_n$, $t_1,...,t_n$ are of types $atype_1,...,atype_n$ respectively.

2.4   SEMANTICS

Introduction

The main goal of semantics in this work is to illuminate the meanings of expressions, assertions and arguments so that we may understand which arguments are true and which are erroneous. To start with, we need a *model* to give meanings to type symbols, constant, predicate and function symbols. In Chapter III, when we treat the theory of integers and strings, we will focus on one particular model, but for the pure predicate calculus we are interested in the meanings of expressions, assertions, and arguments in terms of all possible models. Meanings of variable symbols may change within an argument, and even within a single assertion, so they are assigned outside of any model, by a function which logicians call a valuation, assignment or interpretation. To capture more of a computational intuition, we refer to the correspondence of meanings to variable symbols as a *state*.

Given a model and a state, the process of defining meanings for expressions and assertions has already been studied in detail (see [Tarski 35], [Chang and Keisler 73], [Enderton 72]). The definitions, which operate inductively on the syntactic structures of expressions and assertions, are repeated below. Meanings of arguments could be defined by a simple extension of the same basic inductive process. Since arguments are usually appreciated intuitively in a line by line fashion, rather than by an inductive analysis, and also to pave the way for more general kinds of arguments in the future, we use a different approach. Every position in an argument defines a context, that is, a set of states which are relevant to the meanings of assertions in that position. This set is affected by assumptions and bindings of variables. The meaning of an assertion within an argument is then defined in terms of its context. Finally, the meaning of an argument is simply the conjunction of the meanings (in context) of all of its assertions.

17

Models and States

A *model* is a function from the type, constant, function and predicate symbols of a language to abstract mathematical objects which serve as their meanings. These symbols are called *uninterpreted* symbols since they can be given any meaning in a model.

Definition: A *model* is any function $\mathcal{M}$ such that

$\mathcal{M}$ (*atype*) is a set, for each type symbol

$\mathcal{M}$ (c) ε $\mathcal{M}$ (*atype*) for each constant symbol c of type atype,

$\mathcal{M}$ (f): $\mathcal{M}$ ($atype_1$)$\times \ldots \times$ $\mathcal{M}$ ($atype_n$) $\rightarrow$ $\mathcal{M}$ (btype)

for each function symbol f of type $atype_1 \times \ldots \times atype$ $\rightarrow$ *btype*, (note (f) is a total function here.)

$\mathcal{M}$ (P) $\subseteq$ $\mathcal{M}$ ($atype_1$)$\times \ldots \times$ $\mathcal{M}$ ($atype_n$) for each predicate symbol P of type $atype_1 \times \ldots \times atype_n$.

$\mathcal{M}$(*boolean*) = {true,false} and $\mathcal{M}$(*true*) = true,

$\mathcal{M}$(*false*) = false.

For an arbitrary model $\mathcal{M}$, let

Values = {x $\mid$ x ε $\mathcal{M}$ (*atype*) for some simple-type symbol *atype*}.

A *state* is an assignment of values to variable symbols of the right type.

Definition: A *state* is any function s: Variables $\rightarrow$ Values

States = {s $\mid$ s is a state}.

Meanings of Expressions and Assertions

Suppose that we have a model and a state to give meanings to individual symbols. Expressions and assertions mean exactly what you think they mean. A formal definition of meaning merely makes our intuitive understanding of expressions and assertions more precise.

Let $\mathcal{M}$ be any model. To avoid proliferation of notation, we extend the use of the symbol $\mathcal{M}$ from primitive symbols to expressions. For each state s, $\mathcal{M}$ (s): Expressions → Values is defined as follows:

(1) $\mathcal{M}$ (s) (constant) = $\mathcal{M}$ (constant)

(2) $\mathcal{M}$ (s) (variable) = s(variable)

(3) $\mathcal{M}$ (s) $(f(exp_1,\ldots,exp_n))$ =
$\mathcal{M}$ (f) ($\mathcal{M}$ (s)(exp_1),..., $\mathcal{M}$ (s)$(exp_n))$

Similarly $\mathcal{M}$ may be extended to give meaning to boolean expressions, by defining $\mathcal{M}$ (s) : Bexp onto {true,false}

(4) $\mathcal{M}$ (s) (boolean constant) = $\mathcal{M}$(boolean constant)

(5) $\mathcal{M}$ (s) (boolean variable) = s(boolean variable)

(6) $\mathcal{M}$ (s) $(P(exp_1,\ldots,exp_n))$ =
$\mathcal{M}$ (P) ($\mathcal{M}$ (s)(exp_1),..., $\mathcal{M}$ (s)$(exp_n))$

(7) $\mathcal{M}$ (s) $(bexp_1$ & $bexp_2)$ = *true* iff
$\mathcal{M}$(s)$(bexp_1)$ = *true* and $\mathcal{M}$(s)$(bexp_2)$ = *true*

(8) $\mathcal{M}$ (s) $(bexp_1 \vee bexp_2)$ = *true* iff
$\mathcal{M}$(s)$(bexp_1)$ = *true* or $\mathcal{M}$(s)$(bexp_2)$ = *true*

(9) $\mathcal{M}$ (s) $(bexp_1$ => $bexp_2)$ = *true* iff
$\mathcal{M}$(s)$(bexp_1)$ = *false* or $\mathcal{M}$(s)$(bexp_2)$ = *true*

(10) $\mathcal{M}$ (s) $(\neg bexp)$ = *true* iff $\mathcal{M}$(s)(bexp) = *false*

The important semantic question about an assertion A is: "Is A true in model $\mathcal{M}$ and state s?" In classical logic, such a question may be answered by extending $\mathcal{M}$ (s) to map assertions to {*true,false*} just as we did with boolean expressions. To emphasize the fact that we don't always know the true value of an assertion, as well as to provide notation for both components of the meaning of a command in Chapter IV, we let < $\mathcal{M}$,s > $\models$ A mean that A is true in model $\mathcal{M}$ and state s.

(11) < $\mathcal{M}$,s > $\models$ $P(exp_1,\ldots,exp_n)$ iff
$\mathcal{M}$(P) ($\mathcal{M}$ (s)(exp_1),..., $\mathcal{M}$(s)$(exp_n))$ = *true*

where p is an n-ary predicate symbol.

In the equations for compound assertions we let A,B denote any assertion.

(12) $<\mathcal{M},s> \models A\&B$ iff $<\mathcal{M},s> \models A$ and $<\mathcal{M},s> \models B$

(13) $<\mathcal{M},s> \models A\lor B$ iff $<\mathcal{M},s> \models$ or $<\mathcal{M},s> \models B$

(14) $<\mathcal{M},s> \models A=>B$ iff $<\mathcal{M},s> \models A$ implies $<\mathcal{M},s> \models B$

(15) $<\mathcal{M},s> \models A<=>B$ iff $<\mathcal{M},s> \models A=>B$ and $<\mathcal{M},s> \models B => A$

(16) $<\mathcal{M},s> \models \neg A$ iff not $(<\mathcal{M},s> \models A)$

(17) $<\mathcal{M},s> \models \exists$ *atype* x [*where* B] . A iff we can find some c in $\mathcal{M}(atype)$ and some $\$$ with $\$(x) = c$ and $\$(y) = s(y)$ for all $y \neq x$ such that [if $<\mathcal{M},\hat{\$}> \models B$ then] $<\mathcal{M},\$> \models A$.

(18) $<\mathcal{M},s> \models \forall$ *atype* x [*where* B] . A iff for every state $\$$ with $\$(x) \epsilon \mathcal{M}(atype)$ and $\$(y) = s(y)$ for all $y \neq x$, we know [if $<\mathcal{M},\$> \models B$, then] $<\mathcal{M},\$> \models A$.

Meaning of Arguments

To understand an argument, we must know the meaning of each occurrence of an assertion in the argument. The meaning of such an occurrence depends on the position of the occurrence as well as the assertion which occurs. The position determines a set of possible states, and the meaning of the assertion is defined in terms of that set.

A down pointing arrow, ↓, will be used to indicate a *position* in an argument. The context of this position is indicated using Greek letters, which denote not necessarily well-formed parts of an argument. Thus, α↓β will denote a position with left context α and right context β. Whenever brackets appear (e.g. *proof-qed*), assume that the context between the brackets is well-formed.

20

$\mathcal{M}[\![\,\alpha\!\downarrow\!\beta\,]\!](S)$ is the set of states possible at the position $\downarrow$ starting from the states in S at the beginning of the left context α.

(19) $\mathcal{M}[\![\,\downarrow\!\alpha\,]\!](S) = S$ i.e. S is the set of states possible at the left of the context α, and

$\mathcal{M}[\![\,\alpha\beta\!\downarrow\!\gamma\delta\,]\!](S) = \mathcal{M}[\![\,\beta\!\downarrow\!\gamma\,]\!](\mathcal{M}[\![\,\alpha\!\downarrow\!\beta\gamma\delta\,]\!](S))$.

(20) $\mathcal{M}[\![\,\alpha A\!\downarrow\!\beta\,]\!](S) = \mathcal{M}[\![\,\alpha\!\downarrow\!A\beta\,]\!](S)$ i.e., an assertion A does not change the state, regardless of context α.

(21) $\mathcal{M}[\![\,\alpha$ *proof* argument *qed*$\downarrow\!\beta\,]\!](S) = \mathcal{M}[\![\,\alpha\!\downarrow$ *proof* argument *qed* $\beta\,]\!](S)$ i.e. proof-groups do not change the set of possible states regardless of context.

(22) $\mathcal{M}[\![$ *proof arbitrary atype* x $\downarrow$ argument *qed* $\beta\,]\!](S)$
     $= \{s \mid \exists\$(\$\epsilon S$ and $\$(y) = s(y)$ for all $y \neq x$

and $s(x)\epsilon\ \mathcal{M}(atype))\}$, i.e. the set of all states with an arbitrary atype assigned to x but all other variables the same is possible at this position.

(23) $\mathcal{M}[\![$ *proof assume* A $\downarrow$ argument *qed* $\beta\,]\!](S) =$
     $\{s \mid s\epsilon S$ and $<\mathcal{M},s> \models A\}$.

(24) $\mathcal{M}[\![$ *proof choose atype* x *where* A $\downarrow$ argument
     qed $\beta\,]\!](S) = \{s \mid \exists\$(\$\epsilon S$ and $\$(y) = s(y)$ for all
     $y \neq x$ and $s(x)\epsilon\ \mathcal{M}(atype)$ and $<\mathcal{M},s> \models A)\}$

Finally we can use this positional semantics to say when an argument is valid. Namely, an argument, arg, is valid for model $\mathcal{M}$ and set of states S when every assertion A in arg is true in every state possible at the position where A occurs. To say this formally we extend $\models$ to set of states S by saying $<\mathcal{M},S> \models A$ iff $<\mathcal{M},s> \models A$ for all $s\epsilon S$. Then formally:

(25) $<\mathcal{M}, S> \models$ arg iff for all contexts α,β and assertions A such that $\alpha A\beta =$ arg,

$<\mathcal{M},\mathcal{M}[\![\,\alpha\!\downarrow\!A\beta\,]\!](S)> \models A.$

Definition: An argument in the pure predicate calculus is called *valid* iff it is valid for all models $\mathcal{M}$ and states s, that is

$$\text{arg is valid iff } \forall \mathcal{M} \, \forall s \; \langle \mathcal{M}, s \rangle \models \text{arg.}$$

2.5 PROOF RULES

The definition of a valid argument captures formally
the informal notion of an argument in which all assertions
are true. Unfortunately, there is no general procedure
for distinguishing valid arguments from invalid ones. It
is not enough to speak the truth; we must be able to convince
ourselves and others that certain assertions are true. So,
we define proofs as the formal equivalents of compelling
arguments. It is essential that all proofs be valid
arguments, but not all valid arguments are proofs. The
desirable *completeness* property holds for a proof system
when all valid assertions have proofs. By results of Gödel,
completeness holds for the classical predicate calculus,
but not for the number theoretic system of Chapter III.

Proofs are traditionally built by starting with assumptions and obviously true assertions (axioms), and adding
assertions which obviously follow from assertions and subarguments which have already been established. The
"obviously follows from" relation is defined by rules of
inference. Rules of inference for the predicate calculus
may be written:

$$\frac{A_1, \ldots, A_n}{B}$$

where $A_1, \ldots, A_n$ are schematic descriptions of assertions
or subarguments, and B is a description of an assertion.
The meaning of such a rule is that any assertion of the form
B (conclusion) obviously follows from assertions and subarguments of the corresponding forms $A_1, \ldots, A_n$ (hypotheses).
The order of $A_1, \ldots, A_n$ is not significant. An axiom B can
be thought of as a rule of inference

$$\frac{}{B}$$

with no hypotheses. In describing rules of inference, it
is understood that upper case letters stand for arbitrary

assertions and that variable symbols may be changed. As in the grammars, square brackets indicate optional phrases, but if one such phrase appears, all must appear.

Pure Predicate Calculus

For the pure Predicate Calculus, Gentzen found an elegant way to organize the rules of inference. Each of the logical connectives, $\&$, $\vee$, $=>$, $\neg$, $\forall$ and $\exists$, has two rules: an Introduction Rule whose conclusion uses the given connective, and an Elimination Rule which allows inferences to be drawn from assertions containing the given connective. In the following list, I and E abbreviate Introduction and Elimination.

Introduction Rules	*Elimination Rules*

($\&$I)
$$\frac{A_1,\ldots,A_n}{A_1\,\&\ldots\&A_n}$$

($\&$E)
$$\frac{A_1\,\&\ldots\&A_n}{A_i}$$

($\vee$I)
$$\frac{A_i}{A_1\vee\ldots\vee A_n}$$

($\vee$E)
$$\frac{A_1\vee\ldots\vee A_n,\quad \begin{array}{c}proof\\assume\ A_1;\\ \vdots\\ Q;\\qed\end{array}\ ,\ldots,\ \begin{array}{c}proof\\assume\ A_n;\\ \vdots\\ Q;\\qed\end{array}}{Q}$$

($=>$I)
$$\frac{\begin{array}{l}proof\\ \quad assume\ A;\\ \qquad \vdots\\ \quad B;\\ \quad qed\end{array}}{A => B}$$

($=>$E)
$$\frac{A => B,\ A}{B}$$

($\neg$I)
$$\frac{\begin{array}{l}proof\\ \quad assume\ A;\\ \qquad \vdots\\ \quad false\\ \quad qed\end{array}}{\neg A}$$

($\neg$E)
$$\frac{A,\ \neg A}{false}$$

Introduction Rules (cont.)   Elimination Rules (cont.)

($<=>$I)
$$\frac{A=>B, \ B=>A}{A<=>B}$$

($<=>$E)
$$\frac{A<=>B}{A=>B, \ B=>A}$$

($\forall$I)
proof
    arbitrary α;
    $\vdots$
    A;
$$\frac{qed}{\forall\alpha.A}$$
α is a variable list

($\forall$E)
$$\frac{\forall\alpha.A}{A(t_1/x_1,\ldots,t_n/x_n)}$$
$x_1,\ldots,x_n$ are the variables of α, each t_i is a term of the appropriate type and is free for x_i in A.

($\forall$I)
proof
    arbitrary α[where b];
    $\vdots$
    A;
$$\frac{qed}{\forall\alpha[\text{where } B].A}$$
α is a variable list

($\forall$E)
$$\frac{\forall\alpha[\text{where } B].A, \quad [B(t_1/x_1,\ldots,t_n/x_n)]}{A(t_1/x_1,\ldots,t_n/x_n)}$$
$x_1,\ldots,x_n$ are the variables of α, each t_i is a term of the appropriate type and is free for x_i in A and B.

($\exists$I)
$$\frac{A(t_1/x_1,\ldots,t_n/x_n), \quad [B(t_1/x_1,\ldots,t_n/x_n)]}{\exists\alpha[\text{where } B].A}$$
$x_1,\ldots,x_n$ are the variables of α, each t_i is a term of the appropriate type and is free for x_i in A and B.

($\exists$E)
           proof
$\exists\alpha$[where B].A, choose α
           where [B&]A;
           $\vdots$
           C;
$$\frac{qed}{C}$$
the variables of α are not free in C.

A trivial rule for repeating assertions, and two rules concerning arguments by contradiction, do not fit nicely into the Introduction-Elimination scheme.

Trivial
$$\frac{A}{A}$$

False-elim.
$$\frac{false}{A}$$

Contradiction   *proof*
(Indirect)   *assume* ¬A;

                        ·

                        ·

                        ·

$$\frac{\begin{array}{c} false \\ qed \end{array}}{A}$$

The Indirect rule commits us to classical logic. Intuitionists accept all of the above rules except the last. The rules may also be classified into *inference rules*, whose hypotheses are all simple assertions, and *deduction rules*, whose hypotheses include arguments.

The rules of inference above will produce intolerably cumbersome proofs if every step is written down. Certain types of reasoning, such as the reasoning involved in &E and &I, are so elementary and immediate that they may be performed mentally without writing anything. We do not know at present what types of reasoning ought to be done mentally, so we can only choose something plausible and revise our definition later when we have more experience with proofs. The rules &I, ∨I, &E, =>E, ¬E, <=>I, <=>E and false-elim. are *immediate* rules of inference. (Also two special cases of =>I, are immediate, namely from ¬A, A=>B and from B, A=>B. These can be regarded as instances of ∨I.)

Definition: Let 𝒜 be a set of assertions, and B a single assertion.

25

1. If B∈$\mathscr{A}$, then B *follows immediately* from $\mathscr{A}$.

2. If $A_1,\ldots,A_n$ follow immediately from $\mathscr{A}$ and B follows from $A_1,\ldots,A_n$ by an immediate rule, then B *follows immediately* from $\mathscr{A}$.

3. B does not *follow immediately* from $\mathscr{A}$ unless so required by (1) and (2).

In simple linear proofs (without subarguments), the conclusion of a rule of inference may be deduced whenever the hypotheses follow immediately from previous lines of the proof. In the presence of subarguments, the meaning of an assertion may depend on its position with respect to assumptions and local names, so we must also ensure that hypotheses still hold in the context where we intend to write the conclusion. The following two examples of *incorrect* inferences illustrate the problem:

```
proof
      assume A => B;
      proof
            assume (C => A)&C;
            C;
            A
            qed;
      B;
      qed;
  (A => B) => B;
```

In this example, every assertion follows correctly from previous assertions, except that B does not follow from A and A => B since A holds only under the assumption (C => A) & C, while B is asserted outside the scope of that assumption.

```
proof
      assume P(x) => Q(x);
      proof
            arbitrary integer x where P(x);
            Q(x)
            qed;
      V integer x where P(x) . Q(x)
      qed;
  (P(x) => Q(x)) => V integer x where P(x) . Q(x);
```

Again, all assertions follow correctly except that $Q(x)$
does not follow from $P(x) => Q(x)$ and $P(x)$, because x has
a different (global) meaning in $P(x) => Q(x)$ than its
(local) meaning in $Q(x)$.

The notion of *accessibility* is designed precisely to
eliminate those two forms of incorrect reasoning. Intuitively, an assertion or argument A is accessible from a
later position in an argument when the assertion or argument obviously continues to hold in the later position.

Definition: An instance of assertion or argument A at
position q with free variables $x_1,\ldots,x_n$ is *accessible*
from a position p in a Predicate Calculus argument iff

    1.   A at q occures lexically before p.

    2.   Any subargument containing A at q also contains
        p.

    3.   Any subargument containing p which qualifies any
        of $x_1,\ldots,x_n$ also contains A at q.

An assertion A is *immediate* at a line ℓ in an argument
iff A follows immediately from assertions which are
accessible from ℓ.

Definition: A *proof* is an argument in which every
assertion is either an assumption, or follows from accessible lines and immediate assertions by a rule of inference. To aid in writing, understanding and checking proofs,
we may annotate some or all assertions with a *justification*
consisting of the name of the rule of inference and
citations of some of the earlier lines and expressions
used to infer the assertion.

A proof in which every assertion is so annotated is
called a *justified proof*. The precise syntax of justified
proofs is still a matter for some experimentation. For
the purpose of this work, a line in a justified proof will
have the form, assertion *by* rule name, {citations §,}*.
PL/CV justifications are precisely defined in the appendix.

2.6 THE PREDICATE CALCULUS WITH EQUALITY

When we think of the predicate calculus as a language for describing the most primitive and universal properties of mathematical structures, then it is natural to consider equality, =, as an interpreted predicate. That is, a predicate whose meaning is the same in all models, rather than varying arbitrarily as the other precicate symbols. In many logic texts, equality is considered to be a basic logical notion along with propositional connectives and quantifiers. The classical theory of the predicate calculus with equality is complete.

A syntax for the predicate calculus with equality is obtained by adding equality as a new logical symbol. Thus the class of boolean expressions is enlarged by adding the production

$$bexp \rightarrow exp = exp.$$

Semantics

The meaning of $exp_1 = exp_2$ in model $\mathcal{M}$ with state s is defined by

$$\mathcal{M}(s)(exp_1 = exp_2) = \textit{true if } \mathcal{M}(s)(exp_1) \text{ is the same as } \mathcal{M}(s)(exp_2)$$
$$\textit{false otherwise}$$

Proof rules

Many traditional presentations of equality involve the following rules of inference.

= Reflexivity

$$\overline{t = t}$$

= Symmetry

$$\frac{t_1 = t_2}{t_2 = t_1}$$

= Transitivity
$$\frac{t_1 = t_2, \ t_2 = t_3}{t_1 = t_3}$$

= Substitution
$$\frac{t_1 = t_2, \ A(t_1/x)}{A(t_2/x)}$$

These rules are all *immediate*, so they may be used freely in a proof without explicitly writing down the steps.

The treatment of = by these immediate rules suggests a more powerful set of rules for <=>, which are also *immediate*:

<=> Reflexivity
$$\frac{\rule{3cm}{0.4pt}}{A <=> A}$$

<=> Symmetry
$$\frac{A <=> B}{B <=> A}$$

<=> Transitivity
$$\frac{A <=> B, \ B <=> C}{A <=> C}$$

<=> Substitution
$$\frac{A <=> B, \ C}{C'}$$

where C' is C with some occurrences of A replaced by B.

2.7 USING DEFINITIONS TO ABBREVIATE ASSERTIONS

Informal proofs are made much easier to read and to write with judicious use of definitions of important concepts which appear repeatedly. Most uses of definitions may be formalized by the syntax

definition → *define* defined-symbol({variable §,}$^+$) = assertion

29

For instance, a useful defined concept in arithmetic is the notion that one number is a factor of another:

define factor(x,y) = ∃*integer* z . x∗z = y

Rather than giving semantics to an argument containing a definition, *define* $P(x_1,\ldots,x_n)$ = A, we consider such an argument to be an abbreviation for another argument in which the definition has been removed, and each occurrence of $P(t_1,\ldots,t_n)$ has been replaced by $A(t_1/x_1,\ldots,t_n/x_n)$.[†] If $t_1,\ldots,t_n$ are not free for $x_1,\ldots,x_n$ in A, the bound variables of A are to be changed to make the substitution legal. For example, the following argument (1) abbreviates argument (2).

1. *define* factor(x,y) = ∃*integer* z . x∗z = y;
   proof arbitrary integer x *where* factor$(4,x)$
       proof choose integer z *where* 4∗z = x;
           2∗(2∗z) = x;
           factor$(2,x)$;
           qed;
       factor$(2,x)$
       qed ;
   ∀*integer* x *where* factor$(4,x)$. factor$(2,x)$

2. *proof arbitrary integer* x *where* ∃ *integer* z.4∗z = x;
                                       integer x;
       proof choose integer z *where* 4∗z = x;
           2∗(2∗z) = x;
           ∃*integer* z . 2∗z = x
           qed;
       ∃*integer* z . 2∗2 = x
       qed;
   ∃*integer* x *where* ∃*integer* z . 4∗z = x
                       ∃*integer* z . 2∗z = x

[†] In accordance with this informal treatment of definitions, we do not specify separate declarations of parameters to a definition. The parameters occurring in a define statement, as x,y in *define* p(x,y) are only place markers. They do not have types, but of course when the definition is expanded, typed expressions are substituted for them and the resulting expansion must be type correct.

Definitions may occur anywhere in an argument as long as
they precede each use of the defined symbol, and no use of
a defined symbol occurs outside of a block containing the
definition.

2.8 AUTOMATIC RECOGNITION OF CORRECT PROOFS

In any reasonable formal system of proof it must be
theoretically possible to automatically distinguish
correct proofs from faulty arguments. Proofs in the formal
system of this monograph are intended to be recognizable
by a thoroughly practical automatic verifier. Such a
verifier is presently under construction at Cornell University, and will be released with the new PL/CS subset of PL/C.
The verifier recognized justified proofs in PL/CV, a
language which varies slightly from that of this work in
order to match the syntax of PL/CS.

In developing PL/CV, we are finding ways to increase
the expressive convenience of the formal system. The im-
provements are not finalized, but they will probably include more powerful rules, a more general ability to define
parameterized abbreviations for assertions which occur
repeatedly, and the ability to leave out certain intuitively
redundant steps in proofs. See Appendix for a description
of PL/CV.

2.9 EXERCISES

Section 2.1

(2-1) For boolean expressions $bexp_1$, $bexp_2$, the compound $bexp_1 \Rightarrow bexp_2$ is equivalent to $\neg bexp_1 \lor bexp_2$. Translate the following expressions into equivalent versions without $\Rightarrow$.

      (a)   x => (y=>x)
      (b)   x => x
      (c)   (x=>y) => (x=>(y=>z)) => (x=>z)
      (d)   x => (y=>x&y)

(2-2) A boolean expression quantified over a finite set of objects, say the nonnegative integers $\{0,1,\ldots,n\}$, is equivalent to a boolean expression without quantifiers. Specifically let $D(x)$ be the relation
$x=0 \lor x=1 \lor \ldots \lor x=8 \lor x=9$. Then $\forall$ *integer* x *where* $D(x)$. $A(x)$ is equivalent to $A(0)$ & $A(1)$ & $\ldots$ & $A(9)$, and
$\exists$ *integer* x *where* $D(x)$. $A(x)$ is equivalent to
$A(0) \lor A(1) \lor \ldots \lor A(9)$. Translate the following quantified boolean expressions into equivalent forms without quantifiers.

      (a) $\forall$ *integer* x *where* $D(x)$. $(x<0 \lor x \geq 0)$
      (b) $\exists$ *integer* x *where* $D(x)$. $x>5$
      (c) ($\exists$ *integer* x *where* $D(x)$. $\forall$ *integer* y *where* $D(y)$.
            $x \geq y$) => ($\forall$ *integer* x *where* $D(x)$.
        $\exists$ *integer* y *where* $D(y)$. $x \geq y$)

(2-3) Bounded quantifiers of the type suggested in exercise (2-2) can be added to the operators for forming the boolean expressions of a programming language because expressions formed with them are all computable The language PL/CS allows such quantifiers in assertions in the form:

      ASSERT (boolean_expression)
      FOR ALL index_variable = exp_1 TO exp_2 BY exp_3;

      ASSERT (boolean_expression)
      FOR SOME index_variable = exp_1 TO exp_2 BY exp_3;

Such an assertion is treated as a condition to be evaluated at run-time, producing a message whenever the condition is false.

    (a)   Show how expressions with bounded quantification may be translated into commands with the same effect.

    (b)   Show how expressions with bounded quantification may be translated into assertions of the form of question (2-2).

    (c)   In what essential ways do these quantified boolean expressions differ from the assertions of the predicate calculus? Why is it not possible to use arbitrary quantified assertions as boolean expressions in a programming language? (See Section 2.4 for the answer.)

Section 2.2

(2-4) Let P be the statement "Programs are subtle." Let F be the statement "Correct reasoning is fragile." Let E be the statement "There is an error in the program." Using the logical connectives, $\&, \vee, \neg, =>$, write assertions which symbolize the following statements:

    (a)   Programs are subtle and correct reason is fragile.

    (b)   If correct reason is fragile and programs are subtle, then there is an error in the program.

    (c)   If it is not the case that there is an error in the program, then either programs are not subtle or reasoning is not fragile.

(2-5) Symbolize the following arguments and analyze their structure:

    (a)   If a decimal number ends in zero, it is divisible by 5; a given number ends in zero. Therefore it is divisible by 5.

    (b)   If a decimal number ends in zero, it is divisible by 5; a given number is divisible by 5. Therefore, it ends in zero.

(c)   If a decimal number ends in zero, it is divisible
by 5; a given number does not end in zero.
Therefore, it is not divisible by 5.

(d)   If a decimal number ends in zero, it is divisible
by 5; a certain number is not divisible by 5.
Therefore, it does not end in zero.

(2-6)   The following type of reasoning is called a
syllogism.

all squares are rhombuses,
some rectangles are not rhombuses;
_____

consequently, some rectangles are not squares

It can be formalized by letting x range over two dimen-
sional figures and letting Sq(x) mean "x is a square",
Rh(x) mean "x is a rhombus" and R(x) mean "x is a rectangle."
Then the structure is

$(\forall$ *polygon* x . (Sq(x) => Rh(x)) &
$\exists$ *polygon* x . (R(x) & $\neg$Rh(x))) =>
$\exists$ *polygon* x . (R(x) & $\neg$Sq(x)).

Formalize the following syllogisms and determine which are
valid. $P\lambda (x)$ ... x is a polygon

(a)   All squares are regular polygons,
no trapezoid is a regular polygon;
_____

consequently, no trapezoid is a square.

(b)   All rhombuses are parallelograms,
all rectangles are parallelograms;
_____

consequently, all rectangles are rhombuses.

(c)   No trapezoid is a regular polygon,
no triangle is a trapezoid;
_____

consequently, no triangle is a regular polygon.

(d)   No trapezoid is a regular polygon,
some triangles are regular polygons;
_____

consequently, no triangle is a trapezoid.

(2-7) If we add the type *real* for real numbers, we can formalize the definition of continuity of a function f at a point x_0 as:

$$\forall \text{ real } \varepsilon \ . \ \exists \text{ real } \delta \ . \ \forall \text{ real } x \ . \ (|x-x_0|<\delta \Rightarrow$$
$$|f(x) - f(x_0)|<\varepsilon).$$

Formulate the definition of uniform continuity on an interval a≤x≤b.

(2-8) Let L(x,y,t) mean "x loves y at time t". Formulate the statements:

(a) everybody loves somebody sometime (and write the melody)
(b) somebody is liked by everybody always ,
(c) nobody likes everybody always.

(2-9) Let P(x) mean "x is a person", let T(y) mean "time y", and let F(x,y) mean "x fools y". Formulate the statements:

(a) You can fool some of the people all of the time.
(b) You can fool all of the people some of the time.
(c) You can't fool all of the people all of the time.

Section 2.3

(2-10) The grammatical form of assertion A => B => C is ambiguous without precedence rules. It can be equivalent either to (A => B) => C or to A => (B => C). Give examples of specific assertions for which the meaning of the two forms are different. (For an answer, see exercise (2-13)).

(2-11) Is the grammatical form of A <=> B <=> C ambiguous according to our rules? Should (A <=> B) <=> C mean the same as A <=> (B <=> C)? (You may need to consult the semantics or proof rules.)

(2-12) The grammar for assertions in PL/CV is unambiguous, that is, each assertion has a unique grammatical form, e.g. A => B => C has the outer form

implicant => equivalent .

How can you prove that every assertion has a unique grammatical form?   (This is a nonroutine question.   See [Enderton 72] for a logic textbook's approach.   See [Aho, Ullman 72] for a formal language theory approach.)

(2-13)   Rewrite (A => B) => C and A => (B => C) in terms of ∨ and ¬.

(2-14)   Classify all occurences of variables in the following assertions and arguments as binding, bound or free.

     (a)   x>10 & ∀ *integer* x . x>10 ∨ x≤10
     (b)   ∃ *string* z *where* P(y,z) .
                  ∀ *string* w *where* Q(y,z,w) . R(w,z)
     (c) *proof choose integer* a,b *where* P(a);
           Q(x,b);
           ∀ *string* s . ∃ *integer* ℓ *where* ℓ≥0 . L(x,ℓ);
           R(a,b,s,y)
           qed

(2-15)   Let P be the assertion

   x≥0 & x*x≤y & ∀ *integer* z *where* z*z≤y . z≤x

Perform the following substitutions.   In which cases are the replaced variables free for their replacements?

   (a)   P(x+y/x, 100*v+w/y)

   (b)   P(x+y/x)(100*v+w/y)

   (c)   P(x+z/x, y+1/y, 50/z)

   (d)   P(x+z/x)(y+1/y)(50/z)

Section 2.4

(2-16)   Show that there is an LL(1) grammar to generate the language defined in 2.3.   All LL(k) grammars are unambiguous, so there is an unambiguous grammar for the predicate calculus.   (See [Aho, Ullman 72].)

(2-17) Prove that the following inductive definition of the concept *variable x occurs free in assertion A* is equivalent to our definition of free variable.

(i) if A is a boolean expression, and x occurs in A

(ii) if A is $B_1 \& \ldots \& B_n$ and x occurs free in some B_i

(iii) if A is $B_1 v \ldots v B_n$ and x occurs free in some B_i

(iv) if A is $B_1 <=> \ldots <=> B_n$ and x occurs free in some B_i

(v) if A is $B_1 => \ldots => B_n$ and x occurs free in some B_i

(vi) if A is $\neg B$ and x occurs free in B

(vii) if A is $\forall$ atype $y_1, \ldots, y_m$. B and x occurs free in B and $x \neq y_j$, $j = 1, \ldots, m$

(viii) if A is $\exists$ atype $y_1, \ldots, y_m$. B and x occurs free in B and $x \neq y_j$, $j = 1, \ldots, m$.

Section 2.5

(2-18) Although the constructive meaning of implication, say A => B, is rather subtle when A and B are complex assertions involving quantifiers, the meaning is reducible to a very simple idea when A and B are boolean expressions. In this case, the values of A and B can be computed; they are either *true* (say T for short) or *false* (say F for short). Whatever A => B means in general, in the case when B evaluates to *true* the implication should be *true*. Likewise when A evaluates to *false*, the implication should be *true*. We express this in a *truth table* as follows:

A	A => B	B
T	T	T
T	F	F
F	T	T
F	T	F

Similar reasoning reveals that the following truth table characterizes all the connectives *on boolean expressions*.

A	B	A&B	A∨B	¬B	A=>B	A<=>B
T	T	T	T	F	T	T
T	F	F	T	T	F	F
F	T	F	T	F	T	F
F	F	T	F	T	T	T

Construct and analyze the truth tables of the following assertions:

- (a) a&b => a
- (b) a∨b => a
- (c) a=>b => a
- (d) ¬(a=>b) => a
- (e) a&(b∨c) => a&b ∨ a&c
- (f) a∨(b&c) => (a∨b) & (a∨c)

Note, it is known that the constructive meaning of arbitrary assertions cannot be described by truth tables, even if more than two "truth values" are used.

(2-19) Notice that not all connectives of conversational English can be rendered as truth functional statements even if they connect only simple assertions. Choose assertions for a,b such that *a because b* is *true* when a,b are true and *a because b* is *false* when a,b are true.

(2-20) DeMorgan's laws are

1. ¬(a&b) = ¬a ∨ ¬b
2. ¬(a∨b) = ¬a & ¬b

These are constructively valid for boolean expressions. Show this by a truth table analysis. For arbitrary assertion only

1. ¬a ∨ ¬b => ¬(a&b)
2. ¬(a∨b) = ¬a & ¬b

(2-21) Prove that the structure

$$<\{true, false\}, ∨, \&, true\ false>$$

forms a commutative ring with unit.

(2-22) Call a boolean variable or its negation a *literal*. An assertion involving only connectives and literals is said to be in *conjnctive normal form* (CNF) iff it has the structure

$$(a_{11} v a_{12} v \ldots) \ \& \ (a_{21} v a_{22} v \ldots) \ \& \ldots \& \ (a_{n1} v a_{n2} v \ldots)$$

for a_i literals. Classically every formula is equivalent to a formula in conjunctive normal form. Reduce each of the assertions in (2-18) to CNF.

(2-23) An assertion involving only literals and connectives is said to be in disjunctive normal form(DNF) iff is has the form

$$(a_{11} \& a_{12} \& \ldots) \ v \ (a_{21} \& a_{22} \& \ldots) \ v \ldots v \ (a_{n1} \& a_{n2} \& \ldots)$$

where a_i are literals. Classically every assertion is equivalent to one in DNF. Put the formulas of (2-18) into DNF.

Section 2.6

(2-24) Prove the following (classical) tautologies. Which are constructively true (i.e. true without using the contradiction rule)?

1. $\neg(a=>b) => a$
2. $\neg(a=>b) <=> a \& \neg b$
3. $(a=>(b=>c)) => (a=>b) => (a=>c)$ (self distributive law for =>)
4. $(a \& b=>c) <=> a=>b=>c$ (exportation for =>)
5. $((a=>b)=>a) => a$
6. $\neg\neg a <=> a$ (double negation)
7. $((a=>b) \& \neg b) => \neg a$
8. $(a v b) => c <=> (a=>c) v (b=>c)$
9. $((a=>b) \& (a=>c)) => a => b \& c$
10. $((a=>b)=>c) => (c=>a) => (b=>a)$
11. $(a=>\neg a) => \neg a$
12. $a => b => ((b=>d) > (a=>d))$ (transitivity of =>)
13. $(a=>\neg b) => (b=>\neg a)$
14. $a => b <=> \neg b => \neg a$ (contra-positive)
   (note $a => b => \neg b => \neg a$ is constructively valid).

15. av¬a (excluded middle)
16. a & (b∨c) <=> a&b | a&c (distributivity)
17. a ∨ (b&c) <=> (a∨b) & (a∨c) (distributivity)

(2-25) Prove the following constructivey true assertions of the predicate calculus.

1. ∀ *integer* x . (A(x)=>B(x)) =>
    ∃ *integer* x . (A(x)=>B(x))
2. ∃ *integer* x . (A(x)=>C) =>
    ∀ *integer* x . A(x) => C (converse is true classically)
3. ∃ *integer* x . ¬A(x) => ¬∀ *integer* x . A(x)
    (converse is true classically)
4. ∀ *integer* x . A(x) => ¬∃ *integer* x .¬A(x)
    (converse is true classically)
5. ∀ *integer* x . (A(x)&B(x)) <=> ∀ *integer* x . A(x)
    & ∀ *integer* x . B(x)
6. ∃ *integer* x . (A(x)∨B(x)) <=> ∃ *integer* x . A(x)
    ∨ ∃ *integer* x . B(x)
7. ∀ *integer* x . A(x) ∨ ∀ *integer* x . B(x) =>
    ∀ *integer* x . (A(x)∨B(x))
8. ∃ *integer* x . (A(x)&B(x)) => ∃ *integer* x . A(x) &
    ∃ *integer* x . B(x)
9. ∃ *integer* x . ∀ *integer* y . P(x,y) =>
    ∀ *integer* x . ∃ *integer* y . P(x,y)

(2-26) Suppose the following rule called *extended and introduction* is added to the (constructive) rules. Show how to replace any proof using this rule by a proof without it.

$$\frac{¬(A∨B)}{¬A&¬B}$$

(2-27) The inference ¬(A&B) => ¬A∨¬B cannot be proved without the rule of contradiction. Give a proof using contradiction. Suppose we add the classical rule called *extended or introduction*,

$$\frac{¬(A&B)}{¬A∨¬B}$$

40

(a) Show how any proof using this rule can be trans-
     formed to a proof without it (but using the
     contradiction rule).
(b) Show how any proof using the contradiction rule
     can be transformed into a proof which uses the
     above rule instead.

(2-28) The entended rules of inference discussed above
when adjoined to the ordinary rules for &,∨,¬ form a proof
system in which every theorem involving only the propositional connectives (so called *tautologies*) can be proved
in a very stylized manner. Every theorem can be proved by
contradiction. Moreover, the proof can proceed by decomposing every assertion into smaller parts until only a
conjunction of contradictory atomic assertions remains.
These are called *tableau style* proofs. Here is an example
of one such proof.

```
/* (a∨b) ∨ ¬a&¬b */
proof;  /* by contradiction */
     assume ¬((a∨b) ∨ ¬a&¬b);
          ¬(a∨b) & ¬(¬a&¬b)  /* extended & intro */
          ¬a&¬b & ¬(¬a&¬b)  /* extended & intro */
          ¬¬a ∨ ¬¬b  /* entended or intro */
          proof; assume ¬¬a; false; qed;
          proof; assume ¬¬b; false; qed;
          false
qed
```

Prove ¬(a&(b∨c)) ∨ (a&b ∨ a&c) by the tableau method.

(2-29) A flexible existential elimination rule is used
in PL/CV. It has the form

$$\frac{\exists\ atype(x_1,\ldots,x_n)\ .\ P}{choose\ atype(x_1,\ldots,x_n)\ where\ P}$$

The bound variables $x_1,\ldots,x_n$ have scope equal to the
smallest proof block in which the choose statement appears.
Here is an example of how to use this rule in a proof.

```
/* ∃ integer y . ∀ integer x . P => ∀ integer x
   ∃ integer y . P */
proof assume ∃ integer y . ∀ integer x . P(x,y);
     choose integer y where ∀ integer x . P(x,y);
          proof arbitrary integer w;
                    P(w,y) by ∀E;
                    ∃ integer y . P(w,y) by ∃I
          qed;
          ∀ integer x . ∃ integer y . P(x,y)
   qed;
∃ integer y . ∀ integer x . P => ∃ integer x .
∃ integer y . P
```

Show how to convert this to a proof using the rules of this chapter.

(2-30) The above existential elimination rule can be made even more flexible in the following form.

$$\frac{∃ \; atype(x_1,\ldots,x_n) \; . \; P}{P(a_1/x_1,\ldots,a_n/x_n)}$$

where a_i are *new*.

To say a_i are *new* means that they have not occurred elsewhere in the proof. This is the existential elimination rule used in tableau systems of the predicate calculus. Indeed, in the classical tableau system the following rules are allowed:

$$\frac{∃ \; atype \; x \; . \; P(x)}{P(a/x) \; a \; new}$$

$$\frac{¬∀ \; atype \; x \; .}{¬P(a/x) \; a \; new}$$

Examine the proofs in exercises (2-24)(2-25) and rewrite them using the new tableau rules.

(2-31) The tableau rules of exercises (2-28),(2-29), (2-30) permit the following *systematic tableau proof procedure*:

42

Whenever the or elimination rule is being used, the proof splits into independent proof blocks, one for each disjunct. Thus for A∨B, there is a block

proof assume A   *proof assume* B
        .   .
        .   .
        .   .
qed   *qed*

These blocks can be viewed as branches of a proof tree which splits at the assertion A∨B.

As the proof proceeds certain assertions are *used* as hypotheses of rules. When they are used, we will mark them with a check.

To prove assertion A, write it in an equivalent form not involving =>, then proceed by contradiction, i.e. assume ¬A. Continue in stages (assume ¬A is the first stage). If n stages are completed, then if a contradiction is already provable stop. Otherwise, consider one of the branches (independent proof blocks) of the proof and pick the lexically earliest unused assertion (in traversing the proof from its origin at ¬A). The next action depends on the form of this formula, call it M. (Whenever ¬¬B occurs as a subformula, replace it by B.)

(1) (a) if M is B&C then add the assertions B,C as lines of the proof and mark M as used.
    (b) if M is ¬(B∨C) then add ¬B, ¬C as new lines and mark M as used
(2) (a) if M is B∨C, then start subproofs by or elimination (e.g. *proof assume* B and *proof assume* C), and mark M as used.
    (b) if M is ¬(B&C), then deduce ¬B∨¬C and proceed as in (2)(a).
(3) (a) if M is ∃ *atype* x . B, then pick the first new variable a (in some ordering of variables), add the line B(a/x), and mark M as used.
    (b) if M is ¬∀ *atype* x . B, then deduce ∃ *atype* x . ¬B and proceed as in (3)(a).

43

(4) (a) if M is ∀ *atype* x . B, then take the first
variable a for which B(a/x) does not already occur on the branch, and add the assertions B(a/x) and ∀ *atype* x . B, and
mark M as used. (If there are terms in the
language, they must be substituted as well.)

(b) if M is ¬∀ *atype* x . B, then deduce
∀ *atype* x . ¬B and proceed as in 4(a)

These actions complete stage n+1. If the only unused assertions on each branch are atomic assertions, then the
procedure stops.

Here is an example of this procedure. Given the formula ∀ *atype* x . (A(x)&B(x)) => ∀ *atype* x . A(x) &
∀ *atype* x . B(x),
first write it in an equivalent form not involving =>.

/* to prove (¬∀ *atype* x . (A(x)&B(x))∨ ∀ *atype* x . A(x) &
∀ *atype* x . B(x)) */
proof assume ¬(¬∀ *atype* x . (A(x)&B(x))∨ ∀ *atype* . A(x) &
∀ *atype* x . B(x));
L1: ¬(∀ *atype* x . A(x) & ∀ *atype* x . B(x));/*step (1)(b) */
L2: ∀ *atype* . (A(x)&B(x)); /* step (1)(b) */
L3: ¬∀ *atype* x . A(x) ∨ ¬∀ *atype* x . B(x);/*step (2)(b) on L1
     proof assume ¬∀ *atype* x . A(x);/*step (2)(a) on L3*/
          A(a) & B(a); /* from L2, assuming alphabetical
                              order of variables */
          ∀ *atype* x . (A(x)&B(x)); /* line L2 carried down */
          ∃ *atype* x . ¬A(x); /* step (3)(b) */
          ¬A(b);
          A(b) & B(b);
          false
     qed;
     proof assume ¬∀ *atype* x . B(x); /* step (2)(a) on L3 */
          A(a) & B(a); /* from L2, assuming alphabetical
                              order of variables */
          ∀ *atype* x . (A(x)&B(x)); /* line L2 carried down */
          ∃ *atype* x . ¬B(x); /* step (3)(b) */
          ¬B(b);
          A(b) &B(b);
          false
     qed
qed;

Notice that following the procedure literally may involve
introducting extra variables, such as a. If we had de-
layed instantiating ∀ *atype* x . (A(x)&B(x)) until after
instantiating ∃ *atype* x . ¬A(x) inside the proof blocks,
then we could have used a as the only new variable.
    Try this systematic procedure on the assertions in
exercises (2-24)(2-25).

(2-32)* The interesting fact about the systematic
tableau proof procedure is that if there is a proof of a
classical predicate calculus formula, this procedure will
find it. Try to convince yourself of this rather deep
fact. For a proof, see [Smullyan 71].

(2-33)* There is a tableau proof system for the constructive part of the predicate calculus, and there is
a corresponding systematic tableau procedure. See if you
can discover them. For an asnser to this difficult
exercise, see [Fitting 69].

Section 2.7

(2-34) Write an axiom guaranteeing that a domain, *atype*,
consists of precisely three elements.

(2-35) Write an assertion which is valid only in infinite domains.

(2-36) Prove the following assertion:

∃ *atype* (x_1, x_2, x_3) . where $x_1 \neq x_2$ & $x_2 \neq x_3$ & $x_1 \neq x_3$
∀ *atype* y $(y=x_1 \lor y=x_2 \lor y=x_2)$ =>

∀ *atype* (z_1, z_2, z_3, z_4) . $((z_1 \neq z_2$ & $z_2 \neq z_3$ & $z_1 \neq z_3)$ =>
        $(z_4=z_1 \lor z_4=z_2 \lor z_4=z_3))$

(2-37) Given formulas $t_1 = t_2$, x>0 & p(x) show how to conclude $t_1 > 0$ & $p(t_2)$ from the substitution rule given
$t_1 > 0$ & $p(t_1)$.

45

(2-38) Show that the substitution rule is equivalent to this apparently stronger form

$$\frac{t_1 = t_2, \; P}{P'}$$

where P' is like P expect t_1 is substituted for t_2 at some occurrences.

Section 2.8

(2-39) When free variables occur in definitions, their value can be determined at the point of definition (static scope) or at the point where the definition is expanded (*dynamic scope*). Consider the example:

```
proof choose integer x where x=2;
      define q(z) = r(x,2);
      proof arbitrary x,y where x=3 & y=4;
            p(x) => q(y)
      qed
qed;
```

Explain why the statement p(x) => q(y) is equivalent to p(3) => r(2,4) if values are determined at the point of definition. PL/CV uses static scope to agree with PL/I.

Section 2.9

(2-40) One change of style allowed in PL/CV is that statements of theorems occur before the proof. Thus *proof; assume A;...;B; qed; A=>B* can be written essentially as *A=>B by proof; assume A;...;B; qed*. This format permits writing proofs in which "*assume A*" is suppressed because it can be inferred from the structure of the theorem being proved. The new format causes a change in the definition of accessibility because now assertions appear in a proof before they are proved. How exactly must the definition change?

3

THE THEORY OF INTEGERS
AND STRINGS

3.1 EXTENSIONS OF THE PREDICATE CALCULUS

In order to express interesting arguments concerning
programs, we must be able to refer to the data objects
which these programs manipulate. Elementary programming
tasks commonly involve integers (fixed point numbers),
floating point numbers, and character strings. Traditional
mathematical logic supplies straightforward methods for extending the syntax and semantics of our predicate calculus
language to cover all of these types of objects. Traditional methods for extending the proof rules of the predicate
calculus are severely deficient for our purposes.

We want a set of proof rules which will allow intuitively obvious inferences to be drawn in a single step, even
though they may involve many applications of traditional
axioms and rules. But the rules must also be easy to understand, and practical mechanical means should be available
to check whether a rule has been applied correctly. To
satisfy these three constraints simultaneously is in general quite difficult. We present a solution for the theory
of integers with $+,-,*,0,\pm 1,\pm 2,\ldots,<,\leq,=,\neq,\geq,>$. Similar
solutions for integers with $**$ (exponentiation) and $\div$, as
well as character strings should be attainable by hard
work. A good set of proof rules for floating point numbers may require a significant inspiration.

3.2 NUMBER THEORY SYNTAX

In this formal language of number theory, there are
symbols to talk about the integers, symbols for the operations of addition, subtraction and multiplication and sym-

bols for the predicates of order and equality. These symbols are a subset of the symbols of the right type in the
pure predicate calculus of Chapter II. The precise
syntax is:

$$
\begin{array}{ll}
\text{constant} & \rightarrow \ \ldots|-3|-2|-1|0|1|2|3|\ldots \\
\text{infix operator} & \rightarrow \ +,-,* \\
\text{infix relation} & \rightarrow \ <,\leq,=,\neq,\geq,> \\
\text{simple-type} & \rightarrow \ \textit{integer}
\end{array}
$$

The infix operators are of type $\textit{integer} \times \textit{integer} \rightarrow \textit{integer}$. The relations are of type $\textit{integer} \times \textit{integer}$.

When $\rho_1,\ldots,\rho_n$ are among $<,\leq,=,\neq,\geq,>$, then the
assertion $t_0\rho_1 t_1\rho_2 t_2\rho_3\ldots\rho_{n-1}t_{n-1}\rho_n t_n$ will be used to
abbreviate $t_0\rho_1 t_1 \ \& \ t_1\rho_2 t_2 \ \& \ t_{n-1}\rho_n t_n$.

3.3   NUMBER THEORY SEMANTICS

Everyone understands intuitively what integer expressions and assertions mean. In order to discuss arguments
about the integers within the formal semantics of (2.4),
we restrict attention to those models which agree with our
intuitive understanding.

Definition: A model $\mathcal{J}$ is an *integer model* iff
$$\mathcal{J}(\textit{integer}) = \mathbf{Z} = \{i|\ i \text{ is an integer}\}$$

.
.
.

$\mathcal{J}(-2)$ = the number negative two

$\mathcal{J}(-1)$ = the number negative one

$\mathcal{J}(0)$ = the number zero

$\mathcal{J}(1)$ = the number one

.
.
.

$\mathcal{J}(+)$ = the addition operation

$\mathcal{J}(-)$ = the subtraction operation

$\mathcal{Z}(*)$ = the multiplication operation

$\mathcal{Z}(<)$ = the less than relation

$\mathcal{Z}(\leq)$ = the less than or equal relation

$\mathcal{Z}(\geq)$ = the greater than or equal relation

$\mathcal{Z}(>)$ = the greater than relation.

An integer argument Arg is *valid* iff $< \mathcal{Z},s> \models$ Arg for all integer models $\mathcal{Z}$ and all states s.

3.4   PROOF RULES

Informal proof rules draw heavily on the rich intuitive experience which most people have with the integers. Certain reasonable restrictions may be placed on the application of this intuition. Any induction or argument involving a quantifier should be made explicit, since these kinds of reasoning are so error prone. A single step in a proof should not involve both arithmetic reasoning and a complicated propositional argument, since these two kinds of reasoning require quite different styles of thought. So, it is reasonable to formalize arithmetic proofs with an induction rule and a few rules which allow simple assertions (containing few, if any, logical connectives) to be inferred from other simple assertions.

Induction is a powerful tool, but quite simple to describe.

Positive induction:
    P(k/x);
    proof arbitrary integer x where x≥k & P;

.
.
.

P(x+1/x)
qed;

∀ integer x where x≥k . P

Many informal inductions fit the following form, where the term t with free variables α (not necessarily integer valued) defines a function into the nonnegative

49

integers. For instance, induction on the length of a
character string fits the form as we will see later.

Induction on a term:
proof [**assume** Q] *arbitrary* α;
            t≥k
        qed;
proof **assume** t = k) [& Q] *arbitrary* α;
            .
            .
            .
            P
        qed;
proof **assume** ∀α *where* t<n [& Q] . P
                    & t = n>k [&Q] *arbitrary* α;
            .
            .
            .
            P
        qed;

∀α [*where* Q] . P

In order to describe the rules for quantifier free
arithmetic reasoning, it is convenient to first consider a
traditional style axiomatization and divide the axioms into
categories.

1. Ring axioms and the definition of -.
    ∀ *integer* x,y,z .

(x+y = y+x & x∗y = y∗x	commutativity
& (x+y)+z = x+(y+z) & (x∗y)∗z = x∗(y∗z)	associativity
& x∗(y+z) = x∗y+x∗z	distributivity
& x+0 = x & x∗1 = x	identity
& x+(-x) = 0	additive inverse
& x-y = x+(-y))	subtraction

2. Discrete linear order
   ($\forall$ *integer* x,y,z

       $\neg$ x<x   irreflexivity

     & (x<y) $\vee$ (y<x) $\vee$ (x=y)   trichotomy

     & (x<y&y<z) => x<z   transitivity

     & $\neg$ (x<y<x+1))   discreteness

3. Definitions of $\leq, >, \geq, \neq$
   $\forall$ *integer* x,y,z .

   (x$\leq$y <=> x<y $\vee$ x=y

     & x>y <=> y<x

     & x$\geq$y <=> x>y $\vee$ x=y)

4. Monotonicity of + and *
   $\forall$ *integer* w,x,y,z .

   ((x$\geq$y&z$\geq$w) => x+z $\geq$ y+w

     & (x$\geq$y&z$\leq$w) => x-z $\geq$ y-w

     & (x$\geq$0&y$\geq$z) => x*y $\geq$ x*z

     & (x>0&x*y$\geq$x*z) => y$\geq$z)

    The inference rule *Arithmetic* takes any number of hypotheses of the forms $t_1 < t_2$, $t_1 \leq t_2$, $t_1 = t_2$, $t_1 \geq t_2$, $t_1 > t_2$, $t_1 \neq t_2$ and allows them to be first added, subtracted, and multiplied in any of the ways given by the Monotonicity axioms, then used along with the axioms of categories 1, 2 and 3 to derive either a contradiction (*false*) equality or inequality (including $<, \leq, \neq, \geq, >$), or else a disjunction of equalities and inequalities. *Arithmetic* is the hardest rule to describe precisely, but it captures so many of the intuitively obvious steps in informal proofs that a working understanding of the rule may be acquired by following the examples in the next section.

    By Gödel's famous incompleteness result [Kleene 52] there is no hope that all valid integer assertions will be proved using Arithmetic, and Induction. It is easy to show that all the Peano axioms follow from these two rules, so any arithmetic proof arising in a practical programming context can probably be formalized in our system.

3.5 EXAMPLES OF FORMAL PROOF

Here is an example of a complete formal proof establishing the Euclidean division theorem. A version of

> ∀ *integer* a,b *where* a≥0 & b>0.
> ∃ *integer* q,r *where* 0≤r<b . a = b*q+r.

In Chapter IV section 4.3 there is another proof of this using a program to compute q and r.

First consider an informal argument for this theorem.

Theorem: For all integers a≥0 and b>0 there exist integers q and r with 0≤r<b such that a = b*q+r.

Proof by induction on a.

Induction assertion: ∃ *integer* q,r *where*
0≤r<b . a = b*q+r.

Basis step.
Let a = 0.
0≤0<b and a = b*0+0.
So ∃ *integer* q.e *where* 0≤r<b . a = b*q+r.

Induction step.
Assume for all a<n that
∃ *integer* q,r *where* 0≤r<b . a = b*q+r.
Let a = n.

By the induction hypothesis we know
∃ *integer* q,r *where* 0≤r<b . a-1 = b*q+r.
Either r+1<b or r+1 = b.
If r+1<b, then we have 0≤r+1<b and
a = b*q+(r+1).
So ∃ *integer* q,r *where* 0≤r<b . a = b*q+r.
If r+1 = b, then we have 0≤0<b and
a = b*(q+1)+0.
So ∃ *integer* q,r *where* 0≤r<b . a = b*q+r.

In either case the induction assertion is proved.
By induction on a, ∀ *integer* a,b *where* a≥0 & b>0.
∃ *integer* q,r *where* 0≤r<b . a = b*q+r.

Now the formal proof.

```
/* Theorem: ∀ integer a,b where a≥0 & b>0 .
           ∃ integer q,r where 0≤r<b . a = b*q+r */
/* Proof:  by induction on a */
/* First, prove that a is an acceptable term for induction,
   that is, a≥0 */
```

```
1:   proof assume a≥0 & b>0 arbitrary a,b;
2:        a≥0
        qed;
/* Next, the basis step, letting a = 0 */
3:   proof assume a=0 & a≥0 & b>0        arbitrary integer a,b;
4:   0≤0<b                               by arith b>0;
5:   a = b*0+0                           by arith a=0;
6:   ∃ integer q,r where 0≤r<b . a = b*q+r
                                         by ∃I, 4, 5;
        qed; /* end of basis step */

/* Induction step:  Assume the theorem holds when a<n */
/* Prove the theorem for a=n */

7:   proof assume (∀ integer a,b where a<n & a≥0 & b>0 .
                   ∃ integer q,r where 0≤r<b . a = b*q+r)
                   & a = n>0 & a≥0 & b>0
                                         arbitrary integer a,b;
8:   a-1<n                               by arith, 7;
9:   a-1≥0                               by arith, 7;
10:  ∃ integer q,r where 0≤r<b . a-1 = b*q+r
                                         by ∀E, 7, 8, 9;
11:  proof choose integer q,r where 0≤r<b & a-1 = b*q+r;
12:  r+1<b ∨ r+1 = b                     by arith, 11;

/* Prove by cases that ∃ integer q,r where 0≤r<b .
   a = b*q+r */

13:  proof assume r+1<b;
14:  0≤r+1<b                            by arith, 11, 13;
15:  a = b*q+(r+1)                      by arith, 11;
16:  ∃ integer q,r where 0≤r<b . a = b*q+r
                                         by ∃I, 14, 15;
        qed; /* first case */

17:  proof assume r+1 = b;
18:  0≤0<b                               by arith, 7;
19:  a = b*q+(r+1)                      by arith, 11;
20:  a = b*q+b
21:  a = b*(q+1)+0                      by arith, 20;
22:  ∃ integer q,r where 0≤r<b . a = b*q+r
                                         by ∃I, 18, 21;
        qed; /* second case */
```

23: ∃ *integer* q,r *where* 0≤r<b . a = b*q+r
> *by* VE, 12, 16, 22;

    qed;
24: ∃ *integer* q,r *where* 0≤r<b . a = b*q+r
> *by* ∃E, 10, 23;

    qed; /* end of induction */

25: ∀ *integer* a,b *where* a≥0 & b>0 .
    ∃ *integer* q,r *where* 0≤r<b . a = b*q+r
> *by Induction on* a, 2, 6, 24

In this next example, we develop a proof in several steps, filling in more detail each time. Although a proof by contradiction that there is no largest prime is fairly simple, a constructive proof that arbitrarily large primes exist has one subtlety. Given n, we need to prove that n!+1 is either prime or has a prime factor larger than n. To show constructively that any number is prime or has a prime factor involves describing a procedure to find factors. We must describe this procedure without the benefit of commands.

define   prime(x) = ∀ *integer* y *where* y>1 & factor(x,y) .
      y=x;

define factor(x,y) = ∃ *integer* z . x = y*z;

/* Euclid's Theorem: ∀ *integer* n *where* n≥1 . ∃ *integer* x
               where x>n . prime(x) */

To prove a universally quantified theorem about integers, we may apply either ∀I or induction. Since knowing a prime larger than n-1 doesn't seem to help us find one larger than n, we choose ∀I.

P.1:   *proof arbitrary integer* n *where* n≥1;

We do not have the symbol !, but we may choose an integer m with the essential properties of n!.

P.2:∃ *integer* m *where* m≥n & m≥1 . ∀ *integer* i *where* 1≤i≤n .
   factor(m,i);

(The proof of P.2 will be provided below.)

P.3: *proof choose integer* m *where* m≥n & m≥1 &
         ∀ *integer* i *where* 1≤i≤n . factor(m,i);

P.4: prime(m+1) ∨ ∃ *integer* i *where* prime(i) & i>1 .
    factor(m+1,i)
    /* Prove by cases that ∃ *integer* x *where* x>n .
      Prime(x) */
    /* The first case is trivial */

P.5: *proof assume* prime(m+1);

P.6:   ∃ *integer* x *where* x>n . prime(x) *by* ∃I
    qed; /* First Case */

P.7: *proof assume* ∃ *integer* i *where* prime(i) & i>1 .
    factor(m+1,i);

P.8:   *proof choose integer* i *where* prime(i) & i>1 &
    factor(m+1,i);
    /* Since no number ≤n may divide m+1 ... */

P.9:   i>n;

P.10:   ∃ *integer* x *where* x>n . prime(x) *by* ∃I
    qed
    qed; /* Second Case */

P.11:   ∃ *integer* x *where* x>n . prime(x) *by* VE;
    qed; /* Choice of m */

P.12: ∃ *integer* x *where* x>n . prime(x) *by* ∃E;
    qed; /* Arbitrary n */

P.13: ∀ *integer* n *where* n≥1 . ∃ *integer* x *where* x>n .
    prime(x) *by* ∀I;

Lines P.2, P.4 and P.9 do not follow directly from earlier
lines. P.2 and P.4 are special cases of two general
theorems:

∀ *integer* n *where* n≥0 . ∃ *integer* m *where* m≥n .
       ∀ *integer* i *where* 1≤i≤n . factor(m,i)

and

∀ *integer* k *where* k≥2 . prime(k) ∨∃ *integer* i *where*
      prime(i) & 1<i<k . factor(k,i);

These two theorems will be proved by induction and added as lemmas (1 and 2) to the beginning of the proof. P. 9 may be proved by adding:

> /* Prove that i>n */

P.8.1: $i \leq n \lor i > n$ by arith;

> /* The first case, $i \leq n$ is impossible */

P.8.2: *proof assume* $i \leq n$;

P.8.3: factor(m,i) *by* VE;

P.8.4: ¬factor(m+1,i); /* proved below */

P.8.5: *false*   /* contradicts P.8. */
qed; /* Contradiction */
/* The second case is exactly what we want */

P.8.6: *proof assume* i>n
qed;

P.9:   i>n by VE;

The only unjustified line, P8.4 is also suitable to be proved by a lemma:

∀ *integer* x,y *where* y>1 & factor(x,y) . ¬factor(x+1,y)

L3.1: *proof arbitrary integer* x,y *where* y>1 & factor(x,y);

L3.2: *proof assume* factor(x+1,y);

L3.3: *proof choose integer* z_1 *where* x+1 = z_1*y;

L3.4: *proof choose integer* z_2 *where* x = z_2*y;

$$(z_2*y)+1 = z_1*y; \text{ /* by equality */}$$

$$1 = (z_1-z_2)*y \text{ by arith};$$

$$1 \neq (z_1-z_2)*y \text{ by arith, y>1}$$

qed /* end choice of z_2 */
qed /* end choice of z_1. */

qed; ¬factor(x+1,y)
qed;

lemma 3: ∀ *integer* x,y *where* y>1 & factor(x,y) .
¬factor(x+1,y)

Now to prove the remaining two lemmas.

/* Lemma 1: ∀ *integer* n *where* n≥0 .
              ∃ *integer* m *where* m≥n & m≥1 .
              ∀ *integer* i *where* 1≤i≤n . factor(m,k) */

/* Prove by induction */

/* Basis: ∃ *integer* m *where* m≥0 & m≥1 .∀ *integer* i *where*
              1≤i≤0 . factor(m,i) */

/* The basis step is vacuous, since there is no i with
   1≤i≤0 */

L1.1: *proof arbitrary integer* i *where* 1≤i≤0;

L1.2: *false by arith;*
        qed;

L1.3: ∀ *integer* i *where* 1≤i≤0 . factor(m,i) *by* ∀I;

L1.4: ∃ *integer* m *where* m≥0 & m≥1 . ∀ *integer* i *where*
              1≤i≤0 . factor(m,i);

/* Induction step: Assume the lemma for n and prove n+1 */

L1.5: *proof arbitrary integer* n *where* n≥0 &
              ∃ *integer* m *where* m≥n & m≥1 .
              ∀ *integer* i *where* 1≤i≤n . factor(m,i);

L1.6: *proof choose integer* m *where* m≥n & m≥1 &
              ∀ *integer* i *where* 1≤i≤n . factor(m,i);

L1.7:   m*(n+1)≥n+1 by arith, n≥0, m≥1;

L1.8:   ∀ *integer* i *where* 1≤i≤n+1 . factor(m*(n+1),i);

L1.9:   ∃ *integer* m *where* m≥n+1 & m≥1 . ∀ *integer* i *where*
                       1≤i≤n+1 . factor(m,i) *by* ∃I
           qed;

L1.10:   ∃ *integer* m *where* m≥n+1 & m≥1 . ∀ *integer* i *where*
                       1≤i≤n+1 . factor(m,i) *by* ∀I;
           qed;

L1.11: ∃ *integer* m *where* m≥n+1 & m≥1 . ∀ *integer* i *where*
                       1≤i≤n+1 . factor(m,i) *by* ∃E
           qed; / Induction step */

L1.12: ∀ *integer* n *where* n≥0 . ∃ *integer* m *where* m≥n & m≥1 .
          ∀ *integer* i *where* 1≤i≤n . factor(m,i)
                                              by Induction;

Line L1.8 still needs to be proved, so we add:

          /* Prove ∀ *integer* i *where* 1≤i≤n+1 .
             factor(m*(n+1),i) */

L1.71:   *proof arbitrary integer* i *where* 1≤i≤n+1;

L1.72:   i≤n ∨ i=n+1 *by* arith;
          /* The first case uses the induction hypothesis */

L1.73:   *proof assume* i≤n;

L1.74:   factor(m,i) *by* ∀E

L1.75:   factor(m*(n+1),i);
            qed;

L1.76:   *proof assume* i = n+1;

L1.77:   factor(m*(n+1),i)
            qed;

L1.78:   factor(m*(n+1),i) *by* ∀E
          qed;

L1.8:   ∀ *integer* i *where* 1≤i≤n+1 . factor(m*(n+1),i);

All that remains to complete the proof is lemma 2. In
order to prove lemma 2 we use lemmas 2.1 and 2.2. Lemma
2.1 tells us constructively that every integer greater
than one has a factor less than itself or it does not.
Lemma 2.2 treats an alternative characterization of primes
as those numbers p which have no factors y where 1<y<p.
(Actually the lemma establishes only half of the characterization.)

/* Lemma 2.1: ∀ *integer* m . ∀ *integer* b *where* b>1.
                (∀ *integer* k *where* 1<k<b . ¬factor(m,k)) ∨
                 ∃ *integer* k *where* 1<k<b . factor(m,k)) */

/* proof by induction on b, ∀I on m */

```
lemma 2.1:  proof arbitrary integer m;
/* basis step */
 proof arbitrary k where 1<k<0;
        false by arith;
 qed;  /* basis case */
 V integer k where 1<k<0 . ¬factor(m,k) v
 ∃ integer k where 1<k<0 . factor(m,k);


/* induction step, induction on n */
 proof assume
       (V integer k where 1<k<n . ¬factor(m,k)) v
       (∃ integer k where 1<k<n . factor(m,k));

/* show factor(m,n) v ¬factor(m,n) */

/* apply the Euclidean division theorem from 3.5 */

        ∃ integer q,r where 0≤r<n . m = q*n+r by VE,m,n;
  proof choose integer q,r where 0≤r<n & m = q*n+r;
        r=0 v r≠0 by arith;

/* divisibility is determined by r, analyse cases r=0, r≠0 */

    proof assume r=0;
      m = q*n by arith;
      ∃ integer z . m = z*n by ∃I;
        factor(m,n) v ¬factor(m,n)
    qed;  /* end case r=0 */
    proof assume r≠0;
    /* for contradiction, assume factor(m,n) */
     proof assume ∃ integer z . m = z*n;
      proof choose integer z where m = z*n;
      m = q*n+r;
      m = z*n;
      z*n = q*n+r by arith;
      (z-q)*n = r by arith;
      (z-q)<0 v (z-q)>0 v (z-q) = 0 by arith;
       proof assume z-q<0;
                    (z-q)*n<0 by arith, n>0;
                    r≥0;
                    false by arith
        qed;
```

```
        proof assume z-q>0;
                    (z-q)*n>n by arith;
                    r>n by arith;
                    r<n;
                    false
      qed;
      proof assume (z-q) = 0;
                    (z-q)*n = 0 by arith;
                    r≠0;
                    false
      qed;
      false by VE;   /* end of case analysis on r */
      qed;   /* end choice of z */
    qed;   /* end of contradiction proof */
    ¬ ∃ integer z . m = z*n by ¬I;
    main_disjunct:factor(m,n)∨¬factor(m,n) by VE, r=0∨r≠0;


/* finish lemma by a case analysis on factor(m,n) */

    proof assume factor(m,n);
          1<n<n+1;
          ∃ integer k where 1<k<n+1 . factor(m,k) by ∃I;
      (∃ integer k where 1<k<n+1 . factor(m,k)) ∨
      (∀ integer k where 1<k<n+1 . ¬factor(m,k)) by VI
    qed;   /* end of factor(m,n) case */
    proof assume ¬factor(m,n);
      proof arbitrary integer k where 1<k<n+1;
            1<k<n ∨ k=n by arith;

            /* case analysis on value of k */

      proof assume 1<k<n;
            ¬factor(m,k) by ∀E,k
      qed;
      proof assume k=n;
            ¬factor(m,k)
      qed;
      ¬factor(m,k) by VE   /* 1<k<n ∨ k=n */
    qed;
    ∀ integer k where 1<k<n+1 . ¬factor(m,k) by ∀I;
  qed;
  (∀ integer k where 1<k<n+1 . ¬factor(m,k))∨
  (∃ integer k where 1<k<n+1 . factor(m,k)) by VI;
```

```
  qed;   /* end of r≠0 case */
 qed;   /* end of choice of q,r */
qed;   /* end of induction step */
∀ integer b where b>1 . (∀ integer k where 1<k<n+1 .
    ¬factor(m,k)) ∨ (∃ integer k where 1<k<n+1 . factor(m,k))
   by induction;
qed;   /* end of lemma 2.1 */
∀ integer m . ∀ integer b where b>1 . (∀ integer k where
   1<k<n+1 . ¬factor(m,k)) ∨ (∃ integer k where 1<k<n+1 .
   factor(m,k)) by VI;

/* lemma 2.2:  ∀ integer n . (∀ integer k where 1<k<n .
                                ¬factor(n,k)) => prime(n) */

proof arbitrary integer n;
 proof assume ∀ integer k where 1<k<n . ¬factor(n,k);

/* use definition of prime */

 proof arbitrary integer y where y>0 & factor(n,y);
 disjunct: y=1 ∨ y=n ∨ 1<y<n ∨ y>n by arith;

 /* analyse each case of the disjunction */

 proof assume y=1;
       y=1 ∨ y=n
 qed;
 proof assume y=n;
       y=1 ∨ y=n
 qed;
 proof assume 1<y<n;
       factor(n,y);
       -factor(n,y) by ∀E        /* from hypothesis */
       false;
       y=1 ∨ y=n
 qed;
 proof assume y>n;
  proof choose integer z where n = z*y;
        z<0 ∨ z=0 ∨ z>0 by arith;
        y>0 by arith, y>n, n>1;
   proof assume z<0;
         z*y<0 by arith;
         n<0;
         n>0 by arith n>1;
         false
```

61

```
    qed;
    proof assume z=0;
         n=0;
         n>0 by arith, n>1;
         false
    qed;
    proof assume z>0;
         z*y>n by arith, y>n, z≥1;
         z*y = n;
         false
    qed;
    false by VE, z<0 ∨ z=0 ∨ z>0;
    qed;
    false by ∃E;  /* from factor(n,y) */
    y=1 ∨ y=n
   qed;
```

/* end of case analysis */

```
y=1 ∨ y=n by VE, disjunct
  qed;
  ∀ integer y where y>0 & factor(n,y) . (y=1 ∨ y=n) by ∀I
  qed;
  ∀ integer k where 1<k<n . ¬factor(n,y) =>
  ∀ integer y where y>0 & factor(n,y) .(y=1 ∨ y=n) by ∀I
qed;
∀ integer n . ∀ integer k where 1<k<n . ¬factor(n,y) =>
    ∀ integer y where y>0 & factor(n,y) .(y=1 ∨ y=n) by ∀I;
```

/* end of lemma 2.2 */

We now prove lemma 2 by a so called "course of values" induction.

For a "course of values" induction, we prove ∀ *integer* n *where* n≥k . P(n) by assuming as induction hypothesis ∀ *integer* x *where* k≤x<n . P(x) and concluding P(n). We need just such an induction below because we must assume that for all integers x where 2≤x<k, x is prime or x has a prime factor. We need this stronger assumption rather than the weak assumption k-1 prime or k-1 has a prime factor because when we choose a factor of k, it will be some x<k, not necessarily k-1.

This apparently stronger form of induction can be derived from ordinary induction in a simple way, namely we prove ∀ *integer* x *where* 2≤x<k ... by induction on k.

The details appear below.

/* basis step */

L2.1:   *proof arbitrary* x *where* 2≤x<0;
            false by arith, 2≤x<0;
            prime(x) ∨ ∃ *integer* j *where* prime(j) & j>1 .
              factor(x,j)
        qed;

/* induction step */

L2.2:   *proof arbitrary* x *where* k≥0 &
            ∀ *integer* x *where* 2≤x<k .
            (prime(x) ∨ ∃ *integer* j *where* prime(j) & j>1 .
              factor(x,j))

/* goal: prove prime(k) ∨ ∃ *integer* j *where* prime(j) &
          j>1 . factor(k,j) */

/* by lemma 2.1 we know */

L2.3:   (∀ *integer* y *where* 1<y<k . ¬factor(k,y)) ∨
        (∃ *integer* y *where* 1<y<k . factor(k,y))

/* begin a case analysis on the disjunction to prove
   prime(k) ∨ ∃ *integer* i *where* prime(i) & i>1 .
   factor(k,i) */

L2.4:   *proof assume* ∀ *integer* y *where* 1<y<k . ¬factor(k,y);

        /* now apply lemma 2.2 with k for n */

L2.5:   ∀ *integer* y *where* 1<y<k . ¬factor(k,y) =>
        prime(k) by ∀E
        prime(k);

L2.6:   prime(k) ∨ ∃ *integer* i *where* prime(i) & i>1 .
        factor(k,i)
        qed; /* end of first case for k from L2.4 */

L2.7:   *proof assume* ∃ *integer* y *where* 1<y<k . factor(k,y);

L2.8:   *proof choose* y *where* 1<y<k & factor(k,y);

        /* now apply induction hypothesis */

        2≤y<k *by arith*, 1<y<k;

L2.9:   prime(y) ∨ ∃ *integer* j *where* prime(j) & j>1 .
        factor(y,j);

L2.10:   *proof assume* prime(y); /* first case of L2.9 */
          prime(y) & y>1 & factor(k,y);
          ∃ *integer* i *where* prime(i) & i>1 . factor(k,i)
          by ∃I
          qed;

L2.11:   *proof assume* ∃ *integer* j *where* prime(j) & j>1 .
          factor(y,j); /* second case of L2.9 */

L2.12:   *proof choose integer* j *where* prime(j) & j>1 &
          factor(y,j);
          factor(k,y);
          factor(y,j);
          factor(k,j);   /* by previous lemma */
          prime(j) & j>1 & factor(k,j);
          ∃ *integer* i *where* prime(i) & i>1 . factor(k,i);
          qed;   /* end of second case y */

L2.13:   ∃ *integer* i *where* prime(i) & i>1 . factor(k,i)
          by VE; /* by above case analysis on L2.9 */
          qed;

L2:14:   ∃ *integer* i *where* prime(i) & i>1 . factor(k,i)
          by ∃E;
        qed;   /* end of choice of y */

L2.15:   prime(k) ∨ ∃ *integer* i *where* prime(i) & i>1 .
          factor(k,i);
        qed;   /* end of second case for k from L2.3 */

   proof arbitrary integer x *where* 2≤x<k+1;
        2≤x<k ∨ x=k by arith, 2≤x<k+1;
        proof assume 2≤x<k;
        prime(x) ∨ ∃ *integer* i *where* prime(i) & i>1 .
        factor(x,i) by VE   /* substitute in induction
                              hypothesis */
        qed;
        proof assume x=k;/* we have done all the work above */
        prime(k) ∨ ∃ *integer* i *where* prime(i) & i>1 .
        factor(k,i) /* form L2.15 */
        qed
   qed;

V *integer* x *where* 2≤x<k+1 . prime(x) ∨ ∃ *integer* i *where*
   prime(i) & i>1 . factor(x,i) by VI;
qed; /* end of induction proof on k */

step 1: V *integer* k *where* k≥0 . V *integer* x *where* 2≤x<k .
           prime(x) ∨ ∃ *integer* i *where* prime(i) & i>1 .
           factor(x,i) *by* induction; /* on k */

/* now prove lemma 2 from step 1 */

proof arbitrary integer k *where* 2≤k;
    k≥0 *by* arith, k≥2;
    k<k+1 by arith;
    V *integer* x *where* 2≤x<k+1 .
    prime(x) ∨ ∃ *integer* i *where* prime(i) & i>1 & fact
    factor(x,i);
    by VE, k+1 /* substitute in step 1, k+1 for k */
    prime(k) ∨ ∃ *integer* i *where* prime(i) & i>1 &
    factor(k,i)
    by VE, k /* substitute k for x above */
qed

lemma 2: V *integer* k *where* k≥2 . prime(k) ∨
         ∃ *integer* i *where* prime(i) & i>1 . factor(k,i)

Remarks 1: In a classical proof of this theorem, we would
not need to prove lemma 2. It would follow from the general
logical theorem A∨¬A and basic properties of the quantifiers.
However, such a proof would not supply the information to
decide whether a given number is a prime. † (See part III
of appendix for a classical proof similar to this.)

2. With a proof of this size the advantages of the
PL/CV proof style discussed in the appendix become
quite clear. It is very useful to have the statement of a
theorem before its proof and to have the cases of a case
analysis clearly delineated.

---

† There is a metatheorem, which will be a rule of PL/CV,
that for any assertion A with no quantifiers or bounded
quantifiers, A∨¬A is constructively valid.

3.6   STRING THEORY

String theory is a less common mathematical enterprise than number theory. It has not been developed from several points of view and axiomatized as number theory has been. So we cannot turn to established logic to guide our presentation. The theory of formal languages, developed in linguistics and computer science, is an important part of string theory and will supply us with examples, but it has not been developed axiomatically. Moreover, we choose to use use PL/I - like primitives as the basis of the theory. They are not necessarily the most convenient ones, but they are dictated in the implemented logic by the decision to make PL/CV compatible with PL/I.

The syntax for string theory uses these categories:

character $\rightarrow$ ⌿ | . | < | (| + | ¦ | & | \$ | * |) | ; | ¬

$\rightarrow$ - | / | , | % | _ | > | ? | : | # | @ | ' | = | "

$\rightarrow$ A | B | C | D | E | F | G | H | I | J | K | L | M | N | O | P | Q | R | S | T | U | V | W | X | Y | Z |

$\rightarrow$ 0 | 1 | 2 | 3 | ... | 8 | 9.

(where ⌿ denotes the *blank* character). For convenience let $\Sigma_{PL/I}$ denote the set of all these characters.

character string $\rightarrow$ {character}*   This is $\Sigma^*_{PL/I}$.

literal $\rightarrow$ 'character string'

Literals are the *constants* among the string expressions. The other expressions are defined below. Notice, a character string can be empty, so a literal can be an apostrophe immediately followed by another apostrophe. This "empty" literal denotes the *null string*.

infix operator $\rightarrow$ | |

function symbol $\rightarrow$ *substr*

$\rightarrow$ *len*

simple type $\rightarrow$ *string*

The relations $<, \neq, >, \geq, \neq$, are extended to strings. The type of the string operators and relations is given by:

66

symbol	type description
'character string'	*string*
||	*string × string → string*
substr	*string × integer → string*
	string × integer × integer → string
len	*string → integer*
$<, \leq, >, \geq, \neq$	*string × string*

These operations and relations are regarded as special instances of those of the predicate calculus. Just as arithmetic expressions are those expressions involving operators of relations of type integer, so string expressions are those with operators and relations of type string. An expression such as $substr(s, t_1)$ is of mixed type, string and integer.

The type of an expression is the type of its value. Thus length(exp) is of type integer and $substr(exp_1, exp_2)$ is of type string.

3.7   SEMANTICS OF STRING THEORY

A string model is a sepcial type of integer model. To define the intended meaning, we first specify the basic operations and predicates. These are defined over the domain of integers, $\mathcal{M}(integer) = \mathbf{Z}$, and the domain of character strings, $\mathcal{M}(string) = \Sigma^*_{PL/I}$.

The concatentation function $\|: string × string → string$ maps $\Sigma^*_{PL/I} × \Sigma^*_{PL/I}$ to $\Sigma^*_{PL/I}$. It takes strings x_1 and y and forms $x\|y$, their *concatenation*. For example 'star'\|'wars' = starwars.

The function substr $(-,-,-): string × integer × integer → string$ takes a string x and two integers p and ℓ and selects from x the *substring* of length ℓ starting at position p (regarding the *leftmost* character as the first position and counting to the right). If p is not a position in x or if $\ell \leq 0$, then the value is the empty string. If ℓ is too large (greater than len(x)-p+1), then len(x)-p+1 is used instead.

For example:
$$substr('abcde', 5, 1) = e$$
$$substr('abcde', 5, 2) = e$$
$$substr('abcde', 6, 1) = ' '$$
$$substr('abcde', 2, 3) = 'bcd'.$$

If the last argument to substr (-,-,-) is omitted, then the value len(x)-p+1 is taken, which defined the substring from position p to the right end of the string.

The function *len: string → integer* maps $\Sigma^*_{PL/I}$ to **Z**. It gives the length of the string. For instance, len('aℏaℏaℏℏℏ') = 8.

The equality predicate of type *string × string* is peculiar (and poorly conceived) in PL/I. Namely x=y iff x and y are equal *except for rightmost blanks*. Thus STAR = STARℏℏ but ℏSTAR ≠ STAR.

Our approach to restoring clarity is to introduce another basic equality operation (which in PL/CV must be defined as a function) called *relative equality*. We use

$$x=y\ mod(a)$$

for character a or the null string to mean that when all occurrences of 'a' are removed from both x and y then they are really equal. So normal equality is x=y *mod*( ), i.e. equality with no character removed. Relative equality is very useful in string theory and probably should be a primitive regardless of its value in clarifying the PL/I primitives.

The order in which the individual characters were presented in the grammar is called the "collating sequence" for the alphabet. We repeat it here without the intervening vertical bars used in the grammar:

$$\text{ℏ . < (+ | \& \$ *) ; ¬ - / , \% \_ > ? : \# @ ' = "}$$
$$\text{ABCDEFGHIJKLMNOPQRSTUVWXYZ0123456789.}$$

This order relation can be extended to all strings in the obvious manner, namely it is the basis for *alphabetical* order (also called *lexicographic* order). To compare two strings of unequal length, the shorter is extended to the length of the longer by adding *rightmost* blanks. Then the strings are compared from the left character by character. For example, AB < ABA because ABℏ < ABA since ℏ < A. In general, $a_1 \ldots a_n < b_1 \ldots b_n$ iff for some p $a_p < b_p$ and for all i < p, $a_i = b_i$. The relations ≤, >, ≥ are defined in the obvious way from < (e.s. x≥y iff y<x or y=x).

We are now ready to define a string model.

Definition: A string model $\mathscr{S}$ is an integer model with the additional properties that:

$\mathscr{S}(string)$	=	$\Sigma^*_{PL/I}$
$\mathscr{S}('x')$	=	x for $x\epsilon\Sigma^*_{PL/I}$
$\mathscr{S}(\|\|)$	=	concatenation
$\mathscr{S}(substr)$	=	PL/I substring function
$\mathscr{S}(len)$	=	PL/I length function
$\mathscr{S}(=)$	=	strange PL/I equality
$\mathscr{S}(= mod(a))$	=	equality mod $a\epsilon\Sigma_{PL/I}$
$\mathscr{S}(<)$	=	collating sequence order

3.8 BASIC FACTS ABOUT STRINGS

We have not formulated all the details of a workable axiomatic string theory based on the PL/I primitives, so in place of axioms and inference rules, there is a collection of basic facts from which a set of three or four high level axioms, in the spirit of *arithmetic*, could emerge.*

(1) Relative equality

$\forall$ *string* x,y,z,a *where* len(a) $\leq$ 1.

    (x=x mod(a) &   reflexivity

    (x=y mod(a) &

    y=z mod(a)) => x=z mod(a) &   transitivity

    x=y mod(a) <=> y=x mod(a))   symmetry

(2) Concatenation

$\forall$ *string* x,y,u,v, a *where* len(a) $\leq$ 1.

  (''||x = x   null string is left identity

 & x||'' = x   null string is right identity

 & 'a'||x = ax   left successor

 & x||'a' = xa)   right successor

---

*The article "String Theory" [Corcoran, Frank, Maliney 74] presents an axiomatic string theory from the logician's point of view.

$$\& \quad x||y = \text{''} \ => x = \text{''} \ \& \ y = \text{''}$$

$$\& \quad x||y = u||v \ => \ \exists \ string \ z \ . \ (x=u||z \ \& \ v=z||y) \ \lor$$
$$\exists \ string \ z \ . \ (u=x|\cdot|z \ \& \ y=z||v)$$

(3) Length

$\forall \ string \ x,y,a \ .$

$$\text{len}(x) \geq 0 \qquad\qquad\qquad \text{length is nonegative}$$

$$\& \quad \text{len}(x) = 0 <=> x = \text{''} \qquad\qquad \text{length of null string is 0}$$

$$\& \quad \text{len}(x) = 1 <=>$$
$$x = '\cancel{b}' \ \lor \ x = '.' \ \lor \ \ldots \ \lor \ x = '9'$$

$$\& \quad \text{len}(x) > 1 \ => \ \exists \ string \ a,y \ . \ (x=a||y \ \& \ \text{len}(a)=1)$$

$$\& \quad \text{len}(x||y) = \text{len}(x) + \text{len}(y)$$

(4) Substring

$\forall \ string \ x,y,a \ . \ where \ \text{len}(a) \leq 1$

$$1 \leq i \leq \text{len}(x) \ => \ \text{substr}(x||y, \exp_1, \exp_2) = \text{substr}(x, \exp_1, \exp_2)$$

$$\& \quad \text{len}(x) < \exp_1 \leq \text{len}(x) + \text{len}(y) \ => \ \text{substr}(x||y, \exp_1, \exp_2) =$$
$$\text{substr}(y, \exp_1 - \text{len}(x), \exp_2)$$

$$\& \quad \text{substr}(x, \exp_1, \exp_2) \neq \text{''} \ <=> \ 1 \leq \exp_1 \leq \text{len}(x) \ \&$$
$$1 \leq \exp_2 \leq \text{len}(x) - \exp_1 + 1$$

$$\& \quad \text{substr}(x, 1, \exp) \ || \ \text{substr}(x, \exp+1, \ \text{len}(x) - \exp) = x$$

$$\& \quad \text{substr}(x||y, \text{len}(x)+1, \text{len}(y)) = y$$

$$\& \quad \text{substr}('a', 1, 1) = 'a'$$

$$\& \quad \text{substr}(x, 1, \exp_1 - 1) \ || \ \text{substr}(x, \exp_1, \exp_2) \ ||$$
$$\text{substr}(x, \exp_1 + \exp_2 + 1, \text{len}(x) - (\exp_1 + \exp_2)) = x$$

$$\& \quad 1 \leq \exp_1 \leq \text{len}(x) \ \& \ 1 \leq \exp_2 \leq \text{len}(x) - \exp_1 + 1 \ =>$$
$$\text{len}(\text{substr}(x, \exp_1, \exp_2)) = \exp_2)$$

(5) Lexicographical order

$$'\cancel{b}' < '.' < \ldots < 'A' < \ldots < 'Z' < '0' < \ldots < '9'$$

$$\& \ \forall \ string \ x,y,z,w,a,b \quad where \ \text{len}(a) = \text{len}(b) = 1 \ \& \ a < b . \ ($$

>   x<y => x≠y   distinctness of characters
>
> &   x<y & y<z => x<z   transitivity of <
>
> &   x≤y <=> x<y ∨ x=y   definition of ≤
>
> &   x≥y <=> y≤x   definition of ≥
>
> &   x||a||z < x||b||w)   lexicographic property

(6)   Induction

> P(''/x), *proof arbitrary string a,x where* len(a)=1 & P;
>
> .
>
> .
>
> .
>
>   P(x||a/x)
>   *qed*

∀ *string* x . P

This induction rule can be derived from induction on t presented in 3.4

As in the case of number theory, no one can hope to find a complete set of axioms because of the famous Gödel incompleteness results. (Number theory can be formulated in relatively primitive parts of the string theory.) However, the basic facts listed above should be adequate for all common arguments about strings. They will be used in example proofs as if they were axioms with the heading name as a rule name. Enough information will be supplied in the justification of steps using these rules to allow mechanical determination of precisely which facts were used.

3.9 EXAMPLES

Theorems in any first order string theory lack a certain mathematical sophistication and heritage, but we have devised an example to illustrate the axiomatic role of the basic facts. This example and the exercises prepare the way for analysing programs which manipulate strings.

A Programming Logic

Example:

/*Theorem ∀ *string* a,x,y *where* len(a)=1 .

        ((¬ ∃ *integer* i . substr(x,i,1)=a &

         ¬ ∃ *integer* j . substr(y,j,1)=a) =>

         ¬ ∃ *integer* k . substr(x||y,k,1)=a)*/

proof arbitrary string a,x,y *where* len(a)=1

proof assume ¬ ∃ *integer* i . substr(x,i,1)=a & ¬ ∃ *integer*
j . substr(y,j,1)=a

/* for contradition assume the negation of the conclusion */

proof assume ∃ *integer* k . substr(x||y,k,1)=a;

      a≠ '' *by len*;/* from len(a)=1 */

      1≤k≤len(x||y);   *by substr*

      len(x||y) = len(x)+len(y) *by len*;

D: k≤len(x) ∨ len(x)<k *by arith*;

/* now argue by cases on k */

B1:   *proof assume* k≤len(x);

          1≤k≤len(x);

          substr(x||y,d,1) = substr(x,k,1)   *by substr*;

          substr(x,k,1) = a   *by sub*;

          ∃ *integer* i . substr(x,i,1) = a   *by* ∃ I;

            false

    qed;

B2:   *proof assume* len(x)<k;

          len(x)<k≤len(x)+len(y)   *by arith*;

          substr(x||y,k,1) = substr(y,k-len(x),1)*by substr*;

          substr(y,k-len(x),1) = a   *by substr*;

          ∃ *integer* j . substr(y,j,1) = a;

            false

    qed;

    false   *by*   VE, D, B1, B2

qed;

    ¬ ∃ *integer* k . substr(x||y,k,1) = a

qed

   (¬ ∃ *integer* i . substr(x,i,1) = a &

    ¬ ∃ *integer* j . substr(y,j,1) = a) =>

    ¬ ∃ *integer* k . substr(x||y,k,1) = a

   qed

∀ *string* a,x,y *where* len(a) = 1 .

$((\neg \exists$ *integer* i . substr(x,i,1) = a &
$\neg \exists$ *integer* j . substr(y,j,1) = a) =>
$\neg \exists$ *integer* k . substr(x||y,k,1) = a)

One systematic part of string theory is the theory of formal languages, but much of this is not naturally formulated in the first order theory of strings. However, we can treat certain concepts quite directly. We illustrate one of these.

The Kleene star operator, *, allows building a new set of strings from an initial set. Given $S = \{x_1,\ldots,x_n\}$, the set S* is the collection of all finite (including empty) strings over S. The star indicates the union of the finite concatenations $S^n = \{z_1 z_2 \ldots z_n \mid z_i \epsilon S\}$. The star offers a concise way of describing certain patterns. For example, if x is in (aba)*, then it looks like the empty string, or aba or abaaba or abaabaaba, etc.

There is a predicate in the string theory such that

$$p(x) \text{ iff } x\epsilon(aba)*.$$

Namely

$\exists$ *integer* k *where* k≥0 . len(x) = 3*k &

$\exists$ *integer* i *where* i≥0 .(((mod(i,3)=0 & 1≤i≤len(x)) =>
      substr(x,i,1)=a) &
     ((mod(i,3)=1 & 1≤i≤len(x)) =>
      substr(x,i,1)=a) &
     ((mod(i,3)=2 & 1≤i≤len(x)) =>
      substr(x,i,1)=b))

The relation mod(i,3)=x can be precisely defined in arithmetic, namely eqmod(i,3,x) iff
$\exists$ *integer* k . i = 3.k+x.

We can easily define the operations common in formal language theory. For example, the reverse of a string x, written x^R, is defined by the predicate reverse (x,y) iff
len(x) = len(y) &
$\forall$ *integer* i *where* 1≤i≤len(x).

   substr(x,i,1) = substr(y,len(x)+1-i,1).

With operations like reverse and Kleene star we can pose in the exercises some simple theorems which further illustrate elementary string theory.

Proposition: ∀ *string* x,y,z . z||x = z||y => x=y

Define palindrome(x) = ∀ *string* y *where* reverse(x,y) . y=x.

Proposition: ∀ *string* x,y *where* reverse(x,y)ˋ.
palindrome(x||y).

3.10 EXERCISES

Section 3.1

(3-1) Which of these assertions about integers is provable in one step from the rules of Chapter II?

(i)   2+1 = 2+1   (ii)   2+1 = 1+2   (iii)   x+1 ≥ x+1
(iv)   x+1 > x   (v)   ∀ *integer* x. ∃ *integer* y. y>x
(vi)   2*(x+y) = 2*x + 2*y   (vii)   x*y = y*x
(viii)   x*y = y*x => x*y*z = y*z*x

(3-2) The theory of integers whose absolute value is bounded by $10^{10^{10}}$ clearly includes all "useful" statements about numbers. Moreover, every assertion about these numbers can in principle be decided by a simple algorithm (which examines all possible cases). Does such a theory meet the requirements discussed in (3.1)?

Section 3.2

(3-3) Show how the rules of Chapter II, (2.3) *type restrictions* determine the types of the expressions in the following assertions:

(i)   ∀ *integer* x,y,z. ((x+y) > x => x > (z-y))
(ii)   ∀ *integer* x,y. (0<w & x<y => x+w < y+w)

(3-4) Expand the relations below to their unabbreviated forms:

(i)   0≤x<y≤z   (ii)   0<x ≠ y<w
(iii)   0<x>y ≠ z.

Section 3.3

(3-5) Let $\mathcal{Q}$ denote the set of rational numbers, $\{0,\pm1,\pm2,\pm1/2,\pm3,\pm1/3,\pm2/3,\pm3/2,\ldots\}$. Is $<\mathcal{Q},+,-,*,<,\le,\ge,>>$ an integer model?

(3-6) Let $\mathcal{Z}_n$ denote the finite set $\{-n,-n-1,\ldots,-1,0,+1,\ldots,n-1,n\}$. Can $<\mathcal{Z}_n,+,-,*,<,\le,\ge,>>$ be an integer model?

(3-7) Verify that the following are correct applications of the rule *arithmetic*.

> (i)   x+2 > 0 *by arith*, x>0,+,2>0;
> (ii) x*x > 0 *by arith*, x>0,*,x>0;
> (iii) x+y ≥ 2 *by arith*, x≥1,+,y≥1;
> (iv) 2≤xvx<0 *by arith*, x<x*x,/,x≠0;
> (v)   3*x+y ≥ 2*z-1 *by arith*, x+y > z,+,2*x ≥ z;
> (vi) x=y ∨ y=z ∨ z=x *by arith*, x-1 ≤ y ≤ x+1,
>   x-1 ≤ z ≤ x+1, y-1 ≤ z ≤ y+1.

(3-8) Which of the axioms of 3.4 apply to the rationals $\mathcal{Q}$ as well as the integers $\mathcal{Z}$?

(3-9) Formalize the argument and detect the error.

> Suppose a = b+c, multiply both sides by a-b, i.e.,
> $a^2-ab = ab+ac-b^2-bc$ *by arith*, a = b+c,*,a-b;
> $a^2-ab-ac = ab-b^2-bc$ by arithmetic from above line;
> a(a-b-c) = b(a-b-c) by arithmetic from above line.
> Cancel a-b-c from each side to obtain
>   a=b.

(3-10)* Using the celebrated result that there is no decision procedure to determine whether a polynomial with integer coefficients has a solution in the integers (Hilbert's tenth problem, see [Matiyasevich 70]), show that the quantifier free theory of arithmetic of this chapter is not decidable.

(3-11) Absolute value, |x|, can be included in arithmetic by adding the defining axiom:

$$\forall \text{ integer } x. \; ((x \geq 0 \implies x = |x|) \; \& \; (x \leq 0 \implies |x| = -x) \; \&$$
$$(x = 0 \implies |x| = 0))$$

Prove the following properties of absolute value.

(a) $|x| \geq 0$
(b) $|x+y| \leq |x| + |y|$
(c) $|x*y| = |x| * |y|$
(d) $||x|| = |x|$
(e) $|x*x| = x*x$
(f) $|x/y| = |x|/|y|$

(3-12) Integer division, x/y, and the modulus function, mod(x,y), can be introduced in the arithmetic by adding the following axioms for the infix operator / and the function symbol "mod".

$\forall$ *integer* a,b.

$(a \geq 0 \; \& \; b \neq 0 \implies a = b*(a/b) + \text{mod}(a,b) \; \&$
$a \leq 0 \; \& \; b \neq 0 \implies a = b*(a/b) - \text{mod}(a,b) \; \&$
$\forall$ *integer* q,r.
$((a \geq 0 \; \& \; b \neq 0 \implies$
$\quad a = b*q+r \; \& \; 0 \leq r < |b| \implies q = a/b \; \& \; r = \text{mod}(a,b))$
$\& \; (a \leq 0 \; \& \; b \neq 0 \implies$
$\quad a = b*q-r \; \& \; 0 \leq r < |b| \implies q = a/b \; \& \; r = \text{mod}(a,b)))$
$\& \; (a > 0 \; \& \; 0 < b \leq a \implies a/b > 0)$
$\& \; (a < 0 \; \& \; a \leq b < 0 \implies a/b > 0)$
$\& \; (a > 0 \; \& \; -a \leq b < 0 \implies a/b < 0)$
$\& \; (a < 0 \; \& \; 0 < b \leq a \implies a/b < 0)$
$\& \; (a = 0 \; \& \; b \neq 0 \implies a/b = 0)$
$\& \; (a \neq 0 \; \& \; 0 < |a| < |b| \implies a/b = 0))$

For mod we also have

$\forall$ *integer* q,r. $(a = b*q+r \; \& \; 0 \leq r < |b| \implies$
$\qquad\qquad r = \text{mod}(a,b)) \&$
$\exists$ *integer* q. $(a = b*q + \text{mod}(a,b)) \; \& \; 0 \leq \text{mod}(a,b) < |b|.$

Prove the following properties of division and modulus using the above axioms:

(i) $(x*y)/x = y$
(ii) $y/x + z/x = (y+z)/x$
(iii) $y/x * z/x = (y*z)/x*x$
(iv) $x/y + z/w = (x*w + z*y)/y*w$
(v) $mod(y,x) = |y| - (|y|/|x|) * |x|$
(vi) $mod(y,x)=0 \Rightarrow \exists$ *integer* $z.\ y = z*x$
(vii) $y \geq 0\ \&\ x \geq 0 \Rightarrow y = x*(y/x) + mod(y,x)$
(viii) $y<0\ \&\ x \neq 0\ \&\ y = q*x+r\ \&\ 0 \leq r < |x| \Rightarrow$
$$r = |x| - mod(y,x)$$

(3-13) Exponentiation can be included in arithmetic by adding the infix operator ** and the axioms:

$\forall$ *integer* $b,e.\ (|b| \geq 1 \Rightarrow b**0 = 1\ \&$
$|b| \geq 1\ \&\ e \geq 1 \Rightarrow (b**e = b*(b**e-1)\ \&$
$(b**e)/b = b**e-1))$

Prove the following properties of exponentiation:

(i) $x**(y+z) = (x**y)*(x**z)$
(ii) $x**(y*z) = (x**y)**z.$

(3-14) Prove that for all integers x,y,z and $n>0$

$mod(a,n) = mod(b,n)\ \&\ mod(c,n) = mod(d,n) \Rightarrow$
$\qquad mod(a+c,n) = mod(b+d,n)\ \&\ mod(a*c,n) = mod(b*d,n).$

(3-15) Prove that for all integer $n,p,q\ (n = p*q \Rightarrow$
$(mod(a,n) = mod(b,n) \Rightarrow mod(a,p) = mod(b,p))).$

(3-16) Prove that for any integer x,
$\qquad mod(x*x,4) = 0\ \lor\ mod(x*x,4) = 1.$

(3-17) Prove that if x is odd, then its square is of the form $8*q+1$.

(3-18)   For nonnegative integers x,y,g define gcd(x,y,g) to
mean g is the greatest common divisor of x,y.   That is,
mod(x,g) = 0 & mod(y,g) = 0, and if mod(x,u) = 0 &
mod(y,u) = 0, then mod(g,u) = 0.   Show that if 0<y≤x, then
gcd(x,y,g) => gcd(mod(x,y),y,g).

(3-19)   Prove that if p is prime and mod(a*b,p) = 0, then
mod(a,p) = 0 or mod(b,p) = 0.

Section 3.5

(3-20)   Prove that the minimum of a,b is less than the average of a,b.

(3-21)   Suppose $0<x≤9$ and $z = x*9$ and $z = 10*a_1+a_2$, $0<a_i≤9$.
Then show that $a_1 + a_2 = 9$.

(3-22)   Prove that the square of an odd number must be odd.

(3-23)   Prove the following version of Pythagoras' theorem
that $\sqrt{2}$ is irrational: ¬∃ *integer* a,b. $a^2 = 2*b^2$.

(3-24)   Prove Euclid's theorem that there is no largest
prime by assuming that mp is a largest prime.   (See part
III §3.5 of Appendix for the answer.)

(3-25)*   Prove that there are no nonnegative integers x,y,z
such that $x^4 + y^4 = z^4$.   Note, the seventeenth century
French amateur mathematician Pierre Fermat claimed that he
could prove that $x^n + y^n = z^n$ has nonnegative integer solutions x,y,z,n only for n = 2.   This claim is known as
Fermat's Last Theorem.   It has to this day defied the
attempts of numerous mathematicians to prove it.   Fermat
was a great mathematician with exceptional integrity,
nothing which he claimed he could prove has ever been dis-
proved.

(3-26) Prove the sum of two primes greater than 2 is even. In 1742 Goldbach conjectured, in a letter to Euler, that every even number n ≥ 6 can be represented as the sum of two odd primes. This open problem is known as *Goldbach's conjecture*. (Sometimes the conjecture is phrased to say that every even integer n ≥ 4 is the sum of two primes.)

(3-27)* Show that there exist arbitrarily long sequences of numbers which are all composite (nonprime). Note in contrast that it is an open problem to determine whether there are infinitely many primes p such that p + 2 is also prime (so called twin primes). This is called the *twin primes* problem.

(3-28) Is this claim concerning Goldbach's conjecture and twin primes true?

($\forall$ *integer* x. ((even(x) & x≥4 => $\exists$ *integer* p_1, p_2.
  (prime(p_1) & prime(p_2) & $p_1 + p_2$ = x))
 => $\forall$ *integer* z. $\exists$ *integer* p. (prime(p) & p>z &
  prime(p+2))) =>
=> $\exists$ *integer* x.((even(x) & x≥4 => $\exists$ *integer* p_1, p_2.

  (prime(p_1) & prime(p_2) & $p_1 + p_2$=x)) => $\forall$ *integer* z. $\exists$ *integer* p. (prime(p) & p>z & prime(p+2))). (Hint, look at logical structure.)

Section 3.6

(3-29) Decide which of the following expressions is syntactically correct and describe the composition of their type from the component types:

> substr(x,y,z), len(substr(x,2,1)), substr(len(x),1,1),
> x||substr(x,len(z),2) <= x||z, len(x) < len(x||' '),
> substr(substr(x,2,1),3,1), x||len(x||y),
> 'A'||A, 'A'||A+1, 'A+1'||substr(A,1).

Section 3.7

(3-30) What is the meaning of each of the following expressions? substr(substr('ABC',2,1),1),

substr(substr('ABC',2,2),3,1), 'AB'||substr('ABC',3),
'AB'||substr('ABC',3,2), 'AB'||substr('ABC',4)

(3-31) Which of the following equalities is true?
'ABC' = 'BC' mod(A), 'ABACA' = 'BCA' mod(A),
'ABC' = 'ABC' mod(A)

Section 3.8

(3-32) Prove that the null string, '', is the unique concatenation identity.

(3-33) Can substr('a',1,1) = 'a' be deduced from the other rules?

(3-34) Show how to prove that each character is unique, i.e., 'A' ≠ 'B'.

(3-35) Show how to prove that len('ABC') = 3.

(3-36) Show how to derive induction on strings from the rule for induction on terms in 3.4.

(3-37) If you have skipped ahead to Chapter VII to read about arrays, show how to derive the rules of section 3.8 if character strings are regarded as arrays of single characters.

Section 3.9

(3-38) Prove that every string having the structure (aba)* contains twice as many a's as b's.

(3-39) Suppose that letters represent decimal digits uniquely. Prove that (BE)*(BE) = MOB has the unique solution B=1, E=9 (assume no numeral begins with a zero).

(3-40) Using the above techniques, solve (BE)*(BE) = ABE and (BE)*(BE) = ARE.

(3-41)* Find two factors of the number 1001. What is the general principle for finding factors of numbers of the for 10*1. Express this in the logic.

(3-42) Prove that ∀ *string* x,y,z. (z||x = z||y => x=y).

4

SIMPLE COMMANDS
AND PROGRAMS

4.1   INTRODUCTION

The notion of an *action* is fundamental to our intuitive algorithmic thinking. As early as high school geometry we learn to reason carefully about dropping perpendicular lines and bisecting angles.

None of the ordinary formalisms for mathematics, such as set theory, nor the various specialized first order theories such as geometry or number theory directly expresses actions. Instead, actions are embodied in functions. When these functions are defined implicitly from relations, say by proving $\forall x \exists y\ R(x,y)$, then the intuitive connection to the action may be quite remote. When this implicit definition has only classical, not constructive validity, there may be no underlying action at all. So the ordinary function concept from mathematics does not exactly model computing actions.

On the other hand, a sufficiently rich class of constructive functions can be adequate as a programming language. Lisp 1.5, with its recursive function definitions, is an example. Indeed, there are those who vigorously advocate a purely function oriented approach to programming [Backus 73]. However, modern procedural languages such as Algol, Pascal, PL/I, FORTRAN, etc. are organized around the concept of a state and assignment commands to alter the state. We feel that this organization is not an accident of history nor a false step of modern computing practice. It is evident that the notion of a command changing a state faithfully represents the intuitive concept of an action. In our view, this formulation of actions is not to be excluded from our computational thought. Instead it is to be

integrated into the basic framework. Our logic presents
a formal and precise account of the integration. † We
hope it will influence mathematics to deal more directly
with computation. The syntax of arguments about programs
allows assertions to be freely intermixed with the commands
in a program. The meaning of an occurrence of an assertion
now depends on its position with respect to commands, as
well as its inclusion in proof blocks. The exact way in
which commands should affect the meanings of assertions
has been a matter for some debate in the computer science
literature.

Floyd [Floyd 67] suggests a language in which an assertion, A, written inside a program means that every time control passes to that place in the program, A is true of the
state. This language of asserted programs, as well as the
variant introduced by Hoare [Hoare 69], is called a
"partial correctness" language, and is unable to express the
important fact that the execution of a program terminates
successfully. To express termination, "total correctness"
languages have been proposed in which an assertion A after
a program or program segment means that execution of the
program or segment will terminate successfully, and A will
be true of any resulting state [Floyd 67, Manna, Pnueli, 74,
Engeler 68]. The partial correctness approach seems to
give a natural meaning to assertions in programs, but the
added expressive power of total correctness languages is
very attractive.

A third approach, taken here, tries to enjoy the best
of both partial and total correctness worlds. Any argument claiming to draw conclusions about the state produced
by a nonterminating computation is intuitively wrong. For

---

† We considered developing first a recursive predicate calculus obtained by adding recursive function definitions to
the predicate calculus. But the notion of iterated
actions is more central to this work and is more primitive
than the general notion of recursion. In Chapter VI we
define functions in the broader context of commands, and
from this account those interested in purely function
theoretic (in applicative style) programming can extract
a treatment of the recursive predicate calculus.

82

example, consider the informal program and argument:

```
x := 1;
while x is not even do
      x := x+2
      od ;
x is even and odd;
```

A naive intuitive appreciation of this argument tells us that it is nonsense, there is no even odd number.

Partial correctness semantics makes this bizarre argument valid; total correctness semantics makes the final assertion invalid. We prefer to say that the nonterminating loop itself is invalid. That is, giving a command includes an implicit assertion that the command may be executed successfully. An impossible command is erroneous, and leads to nonsensical conclusions just as any erroneous assumption.

There is a basis for our point of view in natural language. We can say: "Draw a line from A to B". If A and B coincide, then we regard the command as erroneous. Consider this command in an argument: "Draw a line from A to B. Since $\overleftrightarrow{CD}$ is a line, either $\overleftrightarrow{AB}$ and $\overleftrightarrow{CD}$ are parallel or they will intersect." If A and B coincide, this argument is false. A valid argument is: "Suppose A and B are on opposite sides of line $\overleftrightarrow{CD}$, then draw a line from A to B, the lines $\overleftrightarrow{AB}$ and $\overleftrightarrow{CD}$ intersect at a point we will call E." This argument mixes commands and assertions in an acceptable manner.

The presence of commands complicates our reasoning in several ways. Although the rules of inference for the Predicate Calculus with integers and strings remain the same, the notion of accessibility, which determines which assertions may be used as hypotheses in applying a rule, becomes stricter. The meaning of an assertion A may be changed not only by entering and exiting proof blocks, but also by encountering assignments which change the meanings of free variables in A. Also, we need additional rules for reasoning about individual commands and control structures, and these new rules will be more complicated since the order of hypotheses is significant.

4.2 ASSIGNMENT AND CONDITIONAL

Discussion of Assignment

Every action is a change of state. One might imagine
very complex states, such as geometrical configurations in
Euclidean space, but for our purposes a state is a mapping
from variables to objects (as defined in Chapter II).
These states are changed in two steps, a basic object is
constructed using functions, and then it is named. Such
an action is called *assignment*. Assignments are the only
atomic actions. They are written

variable := expression.

The expression denotes the constructed object, ":=" is the
assignment operator, and the variable is the name. Temporary names are quite useful and economical, so we include assignments of the form x := x+1, read "x gets x+1". Here x
is reused to name a new object. When x does not appear on
the right hand side of x := exp, then the assignment is said
to be *simple*. The occurrence of a variable x on the left-
hand side of an assignment is a binding occurrence, not a
free occurrence. At the beginning of the next chapter we
see how the analysis of free and bound variables and substitution is complicated by the presence of assignments.

Discussion of Conditionals

All actions are built as sequences of assignments.
Variety of action is determined by the order of combining
assignments. This order is controlled by the result of
evaluating properties of the state (using boolean expressions). This conditional control over actions is provided
by the conditional statement and the select statement. The
conditional is written:

if boolean expression *then* argument [*else* argument] *fi*.

The select is written:

select
        when(bexp$_1$) *do* argument$_1$ *od*
          .
          .
          .

$$when(\text{bexp}_n) \ do \ \text{argument}_n \ od$$

$$otherwise \ do \ \text{argument}_{n+1} \ od$$

Syntax

Commands and assertions can mix freely in arguments, but in this monograph commands are not allowed within assertions, so commands may never be joined together by the propositional connectives ($\S, \vee, \neg, =>, <=>$). The grammar now contains the new category *command*, the syntax for arguments is extended to include commands. We also introduce a category of main argument whose format is close to that of an ordinary asserted program (and which is especially similar to PL/CV's notion of main argument).

command	→	[label:] variable := exp
	→	[label:] *if* bexp *then* argument
		[*else* argument] *fi*
	→	[label:] *select*
		{*when* bexp *do* argument *od*}*
		otherwise do argument *od*
argument	→	command | argument
proof-group	→	[label:] *proof*
		qualifier;
		{declaration §;}*
		argument
		qed
declaration	→	[*declare*] variable list
main argument	→	[label:] *proof* [*main*]
		[*arbitrary* variable list
		where assertion;]
		{declaration §;}*
		{definition §;}*

> [*assume* assertion;]
>
> [*conclude* assertion;]
>
> {declaration §;}*
>
> argument
>
> qed [label];

The conclude statement is a redundant piece of information which puts the conclusion of the argument in the heading for readability. The conclusion will also occur in the argument.

It might seem reasonable to allow commands to mix freely with formulas, as in x := 1 => x>0. But serious questions arise in interpreting such hybrids. For instnace, given x := 1 => x>0 we would expect by the laws of the propositional calculus (either classical or constructive since the primitive assertions are decidable) for this to mean x>0 ∨ ¬(x := 1) which is not intuitively equivalent. The difficulty is that for commands, order of appearance is significant and is not expressible using ordinary connectives. See [Constable 77, Kroeger 77, Rasiowa 77] for attempts to integrate commands and assertions using a new kind of primitive connective involving a notion of order. (Also see exercises 4.2 number (4) below.)

Here is a typical (schematic) example of a main argument.

scheme: *proof main*
$\quad$ *arbitrary atype* x;
$\quad$ *define* D(x) = ∃ *atype* y R(x,y);
$\quad$ *assume* A(x) & D(x);
$\quad$ *conclude* B(x);
$\quad$ *declare atype* y_1, y_2;
$\quad\quad$ y_1 := f(x)
$\quad\quad$ *if* b(x, y_1) *then* y_2 := g(y_1, x); B(x)
$\quad\quad\quad\quad$ *else* y_2 := h(x); B(x) *fi*

$\quad$ *end* scheme

Semantics

The meaning of commands is well understood informally. We need a precise notation to capture that meaning. Since a command is an action, we use an active mathematical concept to describe its meaning, namely a function (rather than a relation). Since the informal meaning of a command is a state to state transformation, the natural type for the meaning of a command is States → States. Since the value of expressions in commands depends on a model $\mathcal{M}$, it is appealing to write the map as

$$\mathcal{M}: \quad \text{Commands} \to (\text{States} \to \text{States}).$$

But to distinguish the use of $\mathcal{M}$ in command meanings from that in expression meanings, we write the command argument in bold braces, $[\![\ ]\!]$, as in $\mathcal{M}[\![\text{command}]\!]$. (This follows the style of notation in [Milne, Strachey 76, Stoy 77].) The meaning of a command may be extended to $\mathcal{P}(\text{States}) \to \mathcal{P}(\text{States})$ in the usual way:

$$\mathcal{M}[\![\text{command}]\!](S) = \{ \mathcal{M}[\![\text{command}]\!](S) \mid s \varepsilon S \}$$

for any S a subset of States, $s \varepsilon S$.

1. $\mathcal{M}[\![x := exp]\!](s) = s'$ where $\{ s'(x) = \mathcal{M}(s)(exp)$
    $s'(y) = s(y) \ y \neq x \}$

2. $\mathcal{M}[\![\textit{if } bexp \textit{ then } arg_1 \textit{ else } arg_2 \textit{ fi}]\!](s)$

    $= \mathcal{M}[\![arg_1]\!](s)$ if $\mathcal{M}(s)(bexp) = \textit{true}$

    $\mathcal{M}[\![arg_2]\!](s)$ if $\mathcal{M}(s)(bexp) = \textit{false}$

3. $\mathcal{M}[\![\textit{select when } (bexp_1) \textit{ do } arg_1 \textit{ od}$

    $\vdots$

    $\textit{when } (bexp_n) \textit{ do } arg_n \textit{ od}$

    $\textit{otherwise do } arg_{n+1} \textit{ od}]\!](s) =$

    $\mathcal{M}[\![arg_1]\!](s)$ if $\mathcal{M}(s)(bexp_1) = \textit{true}$

    $\mathcal{M}[\![arg_2]\!](s)$ if $\mathcal{M}(s)(bexp_1) = \textit{false} \ \&$

    $\vdots \qquad \qquad \mathcal{M}(s)(bexp_2) = \textit{true}$

$$\mathcal{M} [\![\text{arg}_{n+1}]\!] (s) \quad \text{if} \quad \mathcal{M}(s)(\text{bexp}_1) = \textit{false} \ \text{\&} \ldots \text{\&}$$
$$\mathcal{M}(s)(\text{bexp}_n) = \textit{false}$$

With the arithmetic and string operations of Chapter III, assignment commands and boolean expression evaluations always terminate. So assignments are always valid. However after defined functions and arrays are introduced (Chapter VI, VII) this is no longer true. Anticipating this problem we explicitly provide notation to state the validity of assignment and conditional.

The satisfaction relation, $\models$, must be extended to arguments with commands. Intuitively, $<\mathcal{M}, s> \models$ argument means that in the world $\mathcal{M}$, if the commands in the argument are executed starting in state s, then every command will terminate successfully and every assertion will be true of each state which occurs as control passes that assertion.

4. $<\mathcal{M}, s> \models x := \text{exp}$ iff $\mathcal{M}(s)(\text{exp})$ is defined

5. $<\mathcal{M}, s> \models \textit{if}$ bexp $\textit{then}$ arg_1 $\textit{else}$ arg_2 $\textit{fi}$
   iff $\mathcal{M}(s)(\text{bexp})$ is defined
   if $\mathcal{M}(s)(\text{bexp}) = \textit{true}$ then $<\mathcal{M}, s> \models \text{arg}_1$
   otherwise $<\mathcal{M}, s> \models \text{arg}_2$

6. $<\mathcal{M}, s> \models \textit{select}$
   $\textit{when}$ bexp_1 $\textit{do}$ arg_1 $\textit{od}$
   .
   .
   .
   $\textit{when}$ bexp_n $\textit{do}$ arg_n $\textit{od}$
   $\textit{otherwise do}$ arg_{n+1} $\textit{od}$
   iff $\mathcal{M}(s)(\text{bexp}_1)$ is defined and if
   $\mathcal{M}(s)(\text{bexp}_1) = \textit{true}$ then $<\mathcal{M}, s> \models \text{arg}_1$
   and if $\mathcal{M}(s)(\text{bexp}_1) = \textit{false}$ and $\ldots$ and $\mathcal{M}(s)$
   $(\text{bexp}_i) = \textit{false}$, then $\mathcal{M}(s)(\text{bexp}_{i+1})$ is
   defined and of type boolean and if
   $\mathcal{M}(s)(\text{bexp}_{i+1}) = \textit{true}$ then $<\mathcal{M}, s> \models \text{arg}_{i+1}$

and if all $\mathcal{M}(s)(\text{bexp}_j) = \textit{false}$ $j=1,\ldots,n,$ *then*
$<\mathcal{M},s> \models \text{arg}_{n+1}.$

The meaning of an argument depends on the meanings of assertions in it. Their meaning in turn depends on the set of states possible at their positions in the argument. Commands affect the meanings of arguments by modifying the set of states possible at a position in the obvious way, i.e., if S is the set of states possible before command c,

then $\mathcal{M}[\![\,c\,]\!](S)$ is the set of states possible after c. Also, commands create new nested positions in an argument, namely those in the branches of the select and conditional commands. So to completely specify the positional semantics of arguments, we must describe the set of states possible inside conditional and select commands. This is done by the equations below which are to be regarded as addtions to the equations in Chapter II, (2.4).

The states possible in an argument at a position p determined by left context α, right context β are exactly those which may be produced by executing the commands up to that position, satisfying all assumptions along the way (and regarding assertions and proof-groups as identity transformations). Formally:

7. $\mathcal{M}[\![\text{ assertion } \downarrow]\!](S) = \mathcal{M}[\![\downarrow \text{ assertion }]\!](S) = S$
i.e. assertions never change states

$\mathcal{M}[\![\text{ proof-group } \downarrow]\!](S) = \mathcal{M}[\![\downarrow \text{ proof-group }]\!](S) = S$
i.e. proof-groups never change states

8. $\mathcal{M}[\![\text{ command } \downarrow]\!](S) = \mathcal{M}[\![\text{ command }]\!](S)$
i.e. the states possible after a commnad are just those obtained by applying the command to those states possible before the command.

9. $\mathcal{M}[\![\textit{ if }\text{bexp}\textit{ then }\downarrow \beta]\!](S) = \{s \mid s\varepsilon S$ &
$\mathcal{M}(s)(\text{bexp}) = \textit{true}\}$

10. $\mathcal{M}[\![\textit{ if }\text{bexp}\textit{ then }\text{argument}\textit{ else }\downarrow \beta]\!](S) =$
$\{s \mid s\varepsilon S$ & $\mathcal{M}(s)(\text{bexp}) = \textit{false}\}$

11. $\mathcal{M}[\![$ *select*

$\cdot$

$\cdot$

$\cdot$

   when bexp_i *do* $\downarrow$ *argument od*

$\cdot$

$\cdot$

$\cdot$

   otherwise do argument od $]\!](S)$ =

   $\{s \mid s \varepsilon S \ \& \ \mathcal{M}(s)(\text{bexp}_j) = \textit{false} \text{ for } j=1,\ldots,i\text{-}1 \text{ and}$
   $\mathcal{M}(s)(\text{bexp}_i) = \textit{true}\}$

12. $\mathcal{M}[\![$ *select* ... *otherwise do* $\downarrow$ *argument od* $]\!](S)$ =

   $\{s \mid s \varepsilon S \ \& \ \mathcal{M}(s)(\text{bexp}_j) = \textit{false} \ j=1,\ldots,n\}$

In order to use these positional equations of the form $\mathcal{M}[\![\,\beta\downarrow\gamma\,]\!](S) = \ldots$ to carry information deep inside an argument, say to position $\alpha\beta\downarrow\gamma\delta$, we need to say that $\mathcal{M}[\![\,\downarrow\alpha\,]\!](S) = S$ holds for any α (this gets information S inside), and that for all contexts $\alpha,\beta,\gamma,\delta$, $\mathcal{M}[\![\,\alpha\beta\downarrow\gamma\delta\,]\!](S) = \mathcal{M}[\![\,\beta\downarrow\gamma\,]\!](\mathcal{M}[\![\,\alpha\downarrow\beta\gamma\delta\,]\!](S))$. This tells us what states to use when placing $\mathcal{M}[\![\,\beta\downarrow\gamma\,]\!](S)$ into the context $\alpha \ \delta$. Thus we add:

13. $\mathcal{M}[\![\,\downarrow\alpha\,]\!](S) = S$

14. $\mathcal{M}[\![\,\alpha\beta\downarrow\gamma\delta\,]\!](S) = \mathcal{M}[\![\,\beta\downarrow\gamma\,]\!](\mathcal{M}[\![\,\alpha\downarrow\beta\gamma\delta\,]\!](S)).$

These equations are illustrated by the following simple example showing in brackets the set of states possible at various positions in an argument with commands, assuming that initially only two states are possible, s_1 and s_2.

$\{<s_1(x)=10, \ s_1(y)=5, \ s_1(z)=0>, \ <s_2(x)=3, \ s_2(y)=6,$
$s_2(z)=1>\}$

$z \geq 0;$
 proof arbitrary integer y where y=2;

$\{<s_1'(x)=10, \ s_1'(y)=2, \ s_1'(z)=0>$
$<s_2'(x)=3, \ \dot{s}_2'(y)=2, \ s_2'(z)=1>\}$

if z=0 then

$\{<s_1'(x)=10, s_1'(y)=2, \ s_1'(z)=0>\}$

$$x := 2;$$
$$y = x+z;$$

$\{<s_1''(x)=2, \ s_1''(y)=2, \ s_1''(z)=0>\}$

    else

$\{<s_2'(x)=3, \ s_2'(y)=2, \ s_2'(z)=1>\}$

$$x := 0;$$
$$y+z > x;$$

$\{<s_2''(x)=0, \ s_2''(y)=2, \ s_2''(z)=1>\}$
fi

$\{<s_1''(x)=2, \ s_1''(y)=2, \ s_1''(z)=0>, \ <s_2''(x)=0, \ s_2''(y)=2, \ s_2''(z)=1>\}$
  $y = x+z \ \vee \ y+z > x$

 qed ;

  The assignment and conditional commands theoretically
do not add expressive power to arguments. Any argument
with these commands can be transformed to an equivalent
(but longer) argument without commands. To see this,
consider first the case where there are no assignments, only
conditionals, say *if* bexp *then* argument$_1$ *else* ar-
gument$_2$ *fi*. This construct is clearly equivalent to the
following argument:

> bexp ∨ ¬ bexp
>
> *proof assume* bexp;
>
> > argument$_1$
>
> *qed* ;
>
> *proof assume* ¬ bexp;
>
> > argument$_2$
>
> *qed*;

A simple assignment x := exp in an argument can be replaced by an assumed equation and a declaration that x is arbitrary, e.g.

proof ...	becomes	*proof*
integer x;		*proof arbitrary integer* x
.		*where* x = exp;
.		.
.		.
x := exp		.
qed		*qed*
		qed;

These two methods can be combined to replace both conditionals and assignments in arguments. It is easy to see this if variables are first renamed so that no variable is used more than once on the left of an assignment. Here is a simple example.

> z≥0;
> *proof arbitrary integer* y *where* y=2;
> > integer x;
> > if z=0 then x := 2; y = x+z
> > > else x := 0; y+z > x+2 *by arith*, z≥0,z≠0,x=0;
> > fi;
> *qed*;

> becomes,

$z \geq 0$;
proof arbitrary integer y *where* $y=2$;
 arbitrary integer x_1, x_2 *where* $x_1=2$, $x_2=0$;
 proof assume $x=0$;
  $x_1=2$;

  $y=x_1+z$
 qed
 proof assume $z \neq 0$;
  $x_2=0$;

  $y+2 > x_2+2$ *by arith*, $z \geq 0$, $z \neq 0$, $x_2=0$;
 qed
 $y = x_1+z \lor y+z > x_2+2$;

Proof rules

A correct argument has a great deal of structure, assertions must appear in a certain order since hypotheses of a rule must be known before a rule can be applied. Moreover in block structured proofs, hypotheses must be accessible. They must be in the right part of the argument (not buried in a proof block), and they must mean the same thing where they are needed as they do where they are written.

Arguments with commands have even more structure. First, conditional commands introduce a further type of block structure, creating independent segments of the proof (in one block bexp is assumed, in the other, ¬ bexp). Secondly, assignments cause a different type of qualification which can change the meaning of an assertion from one position to the next. Consider the following invalid argument:

 $x>0$;
 $y>z$;
 $x := w$;
 $x*y > x*z$ by arithmetic, $x>0$, $*$, $y>z$;

This argument is invalid because w may be zero or negative. The assignment x := w changed the meaning of the assertion x>0 at the point it was needed to justify multiplication by a positive number.

The nature of the independent blocks caused by conditionals is illustrated by the next example of an erroneous proof.

> *proof arbitrary integer* x, y *where* x+z > 0;
> > *if* z=0 *then*
> > > minor: x≠0 *by arithmetic*, x+z > 0;
> > >
> > > *else*
> > > z≠0;
> > > major: x≠0 => z≠0;
> >
> > *fi*;
> >
> > > conclusion: z≠0 [by => E, minor, major;]
> *qed*

The minor and major premises of implication elimination appear in the proof and they are in the same proof group, but they are isolated from each other by the independent branches of the conditional. These branches act like proof blocks.

Before we define the notion of proof exactly we should notice that rules of inference are thought to apply *at some particular position* p where an assertion is being introduced, either explicitly or implicitly. It will be useful to have the concept that a deduction is made at a certain point, but the conclusion is not written until later. For example,

> *proof arbitrary integer* u, v *where* (u≥0 & v≥0 &
> > > (u>0 ∨ u>0) & u=x & v=y);
> > *integer* z;
> minor: z := x+y;
>
> major: x+y = z => z>0;
> > > x := 0;
> > > y := 0;
> conclusion: z>0;
>
> *qed*

The conclusion z>0 is valid even though the major and minor premises are not accessible at the conclusion. The argument is valid because it can be rearranged so that z>0 is deduced at the position between the major premise and x := 0. From this position the assertion z>0 is accessible at the position of the conclusion because no free variable contained in it is changed.

To understand more exactly how commands affect proof rules, consider the application of a rule

$$\frac{H_1, \ldots, H_n}{C}$$

at a position q. The hypotheses H_i will be written (or immediate) at position p_i. These positions must be accessible from q in order for the H_i to be used in the rule. The assertions H_i must also mean the same thing at p_i as they do in the rule being applied. That is, if C mentions a variable x or if some H_i mentions x, then the rule format assumes that x is the same at each occurrence. So the meaning of C and H_i must be constant from among the positions $q, p_1, \ldots, p_n$. The assertions will not be constant if some free variable is qualified differently at one of p_i or q than at the others. (Of course, if there are no free variables in an assertion, it is constant over all states.) These ideas are made precise by the following definitions.

A *proof block* is either a proof-group or a conditional-group. A conditional-group has one of the forms:

> *then* argument *else* or *then* argument *fi*
> *else* argument *fi*
> *when* bexp *do* argument *od*
> *otherwise do* argument *od*.

We now extend the definition of accessibility from Chapter II, (2.5).

Definition: An instance of an assertion or argument A (starting) at position p with free variables $x_1, \ldots, x_n$ is *accessible* from a position q in a predicate calculus argument with assignments and conditionals iff:

1. A at p occurs lexically before q, and

2. Any proof block containing A at p also contains q (i.e., p is visible from q), and

95

3. Any proof block containing q which qualifies any $x_1,\ldots,x_n$ also contains A (i.e. $x_1,\ldots,x_n$ are qualified the same way at p and q), and

4. None of x_i is changed on any path from p to q

(A is constant from p to q).

Definition: A *proof* in the *predicate calculus* with assignments and conditionals is an argument in which every occurrence of an assertion A at a position p is either an assumption or follows from accessible lines and immediate assertions by a rule of inference at a position q where A at q is accessible to p.

Predicate calculus rules could be presented in simple format $\dfrac{H_1,\ldots,H_n}{C}$. They described conditions under which a new line could be added to a proof already containing $H_1,\ldots,H_n$. In the presence of conditionals this format is no longer adequate because we may need to specify exactly where a new line can be added, as in adding a line inside a branch of the conditional, e.g. in the rule allowing bexp to be asserted in the *then* branch of *if* bexp *then* arg_1 *else* arg_2 *fi*. Moreover, in the presence of assignments, the order of appearance of hypotheses in a proof is critical and must be reflected in the rule format.

A more appropriate format for rules in this chapter is a two dimensional figure which indicates the relative position of hypotheses and conclusion, and the lexical order of hypotheses. When possible we will use a horizontal line in the rule figure to isolate the conclusion. When this is awkward, we will designate the conclusion in a note. The general shape of a rule figure is either

$$\begin{array}{c} H_{11},\ldots,H_{1n_1} \\ H_{21},\ldots,H_{2n_2} \\ \vdots \qquad \vdots \\ \dfrac{H_{m1},\ldots,H_{mn}}{C}\;_p \end{array} \qquad \text{or} \qquad \begin{array}{c} H_{11},\ldots,H_{1n_1} \\ H_{21},\ldots,H_{2n_2} \\ \vdots \\ [H_{m1},\ldots,H_{mn_p},\; C] \end{array}$$

The vertical order of hypotheses will be important, unless otherwise stated, indicating relative lexical order in the proof. Among hypotheses on the same line, e.g. $H_{21},H_{22}...,$ order is not important. Hypotheses (and conclusions) in brackets are to be instantiated by some schematic representation of a command or proof block or other context depending on the particular rule. This context will show the relative positions of the subarguments (and conclusion).
    Instantiation of such figures requires that:

1. The lexical order of hypotheses must be preserved as indicated by their vertical order in the figure (horizontal order is insignificant).

2. Syntactic segments used to specify context must be instantiated by legal syntax with the same characteristics, i.e. matching delimiters (*if,fi*) must be instantiated by matching delimiters.

3.[†] Contiguous lines in a figure may be separated by formulas and proof blocks but not by commands, and in lines joined by an arrow, say A←B or $\overset{A}{\underset{B}{\uparrow}}$, A must be accessible from B, but A and B may be separated by commands.

    The first rule for assignment has no hypotheses. It says that assignment statements can always be introduced because their right hand sides, as defined so far, must be well-defined.

1. assignment introduction

    $$\frac{}{x := exp}$$

2. assignment (immediate)

    $$\frac{P(exp/x)}{\underset{P}{x := exp}}$$

[†]This condition is unnecessary in paractice because hypotheses need not actually be written at a point, they may be immediate from previous lines. Therefore, we could require contiguous lines in a figure to be instantiated by contiguous but implicit lines in the proof. So arrows,↑, will only be used occassionally for emphasis.

2. conditional introduction

   ---

   if bexp *then else fi*

   This rule says that the schematic structure of a conditional may be introduced. To add content to the branches, other rules must be used.

3. conditional boolean expression introduction (immediate)

if bexp *then*	*if*	*then*
↑		α
bexp conclusion		else
		↑
		¬bexp conclusion

   This rule allows bexp to be concluded in the *then* branch and ¬bexp to be concluded in the *else* branch.

4. conditional elimination

   $$\frac{\text{\textit{if} bexp \textit{then} }\alpha\ Q\leftarrow \text{\textit{else} }\beta\ Q\leftarrow \text{\textit{if}}}{Q} \qquad \frac{\text{\textbf{¬bexp => Q}}\quad \text{\textit{if} bexp \textit{then} }\alpha\ Q\leftarrow \text{\textit{fi}}}{Q}$$

5. selection introduction

   The select command scheme can be introduced at any point. (We omit the obvious rule figure.)

6. select boolean expression introduction (immediate)

   select
      α   (α contains the branches for
         $bexp_1, \ldots, bexp_{i-1}$)

      when $bexp_i$ *do*
         ↑ $\neg bexp_1$ & $\neg bexp_2$ & $\ldots$ & $\neg bexp_{i-1}$ &
         $bexp_i$ conclusion

   This rule allows $\neg bexp_1$ & $\ldots$ & $bexp_i$ as an immediate conclusion in the appropriate branch. In the *otherwise* branch, $\neg bexp_1$ & $\ldots$ & $\neg bexp_n$ is allowed.

7. select elimination

$$
\begin{array}{l}
select \\
\quad when\ \text{bexp}_1\ do\ \alpha_1\ Q \leftarrow od \\
\qquad \vdots \\
\quad when\ \text{bexp}_n\ do\ \alpha_n\ Q \leftarrow od \\
\quad otherwise\ do\ \beta\ Q \leftarrow od \\
\hline
\qquad\qquad Q
\end{array}
$$

Here is an example of an argument using these rules.

Example:

```
/* every three integers have a maximum */
maximum: proof
        arbitrary integers a,b,c;
        integer max;
        define d = max=a ∨ max=b ∨ max=c;
        conclude a≤max & b≤max & c≤max & d;
        max := a;

        if b>max then a<b; max := b; b≤max & a≤max & d fi;
         a≤max & b≤max & d;
        if c>max then c>a by arith, a≤max;
                      c>b by arith, b≤max;
                      max := c;
                      a≤max & b≤max & c≤max & d
        fi;
         a≤max & b≤max & c≤max & d;
qed maximum;
```

4.3 ITERATION

Think of each state with its associated assertions as a state or a symbolic world. The principal advantage of the computer is that it can rapidly take us to new states of knowledge. But this is no real advantage if we must specify in a long list of assignments and conditionals precisely the worlds we want to visit. The gain comes when we can describe in some small pattern a long trip. The most primitive way to do this is in terms of repetition, we say "do

this pattern over and over while some condition is true"
or "until some condition is true."

The concept of simple repetition is fundamental to
any form of constructive numerical thought. It appears in
the ancient algorithms for division, greatest common
divisors, etc. Indeed it is so fundamental that its semantics may be considered primitive. In ordinary mathematics
(without commands) this primitive idea is manifest in the
principle of *mathematical induction*. We will see shortly
the connection between repetition and induction.

Syntax

The iteration commands, like conditionals, form new
block structures. These blocks begin with the key words
while and *for* and are thus called "while-groups" and "for-
groups." We allow also as a variant "repeat-groups."
The precise syntax is:

iterative-group   →   while-loop
                        for-loop
                        until-loop

while-loop   →   *while* bexp
                   do
                        [loop-qualifier]
                        argument
                   od

for-loop   →   *for* variable = $\exp_1$ *to* $\exp_2$
                 [*by*{+1,-1,1}]
                 do
                      [loop-qualifier]
                      argument
                 od

until-loop   →   *repeat*
                   [loop qualifier]
                    argument
                   until bexp

loop-qualifier   →   {*assume* assertion §;}*
                       arbitrary variable list
                       [*where* assertion];

In the for-loop, the leftmost exp is called the *lower bound*, the rightmost is the *upper bound*. Neither the index variable nor any variable in the upper and lower bounds can appear on the left side of an assignment in the loop and the index variable connot appear in the bounds.

Arguments now may contain iterative groups as commands through the addition to the syntax for commands.

command $\rightarrow$ iterative-group

The loop-qualifier contains information needed to prove that assertions are invariant and the loop terminates. The standard form for loop termination is

arbitrary integer $x_1, \ldots, x_n$ *where* assertion.

The use of this statement is described in the proof rules. If this termination portion of the qualifier is absert, then there is an implicit assumption that the loop terminates.

Semantics

The meaning of a for-loop is quite straightforward. We give the definition for the case where the index is increasing. Starting in state s, a for-loop computes a sequence of states $s_0, s_1, \ldots, s_n$ where s_0 (index variable) = $\mathcal{M}(s)$ (lowerbound), $s_0(x) = s(x)$ for $\neq$ index variable

$$s_{i+1}(\text{index variable}) = s_i(\text{index variable})+1$$
$$s_{i+1}(x) = \mathcal{M}[\![\text{argument}]\!](s_i)$$
$$s_n(\text{index variable}) > \mathcal{M}(s_i)(\text{upperbound})$$
$$n = \mathcal{M}(s)(\text{upperbound}) \doteq \mathcal{M}(s)(\text{lowerbound})$$

The sequence is always finite becasue $\mathcal{M}[\![\text{argument}]\!]$ cannot change the index variable or the upper bound, so eventually $s_i(\text{index variable}) > \mathcal{M}(s_i)(\text{upperbound})$.

To state this precisely, we let $s_0, s_1, \ldots, s_{n-1}$ produce possible states at the beginning of the loop body, and s_n becomes a possible state after the loop, as follows:

1. $\mathcal{M}[\![$ *for* i=exp$_1$ *to* exp$_2$

    do [*assume* assertion;] ↓ body *od* $]\!]$(S) =

    {s | $\mathcal{M}$(s)(exp$_1$) ≤ $\mathcal{M}$(s)(exp$_2$) & ∃ŝ(ŝϵS & s(z) =
    ŝ(z) for z different from i and arbitrary vari-
    ables of the loop qualifier & s̆(i) = $\mathcal{M}$(ŝ)(exp$_1$)
    [& <$\mathcal{M}$,s> ⊨ assertion]} ∪

    {s | s(i) ≤ $\mathcal{M}$(s)(exp$_2$) & ∃ŝ(ŝϵ$\mathcal{M}[\![$ *for* i=exp$_1$
    to exp$_2$ do; [*assume* assertion;] body ↓ *od* $]\!]$(S)
    & s(z) = ŝ(z) for z different from i and arbi-
    trary variables of the loop qualifier &
    s(i) = ŝ(i)+1)} (Recall the syntactic conditions
    on exp$_1$, exp$_2$.)
    An argument of the form *for* i=exp$_1$ *to* exp$_2$ do body *od*
is valid iff the body is valid for all states possible
before it. Since *for* iteration is always finite, the loop
terminates whenever the body does.

2. <$\mathcal{M}$,s> ⊨ *for* i=exp$_1$ *to* exp$_2$ do body *od* iff

    <$\mathcal{M}$,$\mathcal{M}[\![$*for* i=exp$_1$ *to* exp$_2$ do ↓ body *od*$]\!]$(s) ⊨ body

The meaning of a while loop is easy to express.
Namely, the body is repeated over and over until the condition becomes false.
    In the equations below, let α be the initial while
loop assumption, bexp does not contain x̄.

α = *assume* A$_1$;...;*assume* A$_n$, *arbitrary integer* x̄ *where* T

3. $\mathcal{M}[\![$ *while* bexp *do* α ↓ body *od* $]\!]$ (S) =

    {s | ∃ŝ(ŝϵS & $\mathcal{M}$(ŝ)(bexp) = *true* & for all z not
    in x̄ s(z) = ŝ(z) & <$\mathcal{M}$,s> ⊨ A$_1$&...&A$_n$&T)}

$$\cup \; \{s \mid \exists \hat{s}(\hat{s}\epsilon \mathcal{M}[\![\textit{while} \; \downarrow \; \exp \; \textit{do} \; \alpha \; \text{body} \; \downarrow \; \textit{od} \;]\!] \,(S)$$
$$\& \; \mathcal{M}(\hat{s})(\text{bexp}) = \textit{true} \; \& \; \text{for all } z \text{ not in } \bar{x}$$
$$s(z) = \hat{s}(z) \; \& \; <\mathcal{M},s> \; \models A_1 \& \ldots \& A_n \& T) \}$$

This is a somewhat disguised *inductive definition* of the set $\hat{S} = \mathcal{M}[\![\textit{while} \; \text{bexp} \; \textit{do} \; \alpha \; \downarrow \; \text{body} \; \textit{od} \;]\!] \,(S)$. In order to determine the states in $\hat{S}$ one needs to know the states possible at *while* bexp *do* α body $\downarrow$od. These are derived from the states possible at *while* bexp *do* α $\downarrow$ body *od*. But this is precisely $\hat{S}$ again. We want the least set (under the set inclusion ordering $\subseteq$) satisfying this definition. There is a least solution because the intersection of solutions is always a solution. Writing the equation above explicitly in terms of $\hat{S}$ leads to :

3´. $\mathcal{M}[\![\textit{while} \; \text{bexp} \; \textit{do} \; \alpha \; \downarrow \; \text{body} \; \textit{od} \;]\!] \,(S) = $ the least $\hat{S}$ such that

$$\hat{S} = \{s \mid \exists \hat{s}(\hat{s}\epsilon S \; \& \; \mathcal{M}(s)(\text{bexp}) = \textit{true} \; \& \; \text{for all } z$$
$$\text{different from } \bar{x} \; s(z) = \hat{s}(z) \; \& \; s(\bar{x})\epsilon \mathbf{Z}^n$$
$$\& \; <\mathcal{M},s> \; \models A_1 \& \ldots \& A_n \& T) \}$$
$$\cup \; \{s \mid \exists \hat{s}(\hat{s} \; \mathcal{M}[\![\text{body} \;]\!] \,(\hat{s}) \; \mathcal{M}(s)(\text{bexp}) = \textit{true}$$
$$\& \; \text{for all } z \text{ not in } \bar{x} \; s(z) = \hat{s}(z) \; \&$$
$$<\mathcal{M},s> \; \models A_1 \& \ldots \& A_n \& T) \}$$

When we are interested only in the state to state behavior of the whole loop, we can give it in terms of an inductive (or recursive) definition of a function. We ask for the least solution to the equation in (4), i.e. the solution with the *smallest domain* in the subset ordering. [†]

4. $\mathcal{M}[\![\textit{while} \; \text{bexp} \; \textit{do} \; \alpha \; \text{body} \; \textit{od} \;]\!] \,(s) = $

if $\mathcal{M}(s)(\text{bexp}) = \textit{true}$

then $\mathcal{M}[\![\textit{while} \; \text{bexp} \; \textit{do} \; \alpha \; \text{body} \; \textit{od} \;]\!] \, (\mathcal{M}[\![\text{body} \;]\!] \,(s))$
else s

where $\mathcal{M}[\![\text{argument} \;]\!]$ gives the state to state meaning of an argument.

[†] To be careful here we must note that there is always a least solution, obtained by intersecting the set of domains of all solutions.

5. $<\mathcal{M}, s> \models$ *while* bexp *do* α body *od* iff the function
$\mathcal{M}[\![$ *while* bexp *do* α body *od* $]\!]$ (s) is defined for all s and
$<\mathcal{M}, \mathcal{M}[\![$ *while* bexp *do* α ↓ body *od* $]\!]$ (s)> $\models$ body.

Now we can define the positional meaning of a full while loop:

6. $\mathcal{M}[\![$ *while* bexp *do* α argument *od* ↓ $]\!]$ (s) =
$\{s \mid \exists \hat{s}(\hat{s} \epsilon S \ \& \ <\mathcal{M}, \hat{s}> \models$ *while* bexp *do* α argument *od*
$\& \ s = \mathcal{M}[\![$ *while* bexp *do* argument *od* $]\!]$ ($\hat{s}$))\}

Unlike assignment and conditional commands, the iterative commands increase the expressive power of the predicate calculus. For instance, we can express in the theory of pure iterative programs over an uninterpreted domain the fact that an arbitrary iterative program always halts. This problem is known to be Π_2^o complete (not partially decidable) whereas validity in the pure predicate calculus is Σ_1^o complete (partially decidable).

A thorough discussion of these results can be found in the literature of program scheme theory (see [Greibach 75, Luckham, Park, Paterson 70, Park 69, Constable, Gries 72, Harel, Meyer, Pratt 77]).

The addition of iterative commands to the elementary number theory of Chapter III, to form iterative number theory, does not increase the expressivness of that theory because the computations of numerical programs can be encoded as integers (arithmetized) as in Gödel's theorem. This topic is discussed extensively in traditional logic books (usually in terms of Turing machines), (see [Kleene 52, Enderton 72]).

Proof rules

Before we present the proof rules for loops, let us consider how we informally analyze a programming problem in terms of iteration. This will highlight the important features of the rules. Suppose we are given nonnegative integers a,b and want to find q and r such that a = b*q+r with $0 \le r < b$. If we start in a state with $q=0$ and $r=a$, then we have $a = b*0+a$. We can reach our goal state if we can bring r into the interval $0 \le r < b$ and hold the relation $a = b*q+r$ invariant as we travel from state to state. If $r < b$, then by subtracting b from r we move closer to the goal, that is $r-b$ is smaller. When $r-b < 0$ then we know $r < b$ and the goal is met. To keep $a = b*q+r$, when we subtract b from r we add 1 to q, that is $a = b*(q+1)+(r-b)$. So our dynamic conception of the problem is to "move r toward b by subtracting b from it and keep $a = b*q+r$ by adding 1 to q while $r-b \ge 0$." This is exactly the meaning of

$$a = b*q+r;$$
$$while \ r-b \ge 0$$
$$do$$
$$\quad a = b*q+r;$$
$$\quad r := r-b;$$
$$\quad q := q+1;$$
$$\quad a = b*q+r$$
$$od$$
$$r-b < 0;$$

A proof that this is correct involves only a few more statements. It will be given in complete detail later.

Iteration is clearly closely connected to the sequence of nonnegative integers. We start the iteration in some initial state s_0 and form a sequence of new states $s_1, s_2, s_3, \ldots$. If we want to prove that a property P is true in each state s_n, for all n $< \mathcal{M}, s_n > \models P$, then *induction* on n is the natural way to proceed.

For example, to prove $a = b*q+r$ in each state produced by the above example, we can consider the sequence of values $<q_n, r_n>$ where $q_0 = 0$, $r_0 = a$. We need to prove $a = b*q_n+r_n$ for all n. The basis step is $a = b*q_0+r_0$ which is $a = b*0+a$. For induction we get to assume $a = b*q_n+r_n$ and we show $a = b*q_{n+1}+r_{n+1}$. To do this we notice that $q_{n+1} = q_n+1$ and $r_{n+1} = r_n-b$. So

$$b*q_{n+1}+r_{n+1} = b*(q_n+1)+(r_n-b) =$$

$$b*q_n+b+r_n-b = b*q_n+r_n = a.$$

105

This type of inductive argument applied to a loop
has a particularly pleasing form. We do not need the integer subscripts. Indeed we do not need explicit mention
of the integers at all. The basis step corresponds to
establishing a = b*q+r just before the loop. The induction
step corresponds to assuming a = b*q+r just before the
loop body and proving that it holds after the body is
executed. So we can write the argument as

```
a = b*q+r;
while r-b≥0
    do
        assume a = b*q+r;
               a = b*(q+1)+r-b by arithmetic;
               r := r-b;
               q := q+1;
               a = b*q+1
    od;
```

But this argument only establishes that the loop is
correct *if it halts*. Before a loop can be introduced
correctly into a program, we must know that it halts. In
fact, writing a loop in an argument in our logic is an
assertion that it halts.

In terms of the sequence notation, the argument that
the loop halts is an argument that the sequence $s_0, s_1, s_2, \ldots$
is finite. This can be expressed by saying that there is
a state in which the loop condition is false. This statement has the informal form

$$\text{for some n } \langle \mathcal{M}, s_n \rangle \models \neg(\text{loop condition})$$

How are statements of this type proved?

As we discussed in Chapter III, a typical way to
prove $\exists \text{integer } n \; P$ is to construct n. Programs are
particularly good for exhibiting such constructions. Let
us see how this is done for the example.

On each iteration the difference between r and b is
decreasing, that is n = r-b is decreasing. If n<0, then
the loop condition, r-b≥0 is false and the loop will terminate. These facts tell us that the loop must terminate
as long as there is some intitial value for n, because
this value of n decreases with each loop iteration, and it

can decrease only finitely often before it reaches 0
(when it does the loop condition is false).
  This example suggests one method of proving loop
termination, namely discover an arithmetic relation T such
that in the initial state T holds for some nonnegative
value n (i.e. ∃*integer* n, n≥0 & T), also T(0/n) => ¬bexp,
and if T holds for any state s, then T(n-1/n) holds for the
state s' obtained by applying the loop body to s. We
formulate this as

> T(0/n) => ¬bexp;
> ∃*integer* n . n≥0 & T(n);
> *while* bexp
>   *do*
>   *arbitrary integer* n *where* T(n);
>   argument
>   T(n-1/n);
>   T(0/n) => ¬bexp;
>   *od*;

In some cases we will need a more general rule than this,
obtained by replacing the integers with more general well-
founded sets (as we do below).
  We can simplify the rule somewhat by noticing that
T(0/n) => ¬bexp is equivalent to bexp => ¬T(0/n). Moreover this need only be proved once inside the loop.
Clearly it must be true in the loop and the only information we can use to prove it must be accessible from inside
the loop. So if it is true inside, it will be true just
before the loop. Thus the loop introduction rule has the
form:

> ∃*integer* n . n≥0 & T
> *while* bexp
>   *do*
>   *arbitrary integer* n *where* T;
>   ¬T(0/n);
>   argument
>   T(n-1/n)
>   *od* ;

  Now let us consider the details of inference rules
for loops and their effect on the definition of proofs.
Adding any new command to the logic may necessitate

amendments to the definition of a proof, in particular to the notion of accessibility. New commands also require new inference rules. In the case of iteration, these changes are major. First, the notion of proof block is now extended to include iteration-groups. Second, the notion of when an assertion at position p is accessible to a position q is complicated in a subtle way. Now paths from p to q can include positions which are lexically beyond q. For instance in

```
p : assertion;
while bexp do
        .
        .
        .
    q : assertion;
    x := exp
od
```

the assignment x := exp lying beyond position q will cause the assertion at p to become inaccessible if that assertion contains x *because that assignment can be executed in the flow of control from p to q*. Third, the rules of inference for a while-loop (or repeat loop) must demonstrate that the loop terminates. This is the first instance encountered (but not the last) where the introduction of commands must be justified. Moreover, the syntax for such a rule will be novel because the conclusion is the loop itself while some of the hypotheses appear within the loop. Finally, the rule for loop invariants, although based on mathematical induction, exhibits the basis and induction steps in a syntactic form which looks quite different from the traditional forms of induction in Chapter III.

This rule should be familiar to those who know mathematical induction, but the syntactic differences may at first be distracting.

In the detailed account of these matters given below we will at first not try to be precise about the possible execution paths from a position p to a position q since the concept is intuitively very clear and immediate to anyone familiar with programming. But after the main definition we discuss these paths more fully.

Definition: An *execution path* from position p to position q is a path from p to q in the flowgraph of the argument. (See below the definition of *control segment* from p to q.)

Definition: A proof block is either a proof block as defined in (4.2) or is an iteration-group.

Definition: An instance of an argument A (starting) at position p with free variables $x_1,\ldots,x_n$ is *accessible* from position q in an iterative argument iff

1. A at p occurs lexically before q, and

2. Any proof block containing A at p also contains q,

3. Any proof block containing q which qualifies any of $x_1,\ldots,x_n$ also contains A,

4. x_i is not changed on any execution path from p to q.

Definition: A proof in the calculus of iterative *arguments* is an argument in which every occurrence of an assertion at a position q is either an assumption or follows from accessible lines and immediate assertions by a rule of inference at a position p accessible to q.

In order to construct an iterative argument we need inference rules for introducing loops and for using loops as induction arguments. There are two intuitive components to an argument about a loop. One, we argue that the loop must halt. Two, we argue that certain assertions are true after the loop. One common problem to both arguments is that the recursive nature of the loop construct seems to lead to circular arguments. We solve this difficulty by making an assumption at the beginning of a loop. Before a loop rule may be applied either to prove termination or to extract an invariant assertion from a loop, all assumptions at the beginning of the loop must be *discharged*. That is, we must insure that no statements outside the loop depend on these assumptions. A loop in which all assumptions are discharged (both before the loop and at the end) is called a *completed loop*. It has the following form:

a completed while-loop

P
↑
∃*integer* i . i≥0 & T;
while bexp *do*
      assume P;
      arbitrary integer i *where* T;
      argument
      P;
      T(i-1/i)
od; i does not occur free in P

a completed for-loop

P(exp$_1$/i)
↑
for i = exp$_1$ *to* exp$_2$ *do*
               assume P;
               argument
               P(i+1/i)
               od

    The exact form of the rules is given below. For
each loop there is an *introduction rule* and an *elimination
rule* (or invariant rule or induction rule as some like to
call it). The introduction rules assume that the body of
the loop has already been introduced. So in the case of
the for-loop the rule is trival. For the while loop,
two introduction rules are given, one using nonnegative integers as the well-founded set and the other using n tuples
of nonnegative integers. For this second rule we need the
lexicographical ordering of n tuples defined below.

Definition:

$$<m'_1,\ldots,m'_n> <(n) <m_1,\ldots,m_n>$$
if for some j where $1\le j\le n$ iff $m'_i=m_i$ for $i<j$ and $m'_j<m_j$

$$<m'_1,\ldots,m'_n> = <m_1,\ldots,m_n> \text{ iff } m'_i=m_i \text{ for } i=1,\ldots,n$$

For example, the $<(2)$ ordering of pairs is
$<0,0>,<0,1>,\ldots,<0,n>,\ldots,<1,0>,<1,1>,\ldots,<1,n>,\ldots<2,0>,$
$<2,1>,\ldots,<2,n>,\ldots,\ldots$.

(For those readers familiar with ordinals, this forms an ω^2 ordering. See [Sierpinski 65] for an account of ordinals.)

a completed loop with n tuples.

$\exists$*integer* $m_1,\ldots,m_n$. $(m_1 \geq 0 \& \ldots \& m_n) \geq 0$ & T;

while bexp
 do
 assume P
 arbitrary integer $x_1,\ldots,x_n$ *where* $x_1 \geq 0 \& \ldots x_n \geq 0$ & T;
 $\neg T(<0,\ldots,0>/<m_1,\ldots,m_n>);$
 argument
 P;
 $T(<m_1',\ldots,m_n'>/<m_1,\ldots,m_n>)$ &
  $<m_1',\ldots,m_n'> <(n) <m_1,\ldots,m_n>$
od

 1. *while loop introduction* (loop termination)
  $\exists$*integer* i . $(i \geq 0$ & T$)$;
  while bexp *do*
   arbitrary integer i *where* T;
   $\neg T(0/i);$
   argument
   $T(n-1/n)$
  od
  The loop itself is the conclusion and must be completed.

 2. *while loop elimination* (*invariant*)
  P;
  while bexp
  do assume P;
   argument
   P;
  od
  ————————————
  P & $\neg$bexp   provided the loop is completed

111

3. while loop introduction (n tuple form)

$\exists integer\ m_1,\ldots,m_n\ .\ (m_1 \geq 0 \&\ldots \& m_n \geq 0\ \&\ T)$;

while bexp *do* {bexp}
    arbitrary integer $m_1,\ldots,m_n$ *where*

$$m_1 \geq 0 \&\ldots \& m_n \geq 0\ \&\ T;$$

$\neg T(0/m_1,\ldots,0/m_n)$;

argument
$T(m_1'/m_1,\ldots,m_n'/m_n)\ \&$

$<m_1',\ldots,m_n'> <(n)\ <m_1,\ldots,m_n>$

od

4. for loop elimination (also see exercise 4-39)

$\neg(exp_2+1 < exp_1)$;　　　　$\neg(exp_2-1 > exp_1)$;
$P(exp_1^2/i)$;　　　　　　　　$P(exp_1^2/i)$;

for i = exp_1 *to* exp_2　　　*for* i = exp_1 *to* exp_2 *by*-1
do　　　　　　　　　　　　　*do*
  assume P(i);　　　　　　　 *assume* P(i);
  argument　　　　　　　　　 argument
      P(i+1)　　　　　　　　　　 P(i-1)
od　　　　　　　　　　　　　*od*
────────────────　　　　───────────────
$P(exp_2+1/i)$　　　　　　　$P(exp_2-1/i)$

upward version　　　　　　　　downward version

5. repeat introduction

$\exists integer\ i\ .\ (i \geq 0\ \&\ T)$
repeat
arbitrary integer i *where* T
argument
$T(i-1/i)$;
$T(0/i)\ =>\ bexp$
until bexp

The loop must be completed. The conclusion is
the loop itself.

6. repeat *elimination*

    P;
    repeat
      assume P;
      argument
      bexp => E;
      -bexp => P
    until bexp
    _____
        E & bexp
    The loop must be completed

Here is an example of an argument with assignment, conditional and iterative commands. The command computes q, r such that a = b*q+r & 0≤r<b for nonnegative integers a, b. The argument formalizes our discussion at the beginning of this section.

Example:

    divide: *proof*
            arbitrary integer a,b *where* a≥0 & b>0;
            integer q,r;
            conclude a = b*q+r & 0≤r<b;
            r := a;
            q := 0;
            a = b*q+r *by arith*, q=0, r=a;

            if a<b
            then a = b*q+r & 0≤r<b;
            else (r-b)+1>0 *by arith*, a≥b, r=a;
                  r-b < (r-b)+1 *by arith*,
                  ∃*integer* i . (i≥0 & r-b < i) ∃I, (r-b)+1;
                  while (r-b)≥0 *do*
                  arbitrary integer i *where* r-b<i;
                  assume a = b*q+r & r≥0;
                  ¬(r-b<0) *by arith*, r-b≥0;
                  a = b*(q+1) + (r-b) *by arith*, a = b*q+r;
                  r-b≥0;
                  (r-b)-b < i-1 *by arith*, r-b<i, b≥1;
                  r := r-b;
                  q := q+1;
                  a = b*q+r & r≥0
                  od;

```
remova:  proof
         arbitrary string x,a where len(a) = 1;
         string y,z,z₁,z₂,w;

         integer j,k,ly;
         define no_a(z,j) = V integer k where 0≤k<j .
                               substr(z,k,1) ≠ a;
         define eq(z₁,z₂,i) = V integer k where 1≤k<i .
                               substr(z₁,k,1) = substr(z₂,k,1);

         conclude y=x mod(a) & no_a(y,len(y)+1);

         /* first prove a lemma needed in the for loop */
         /* begin proof of lemma 1 */

         proof arbitrary string x,w integer k;
            proof; assume eq(x,w,k) & substr(x,k,1) =
                                         substr(w,k,1);
         proof arbitrary integer j where 1≤j<k+1;
         j=k v 1≤j<k by arith;
         proof assume j=k;
            substr(x,j,1) = substr(w,j,1);
         qed;
         proof assume 1≤j<k;
            substr(x,j,1) = substr(w,j,1) by VE,
            1≤j<k,  k;
         qed;
         substr(x,j,1) = substr(w,j,1) by VE;
         qed;
  qed;
  qed;
lemma 1: Vstring x,w integer k . (eq(x,w,k) & substr(x,k,1) =
         substr(w,k,1) => eq(x,w,k+1));
         define invariants(i) =
            y = w mod(a) & len(y) = ly & len(w) = i-1 &
            no_a(y,ly+1) & eq(x,w,i);

         /* establish the invariant(len(x)+1) by a loop */
         /* prove the invariant for initial value, i=1 */
         /* initial values */

         y := ''; w := ''; k := 0; ly := 0;
         substr(y,0,1) ≠ a by string, y = ''

         /* prove no_a(y,ly+1) */
```

```
proof arbitrary integer k where 1≤k<1;
false by arith;
   substr(y,k,1) ≠ a;
qed
no_a(y,1y+1)

/* prove eq(x,w,1) */

proof arbitrary integer k where 1≤k<1;
false by arith;
   substr(x,k,1) = substr(w,k,1)
qed;
eq(x,w,1);
/* prove other easy conjuncts of invariant */
y = w mod(a) by string;
len(s) = 0 by len, w = '';
/* prove for loop bounds are legal */

¬(len(x)+1 < 1) by arith, len(x)≥0;
for i=1 to len(x) do
   assume invariant(i);
   if substr(x,i,1) ≠ a
   then /* there is no a at position i of x */
        y := y||substr(x,i,1);
        w := w||substr(x,i,1);
        substr(w,i,1) = substr(x,i,1) by string;
        y = w mod(a) by string;
len(y) = 1y+1 by len;
substr(y,1y+1,1) ≠ a;
len(w) = i;
eq(x,w,i+1) by VE, x,w,i+1, lemma 1;

/* prove no_a(y,1y+2) */

proof arbitrary k where 0≤k < 1y+2
   k = 1y+1 ∨ 0≤k < 1y+1 by arith;
   case 1:  proof assume k = 1y+1;
              substr(y,k,1) ≠ a
              qed;
   case 2:  proof assume 0≤k < 1y+1;
              substr(y,k,1) ≠ a by VE, no_a(y,1y+1)
              qed;
   substr(y,k,1) ≠ a by VE;
qed;
no_a(y,1y+2);
1y := 1y+1;
invariant(i);
```

```
        else  /* there is an a at position */
              substr(x,i,1) = a;
              len(w||substr(x,i,1) = len(w)+1;
              w := w||substr(x,i,1)
              len(w) = i;
              substr(w,i,1) = substr(x,i,1);
              y = w mod(a) by mod;
              eq(x,w,i+1) by ∀E, x,w,i, lemma 1
        od;
        invariant(len(x)+1) by for elimination;
        x = w mod(a) by string, eq(x,w,len(x)+1),
                                    len(x) = len(w);
        y = w mod(a)   /* part of invariant */
        y = x mod(a) & no a(y,len(y)+1)
qed remova
```

Soundness

From our introductory discussion of while loops and
induction, it is clear that establishing P before the loop
es equivalent to proving the basis step of an induction
(P is true for zero interations of the loop body).   Establishing validity of the completed loop body,

   while bexp *do assume* P; argument: P; *od*

is equivalent to extablishing the induction step

   proof assume P; argument; P; *qed.*

The induction step shows that if P is true of any state
before the loop body (in particular those arising after
n iterations), then it is true for any state possible after
applying the loop body to that state (i.e., after n+1
iterations).   The soundness of the loop elimination rules
is proved by the induction argument just suggested.
   An argument showing the soundness of the loop introduction rules is more involved.   Consider the while introduction rule.   We know from the validity of the assertion
∃ *integer* n . (n≥0 & T) before the loop that among the
states possible before the loop body there is one where
s(i) = m such that m≥0 & T(m/i) (where i is declared in
arbitrary integer i *where* T).   We also know that on
every iteration of the body, T holds on a smaller value, so
that the sequence s(i) = m, s(i) = m-1, s(i) = m-2, ...

appears among the possible states before the loop body.
We also know from the assertion ¬T(0/i) that the state
s(i) = 0 is not among the states possible just before the
loop body. We conclude from the fact that the integers are
well ordered that the loop body can be executed at most m
times under these conditions. (This argument is entirely
constructive if the proof of ∃ *integer* n . (n≥0 & T) is. We
can in fact determine from it an upper bound on the running time of the loop, namely m iterations. One way to
see the computational content of the argument is to
notice that it is decidable whether a loop runs in more
or less than m steps. Therefore if we know that it does
not run more than m steps, we know it runs in m or fewer
steps.}

4.4   GOTO PUNCTUATION

<u>Discussion</u>

The statement *goto* L in a program tells us that the
next statement to be considered is at the position labeled
L. Possibly it is put at L rather than next in line because L logically belongs to a different part of the argument, as for example when we discover that the data contains an error and we invoke special routines to process
the error. Possibly the next command is put at L mainly
to make the program compact, as in using a goto to leave
a loop from the middle. In any case, the goto is not a
basic action, but rather punctuation, telling us how parts
of the program are arranged.

When carefully used, the goto can provide arrangements
of the program which add to its logical clarity and
improve its runtime efficiency. For example, there is a
class of iterations of the form

```
start: S;
          if bexp then goto exit fi;
          F; goto start;
exit:  _____;
```

where S and F may be arguments several statements long.
When S is empty, this iteration has the form of a while

loop : *while* bexp *do* F *od*. When F is empty the iteration has the form of a repeat loop : *repeat* S *until* bexp. If neither is empty, then writing either a while or a repeat loop is awkward. We really want a loop that is performed "n and 1/2 times." Such an iteration can be "handcrafted" with a goto statement such as

```
        while true do
            S;
            if bexp then goto exit fi;
            F
        od;
        exit: _____;
```

We will provide rules for the goto which allows us to prove statements about such programs.

  The goto permits not only helpful rearrangements of an argument but tangled contortions as well. The dangers of unrestricted gotos have been discussed at length in research literature [Dijkstra 68, Dahl, Dijkstra, Hoare 72, Knuth 74] and in introductory programming textbooks [Conway, Gries 75], so we will not belabor the point here. As a guard against these dangers, the language PL/CS allows only forward referencing gotos. [†]

  We will see in our discussion of goto rules that even the simple forward goto significantly complicates our perception of the logical dependencies in a proof. One can then easily imagine how an unrestricted goto would lead to severe logical complexity, largely because circular dependencies arise. In every other case of circular dependency the scope of that dependency is clearly indicated by the syntax, e.g. by the *while, do, od* delimiters for loop proof blocks, *proof, qed* for induction, etc.

Syntax

  Syntax for the goto punctuation is quite simple, it acts syntactically like a command.

[†]In Chapters V and VI we will see that the PL/CS gotos are further restricted to disallow jumping out of procedures and functions.

punctuation   →   *goto* label

argument   →   argument | punctuation

Note, a goto cannot enter any block (conditional, iterative, proof) nor leave a proof-group. Moreover, the label must be lexically beyond the goto punctuation itself (i.e. must be *forward referencing*).

Semantics

The meaning of programs built only from assignments, conditionals and loops can be given by a simple inductive definition which gives the meaning of a statement entirely in terms of the meaning of its simpler constituent parts; moreover, the program can be built from the single binary operation of composition. Once the goto is introduced, this is no longer true. In this case, the meaning of a program is not given as a simple inductive definition but rather separate parts of the program must be defined simultaneously by a set of mutually recursive definitions. (This approach is also needed later when mutually recursive procedures are added to the language.) However, in the case of the *forward* goto, one can preserve the simple inductive nature of the definition giving up only the binary nature of composition (as is done in [Constable, Donahue 76]).

The positional semantics we have been using to define other language features also works well with gotos because the entire program can be kept as an argument to the meaning function. Thus each equation concerning a position can mention the other position needed in the mutual recursion.

The new meaning equations are:

$$\mathcal{M}[\![\ goto\ \ell;\downarrow\beta\ ]\!](S) = \text{empty set}$$

$$\mathcal{M}[\![\ \alpha;\ell:\downarrow\beta\ ]\!](S) = \mathcal{M}[\![\ \alpha\downarrow\ ]\!](S) \cup \mathcal{M}[\![\ \hat{\alpha}\ \downarrow\ goto\ \ell;\hat{\beta}\ ]\!](S)$$
for all *goto* ℓ in α but not in a proof-group,

i.e. the set of states possible immediately after a label with left context α are all those possible immediately before the label and all those possible immediately before any *goto* ℓ appearing in the left context α but not inside any proof-group in α.

A Programming Logic

Proof rules

We have discussed already (in (4.2)) that when a rule of inference is being applied at a position p in an argument, the hypotheses H_i must be accessible (either explicitly or implicitly at positions q_i) and must mean the same thing where they are available as they do where they are being applied. The goto punctuation does not change the meaning of any statements, but it divides the argument into segments (based in the value of boolean expressions controlling the goto). These segments may isolate positions from each other making certain assertions unavailable to certain positions. This happens in a very simple way which we can illustrate with this example:

```
A;
while b₁
   do.
      .
      .        {b₁ does not change
      .
      if b₂ then goto ℓ₁ fi;
      .
      .
      .
   od;
¬b₁;
P;
goto ℓ₂;
ℓ₁: Q₁;
ℓ₂: ;
```

At ℓ_1 we know b_1 & b_2 because of the source of the *goto* ℓ. If we now allowed lexically previous statements to be accessible at ℓ_1 we would also know $\neg b_1$, which would allow us to erroneously conclude b_1 & $\neg b_1$ at ℓ_1.

One way to look at this situation is to notice that the goto extends various dependencies (as occur in block structures) beyond their explicit boundaries. In the example, the position immediately before *goto* ℓ_1 depends on

120

b_1 and b_2. Such an extension creates dependencies which are not explicitly shown by block structures. These dependencies divide the proof into segments (which are like blocks without the delimiters). These segments can join together at labels.

The added condition on accessiblility caused by the goto's segmentation of proofs is that the hypotheses of a rule must all belong to the same segment where the rule is being applied. Informally two positions, p lexically before q are in the same proof segment when they satisfy a consistent set of boolean expressions (i.e. when they are on the same path in the flowchart of the argument). This happens when every path (from the start of the argument) to q must pass through p. We make this precise as:

Definition: A position p in an argument *dominates* a position q iff every execution path in the flow diagram from start to q must pass through p. (This is a generalization of the lexical order.)

We can determine dominance in the linear representation of a program by following the flow from p to q and checking that in addition there are no jumps into the lexical segment from p to q from outside that segment.

We can now give the new definition of accessibility which differs from (4.3) only in that lexical order is replaced by dominance.

Definition: An instance of an argument A starting at position p with free variables $x_1, \ldots, x_n$ is *accessible* from position q in an argument with gotos iff:

1. A at p dominates q (A and q are in the same seqment), and

2. Any proof block containing A at p also contains q (A is visible from q), and

3. Any proof block containing q which qualifies any of $x_1, \ldots, x_n$ also contains A (no x_i is captured at q, so A is free at q), and

4. None of the x_i is changed on any execution path from p to q (A is constant from p to q).

121

That is, from q we can see that A is free to move to q without changing.

The definition of a *proof* for arguments with gotos is the same as for the iterative arguments of (4.3).

The new proof rules for goto's are quite simple. First, for logical completeness we need a rule allowing us to make arbitrary conclusions after gotos. Since no states are possible immediately after a goto, any assertion is valid in that set of states. The rule is:

1.   goto rule

$$\frac{goto \;\; \ell}{false}$$

Although this rule may seem puzzling and unnecessary, it is needed because of the form of the other rules. The example following these rules should make this clear.

2.   label rule

Labeled positions are places where program segments come together. In order to carry information beyond these points we need a special rule because in an ordinary rule, the hypotheses must all be in the same segment. This special rule is called the *label rule*. It says that if we know P before each goto ℓ and before ℓ itself, then we know P at ℓ.

In terms of a flow diagram the rule is simply that P is known at a node iff it is known on every edge entering that node.

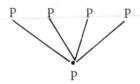

by label

Here is treatment of the division algorithm using goto punctuation to handcraft an iteration.

Example

division: *proof a*
          arbitrary integer a,b *where* a≥0 & b>0;
          integer q,r;
          conclude a = b*q+r & 0≤r<b;
          q := 0;
          a-b*q≥0 *by arith*, a≥0 , q=0;
          (a-b*q)+1≥0 *by arith*;
          a-b*q < (a-b*q)+1;
          $\exists$ *integer* i . (i≥0 & a-b*q < i) *by* I;
          while true *do*
            assume a-b*q≥0;
            arbitrary integer i *where* a-b*q < i;
            ¬(a-b*q<0) *by arith*, a-b*q≥0;
            r := a-b*q;
            r≥0 & r = a-b*q;
            if r<b *then*
                  goto out;
                  a-b*q≥0 *by goto*;
                  a-b*q<i-1 *by goto*;
                  else
                  b≤r;
                  b≤a-b*q;
                  0≤a-b*(q+1) *by arith*, b≤a-b*q;
                  b≥1;
                  (a-b*q)-b < i-1 *by arith*;
                  a-b*(q+1) < i-1;
                  q := q+1
         fi;
        od;
        out: r<b & r = a-b*q & r≥0 *by label*;
        a = b*q+r *by arith*;
        a = b*q+r & 0≤r<b
qed division;

Here is a detailed outline of an argument to construct a prime larger than a given positive integer. It uses Euclid's theorem on primes proved in (3.5). The reader should easily be able to fill in the missing details.

Example:

```
primes: proof
        arbitrary integer x where x>0;
        integer y,z,j,k,i,m,n;
        define factor(z,y) = ∃integer w . z = w*y;
        define prime(z) = ∀integer y where y>0 &
                          factor(z,y) . (y=1 ∨ y=z);
        define T(j,z) = ∃integer p. (j=p-z & p≥x & prime(p)):
        conclude y≥x & prime(y);
        y := x;
        y≥x by arith, y=x;
        ∀integer n where n≥0 .∃ integer p .
        p>n & prime(p) by Euclid's theorem in Chapter III,
          (3.5);
        ∃integer k where k>0 & T(k,y) by ∀E, y;
        /* namely, pick k = p-y */
        repeat
            assume y≥x;
            arbitrary integer i where T(i,y);
            y+1 > x by arith, y≥x;
            T(i-1,y+1); /* note i-1 = p-(y+1) */
            y := y+1;
            ∀integer m where 2≤m<2 . ¬factor(y,m);
            for i=2 to y-1 do
            assume ∀integer m where 2≤m<i . ¬fact(y,m);
                for j=2 to y-1 do
                    assume ∀integer n where 2≤n<j . n*i ≠ y;
                if i*j = y then goto exit fi;
                i*j ≠ y;
                ∀integer n where 2≤n<j . n*i ≠ y
                od;
            ∀integer m where 2≤m<i . ¬factor(y,m);
            od;
            ∀integer i where 1<i<y . ¬factor(y,i);
            prime(y) & y≥x; /* by lemma 2.2 in Chapter III,
                                (3.5) */
            goto found;
            ¬T(0,y); /* by goto rule */
        exit: j*i = y & 1<i & 1<j;
            ¬prime(y);
```

```
    proof assume T(0,y);
        proof choose p where 0 = p-y & p≥x & prime(p);
            p=y;
            prime(y);
            ¬prime(y);
            false
        qed;
        false
    qed;
    ¬T(0,y);
    until false;
    found: prime(y) & y≥x
qed primes;
```

4.5   EXERCISES

Section 4.1

(4-1)   How is the geometric action of constructing a tangent to a curve at a point represented in analytic geometry?

(4-2)   The following relation based in Fermat's conjecture (exercise (3-25)) implicitly defines a function in ordinary number theory, but is there an underlying computational action?

$\forall$integer n *where* n>0 . $\exists$integer y .

$((\exists$integer $x_1,x_2,x_3 . x_1^n+x_2^n=x_3^n)$ <=> y=1) &

$(\neg(\exists$integer $x_1,x_2,x_3 . x_1^n+x_2^n=x_3^n)$ <=> y=0)

(4-3)   Write an informal proof of correctness for your favorite simple algorithm. Analyse the proof to see whether it fits the mold of the inductive assertion method for "partial correctness" of Floyd and Hoare or the mold of "total correctness" or neither.

(4-4)   Read [Manna, Waldinger 78] for a more detailed survey of methods of proving program correctness.

(4-5)   Consider Euclid's proof of Proposition 1, Book I of *Elements* which is paraphrased below. Compare his method of mixing commands and assertions to the one we describe. (The postulates and definitions refer to the *Elements*.)

125

Proposition 1: Construct an equilateral triangle on a given finite straight line.

Proof: Let AB be the given straight line. Using A as center and AB as radius, construct a circle (justified by Postulate 3), call it BCD.
Using B as center and AB as radius, draw another circle (justified by Postulate 3), call it ACE.

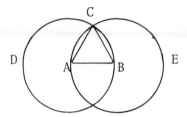

From the point C at which the circles intersect to points A and B draw line segments called CA, CB (justified by Postulate 1).

Now since A is the center of circle CDB, AC is equal to AB (by Definition 15).

Again since B is the center of circle CAE, BC is equal to BA (by Definition 15).

But CA was proved equal to AB, therefore each of the lines CA, CB is equal to AB. Since CA equals AB and CB equals AB, CA equals CB.

Therefore CA, AB, BC are equal to one another, so triangle ABC is equilateral.

QED.

Section 4.2

(4-6) How is a very complex state, such as the geometrical configuration for the proof in exercise (4-5), represented as a state in the precise sense of a mapping from variables to objects?

(4-7) Examine a typical mathematics text book to see how the assignment operator is paraphrased. What other programming language notations for the assignment operator have you seen, any in addition to these: x=exp, *let* x=exp, x←exp?

(4-8)   Allowing a variable to be reused (to appear on the left side of an assignment more than once) saves space in a predicate calculus argument. How many lines can be saved in a sequence of n assignments?

(4-9)   Translate the following argument (scheme) into (an equivalent argument in) the pure predicate calculus of Chapter II.

$$x := f(x)$$
$$\textit{if } b(x) \textit{ then } x := g(x); \; P(x)$$
$$\textit{else } x := f(x); \; Q(x)$$
$$\textit{fi}$$
$$P(x) \lor Q(x)$$

(How would you define the notion of equivalence between arguments that you are using?)

(4-10)   Compare the meaning of these two arguments, A and B.

A	B
$\textit{if } b_1 \textit{ then } P_1 \textit{ fi;}$	$\textit{select}$
$\textit{if } b_2 \textit{ then } P_2 \textit{ fi;}$	$\textit{when } b_1 \textit{ do } P_1 \textit{ od;}$
$\textit{if } b_3 \textit{ then } P_3 \textit{ fi;}$	$\textit{when } b_2 \textit{ do } P_2 \textit{ od;}$
$P_4.$	$\textit{when } b_3 \textit{ do } P_3 \textit{ od;}$
	$\textit{otherwise do } P_4 \textit{ od.}$

(4-11)   Prove that the following sequence of assignments computes ax^2+bx+c:

$$y := a*x$$
$$y := (y+b)*x$$
$$y := y+c.$$

(4-12)   Give an argument in the number theory of Chapter III equivalent to the argument finding the maximum of a,b,c.

(4-13)   Write an argument to find the (lexicographical) maximum of three character strings, x,y,z.

(4-14)   Write an argument to exchange the string values of variables x and y. Notice that it begins as

proof arbitrary string a,b *where* x=a & y=b;
/* conclude x=b & y=a */
$\vdots$
q̇ed

127

(4-15) Given integers A,B,C write an argument to determine whether they are the lengths of the sides of a
triangle. (They are if all are positive and A+B>C, A+C>B
and B+C>A.)

(4-16) Given integers A,B,C write an argument to determine
whether they are lengths of the sides of an equilateral
triangle.

(4-17) Consider the propositional logic obtained by adding
the connective ; and allowing commands as propositions.
If α,β,γ are commands and p,q,r are assertions, then
α;p means α halts and p is true of the resulting state.
Let α alone mean that α halts. Thus $\alpha\&\beta$ means α and β
both halt. p;α means p is true and α is applied to the
state, α;β is the usual notion of composition of commands.
Show that the following formulas are tautologies in this
propositional logic of commands:

$$\alpha;p \Rightarrow \alpha$$
$$p;\alpha \Rightarrow p\&\alpha$$
$$\neg(\alpha;p) <=> \neg\alpha \lor \alpha;\neg p$$
$$\alpha;(p\&q) <=> \alpha;p \& \alpha;q$$
$$\alpha;(p\lor q) <=> \alpha;p \lor \alpha;q$$

(See [Constable 77] for a more detailed treatment of this
calculus.)

(4-18) Describe the set of states possible at the significant positions in the following argument, starting with
the initial set $S_0 = \{s_1(x)=5, s_2(x)=-1\}$

> *proof integer* x;
>   *if* x<0 *then* x := -x; x>0
>   *else* x≥0 *fi*;
>   x≥0
> *qed*

(4-19) Describe the set of states possible at the significant positions in the following argument.

```
    proof arbitrary integer z;
          integer x,y;
    x := 2;
    y := 5;
    x<y;
          proof assume y<z;
                x := 10;
                x<z
          qed;
    y<z => x<z
    qed
```

(4-20) Consider the concept of *concurrent assignment*,
$x_1, \ldots, x_n := exp_1, \ldots, exp_n$. The computational meaning of
this statement is that expressions exp_i are evalutated and
simultaneously assigned $x_1 := exp_1$, $x_2 := exp_2, \ldots, exp_n :=$
exp_n. Thus if x_1 has value 1 and x_2 has value 2, $x_1, x_2 :=$
$x_1 + x_2$, $x_1 + x_2 + 1$ will result in x_1 having value 3 and x_2
having value 4. Notice that x_1, $x_2 := exp_1$, exp_2 need not
be equivalent to either $x_1 := exp_1$; $x_2 := exp_2$ or
$x_2 := exp_1$; $x_1 := exp_2$.
    Describe the effect of x,y := y,x. (See [Dijkstra 76].)

(4-21) Write an assignment rule for concurrent assignment.

(4-22) Given an argument using conditionals and concurrent
assignments, prove there is an equivalent argument of the
type described in section 4.2 (e.g. using ordinary assignments). The concurrent assignment argument may be shorter,
but if it involves n such assignments, how many ordinary
assignments would be necessary, in the worst case, to
replace them.

Section 4.3

(4-23) Why does the loop rule require the hypotheses
∃*integer* n .(n≥0 & T)? (See exercise (4-31) for answer.)

(4-24) Describe the set of states possible at the significant positions of the following loops.

(a) *while* x≠0 *do* x := x-1 *od*
     starting with S = $\{s_1(x)=3, \; s_2(x)=0\}$

(b) *repeat* x := x-1 *until* x=0;
     where S = $\{s_1(x)=3, \; s_2(x)=0\}$

(4-25) Describe the set of states possible at the significant positions in the following arguments.

(a) *proof assume* x>0;
           integer y;
     while x≠0 *do* y := y*y *od*
     qed

     starting with s = $\{s_1(x)=0, \; s_2(x)=3\}$

(4-26) Which of assertions a,b,c is accessible at the position labeled p?

     a: $\forall type$ x . P(x)
     b: Q(x,y)
     c: Q(y,y)
     while b(x) *do* p: ; x := f(x,y) *od*

(4-27) Find the error in the following proof. Notice, we are assuming that the loop terminates, so this is interpreted to be a partial correctness proof.

     proof arbitrary integer a *where* x=a;
           integer y,z;
     y := 0; z := x;
     $y = a^2 - x*a \; \& \; y \geq 0$;
     while x≠0
         do assume $y = z^2 - x.a$;
           $y \geq 0$;
           y := y+z;
           x := x-1;
           $y \geq 0$;
           $y = a^2 - x.a$
     od;
     $x=0 \; \& \; y = a^2 - x.a$;
     $y = a^2$

(4-28) Complete the corrected argument in (4-27) by proving termination of the loop.

(4-29) Prove that the following program computes the greatest common divisor of x and y, nonnegative integers.

```
a := x; b := y;
repeat
    while a>b do a := a-b od;
    while b>a do b := b-a od
until a=b
```

(4-30) Prove that the following program computes the value 91 in the range 0≤x≤101.
(See Appendix for an answer). Termination is the interesting part.

```
proof
        arbitrary integer x where 0≤x≤101;
        conclude x=91;
        integer d;
        d := 1;
        while d>0 do
            if x>100 then x := x-10;
                          d := d-1
                     else
                          x := x+11;
                          d := d+1
        fi
    od
```

(4-31) Show that in either of the above programs, if we assume the condition *arbitrary integer i where i<i* the proof of termination is trivial.

(4-32) Give a detailed proof (by induction) of the soundness of the loop rules.

(4-33) In Hoare's logic the notation {P} α {Q} for command α, assertions P,Q means "if P is true of the input state s and α terminates on s, then Q is true of the output state." In this notation, the following are rules for loop induction. Show that these rules can be derived from ours. (In fact, we derived ours from Hoare's.)

(i)   {P&b} α {P}
     ―――――――――――――――――――――
     {P} *while* b *do* α *od* {P&¬b}

(ii)
$$\frac{\{P\}\ \alpha\ \{Q\}}{\{Q\&\neg b\}\ \alpha\ \{Q\}}}{\{P\}\ repeat\ \alpha\ until\ b\ \{Q\&b\}}$$

(4-34)   Show that the following while rule is correct.

```
P;
∃integer n . (n≥0 & T(n));
T(0/n) => ¬bexp;
while bexp
    do assume P;
       arbitrary integer n where T;
       argument
       T(n-1/n);
       T(0/n) => ¬bexp;
       P
od
```

¬bexp & P

(4-35)   Prove the program in exercise (4-27) is correct using the rule from exercise (4-34). Then show how the proof of $T(0/n)$ => ¬bexp inside the loop is valid outside before the loop.

(4-36)   Try to give a correctness proof of the program in exercise (4-27) in Hoare's logic (exercise (4-33)). You will also need the *rule of consequence*:

$$\frac{\{P\}\ \alpha\ \{Q\}\ ,\ \{Q\}\ \beta\ \{R\}}{\{P\}\ \alpha;\beta\ \{R\}}$$

(4-37) Dijkstra's calculus [Dijkstra 76] is based on the concept of the weakest precondition of a command with respect to an assertion. Precisely,

wp(α,P) = {s | α terminates on s and after executing α on s, P is true of the result}.

Give a definition of wp(α,P) in terms of the formal semantics in section 4.3 for α an iterative program. Notice, wp(α,P) is precisely the predicate α;P

(4-38)   Prove Dijkstra's while axiom using our formal semantics

$$P\&bexp => wp(\alpha,P)$$

P&wp(*while* bexp *do* α *od*,true) => wp(*while* bexp *do* α *od*, P&¬bexp)

(4-39) The *for elimination* rule can also be given in the form

$$P(exp_1-1/i); \neg(exp_2 < exp_1-1);$$
$$for \ i=exp_1 \ to \ exp_2$$
$$\quad do \ assume \ P(i-1);$$
$$\quad \quad argument$$
$$\quad \quad P(i)$$
$$\quad od$$

$$\overline{\quad\quad\quad\quad\quad\quad\quad\quad\quad\quad\quad\quad\quad\quad}$$

$$P(exp_2/i)$$

Show how to derive this form from the rule in 4.3. We will consider this as a legitimate rule in further proofs.

(4-40) Examine the PL/CV do index rule in Part IV of the Appendix and compare it to the for elimination rules in (4-39) and in section (4.3). Notice the PL/CV rules are especially adapted to handle exits from the middle of the loop.

(4-41) Continuing the logic of commands in exercise (4-17), let $b*\alpha$ abbreviate *while* b *do* α *od* and let $b \rightarrow \alpha,\beta$ abbreviate *if* b *then* α *else* β *fi*. Prove the following theorems in this propositional logic of programs:

(1) $(b \rightarrow \alpha,\beta); p <=> (b => \alpha;p) \ \& \ (\neg b => \beta;p)$

(2) $(b*\alpha); p <=> \neg b \& p \lor (b;\alpha); (b*\alpha); p$

(3) $(p => b*\alpha) => p => \neg b \lor \alpha$

(4) $b*\alpha => b*\alpha; \neg b$

5

RECURSIVE PROCEDURES

5.1 INTRODUCTION

Procedures in programs serve a purpose analogous to that of definitions and lemmas in traditional mathematical arguments. Using procedure definitions, we may solve a certain programming problem once, and use the solution repeatedly as a primitive command in varying contexts. This facility not only allows shorter and simpler programs, it also allows a degree of modularity, or isolation of different logical notions. Procedure definitions are a boon to proofs involving programs, since they allow important properties of procedures to be proved once as lemmas, and applied repeatedly in a main program proof at each invocation of the procedure. The simplest kind of procedure is defined by a sequence of assignments, conditionals and loops. Semantics and proof rules for such procedures could be extremely simple. Unfortunately, parameterless, nonrecursive procedures are not very useful for programming.

In Chapter II we saw how the notion of substitution for free occurrences of variables is used to let $P(exp/x)$ assert the same thing about a specified expression exp which P asserted about x. Similarly, we would like to invoke a procedure in such a way that the invocation, or call, *does* the same thing with a particular expression which the sequence of commands in the procedure definition did with a certain variable. This desire leads naturally to procedures with parameters, and a serious new problem. In order to prevent pathological captures of variables, we need to extend the free and bound variable analysis to arguments with commands. Also, certain procedure calls

134

involve deliberate substitution for binding and bound occurrences of variables, requiring a notion of substitution different from the free substitution of Chapter II.

Procedures become more useful when we allow apparently circular, recursive definitions. To prove properties of recursive procedures, and especially to prove termination, we need another version of induction, as we did for loops in Chapter IV.

5.2 SUBSTITUTION IN ARGUMENTS WITH COMMANDS

Recall that the essential problem in substituting expressions for free variables in Chapter II was avoiding capture of variables, that is, placing a variable in a position where it acquires a different meaning from the one it had before substitution. In order to extend the necessary notions of free, binding and bound occurrences of variables in a useful way, we need to reconsider the intuition behind these notions.

A free occurrence of a variable in an argument A is one where the variable obviously has the same meaning in A as it does previous to A. A binding occurrence is one which gives new meaning to a variable symbol, and a bound occurrence in A is one where the variable may have different meaning than it did previous to A. Along with the quantifiers and qualifiers of Chapter II which give new meanings to variables, we now have assignments and *for* loops.

Definition: An occurrence of a variable symbol x of one of the following forms is a *binding* occurrence of x.

1. $\forall$...x, or $\exists$...x

2. *proof arbitrary* ...x or *proof choose* ...x

3. *for* $x=exp_1$ to exp_2

4. x := exp

A nonbinding occurrence of a variable symbol x in an argument A is *bound* in A if any of the following holds:

1. the occurrence is in a subassertion P within
    an assertion

$$\forall \ldots x \ldots P \text{ or } \exists \ldots x \ldots P$$

2. the occurrence is in a subargument B within
    an argument

$$\textit{proof choose} \ldots x \ldots \text{ B } \textit{qed}$$

or

$$\textit{proof arbitrary} \ldots x \ldots \text{ B } \textit{qed}$$

or

$$\textit{while bexp do arbitrary} \ldots x \ldots \text{ B } \textit{od}$$

or

$$\textit{for } x = \exp_1 \textit{ to } \exp_2 \textit{ do } B \textit{ od}$$

3. the occurrence is in an assertion or command L
    where *some* execution path from the beginning of
    A to L contains an assignment

$$x := \exp \text{ or } \textit{call } p(\ldots x \ldots)$$

where x is a readwrite parameter (see 5.3).
    All other occurrences of x in A are *free* in A.
  Clause (3) in the definition of bound occurrences
introduces a few minor subtleties. Note that, in the
argument

$$x \geq 0;$$

$$x := x+1;$$

$$x \geq 1;$$

the occurrence of x in the first line is free, as is the
occurrence on the right-hand side of the assignment. The
left-hand occurrence of x in the assignment is binding,
and the occurrence in the last line is bound. Unlike
quantifiers and qualifiers, which bind variable occurrences
within an explicitly bracketed scope, assignments bind
variable occurrences whenever a conceivable execution path
allows the assignment to affect the meaning of that
occurrence. Thus, in the presence of loops, a bound
occurrence of x may occur lexically *before* an associated
binding occurrence. For example, expanding the argument
above to

> *while* x<100 *do*;
>   x≥0;
>   x := x+1;
>   x≥1
>
> *od*

The left-hand occurrence of x in the assignment is
binding, and all four other occurrences of x are bound.
     In the *while* example above, as well as in conditional
arguments such as

> *if* x<0 *then*
>   x := -x;
>   *end*;
>   x≥0;

There are certain occurrences of variables which are
bound, yet whose meanings still *may* depend on the initial,
or global, interpretation of x. In the predicate calculus,
binding was an all or nothing affair, with commands some
variable occurrences are only loosely bound. To capture
the notion that the meaning of an argument A depends on
the global interpretation of x (i.e., the argument says
something about the global meaning of x), we cannot merely
say, as in Chapter II, that x is free in A. We need a
finer distinction among bound variable occurrences.

Definition: A bound occurrence of x in A is *tightly bound*
in A iff the occurrence is bound by a quantifier or qualifier
or *for* loop, or *every* execution path from the beginning
of A to (but not including) the line containing the
occurrence has an assignment

> x := exp or *call* p(...x...)

where x is a readwrite parameter. Any other bound occurrence is *loosely bound*.
     Notice that an argument says something about x when-
ever x appears free or loosely bound in A.
     The notion of where a given variable occurrence is
bound becomes more complicated with assignments. Intuitively, a bound variable occurrence is *bound by* each
binding which might affect its meaning.

Definition: Every free or loosely bound occurrence of a variable x in argument segments α,β,γ is *bound by* the binding occurrence of x in.

   (i)   ∀...x... α
   (ii) ∃...x... α
   (iii) *proof choose* ...x... α *qed*
   (iv) *proof arbitrary* ...x... α *qed*
   (v)   *while* bexp *do arbitrary* ...x... α *od*
   (vi) *for* x=exp$_1$ *to* exp$_2$ *do* α *od*

   (vii) let c(x) be either x := exp or *call* p(...x...)
         for x a readwrite parameter, then
         (a)   c(x); α
         (b)   *if* bexp *then* ...c(x); α [*else*...] *fi*; β
               if bexp *then* ...*else* c(x); α *fi*; β
         (c)   *for* i=exp$_1$ *to* exp$_2$ *do* α c(x); β *od*; γ

         (d)   *while* bexp *do* α c(x); β *od*; γ
         (e)   *repeat* α c(x); β *until* bexp; γ

Now, suppose we have an argument A which computes with the value of x, and we wish to derive an argument which does the same thing with the value of some expression t. As in Chapter II, we may use syntactic substitution.

Definition: A(t/x) is the argument obtained by simultaneously replacing every free occurrence of x in A by t. A(t$_1$/x$_1$,...,t$_n$/x$_n$) is the argument obtained by simultaneously replacing every free occurrence of every x$_i$ by the corresponding t$_i$.

Syntactic substitution in arguments fails to capture the intuition of doing the same thing with the value of t which was done with x when the substitution causes an accidental binding of a free variable occurence in t. One other type of failure may occur in the presence of commands. Consider the valid argument, on the left where |x| is the absolute value of x. Substituting 3 for free occurrences of x yields the following invalid argument, on the right.

```
y := x;                          y := 3;
if x<0 then                      if 3<0 then
    x := -x                          x := -3
fi;                              fi;
z := x;                          z := x;
z = |y|                          z = |y|
```

The problem is, we cound not substitute 3 for x in z := x, because this occurrence of x is loosely bound by x := -x above; yet, since 3<0 is false, the meaning of x in z := x is the global, unbound meaning.

Substituting for free and loosely bound occurrences also leads to trouble, as when -3 replaces free and loosely bound occurrences of x above:

$$y := -3;$$
$$if\ -3<0\ then$$
$$x := -(-3);$$
$$fi;$$
$$z := -3;$$
$$z = |y|$$

The simplest way out is to disallow substitution in the presence of loosely bound occurrences.

Definition: t is   *free for* (*free occurrences of*) x in A iff x does not occur loosely bound in A, and no free occurrence of a variable in t becomes bound in $A(t/x)$.

We will always insist that t is free for x in A before substituting t for x. Substitution for free occurrences is the mechanism used with readonly procedure parameters. Substitution of y for all (free, binding and bound) occurrences of x should capture the intuition of doing the same thing with y that was done with x. This concept will be used to explain readwrite parameters in procedures.

Definition: $A(y//x)$ is the argument obtained by simultaneously replacing all occurrences of x in A by y. $A(y_1//x_1,\ldots,y_n//x_n)$ is the argument obtained by simultaneously replacing all occurrences of each x_i in A by y_i. y is *free for all occurrences* of x in A iff no variable occurrence in A acquires a new binding in $A(y//x)$.

Mixed substitutions such as $A(t/x, w//u)$ will also be used, with the natural meaning. Notice that, within assertions, it doesn't matter whether we rename quantified variables or not. The following two arguments are semantically equivalent, where α and β are arguments, and A is an assertion:

$$(\alpha;A;\beta)(y//x)$$
$$\alpha(y//x); \ A(y/x); \ \beta(y//x).$$

5.3 SYNTAX

A procedure definition contains a heading with the procedure name and a list of formal parameters (i.e., parameters to be substituted for), an optional sequence of declarations and assumptions, and an argument which is the body of the procedure.

procedure definition →

   procedure-name: *procedure*[(parameter-list)];

        [[dcl] variable-list *readonly*;]

        [[dcl] variable-list [*readwrite*];]

        [[dcl] variable-list *external*;]

        [*assume* assertion;]

        [*arbitrary* variable-list
        [*where* assertion];]

        [*conclude* assertion;]

        [[dcl] variable-list;]

        argument

        end[procedure-name];

parameter-list → {variable §,}$^{+}$

Each variable in the argument must appear exactly once in one of the declarations or in the qualifier. The *conclude* line is a redundant assertion which must appear in the argument, just before each *return* command (see below).

  Two additional commands are needed, given by the following productions:

    command → *return*

      call procedure-name [(expression-list)]

Each *call* command must have an associated procedure
definition, and the expression-list in the *call* must
match the parameter list in the procedure heading in
three ways:

1.   The lengths must be the same,

2.   The types of the expressions in the *call* must
     match the declared types of the procedure in order,

3.   For each variable in the *readwrite* declaration in
     the procedure definition, the corresponding expres-
     sion in the call must be a single variable symbol
     which does not appear elsewhere in the *call*, or in
     the *external* variable-list (of *any* procedure
     reached by the call).

The exact way in which a main argument is joined to procedure
definitions is not crucial; we list the main argument first.

    argument-with-procedures →
            argument; {procedure-definition §;}*

Example: a procedure to swap the values of x,y

        swap: *procedure* (x,y);
              integer x,y;
              integer t;
              arbitrary integers a,b *where* a=x & b=y;
              conclude x=b & y=a; /* exchanges values of x,y */
              t := x;
              t=a;
              x := y;
              x=b;
              y := t;
              y=a;
              return
        end swap

5.4   SEMANTICS

In the presence of procedures we need an additional
parameter in all our meaning functions, consisting of a
list of procedure definitions. This parameter will be
irrelevant for objects not involving procedure calls or

141

A Programming Logic

procedure names, i.e.

$$\mathcal{M}[\![\alpha, \text{proc-defs}]\!] = \mathcal{M}[\![\alpha]\!]$$

$$\mathcal{M}(s)(\beta,\text{proc-defs}) = \mathcal{M}(s)(\beta)$$

$$<\mathcal{M},s> \models A \text{ proc-defs} <=> <\mathcal{M},s> \models A$$

whenever α,β,A do no contain any *call* commands.

Imperative meaning

The meaning of a procedure is a partial function from $\text{Values}^n \times \mathcal{P}(\text{States}) \to \mathcal{P}(\text{States})$. The procedure body determines a partial function $\text{States} \to \text{States}$. The parameters specify certain initial values of the input state (all other values are arbitrary). The correspondence between actual and formal parameters determines the value of the parameters and determines which values of the final state are transferred to which variables of the state in which the procedure was called. All this can be summarized in two simple equations, one for procedure definition, one for procedure call.

Procedure definition: Let proc-defs contain the definition p: *proc*$(\overline{x},\overline{y})$ body *end* p with readonly parameter list $\overline{x}$, readwrite parameter list $\overline{y}$, and external variables $\overline{z}$.

Then $\mathcal{M}(p,\text{proc-defs}) = \lambda,\overline{u},\overline{v},s.$

$$[\mathcal{M}[\![\text{body}]\!](\{s' \mid s'(\overline{x})=\overline{u}, s'(\overline{y})=\overline{v}, s'(\overline{z})=s(\overline{z}), s'(w) \text{ is}$$
$$\text{arbitrary for all other variables } w\})].$$

The result is a single state when the meaning of the body depends only on the initial values of the variables in $\overline{x},\overline{y}$. (This accords with our operational intuition because when the procedure definition is compiled, some arbitrary section of memory will be used to form the state. Only the parameters will be initialized; all other variables have the
of memory.

procedure call

$$\mathcal{M}[\![\text{call } p(\overline{u},\overline{v}), \text{proc-defs}]\!](s) = s' \text{ where}$$

$s'(\overline{v})=\hat{s}(\overline{y})$, $s'(\overline{z})=\hat{s}(\overline{z})$, $s'(w)=s(w)$ for all other variables
w, $\hat{s}\varepsilon.\mathcal{M}(p,$ proc-defs$)(s(\overline{u}),s(\overline{v}),s)$

Notice, $\mathcal{M}[\![$ call $p(\overline{u},\overline{v})]\!]$ is well defined only when all
$\hat{s}\varepsilon.\mathcal{M}(p,$ proc-defs$)(s(\overline{u}),s(\overline{v}),s)$ agree on $\overline{y},\overline{z}$.

When the procedure is recursive, these two meaning
equations are mutually recursive. As usual, we consider
the meaning to be the least partial function solution to
the equations.

The meaning of a set of mutually recursive procedures
and functions can be defined by a straightforward extension of these equations to systems of equations. We give
detailed positional semantics below for mutually recursive
procedures.

assertive meaning

$<\mathcal{M},s> \models_\alpha$ *call* $p(u,v)$ proc-defs iff

$\mathcal{M}(p,$proc-defs$)(s(\overline{u}),s(\overline{v}),s)$

positional semantics

A positional semantics of a program with defined
recursive procedures and functions requires a description
of the states possible after a procedure call, as
α *call* $p \downarrow \beta$.

We describe the position after a procedure call

$\mathcal{M}[\![\alpha$ *call* $p(\overline{u},\overline{v}) \downarrow \beta,$ proc-defs $]\!](S) =$

$\{\mathcal{M}[\![$ *call* $p(\overline{u},\overline{v}),$ proc-defs $]\!](s')$
$|\ s'\varepsilon.\mathcal{M}[\![\alpha\downarrow$ *call* $p(\overline{u},\overline{v})$ $\beta,$ proc-defs $]\!](S)\}$

5.5 DISCUSSION OF PROOF RULES

Fifty years ago logicians labored to correctly formulate the inference rules for the predicate calculus.
Numerous mistakenly unsound or incomplete axiom systems
were published. Computer scientists are experiencing
similar difficulties formulating the rules for procedures.

The rules are subtle. They involve new concepts, yet we
demand their complete integration into a formal logic.
This discussion will try to illuminate some of the errors
that must be avoided.

Basically there are two problems. One is how to
properly substitute for parameters as well as for logical
variables (used to describe the procedure). The other is
how to avoid circular reasoning in dealing with apparently
circular recursive procedure definitions, namely recursive
procedures. First we look at the problem of substitution.

Nonrecursive Procedures

Consider first a definition of a procedure p, containing no *call* commands, with a single *return* at the end.
Suppose we have a proof of the form

$$\textit{proof assume } A;$$
$$\text{Body}$$
$$B$$
$$\textit{qed}$$

where Body is the body of the procedure definition up
to but not including the *return* command. Let $\bar{v}, \bar{w}, \bar{x}, \bar{y}, \bar{z}$
be, respectively, the *readonly, readwrite, external,*
other program variables, and the logical variables of p.
Now, suppose that the form

$$A(\bar{t}/\bar{v},\ \bar{u}/\bar{w});$$
$$\textit{call } p(\bar{t}, \bar{u});$$

appears in an argument. The effect of the call is intuitively the same as the effect of a copy of the body with
$\bar{t}$ replacing $\bar{v}$ and $\bar{u}$ replacing $\bar{w}$, that is, $\text{Body}(\bar{t}/\bar{v},\ \bar{u}//\bar{w})$.
In the hope that

$$\textit{proof assume } A(\bar{t}/\bar{v},\ \bar{u}/\bar{w});$$
$$\text{Body}(\bar{t}/\bar{v},\ \bar{u}//\bar{w})$$
$$B(\bar{t}/\bar{v},\ \bar{u}/\bar{w})$$
$$\textit{qed}$$

is a valid argument, we would like to substitute the
whole subargument

$$\text{Body}(\bar{t}/\bar{v},\ \bar{u}//\bar{w})$$
$$B(\bar{t}/\bar{v},\ \bar{u}/\bar{w})$$

for $call(\overline{t},\overline{u})$. The roundabout development above leads to the following rule of inference:

$$
\begin{array}{ll}
\text{p: } \textit{procedure } (\overline{v},\overline{w}); & \\
\quad \textit{dcl } \overline{v} \textit{ readonly}; & \\
\quad \textit{dcl } \overline{w} \textit{ readwrite}; & \\
\quad \textit{assume } A; & \\
\qquad \text{Body} & \\
\qquad B & A(\overline{t}/\overline{v},\ \overline{u}/\overline{w}) \\
\qquad \textit{return} & call\ p(\overline{t},\overline{u}) \\
\quad \textit{end } p & \\
\end{array}
$$

$$B(\overline{t}/\overline{v},\ \overline{u}/\overline{w})$$

Such a rule should be sound as long as no capture of variables occurs in the substitution

$$
\begin{array}{l}
\textit{proof assume } A(\overline{t}/\overline{v},\ \overline{u}/\overline{w}); \\
\qquad \text{Body}(\overline{t}/\overline{v},\ \overline{u}//\overline{w}) \\
\qquad B(\overline{t}/\overline{v},\ \overline{u}/\overline{w}) \\
\quad \textit{qed}
\end{array}
$$

Capture of variables by assignments in the Body (often called "aliasing") is prevented by the syntactic restriction that no *readonly* variable in $\overline{v}$ occurs on the left-hand side of an assignment, and no variable in $\overline{u}$ may occur more than once in the *call*. Capture of variables by quantifiers and qualifiers may be avoided by renaming qualified and quantified logical variables. The problem of capture by local procedure variable declarations is avoided by a similar renaming process, and by prohibiting free occurrences of local procedure variables in A and B.

When *readwrite* variables appear both free (or loosely bound) and bound in a procedure body, we may need extra variable symbols in the assertions A and B just in order to describe the procedure in a useful way. For example:

```
inc: procedure(x);
        dcl integer x readwrite
        x := x+1;
     end inc
```

No final assertion may express the fact that the new value of x is one larger than the old value without using another variable symbol, as in

```
inc: procedure(x);
        dcl integer x readwrite;
        arbitrary x_0;

        assume x=x_0;

        x := x+1;
        x = x_0+1;
end inc
```

The logical variable x_0 is introduced merely to refer to an old value of x.

5.6 PROOF RULES

All the considerations above lead to the following general rule for nonrecursive procedure *calls*.

nonrecursive procedure call

```
p: procedure(V̄,W̄);
        dcl V̄ readonly;
        dcl W̄ readwrite;
        dcl X̄ external;
        dcl Ȳ;
        arbitrary Z̄;
        assume A;
        Body;
    end                              A(T̄/V̄, ū/w̄, s̄/z̄)
```
_____

$$call\ p(T̄,ū);$$
$$B(T̄/V̄, ū/w̄, s̄/z̄)$$

where s̄ and T̄ are sequences of terms, ū is a sequence of distinct variables not occurring in s̄,T̄,X̄ every *return* command in Body is immediately preceeded by B, the substitutions do not cause any captures.

Note that the conclusion of this rule includes both the termination of the *call* and the assertion $B(T̄/V̄, ū/w̄, s̄/z̄)$ after the *call*. This rule may be applied to procedures containing *call* commands, as long as the procedure definitions can be ordered so that all *calls* in a definition refer to an earlier defined procedure.

Recursion

Suppose that we wish to define a procedure reduce(x,y) which, for x>1 divides out all factors of x from y when y>0. In the case that x does not divide y, the task is trivial. When x divides y, reduce(x,y) should have the same effect as

```
y := y/x;
reduce(x,y);
```

Such observations lead naturally to a recursive definition:

```
reduce: procedure(x,y);
          integer x readonly;
          integer y readwrite;
          if mod(y,x) = 0 then
                y := y/x;
                call reduce(x,y);
          fi;
          return;
        end reduce
```

where mod(y,x) = 0 iff x divides y. [†]

Our confidence in this procedure is based on the fact that, where the *call* command appears within the body of the definition, the size of the problem is reduced; y is replaced by the (usually) smaller y/x. A proof that reduce accomplishes its task should proceed by induction on the value of y. The problem is to represent such an induction, whose hypothesis refers to the whole procedure definition, as an argument within that procedure definition. Fortunately, we know exactly how the induction hypothesis must be applied: it will be used to infer directly after each recursive *call* that the procedure's task has been accomplished. So, instead of assuming that "If y≤n then reduce(x,y) halts with the new value of y being the old value of y divided by the largest possible power of x," we simply prove that y is smaller than n before each recursive call, and assume that the *call* halts with the new value of y as desired. Such an argument might look like

---

[†] We can treat this example without the mod function by using the divide procedure given below as an example.

this:

```
reduce: procedure(x,y);
        integer x readonly;
        integer y readwrite;
        arbitrary integer y0, i where y≤i
        assume x>1, y>0, y=y0;
        if mod(y,x) = 0 then
          y := y/x;
          i>0;
          y≤i-1;
          x>1 & y>0 & y = y0/x;
          assume call reduce(x,y) for reduce;
          assume ∃integer z . y = (y0/x)/x^z &
           mod(y,x) ≠ 0 for reduce;
          ∃integer z . y = y0/x^z & mod(y,x) ≠ 0;
          else mod(y,x) ≠ 0;
               y = y0/x^0;
          ∃integer z . y = y0/x^z & mod(y,x) ≠ 0;
          fi
          ∃integer z . y = y0/x^z & mod(y,x) ≠ 0;
          return;
 end reduce
```

Establishing i>0 before the recursive *call* is the same as showing that, if i≤0, no recursive call will be made - part of the basis step of our implicit induction. The *call* and the following assertion are *assumed* "*for* reduce" to indicate that, although they appear in one branch of a conditional, their scope is the whole definition, and these assumptions will not be discharged at the end of the conditional. Note that, if the assumptions were restricted to the conditional branch containing them, we could not infer

$$\exists \textit{integer } z.\ y = y_0/x^z \ \&\ \mathrm{mod}(y,x) \neq 0$$

after the conditional. (See exercise (5-27) in 5.6 for an interesting syntactic way of indicating the scope of the assumption.) When many mutually recursive procedures are defined together, the necessary argument becomes more intricate, but the underlying induction is essentially the same.

The previous rule for nonrecursive procedure *calls* is used for recursively defined procedures with three changes.

1. The rule may not be applied to recursive *calls* within procedure definitions; these *calls* must be handled by the assumption mechanism sketched above.

2. A new logical variable with special status in the rule is added to prove termination.

3. The inductive assumptions in the mutually recursive procedure definition must be discharged.

A set of definitions with all such assumptions discharged is called a *completed* set of definitions, defined syntactically as follows:

Definition: Let $\mathcal{D}$ be a set of procedure definitions. For each procedure p defined in $\mathcal{D}$ let $\bar{v}_p, \bar{w}_p, \bar{x}_p, \bar{y}_p, \bar{z}_p$ be, respectively, the *readonly, readwrite, external,* local and all but one of the logical variables in the definition of p. Let n be a special logical variable, used in all procedures of $\mathcal{D}$ to prove termination. Let A_p be the assumption at the beginning of the definition of p, and let B_p be the assertion intended as the conclusion after p is executed. The set of definitions $\mathcal{D}$ is *completed* iff:

1. Every assumption following every recursive *call* in procedure q of the form *assume call* $p(\bar{t}, \bar{u})$ *for* q is of the form

$$\textit{assume } B_p(\bar{t}/\bar{v}_p, \ \bar{u}/\bar{w}_p, \ \bar{s}/\bar{z}_p) \textit{ for q}$$

   where $\bar{s}$ and $\bar{t}$ contain terms, $\bar{u}$ contains distinct variables not appearing in $\bar{s}, \bar{t}, \bar{x}_p$.

2. For each such assumption, the corresponding assertion

$$A_p(\bar{t}/\bar{v}_p, \ \bar{u}/\bar{w}_p, \ \bar{s}/\bar{z}_p, n-1/n)$$

   appears immediately before the *call*.

3. In every procedure, the assertion

$$n>0$$

appears immediately before each recursive *call*.

4. The assertion B_p appears immediately before each *return*.

5. $\overline{y}_p$ are not free in A_p and $\overline{y}_p$, n are not free in B_p.

Finally, the new rule for *calls* appearing in the main program is:

p: *procedure*$(\overline{v}_p, \overline{w}_p)$;
  dcl $\overline{v}_p$ *readonly*;
  dcl $\overline{w}_p$ *readwrite*;
  dcl $\overline{x}_p$ *external*;
  dcl $\overline{y}_p$;
  arbitrary $\overline{z}_p$, *integer* n;
  assume A_p;
  conclude B_p;
  Body; $\exists$ *integer* n . $A_p(\overline{t}/\overline{v}_p, \overline{u}/\overline{w}_p, \overline{s}/\overline{z}_p)$
  end p;

---

call $p(\overline{t}, \overline{u})$;

$$B_p(\overline{t}/\overline{v}_p, \overline{u}/\overline{w}_p, \overline{s}/\overline{z}_p)$$

where $\overline{s}$ and $\overline{t}$ contain terms, $\overline{u}$ contains distinct variables not occurring in $\overline{s}, \overline{t}, \overline{x}_p$; the substitutions do not cause captures; $\overline{y}_p$ are not free in A_p; $\overline{y}_p$, n are not free in B_p; the set of procedure definitions associated with this argument is completed.

For certain recursively defined procedures, it is convenient to use induction over well-orderings other than the normal ordering of the integers. The normal way to prove that a set is well-ordered is to map it into the positive integers, so more general forms of induction usually improve the convenience and not the power of a proof system. Given a well-ordering $\prec$, we may allow $\prec$-induction for procedure proofs by generalizing the definition of completed procedure definitions. Simply change the assertion in clause (2) to

$$A_p(\overline{t/v}_p, \overline{u/w}_p, \overline{s/z}_p, m/n) \ \& \ L$$

where L is some assertion which expresses the fact that m n (assume 0 is the least element of this ordering). Interesting examples of other well-orderings, beyond the n-tuple orderings discussed in Chapter IV, must await the introduction of types of objects other than the integers

Here is a simple example of an argument for the division algorithm using a recursive procedure. It is instructive to compare this to the iterative version in Chapter IV and the number theory version in Chapter III.

Example:

```
divide: procedure (a,b,q,r);
        dcl a,b, readonly;
        dcl q,r readwrite;
        assume a≥0 & b>0;
        conclude a = b*q+r & 0≤r<b;
        arbitrary integer n where a+b≤n;
        dcl integer q₀,r₀;

        if a<b then q := 1; r := a;
                    a = b*q+r & 0≤r<b;
                    return fi;
        if a=b then q := 0; r := 0;
                    a = b*q+r & 0≤r<b;
                    return; fi;
        a>b by arith, ¬(a<b), a≠b;
        a-b≥0 & b>0 & (a-b)+b≤n-1 & n>0;
        assume call divide (a-b,b,q₀,r₀) for divide;

        assume a-b = b*q₀+r & 0≤r<b for divide;

        a = b*(q₀+1)+r₀
        q := q₀+1;
        r := r₀;
        a = b*q+r & 0≤r<b;
        return
end divide;
```

completed procedure definitions. Simply change the assertion in clause (2) to

$$A_p(\overline{t/v}_p, \overline{u/w}_p, \overline{s/z}_p, m/n) \ \& \ L$$

where L is some assertion which expresses the fact that m n (assume 0 is the least element of this ordering). Interesting examples of other well-orderings, beyond the n-tuple orderings discussed in Chapter IV, must await the introduction of types of objects other than the integers

Here is a simple example of an argument for the division algorithm using a recursive procedure. It is instructive to compare this to the iterative version in Chapter IV and the number theory version in Chapter III.

Example:

divide: *procedure* (a,b,q,r);

    dcl a,b, *readonly*;

    dcl q,r *readwrite*;

    assume $a \geq 0$ & $b > 0$;

    conclude $a = b*q+r$ & $0 \leq r < b$;

    arbitrary integer n *where* $a+b \leq n$;

    dcl integer q_0, r_0;

    if $a < b$ *then* $q := 1$; $r := a$;

            $a = b*q+r$ & $0 \leq r < b$;

            return fi;

    if $a = b$ *then* $q := 0$; $r := 0$;

            $a = b*q+r$ & $0 \leq r < b$;

            return; fi;

    $a > b$ *by arith*, $\neg(a<b)$, $a \neq b$;

    $a-b \geq 0$ & $b > 0$ & $(a-b)+b \leq n-1$ & $n > 0$;

    assume call divide $(a-b,b,q_0,r_0)$ *for* divide;

    assume $a-b = b*q_0+r$ & $0 \leq r < b$ *for* divide;

    $a = b*(q_0+1)+r_0$

    $q := q_0+1$;

    $r := r_0$;

    $a = b*q+r$ & $0 \leq r < b$;

    return

end divide;

Given x,y>0 we can find their greatest common divisor, a, and factor it out of x and y by the following procedure.

```
qcd:  procedure(x,y,a);
      integer x,y,a;
      integer t;
      arbitrary integer x0,y0,n;
      assume 0<x=x0 & 0<y=y0 & x+y≤n;
      conclude a>0 & x0=x*a & y0=y*a &
      ∀ integer v,w,b where x0=v*b & y0=w*b  . a≥b;
      if x=y
         then a := x;
              x := 1;
              y := 1;
              proof arbitrary integer v,w,b
                    where x0= v*b & y0=w*b;
                    a = v*b;
                    a≥b by arith, a = v*b, a>0, v>0, b>0
              qed
      fi;
      x≠y;
      if y>x

         This case is symmetric to the
         y<x case treated below.  The
         details are left to the reader.


      fi;
      x>y;
      (x-y)+y ≤ n-1 by arith, x+y ≤ n,-,y≥1;
      x-y = x0-y0;
      x := x-y;
      0<x=x0-y0 & 0<y=y0 & x+y≤n-1; 0<n;
      assume call qcd(x,y,a) for qcd;
      ind_hyp:  assume a>0 & (x0-y0) = x*a & y0 = y*a &
         ∀ integer v,w,b where x0-y0 = v*b & y0 = w*b . a≥b
         for qcd;
```

```
/* establish the conclusion */
proof arbitrary v,w,b
      where x_0 = v*b & y_0 = w*b;
            x_0-y_0 = (v-w)*b by arith, x_0 = v*b,-,y_0 = w*b;
            a≥b by VE, ind_hyp
qed;
      x_0 = x*a+y_0 by arith x_0-y_0 = x*a;
      x_0 = (x+y)*a by arith, x_0-y_0 = x*a,+,y_0 = y*a;
      x := x+y;
      x_0 = x*a & y_0 = y*a;
return;
end qcd;
```

5.7 EXERCISES

Section 5.1

(5-1) The lemmas in the proof of Euclid's theorem in Chapter III were not used repeatedly. Most were used only once. Why were they separated from the main argument as lemmas? Are procedures used in an analogous way in any of your programs?

(5-2) Develop the semantics and proof rules for parameterless nonrecursive procedures.

(5-3) Try to formulate a proof rule for parameterless recursive procedures (see exercise (5-17)).

Section 5.2

(5-4) Pick out all binding occurrences of variables in this program scheme (there are 5 of them).

```
p: procedure(x);
   atype x;
   atype y, integer i;
   arbitrary atype n where T(n);
   assume A;
   conclude C;
   y:= x;
   for i=1 to 10 do x:= exp od;
   y:= x;
   return
end p
```

(5-5) Pick out all the bound variables in the above example. Note, there is one free, one binding and one bound occurrence of variable x.

(5-6) Suppose the expression exp in (5-4) contains an occurrence of x, y and i. Which of these occurrences would be bound? Which are tightly bound?

(5-7) For the above example (5-4), what is $p(t/x)$?

(5-8) Consider the example

```
assign: procedure(x);
        integer x;
        arbitrary integer b where b=x;
        conclude x = b+1;
        x+1 = b+1 by arith x = b,+,1;
        x:= x+1;
        x = b+1;
        return
        end assign
```

(a) What substitution rule is violated in producing the following contradiction:

$$b=b; \quad call \ assign(b); \quad b \ = \ b+1?$$

(b) What rule is violated in producing the following contradiction by substituting x for b

$$x=x; \quad call \ assign(x); \quad x \ = \ x+1?$$

(5-9) Consider the example

```
add: procedure(x,y);
     integer x,y;
     arbitrary integer a,b where x=a & y=b;
     conclude y = a+1;
     y:= x+1;
     return
     end add
```

What rule is violated in producing the erroneous conclusion:

$$call \ add(x,x); \quad x \ = \ x+1?$$

(5-10) Consider the procedure

```
p: procedure(x,y);
   integer x,y;
   conclude x=0 & y=1;
   x:= 0;
   y:= 1;
   return
   end p
```

What rule is violated in producing the conclusion $call$ $p(z,z)$; $z=0$ & $z=1$? Compare this to the assertion $\exists x \ \exists y . (x=0 \ \& \ y=1)$ and the substitution for bound variables producing $\exists z \ \exists z . (z=0 \ \& \ z=1)$.

155

(5-11) Consider the example

    d: *procedure* (y_1, y_2);

        integer y_1, y_2;

        arbitrary integer a_1, a_2 *where* $a_1 = y_1$ & $a_2 = y_2$;

        conclude $y_1 = a_1 + 1$ & $y_2 = (a_1 + 1) + (a_2 + 1)$;

        $y_1 := y_1 + 1$;

        $y_2 := y_1 + y_2 + 1$;

        return

        end d

Clearly for $y_2 \geq 0$, *call* $d(y_1, y_2)$; $y_1 < y_2$. But what happens if we substitute $y > 0$ for y_1, y_2, e.g. *call* $d(y, y)$; $y < y$?

Section 5.3

(5-12) Compare the syntax for procedures in this section to the syntax for PL/CV procedures. When is the statement *arbitrary* variable list [*where* assertion] optional? When are the parameter declarations optional?

(5-13) In PL/CV, logical variables can be passed as para-maters (by shielding them) just as they can here. Why is this important ? (The termination variable need not be passed as a parameter, can you anticipate the explanation of this in (5.6)?)

(5-14) Does PL/I require that the types of actual and for-mal parameters agree?

(5-15) Why is restriction 3 placed on the definition of a parameter list?

Section 5.4

(5-16) In this exercise we examine a text book style seman-tics for procedures. Information is passed to procedures through a correspondence between arguments to the procedure at the point it is called (the *actual* parameters) and the arguments to the procedure at its definition (the *formal* parameters). In the usual text book style semantics for

PL/I procedures (see [Gries 71] p. 190 or [Conway and Gries 75] p. 201) the information passed through the correspondence are the *addresses* of the actual parameters (or of certain *dummy arguments*). In Conway and Gries this is explained in terms of drawing arrows from the formal parameters to the locations of the actual parameters. A diagram from their book makes this operational view clear. Suppose swap(I,J) is being called from a main program with variables A(1), A(2), I, J, X, T:

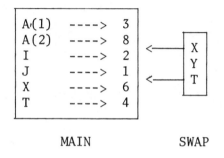

MAIN   SWAP

According to this description, the addresses I,J are given to X,Y which then have access to the *values* of I,J. When the procedure executes, any change in X and Y *results* in changes to I and J.†
     Relate this textbook semantics to the formal semantics of this chapter. Try to outline a proof that they are equivalent.

---

† In the terminology suggested by Algol 60 the arguments are passed by *value result*. To see the origin of the term, consider the semantics of swap((I),(J)). Now the arguments are expressions. Only their value is available. The procedure is said to be *called by value* and changes in X and Y *do not* *result* in changes to I and J. To see how this works operationally we notice that when arguments to a procedure are expressions, dummy locations are created, the values of the expressions are put in them and then the dummy addresses are given to X and Y. When the procedure finishes executing, the dummies vanish (and so does the result of the procedure on those dummy locations).

(5-17)   The meaning of a recursive procedure can be thought of as a *relation* on states. Given p: *procedure*$(\bar{x},\bar{y})$ body *end* p which we described in (5.4) as a mapping $\text{Values}^n \times \text{States} \to \text{States}$, it can also be thought of as a relation R_p on $\text{Values}^n \times \text{States} \times \text{States}$, namely $R_p(\bar{u},\bar{v},s,s')$ iff $\mathcal{M}(p)(\bar{u},\bar{v},s) = s'$.

The relation R_p can be defined *inductively* in a very simple way. The base case for the induction are those values of p obtained with 0 (no) recursive calls. Call them R_p^0. Given the set of values after n recursive calls, my R_p^n, the set of values after n+1 calls is defined essentially as the body applied to R_p^n. This definition can be easily made precise when the body has the simple form

$$if \text{ bexp } then \text{ stmt}_0$$
$$else \text{ stmt}_1; \text{ } call_p; \text{ stmt}_2$$

where stmt_i i=0,1,2 do not contain calls to p. (These are a form of linear recursive procedures.) In this case, R_p^{n+1} is defined as $\langle \bar{u},\bar{v},s,s'\rangle$ where on input $\bar{u},\bar{v},s$, bexp is false and stmt_1 produces a call to p with actual parameters $\bar{z},\bar{w}$ in state s_1, $\langle\bar{z},\bar{w},s_1,s_2\rangle \in R_p^n$ and $s' = \mathcal{M}[\![\text{stmt}_2]\!](s_2)$.

Give the inductive definition of the relation corresponding to the example reduce in (5.6).

(5-18)   Notice that a while loop may be simulated by a recursive procedure with exactly one recursive call at the
end of the body, e.g.,

> *while* bexp *do* body *od*

translates to

> loop: *procedure*;
>   *if* ¬bexp *then return*;
>   body
>   *call* loop
>   *end* loop

If we ignore semicolons, the associated production is

> loop ——> *if* ¬bexp *then return* body loop.

A grammar made up of such productions is regular, and must
generate a regular language.   Show how to transform any set
of recursive procedures with exactly one call at the end of
each definition body into a program which uses while loops
instead of procedures.   Suggest a method by which an opti-
mizing compiler might eliminate many unnecessary recursive
definitions.

(5-19)   Can every recursive procedure be transformed into
an iterative program?

(5-20)*   Suppose we do not specify the types of the basic
functions and operators of our program, so that only a program scheme is determined.   Can every recursive procedure
program scheme be translated into an iterative scheme
(see [Manna 74])?

Section 5.5

(5-21)*   A set of procedure definitions without parameters
is very similar to a context-free grammar.   A definition

> p: *procedure*;
>   body;

corresponds to a production

$$p \longrightarrow body.$$

(Body has the word *call* removed from each *call* command.)
The computation associated with a *call* p instruction may be
divided into:

(1) Using p as the start symbol, left-derive a sen-
tential form x using the appropriate context free
grammar;

(2) Execute x.

Assuming that *call* p halts, step (1) may be carried out far
enough that no *calls* will be executed in step (2).
What changes would occur in the programming language
if in step (1) we
(A) Used right-derivations
(B) Allowed arbitrary derivations
(C) Allowed more than one production for each nonter-
minal.

(5-22)* What kinds of grammars are needed to handle procedures with parameters in a way similar to that in problem
(5-21)?

(5-23) The problems of capture of free variables have
plagued logicians for years. Three general attitudes may
be found:

(1) define substitution ignoring capture problems, and
let the users of substitution take care of the
problems;
(2) restrict substitution so that it may only be performed when no captures occur;
(3) define substitution in such a way that bound variables are automatically renamed to avoid capture.

These three approaches may sometimes be mixed together in one technique. Analyze call by reference, call by name and call by value-result in terms of the three choices above. Where does the treatment in this chapter fit? In each case, what additional restrictions, if any, are needed to prevent capture? In what ways are the restrictions of this chapter stronger than necessary?

Section 5.6

(5-24) Using the method of exercise (5-18) rewrite a procedure with one recursive call "at the end" as a while loop. Then compare the proof rule for the procedure to the proof rule for while loops in Chapter IV.

(5-25) It is informative to compare procedure calls to concurrent assignments (see Chapter IV exercise 4-20). Suppose the readwrite parameters $w_1, \ldots, w_m$ are listed first with readonly parameters $v_1, \ldots, v_m$. The procedure can be thought of as a vector function $p: \text{Values}^{n+m} \rightarrow \text{Values}^m$. Call $p(v_i, w_i)$ corresponds to

$$w_1, w_2, \ldots, w_n := p(v_1, \ldots, v_m, w_1, \ldots, w_n).$$

Write an assignment axiom for this concurrent assignment and compare it to the nonrecursive procedure call rule.

(5-26) Compare the procedure rule to the PL/CV version in the Appendix, part V. Notice that the induction hypotheses, such as *assume call* $p(\bar{u}, \bar{v})$, are not written at all. Describe an algorithm for deducing these hypotheses and writing them (either in the form of the rule or in the notation of exercise (5-27)).

(5-27) In exercise (4-17) of Chapter IV we introduced a
notation for including commands in formulas. .That notation
provides a convenient way to describe procedures.
Introducing procedure p: $procedure(\bar{x},\bar{y})$;

$$assume\ A_p$$

$$conclude\ B_p$$

$$body$$

$$end\ p$$

asserts $A_p(\bar{x},\bar{y}) \Rightarrow call\ p(\bar{x},\bar{y}); B_p(\bar{x},\bar{y})$. Such notation allows us to dispense with the forms *assume call* $p(\bar{x},\bar{y})$ *for* q
and *assume* $B_p(\bar{x},\bar{y})$ *for* q in procedure bodies. That notation
was introduced only to explicitly display the scope of cer-
tain assumptions about the procedure. These scopes could
be specified by writing the induction hypotheses for recursive procedures in the procedure heading along with the input assumptions. For the reduce procedure this results in:

reduce: *procedure*(x,y);

　　　integer x *readonly*;

　　　integer y *readwrite*;

　　　arbitrary integer y_0,i *where* $y{\le}i$

　　　assume x>1 & y>0;

　　　conclude $\exists$ *integer* z. $y = y_0/x^z$ & $mod(y,x) \neq 0$;

hyp: *assume* $y \le i-1 \Rightarrow reduce(x,y)$;

　　　　　　integer z. $y = y_0/x^z$ &

　　　　　　　　　　　　$mod(y,x) \neq 0$;

　　if $mod(y,x) = 0$ then /* y divisible by x */

　　　y:= y/x;

　　　i>0;

　　　y $\le$ i-1;

　　　x>1 & y>0 & $y = y_0/x$;

　　　call reduce (x,y);

　　　$\exists$ *integer* z. $y = (y_0/x)/x^z$ & $mod(y,x) \neq 0$

　　　　　　　　　　　　/* by hyp */

$$\exists \; integer \; z.. \; y = y_0/x)x^z \; \& \; \text{mod}(y,x) \neq 0$$

$$else \; /* \; y \; not \; divisible$$
$$by \; x \; */$$

$$y = y_0/x^0 \; \& \; \text{mod}(y,x) \neq 0$$

$$\exists \; integer \; z. \; y = y_0/x^z \; \&$$
$$\text{mod}(y,x) \neq 0;$$

fi

Write the divide example in this new notation. Rewrite the program to compute z explicitly.

(5-28) Transform the primes example of 4.4 and the arguments in exercises 4-27, 29, 30 in Chapter IV to recursive procedures and prove them correct.

(5-29) The following two mutually recursive procedures define pairing and unpairing operations on integers. Prove that

(a) for all nonnegative integers a,b, pair (a,b,k) is defined and for any nonnegative k, unpair (k,a,b) is defined.
(b) show that *call* pair (a,b,k);
              call unpair (k,c,d);
              a=c & b=d
(c) show that *call* unpair (k,a,b);
              call pair (a,b,n);
              k=n;

The procedures are:

```
pair: procedure(a,b,k);
      integer a,b readonly;
      integer k readwrite;
      assume a≥0 & b≥0;
      conclude [part of exercise]
      if a>b then k = a² + 2*b + 1; return
            else k = b² + 2*a; return fi
end pair
```

```
unpair: procedure(k,a,b);
        integer k readonly;
        integer a,b readwrite;
        assume k≥0;
        conclude [part of exercise]
        integer a1,b1;
        if k=0
            then a:= 0; b:= 0; return
            else
            call unpair (k-1,a1,b1);
            select
                when a1<b1
                do a:= b1; b:= a1; return od
                when a1>b1
                do a:= b1 + 1; b:= a1; return od
                when a1=b1
                do a:= 0; b:= a1 + 1; return od
                otherwise return end
        fi
    end unpair
```

(5-30) A major problem concerning procedures is how to avoid circular reasoning about circular processes. There is only one way people have imagined for doing this—that is to use *mathematical induction*. The practical problem of understanding mutual recursion is how to see through the complexity to the basic underlying use of mathematical induction.

We will discuss induction on the depth of calls. Let us see how this can lead to circularity. Consider the procedure:

```
f: procedure(x,y);
   integer x readonly;
   integer y readwrite;
   if x=0 then y:= 0; return
           else if even (x)
                   then call f(x/2,y); return
                   else call f(3x+1,y); return
                fi
   fi
end
```

To show that y is 0 after any call, argue by ordinary
mathematical induction on n, the depth of recursive call.
If there are 0 calls, then we must have executed y=0, so
y=0. Assume the result is true for any depth n. Consider
a call of depth n+1. Then either f(x/2,y) or f(3x+1,y) are
called. But since f(x,y) halts in n+1 calls, each halts in
n calls, so f(x/2,0) and f(3x+1,0). Thus y=0 for all x.

This argument is fallacious because it is circular.
Will the circularity be detected by our rules?

The argument is false because we expected too much
from it. If we ask the question, "Is the procedure correct
if it terminates?" Then we can use the following type of
argument to get an answer.

We need to write procedures and functions in a way that
exposes the integer parameter which is the basis for the induction. Given any procedure p with body B_p define $p^{[n]}$ as
the new procedure obtained by expanding all recursive calls
to depth n. To be more precise, to define $p^{[1]}$ from p,
first number all occurrences of procedure calls, say $call_1$
p, $call_2$ p,... . Label the statement following them by L_i
(a new distinct label). Replace each $call_i$ $p(\hat{x},\hat{y})$ by the
body of p with $\hat{x}$ substituted everywhere for x, $\hat{y}$ for y.
Rename (if necessary) all local variables to be new. Then
replace *return* by *goto* L_i. Call the result $p^{[1]}$, it is the
depth one expansion of p.

Clearly p is equivalent to $p^{[1]}$, i.e. they perform the
same computation; but if p calls itself only once on inputs
x,y; then $p^{[1]}$ can perform the same computation with *no recursive* calls.

Now we can repeat the above process on $p^{[1]}$ to form
$p^{[2]}$, then repeat it again to form $p^{[3]}$, etc. In each case
$p^{[n]}$ is equivalent to p. Call $p^{[n]}$ the *depth n expansion of*
p.

Now suppose that we want to show that for each $p^{[n]}$, *if it does not call p recursively*, then it is *correct*. Such a proof can be treated as an ordinary mathematical induction on n. In fact, there is an especially appealing induction hypothesis for this proof. It says, "assume that the procedure p is correct whenever it is called in p". If from that assumption we can prove p itself is correct, then we have proved $p^{[n+1]}$ correct from the assumption that $p^{[n]}$ is correct, whenever neither procedure calls itself.

This method of reasoning only allows us to prove that if p halts, then it works correctly. To see the validity of this claim, suppose $p(x,y)$ halts and suppose we know $p^{[n]}$ is correct for all n (if p does not call itself). Then p calls itself recursively for only n steps. It is also equivalent to $p^{[n+1]}$ and $p^{[n+1]}$ never calls itself recursively, so it is correct by the above argument.

Use the argument above to outline a proof of the soundness of our recursive procedure rule when termination is assumed.

(5-31) Give an example of an erroneous proof in which something ridiculous is proved by allowing the termination parameter n to be free in the conclusion B_p of a procedure p.

Change the form of the final conclusion of the *call* rule so that n may be safely allowed to be free in B_p.

(5-32) The simplest way to prove that $\prec$ is a well-ordering of a set S is to give a mapping $f: S \rightarrow \mathcal{N}$ such that, for all x, y∈S,

$$f(x) \geq 0$$
$$x \prec y \iff f(x) < f(y).$$

Given such a mapping f, show how any proof of termination using the well-ordering $\prec$ may be transformed into a proof of the usual integer rule.

(5-33) Define a well-ordering $\prec$ on $\mathcal{N} \times \mathcal{N}$ by $\langle x_1, y_1 \rangle \prec \langle x_2, y_2 \rangle$ iff $x_1 < x_2 \lor x_1 = x_2 \mathbin{\&} y_1 < y_2$. Show that the simple technique of problem (5-28) cannot be applied to the well-ording.

6

RECURSIVE FUNCTIONS

6.1   <u>INTRODUCTION</u>

Defined functions in programming languages are often viewed as merely special sorts of procedures. Such a view is very reasonable for a compiler designer, since the same techniques are generally used to implement both functions and procedures. Logically, procedures and functions have very different status because procedure definitions create new commands in the same syntactic class as assignments, while function definitions create new functions which may appear freely in terms. Function parameters are all readonly (we do not consider the so called "functions with side-effects"), so the intricate problems of variable substitution, which plagued the logic of procedures, do not affect functions. But the possibility that computation of defined functions may not terminate leads to problems in other parts of the logic. For instance, since defined functions occur in assignments, conditionals and loops, additional restrictions must be placed on many of the proof rules to insure that these commands terminate. Moreover, since defined functions appear in assertions, serious questions arise about the underlying assertion logic, the predicate calculus itself. Specifically, what meaning (if any) should we assign to an assertion involving undefined function applications, e.g. what should $x/0 = x/0$ mean?

6.2 SYNTAX

The syntax for function definitions is essentially the same as the syntax for procedure definitions, but new primitive statements of the form *return*(exp) may be included in the body of a function definition, indicating that the computation of a function value is finished, and that the appropriate value is given by exp. Like *goto*, the *return* statement is better thought of as punctuation than as a command.

Function definitions look just like procedure definitions except that

1.   The word *function* is used instead of *procedure*,

2.   a phrase *returns*(*atype*) is used to indicate the type of value produced by the function,

3.   all parameters must be *readonly*,

4.   external variables may not appear on left-hand sides of assignments,

5.   the punctuation *return* carries an expression indicating the value produced by the function.

Grammatically,

function-definition →

>   function-name: *function*[(argument list)] *returns*(atype);

>> [[*dcl*] variable list *readonly*;]

>> [[*dcl*] variable list *external*;]

>> [*arbitrary* variable list;]

>> {*assume* assertion;}*

>> [*conclude* assertion;]

>> [[*dcl*] variable list ;]

>> argument

>> *end* [function name];

>   command → *return*(exp)

Note, the conclude statement and the argument may contain an occurrence of the function being defined.

Here is an example of a simple function definition.

max: *function*(x,y) *returns*(*integer*);
    integer x,y *readonly*;
    /* compute the maximum of positive integers x,y */
    assume x>0 & y>0;
    conclude max(x,y)≥x & max(x,y)≥y &
          max(x,y) = x ∨ max(x,y) = y;
    integer m;
    m := x;
    if m<y *then* m := y *fi*;
    return(m)
    end max

6.3   SEMANTICS

Discussion

A function definition creates a new model in which the defined function is associated with the appropriate function symbol, just as assignment creates a new state with a new value for some variable symbol. Unfortunately, the defined function may only be well-defined on a proper subset of its apparent domain. Consider for example a natural definition of the factorial function.

```
fact: function(x) returns(integer);
      integer x readonly;
      integer y,z;
      z := x; y := 1;
      while z≠0
         do
            y := y*z;
            z := z-1
         od;
      return(y)
      end fact
```

Although, according to the header, the argument x is allowed to be any *integer*, the computation of fact(x) as defined above terminates only if x≥0. It is not clear how to associate with the function symbol fact a total function in *integer* → *integer*. Some mathematicians would say that fact should refer to a partial function. We prefer to think of fact as a total function on a subset of the integers.

fact: {x | x is an *integer* x≥0} → *integer*.

In general we shall assign to every function definition a unique function from a subset of its apparent domain (the domain specified by the type symbols) into its apparent range. This subset is the *domain* of the function. For convenience we call these *partial functions* and use the term *total function* to refer to functions whose domain is their apparent domain.

Meaning of function definitions

The execution of the body of function definition is the same as the execution of any other program segment, except for the *return* commands; *return* simply stops execution of the function body. So

$$\mathcal{M} \; [\![\, return(t)\!\downarrow \,]\!] \, (s) = \emptyset.$$

Now let Defs be a set of function and procedure definitions including one of the form

> f: *function*($\bar{v}_f$) *returns*(atype);
>
>   *btype* $\bar{x}_f$ *external*;
>
>   *ctype* $\bar{v}_f$ *readonly*;
>
>   *arbitrary dtype* $\bar{z}_f$;
>   Body
>   *end* f

The meaning of the symbol f may depend on the state, due to the global readonly variables $\bar{x}_f$, so we extend the meaning function to

$$\mathcal{M} : \text{States} \to ((\text{function-symbols} \times \text{definitions}) \to$$
$$\bigcup_{n\geq 0} (\text{values}^n \to \text{values})$$

The graph of the function $\mathcal{M}(s)(f,\text{Defs})$ is equal to the union, taken over all contexts α, β such that α returns$(t)\beta$ = Body, of the graphs of the functions

$\lambda\bar{u} \cdot \mathcal{M}(\mathcal{M}[\![\alpha\!\downarrow\ return(t)\ \beta]\!](s'))(t)$ where s'=s except that $s'(\nabla_f)$ = u, $s'(\bar{x}_f)$, $s'(\bar{y}_f)$ are initialized, and $s'(\bar{z}_f)$ are arbitrary. Symbolically (and identifying a function with its graph),

$\mathcal{M}(s)(f,\text{Defs})$ =

$\quad \lambda\bar{u} \cdot \mathcal{M}(\mathcal{M}[\![\alpha\!\downarrow\ return(t)\ \beta]\!](s'))(t)$ where

$\alpha\ return(t)\ \beta$ = Body $\quad$ and $s'(\bar{x}_f)$ = $s(\bar{x}_f)$, $s'(\bar{v}_f)$ = $\bar{u}$,

$s'(\bar{z}_f)$ are arbitrary, and $s'(\bar{y}_f)$ are uniformly initialized. [†]

A function definition is only meaningful when the value returned does not depend on the initial values of local variables. We know this from the behavior of the compiler (see Appendix). The fancy definition above merely says that f denotes the function computed by running Body on a state in which the formal parameters have been initialized to the values of the arguments of f, and taking the value of the term t in the *return*(t) punctuation when control reaches such a position.

Meaning of expressions

Since the meanings of defined functions depend on the state, the semantics of terms must be modified slightly as follows:

$\quad \mathcal{M}(s)(f\ (t_1,\ldots,t_n),\text{Defs})$ =

$\quad (\mathcal{M}(s)(f,\text{Defs}))((\mathcal{M}(s)(t_1,\text{Defs})),\ldots,\mathcal{M}(s)(t_n,\text{Defs}))$

where $<t_1,\ldots,t_n>$ belongs to the domain of $\mathcal{M}(s)(f,\text{Defs})$. If the arguments are not in the domain, the meaning function is undefined.

As with procedure definitions, the Defs parameter is irrelevant to the meanings of objects not containing function or procedure names. Without global variables,

---

[†] This method is equivalent in principle to the popular least fixed point method (see [Scott 70, Milne, Strachey 76, Stoy 77]).

$\mathcal{M}(s)(f,Defs)$ may be written $\mathcal{M}(f,Defs)$.

Meaning of commands

In the presence of function definitions, equations for commands must include the definitions as a parameter, and in order for the command to be meaningful, functions must be applied only to arguments in their domains. A typical semantic equation for commands is:

$\mathcal{M} [\![x{:}{=}exp,Defs]\!] (s) = s'$ where

$s'(x) = \mathcal{M}(s)(exp,Defs)$ and $s'(y) = s(y)$ for $y{\neq}x$.

Meaning of assertions - discussion

Unfortunately, the inclusion of functions over subsets of domains introduces a new problem into the Predicate Calculus. We must decide how to treat assertions containing undefined terms, such as $x/0$. Such assertions arise commonly in calculus as well because the special functions like logarithm, tangent, etc. are partial. We have, in fact, adopted a solution from the logician H.J. Keisler's calculus book, [Keisler 76].

Reasoning about partial functions, though it is an old problem, has lately received fresh attention in computer science. We benefit from a variety of detailed new studies of the question, for instance [McCarthy 63, Scott 70,76, deBakker 70, Manna 74, Vuillemin 75, Cartwright 76]. But none of the approaches in the literature is overwhelmingly superior to any other. All of them involve incorporating new concepts in the underlying logic, a step we would take with great reluctance.

Everyday rules for reasoning about partial functions are free to use the best features of several essentially equivalent but formally distinct conceptions. This freedom is too costly in an implemented formalism, so one must make painful choices. We considered the ramifications of two diametrically opposite approaches. In one, the proof rules of the predicate calculus remain entirely unchanged, a feature obviously attractive to those writing mechanical proof checkers. In the second approach, adopted from Keisler, the semantics remains standard, but the proof rules are altered. In the main text of this monograph we give the required alteration to proof rules, while in the appendix, on PL/CV, we present the logic requiring no alteration of the Predicate Calculus.

Meaning of assertions

The proof rules given below in 6.4 are based on a standard (constructive) computational semantics. Each recursive definition f determines $\mathcal{M}(f)$ as above, i.e. a unique total function from a subset of its apparent domain into its apparent range.

Following Keisler, for atomic relations R we let

$$<\mathcal{M},s> \models R(\exp_1,\ldots,\exp_2) \text{ iff } \exp_1,\ldots,\exp_n$$

are all defined on s and

$$\mathcal{M}(R)(\mathcal{M}(s)(\exp_1),\ldots,\mathcal{M}(s)(\exp_n)) = true$$

That is, an assertion involving a defined function value, say f(x), is valid only if f(x) is defined, say f(x) = y, and the assertion is true of the value. So f(x) = f(x) is true precisely on those x for which $\mathcal{M}(f)$ is defined, i.e. precisely on the domain of $\mathcal{M}(f)$. Notice f(x) ≠ f(x) is never true, but it is not equivalent to ¬(f(x) = f(x)) since the latter may be true where f is undefined. Consider the factorial function, neither fact(-1) = fact(-1) nor fact(-1) ≠ fact(-1) is valid, but ¬(fact(-1) = fact(-1)) and ¬(fact(-1) ≠ fact(-1)) are both valid.
Thus the meanings of assertions are quite sensitive to the exact choice of primitive predicates.

Expressive power

The ability to define functions increases the expressive power of a language. In effect, we gain all the expressive power of a language with recursive equations [Greibach 75, Manna 74]. In addition, the way in which we assimilate possibly ill-defined terms into the logic allows us to directly assert termination and nontermination of a function body in the forms $f(\exp_1,\ldots,\exp_n)=f(\exp_1,\ldots,\exp_n)$ and $¬(f(\exp_1,\ldots,\exp_n) = f(\exp_1,\ldots,\exp_n))$.

With procedures, termination may be expressed by an argument, but not by a single assertion, and nontermination cannot be directly expressed. The additional expressive power of functions is not exploited in this monograph; in fact, we do not provide any way of proving that a function body does not terminate, only a way of proving that it does.

An alternate approach to semantics of partially defined functions

The irritating changes to the predicate calculus rules which were introduced by Keisler's semantics may be avoided entirely by changing the logical status of function definitions. In the previous treatment, a function definition is viewed as defining precisely one partial function; and the computation resulting from invocation of such a definition is viewed as a calculation of the unique value of the defined function. Alternatively, we may think of a function definition as a method for enumerating assertions about an unknown function. A computation, then, is a derivation of one such assertion. In typical procedural languages the generality of this view is not important, since all enumerated assertions turn out to be of the form $f(\overline{u}) = a$ for constants $\overline{u}$ and a. Even so, the ease with which the assertive treatment of definitions merges with our underlying predicate logic may make this approach attractive.

The meaning of a set of function definitions is the set of assertions $f(\overline{u}) = a$ such that the computation of the body of the definition of f on (the value of) $\overline{u}$ yields a.

$\mathcal{M}(s)(\text{Defs}) = \{f(\overline{u}) = a \mid \overline{u}, a \text{ are constant symbols, and}$

$\mathcal{M}'(a) = \mathcal{M}'(\mathcal{M}' [\![\alpha \downarrow \textit{return}(t) \ \beta]\!] (s'))(t)$

where $\alpha \ \textit{return}(t) \ \beta$ is the body of the definition of f, and

$s'(\overline{x}_f) = s(\overline{x}_f)$, $s'(\overline{v}_f) = \overline{u}$, and $s'(\overline{y}_f)$, $s'(\overline{z}_f)$ are arbitrary, and $\mathcal{M}'$ is any model such that

$$< \mathcal{M}, s> \models \mathcal{M}(s)(\text{Defs}), \text{ and}$$

$$\mathcal{M}'(h) = \mathcal{M}(h) \text{ for all primitive functions h}\}.$$

As usual, $\mathcal{M}(s)(\text{Defs})$ is the smallest set satisfying the equation above. Now, an argument with definitions is valid in a model $\mathcal{M}$ if the argument without definitions is valid in all models $\mathcal{M}'$ agreeing with $\mathcal{M}$ on primitive functions and satisfying all the computed assertions about defined functions.

$$<\mathcal{M},s> \models \text{Arg, Defs}$$

$$\text{iff}$$

$$< \mathcal{M}',s> \models \text{Arg for all } \mathcal{M}' \text{ such that}$$

$$< \mathcal{M}',s'> \models \mathcal{M}(s')(\text{Defs}) \text{ and}$$

$$\mathcal{M}'(s')(h) = \mathcal{M}(s')(h)$$

for all states s', primitive functions h. As before, the state component in expressions like $\mathcal{M}(s')(h)$ may be eliminated if we rule out external variables.

Notice that $\mathcal{M}'$ above may associate with a defined symbol f any total function consistent with the values computed by the body of the definition of f. That is,

$\mathcal{M}'(s)(f,\text{Defs})(\overline{u})$ = a if the body of the definition of f, running on $\overline{u}$, returns a. If the body fails to halt on $\overline{u}$, $\mathcal{M}'(s)(f,\text{Defs})(\overline{u})$ might be anything. Assertive semantics requires no change to the logical rules. For instance, $f(\overline{u}) = f(\overline{u})$ is valid whether or not the computation of $f(\overline{u})$ halts. If the computation of $f(\overline{u})$ fails to halt, however, only those assertions which hold for all objects of appropriate type will hold for $f(\overline{u})$. And a command which refers to $f(\overline{u})$, such as $x:=f(\overline{u})$, is still invalid. The assertive approach to function definitions is used by the implementation of PL/CV described in the Appendix. For more discussion of the assertive approach, see [Kleene 52], [O'Donnell 77], [Cartwright 76].

6.4 PROOF RULES

The proof rules for reasoning about function definitions are essentially analogous to the procedure rules. In order to draw conclusions about recursively defined functions, all assumptions about recursive invocations must be discharged. A set of procedure and function definitions is said to be *completed* when all such assumptions are discharged.

Definition: Let $\mathcal{D}$ be a set of procedure and function definitions. For each function f defined in $\mathcal{D}$ let $\overline{v}_f$, $\overline{x}_f$, $\overline{y}_f$, and $\overline{z}_f$ be the readonly parameters, external variables, local variables, logical variables except one. Let n be a distinguished logical variable (the one missing from $\overline{z}_f$) used to prove termination. As for procedures, A_f and B_f are respectively the input assumptions about f and the conclusion about f. The assertion B_f is a statement about f. For convenience we can let r be a special variable standing for the result of f. For a procedure p in this set of definitions, let $\overline{v}_p$, $\overline{w}_p$, $\overline{x}_p$, $\overline{y}_p$, $\overline{z}_p$ be as before in the definition of completed procedures (Chapter V, 5.6). Let A_p, B_p be as before except that A_p need not contain all the assumptions at the beginning of the body of p. $\mathcal{D}$ is *completed* iff

1. Every assumption following every recursive *call* in procedure q of the form *assume call* $p(\overline{t},\overline{u})$ *for* q is of the form

    assume $B_p(\overline{t}/\overline{v}_p,\ \overline{u}/\overline{w}_p,\ \overline{s}/\overline{z}_p)$ *for* q

    where $\overline{s}$ and $\overline{t}$ contain terms, $\overline{u}$ contains distinct variables not appearing in $\overline{s},\overline{t},\overline{x}_p$.

2. For each such assumption, the corresponding assertion

    $A_p(\overline{t}/\overline{v}_p,\ \overline{u}/\overline{w}_p,\ \overline{s}/\overline{z}_p,\ n-1/n)$

    appears immediately before the *call*.

3. In every procedure, the assertion

    $$n>0$$

    appears immediately before each recursive *call*.

4. The assertion B_p appears immediately before each *return* in procedure p.

5. $\bar{y}_p$ are not free in A_p and $\bar{y}_p$, n are not free in B_p.

6. Every assumption at the beginning of p (or f) is of the form A_p (or A_f) or the form

$$\overline{\forall v}, \; \overline{z}(A_{f'}, (n-1/n) \; => \; B_{f'}, (f'(\bar{v})/r)) \text{ for } f' \varepsilon \; \mathcal{D}.$$

7. The assertion n>0 appears immediately before each assumed command containing a recursive reference to a defined function (as in *return(exp) assume for* f).

8. The assertion $B_f(t/r)$ appears immediately before each *return*(t) in f.

9. $\bar{y}_f$, r are not free in A_f and $\bar{y}_f$, n are not free in B_f.

As with procedure definitions ,only a completed set of procedure and function definitions provides an inductive proof of the correct termination of each procedure and function. Clause (6) allows the inductive assumptions about functions, clause (7) provides the basis step. The extra logical variables $\bar{z}_f$ are not needed in function

proofs, but they might prove convenient. Soundness is argued as in Chapter V.

The rule for reasoning about functions within a main program is simply

recursive function call rule

```
f:   function(v) returns(atype);
     v btype readonly;
     x ctype external;
     arbitrary dtype z, integer n;
     assume A;
     conclude B;
     etype y;
     body
     end f          m>0, A(ū/v, w̄/z, m/n)
```

$$\overline{\qquad\qquad\qquad\qquad\qquad\qquad\qquad\qquad}$$

$$B(f(\bar{u})/r, \; \bar{w}/\bar{z}) \; by \; function, \; f(\bar{u})$$

where $\bar{y}$, r are not free in B and $\bar{y}$, n are not free in B. The set of procedures and functions containing f must be completed.

We also need a rule allowing conclusions after *return*(exp).

function return rule

$$return(\text{exp})$$
$$\overline{\hspace{2cm}}$$
$$P$$

where P is any assertion.

In exercise (6-37) we show how to treat the case of partial correctness of recursive functions by adding syntax for assuming termination.

Modifications to rules in presence of functions

The presence of defined functions affects every rule which introduces a new, possibly ill-defined, expression. For example, the assignment x:=f(y) is only valid when y is in the domain of f, so the assignment introduction rule must be modified to

$$m_1 > 0 \ \& \ A_{f_1}(\overline{t}_1/\overline{v}_{f_1}, m_1/n), \ldots, m_k > 0 \ \& \ A_{f_k}(\overline{t}_k/\overline{v}_{f_k}, m_k/n)$$
$$\overline{\hspace{9cm}}$$
$$x := \text{exp}$$

where $f_1(\overline{t}_1), \ldots, f_k(\overline{t}_k)$ are all the subexpressions of exp with f_i a defined function.

We can simplfy writing these hypotheses if we agree to say that an expression is well-defined whenever $m > 0 \ \& \ A_f(\overline{t}/\overline{v}_f, m/n)$ for each defined function application $f(\overline{t})$ appearing in the expression. The rule then can be written

assignment introduction

$$\text{exp is well-defined}$$
$$\overline{\hspace{3cm}}$$
$$x := \text{exp}.$$

Similarly, the ∀E, ∀I, Equality and Arithmetic rules, all of which may introduce new terms not appearing in the hypotheses, and the conditional and while introduction rules, which may use new terms in the conditions, must be changed to include the hypotheses that all new terms (not in the other hypotheses) are well-defined. These added hypotheses are exactly those which are often forgotten, as in the well known erroneous proofs that 1=2 using division by 0 (see exercise (3-9)).

The change to the while loop introduction rule is slightly more complicated than assignment and conditional, since the termination conditions for the boolean expression of a while loop must hold when the expression is evaluated after each execution of the body of the loop. The modified while introduction rule is:

while loop introduction
∃*integer* i . (i≥0 & T), bexp is well-defined

while bexp *do*
assume bexp is well-defined
arbitrary integer i *where* T
    ¬T(0/i);
    argument
    T(i-1/i), bexp is well-defined
od

The PL/CV manual in the Appendix presents all rules with the necessary extra conditions in well-defined expressions.

Relationship to other function rules

The function rule given here looks disturbingly like the unsound function rule proposed in [Clint and Hoare 72] and shown unsound for partial functions in [Ashcroft, Clint and Hoare 75] (see exercise (6-19)). With the partial correctness interpretation of asserted programs, such a rule allows contradictory proofs, and modifications necessary to achieve even formal consistency (no provable contradictions) produce rather complex rules as in [Musser 77]. A strong advantage of the total correctness approach to functions is that the hypothesis to the simple intuitive function rule includes the successful termination of the function body, so the rule is sound even for partial functions.

6.5 EXAMPLES

Suppose we have a fast function to divide a number by 10. Call it tenth(x). It satisfies the conditions

tenth_lemma: ∀ *integer* x,q,r *where* x≥0 & q≥0 & r≥0.
      L1: tenth(10*x) = x,
      L2: x = 10*q+r & 0≤r<10 => tenth(x) = q,
      L3: x>0 => tenth(x)<x.

We will prove in addition that

$$n>0 \Rightarrow tenth(exp(10,n)) = exp(10,n-1)$$

as part of a lemma about the defined function exp.

exp: *function* (b,e) *returns* (*integer*);
    integer b,e *readonly*;
    arbitrary integer n; /* depth of recursion */
    assume e≥0 & e<n & b>1;
    assume induction hyp: ∀ *integer* x . (x≥0 & n-1>x =>
        exp(b,x)>0);

    conclude
      P1: e>0 => b*exp(b,e-1) = exp(b,e),
      P2: exp(b,e)>0,
      P3: e=0 => exp(b,e) =1,
      P4: b=10 & e>0 => tenth(exp(b,e)) = exp(b,e-1);

    if e=0 *then*
        ¬e>0 *by arith*, e=0;
        e>0 => b*exp(b,e-1) = 1;
        b=10 & e>0 => tenth(1) = exp(b,e-1);
        e=0 => 1=1;
        1>0;
        return(1);

```
        else
        e>0 by arith, e≠0, e≥0;
        /* set up for recursive call */
        e-1≥0 by arith, e>0;
        e-1<n-1 by arith, e<n;
        /* establish properties P1-P4 for call */
        /* establish P1 */
        e>0 => b*exp(b,e-1) = b*exp(b,e-1);
        /* establish P2 */
        exp(b,e-1)>0 by VE, induction_hyp;
        b*exp(b,e-1)>0 by arith, b>0,*,exp(b,e-1)>0;
        /* establish P3 */
        e=0 => b*exp(b,e-1)=1;
        /* establish P4 */
        proof assume b=10 & e>0;
            tenth(b*exp(b,e-1)) = exp(b,e-1) by VE,
                                            tenth_lemma
        qed;
        b=10 & e>0 => tenth(b*exp(b,e-1)) = exp(b,e-1);
        return(b*exp(b,e-1))
    fi
end exp
```

We now use the function exp in an efficient version of the well-known Euclidean division algorithm. This algorithm corresponds rather closely to the method of "long division by hand" taught in school.

It is a very worthwhile exercise to examine the un-asserted program given below and try to convince yourself that it is correct - by whatever means.

```
assume a≥0 & b>0;
r := a; q := 0; w := b; m := 0;
while w≤r do w := 10*w; m := m+1 od;
while w≠b do
        q := q*10;
        w := tenth(w);
        m := m-1;
        if w≤r
        then for i=2 to 10 do
                if r<i*w
```

```
            then r := r-(i-1)*w;
                 q := q+(i-1);
                 goto exit fi
          od;
          exit: ;
      fi
  od;
  a = b*q+r & 0≤r<b
```

The crucial assertions are

```
  while w≤r do w := 10*w; m := m-1 od;
  w>r & w = exp(10,m)*b & m≥0;
```

and that

```
  a = w*q+r & 0≤r<w & w≥b &
  w = exp(10,m)*b & m≥0
```

is the invariant of the *while* w≠b loop. Most of the reasoning is involved with showing that

```
  q := q*10; w := tenth(w); m := m-1
```

preserve this invariant.
     Let us now examine the details of this argument.

```
div:  function (a,b) returns(integer);
      integer a,b readonly;
      assume a≥0 & b>0;
      conclude ∃ integer r . (a = div(a,b)*b+r & 0≤r<b);
      integer q,r,w,m;
      r:=a; q:=0; w:=b; m:=0;
      m=0 => exp(10,m) = 1 by function, exp(10,m);
      exp(10,m) = 1;
      w = exp(10,m)*b by arith, exp(10,m) = 1,w=b;
      r-w<r by arith, b>0, w=b;
      r≥0 & r-w<r;
      ∃ integer k . (k≥0 & r-w<k) by ∃I;
      while w≤r do
          assume w = exp(10,m)*b & m≥0;
          arbitrary integer k where r-w<k;
          10*w>w by arith, w≥1;
          r-10*w<k-1 by arith, 10*w>w, r-w<k;
          10*exp(10,m) = exp(10,m+1) by function,
                         exp(10,m+1);
          10*w = exp(10,m+1)*b;
```

182

```
        w:=10*w;
        m+1≥0 by arith, m≥0;
        m:=m+1;
        w = exp(10,m)*b & m≥0;
        r-w<k-1
    od
    w>r by arith, ¬(w≤r);
    w>r & w = exp(10,m)*b, m≥0;
    m≥0 & 10>0 => exp(10,m)>0 by function, exp(10,m);
    exp(10,m)>0;
    w≥b by arith, exp(10,m)≥1, w = exp(10,m)*b;
    (w-b)+1≥0 by arith, w≥b;
    w-b < (w-b)+1 by arith;
    ∃ integer k . (k≥0 & w-b<k) by ∃I;
    a = w*q+r by arith, q=0, r=a;
    while w≠b do
        assume a = w*q+r & 0≤r<w & w≥b & w = exp(10,m)*b
                        & m≥0;
        arbitrary integer k where w-b<k;
        ¬(w-b<0) by arith, w≥b;
        w≠b => m>0; m>0;
        10*exp(10,m-1) = exp(10,m) by function, exp(10,m);
        10=10 & m>0 => tenth(exp(10,m)*b) = exp(10,m-1)*b
        by function, exp(10,m);

        w = 10*tenth(w);
        w>0 => tenth(w)<w by ∀E, tenth_lemma;
        tenth(w)<w;
        a = tenth(w)*10*q+r by arith, w = 10*tenth(w);
        tenth(w)-b k-1 by arith, tenth(w)<w, w-b<k;
        q:=q*10;
        w:=tenth(w);
        m:=m-1;
        a = w*q+r & 0≤r<10*w & w≥b;
        w = exp(10,m)*b & m≥0;
        w-b<k-1
    if w≤r
    then w≤r<10*w;
/* relying on order of evaluation, determine the
   interval w*n≤r<w*(n+1)   */
```

```
for i=2 to 10 do
    assume (i-1)*w≤r<10*w;
    if r<i*w then (i-1)*w≤r<i*w;
                   a = w*(q+i-1)+r-(i-1)*w by arith;
                   r := r-(i-1)*w;
                   q := q+(i-1);
                   a = w*q+r & 0≤r<w;
                   goto exit;
                   i*w≤r<10*w fi;
        i*w≤r<10*w
od;
  (10+1)*w≤r<10*w;
   false by arith, (10+1)*w≤r<10*w;
exit:  a = w*q+r & 0≤r<w;

else ¬(w≤r);
       r<w by arith, ¬(w≤r);
       0≤r<w by arith, r≥0;
       a = w*q+r & 0≤r<w
fi
od;

w=b & a = w*q+r & 0≤r<w;
a = b*q+r & 0≤r<w;
∃ integer r . (a = b*q+r & 0≤r<w) by ∃I;
return(q)
end div
```

A well-known example of a recursive function whose termination proof is interesting is John McCarthy's ninety-one function:

f91(x) = *if* x>100 *then* x-10 *else* f91(f91(x+11)) *fi*

This function is total and is equivalent to the function g defined by

g(x) = *if* x>100 *then* x-10 *else* 91 *fi*

How can we show that f91 terminates? We cannot simply use induction on x since f91 is evaluated on larger elements. But we can use induction on the term $n = 101 \doteq x$ (where $a \doteq b = $ if $a \geq b$ then a-b else 0).

Suppose $n = 101 \doteq x$ is 0, then x>100 and we know f91(x) terminates. That is, f91(x) terminates for all $n \geq 101 \doteq x$. Suppose for induction that f91(x) terminates when $n \geq 101 \doteq x$ then we show it terminates for $(n+1) \geq 101 \doteq x$.

Suppose $(n+1) \geq 101 \doteq x$, then clearly $n \geq 101 \doteq (x+11)$, so f91(x) must halt. But what can we say about f91(f91(x+11))? We must know something about the value f91(x+11). Thus to solve the termination problem, we need some correctness information.

We get what we need by analyzing cases. If $90 \leq x \leq 100$, then x+11>100 so f91(x+11) = x+11-10 = x+1. Thus in this range we know f91(f91(x+11)) = f91(x+1). But we know $101 \doteq (x+1) \leq n$, so the induction hypothesis holds.

If x<90, then we need even more information, namely that f91(x) = g(x). We can establish this also by induction on n (see proof below in the program). So we know f91(x+11) = g(x+11), x<90. Notice g(x+11) = 91 = g(x). So f91(f91(x+11)) = f91(91). We can determine that f91(91) = 91.

This entire argument can be easily represented inside the function as follows:

```
g:  function(x) returns(integer);
    integer x;
    assume x≥0;
    conclude (x>100 => g(x)=x-10) & (x≤100 => g(x)=91);
    if x>100 then return (x-10) else return (91) fi
    end g;
```

```
f91:   function(x) returns(integer);
       integer x;
       assume x≥0;
       arbitrary integer n where n>100÷x & n≥0;
       conclude ninety_one_lemma:   f91(x)=g(x);
       assume ind_hyp:  ∀ integer y . (n-1)>100÷y =>
                          f91(y)=g(y);
       if x>100
       then x-10 = g(x); /* by definition of g */
            return(x-10);
       else x≤100;
          x<90 ∨ 90≤x by arith;
          proof assume 90≤x;
          90≤x≤100;
          x+11 > 100 by arith, 90≤x;
          n-1 > 100-(x+11) by arith, n > 100-x;
          f91(x+11) = g(x+11) by ∀E, ind_hyp;
          g(x+11) = x+1; /* by definition of g */
          f91(f91(x+11)) = f91(x+1); /* substitution */
          n-1 > 100-(x+1) by arith, n > 100-x;
          f91(x+1) = g(x+1) by ∀E, ind_hyp;
          x+1 ≤ 101 by arith, x≤100;
          x+1=101 ∨ x+1≤100;
          proof assume x+1 = 101;
            x+1 > 100 by arith, x+1 = 101;
            g(x+1) = 101-10; /* by definition of g */
            101-10 = 91 by arith;
            x = 100 by arith, x+1 = 101;
            g(x) = 91; /* by definition of g */
            g(x) = g(x+1) /* by definition of g */
          qed;
          proof assume x+1 ≤ 100;
            g(x+1) = 91; /* by definition of g */
            x < 100 by arith, x+1≤100;
            g(x) = 91;
            g(x+1) = g(x)
          qed;
          g(x) = g(x+1) by ∀E; /* on x+1=101 ∨ x+1≤101 */
          f91(f91(x+11)) = g(x); /* substitution */
```

```
proof assume x<90;
   x+11 < 101 by arith, x<90;
   x+11 ≤ 100
   n-1 > 100-(x+11) by arith, n > 100-x;
   f91(x+11) = g(x+11) by ∀E, ind_hyp;
   g(x+11) = 91;  /* by definition of g */
   g(x) = 91;
   f91(x+11) = 91;
   f91(f91(x+11)) = f91(91);
   x+1 < 91 by arith, x<90;
   100-x-1 > 100-91 by arith, 100≥100, -, x+1<91;
   n-1 > 100-x-1 by arith, n > 100-x,
   n-1 > 100-91 by arith, n-1 > 100-x-1, 100-x-1 >
         100-91;
   f91(91) = g(91) by ∀E, ind_hyp;
   f91(f91(x+11)) = g(x);
qed;
f91(f91(x+11)) = g(x) by ∀E, x<90 ∨ 90≤x;
return (f91(f91(x+11))) assume for f91
end f91;
```

Mutually recursive functions example

Suppose that we want to count the number of expressions, of a limited size, which may be constructed from the operations LENGTH, +, || (concatenation), SUBSTR and some set of integer and string constants. By "limited size" we mean that the depth (nesting level) of each expression is bounded by some chosen integer. The easiest way to characterize the number of such expressions is to use a pair of functions with mutually recursive definitions:

$$Intexp(I,S,D)$$
         and
$$Strexp(I,S,D)$$

should be the numbers of integer valued and string valued expressions with I integer constants, S string constants, and maximum depth D. Since an expression of depth 0 must be a single symbol,

$$Intexp(I,S,0) = I$$
$$Strexp(I,S,0) = S$$

Now, for D>0, an integer valued expression of depth at most D may be either a single symbol, or LENGTH(E) where

187

E is a string valued expression of depth at most D-1, or $E_1 + E_2$ where E_1 and E_2 are integer valued expressions of depth at most D-1. Thus,

$$\text{Intexp}(I,S,D) = I + \text{Strexp}(I,S,D-1) + \text{Intexp}(I,S,D-1)^2$$

for D>0. Similarly, a string valued expression may be a single symbol, $E_1 || E_2$ or $\text{SUBSTR}(E_3, E_4, E_5)$ where E_1, E_2, E_3 are string valued, E_4 and E_5 are integer valued. Thus,

$$\text{Strexp}(I,S,D) = S + \text{Strexp}(I,S,D-1)^2 \\ + \text{Strexp}(I,S,D-1) * \text{Intexp}(I,S,D-1)^2$$

These equations translate directly into the following function definitions.

Intexp: function(I,S,D) *returns(integer)*;
integer I,S,D *readonly*;
if D=0 *then*
    return (I)
else
    return $(I + \text{Strexp}(I,S,D-1) + \text{Intexp}(I,S,D-1)^2)$
fi; *end* Intexp

Strexp: function(I,S,D) *returns* (integer);
integer I,S,D *readonly*;
if D=0 *then*
    return (S);
else
    return $(S + \text{Strexp}(I,S,D-1)^2 + \text{Strexp}(I,S,D-1) *$
                    $\text{Intexp}(I,S,D-1)^2)$

fi; *end* Strexp

To prove that

$$\text{Intexp}(I,S,D) \leq (I+S+4)^{(3^{(D+1)}-1)/2}$$

and

$$\text{Strexp}(I,S,D) \leq (I+S+4)^{(3^{(D+1)}-1)/2}$$

we would need knowledge about exponentiation, which hasn't yet been developed for this logic. So what follows should be taken as a proof sketch which can be filled in once good rules for exponentiation are available. The reader

may verify that the following function arguments are
complete (i.e., all assumptions are discharged).

Intexp: function(I,S,D) *returns* (*integer*);
integer I,S,D *readonly*;
assume I≥1 & S≥1 & D≥0;

conclude Intexp(I,S,D) ≤ (I+S+4)$^{(3^{(D+1)}-1)/2}$;
arbitrary integer R *where* D≤R;
assume ∀ *integer* I,S,D *where* I≥1 & S≥1 & D≥0.

    D≤R-1 => Intexp(I,S,D) ≤ (I+S+4)$^{(3^{(D+1)}-1)/2}$;
assume ∀ *integer* I,S,D *where* I≥1 & S≥1 & D≥0.

    D≤R-1 => Strexp(I,S,D) ≤ (I+S+4)$^{(3^{(D+1)}-1)/2}$;
if D=0 *then*
  $(3^{(D+1)}-1)/2$ ≥ 1;
  I ≤ I+S+4;
  I ≤ (I+S+4)$^{(3^{(D+1)}-1)/2}$;
return (I);
else
  D-1 ≥ 0;
  D-1 ≤ R-1;
  R>0;

  Intexp(I,S,D-1) ≤ (I+S+4)$^{(3^{D}-1)/2}$;

  Strexp(I,S,D-1) ≤ (I+S+4)$^{(3^{D}-1)/2}$;

  I+Strexp(I,S,D-1)+Intexp(I,S,D-1)^2 ≤

    I+(I+S+4)$^{(3^{D}-1)/2}$+((I+S+4)$^{(3^{D}-1)/2}$)^2;

  (I+S+4)$^{(3^{D}-1)/2}$ ≥ 1;

  ((I+S+4)$^{(3^{D}-1)/2}$)^2 ≥ I+(I+S+4)$^{(3^{D}-1)/2}$;
  I+Strexp(I,S,D-1)+Intexp(I,S,D-1)^2 ≤

    ((E+S+4)$^{(3^{D}-1)/2}$)^2*(I+S+4)$^{(3^{D}-1)/2}$;

  I+Strexp(I,S,D-1)+Intexp(I,S,D-1)^2 ≤

    ((I+S+4)$^{(3^{D}-1)/2}$)^3;

$I+Strexp(I,S,D-1)+Intexp(I,S,D-1)^2 \le$

$(I+S+4)^{(3^{D+1}-3)/2}$;

$I+Strexp(I,S,D-1)+Intexp(I,S,D-1)^2 \le$

$(I+S+4)^{(3^{D+1}-1)/2}$;

return $(I+Strexp(I,S,D-1)+Intexp(I,S,D-1)^2)$

assume for Intexp;

fi

end Intexp

Strexp: *function*(I,S,D) *return s(integer)*;
integer I,S,D *readonly*;
assume $I \ge 1$ & $S \ge 1$ & $D \ge 0$;

conclude $Strexp(I,S,D) \le (I+S+4)^{(3^{(D+D)}-1)/2}$;
arbitrary integer R *where* $D \le R$;
assume $\forall$ *integer* I,S,D *where* $I \ge 1$ & $S \ge 1$ & $D \ge 0$.

$\quad D \le R-1 \Rightarrow Intexp(I,S,D) \le (I+S+4)^{(3^{(D+1)}-1)/2}$;
assume $\forall$ *integer* I,S,D *where* $I \ge 1$ & $S \ge 1$ & $D \ge 0$.

$\quad D \le R-1 \Rightarrow Strexp(I,S,D) \le (I+S+4)^{(3^{(D+1)}-1)/2}$;
if $D=0$ *then*

$(3^{(D+1)}-1)/2 \ge 1$;
$S \le I+S+4$;

$S \le (I+S+4)^{(3^{(D+1)}-1)/2}$;
return (S);
else

$D-1 \ge 0$;
$D-1 \le R-1$;
$R>0$;

$Intexp(I,S,D-1) \le (I+S+4)^{(3^D-1)/2}$;

$Strexp(I,S,D-1) \le (I+S+4)^{(3^D-1)/2}$;

$S+Strexp(I,S,D-1)^2+Strexp(I,S,D-1)*Intexp(I,S,D-1)^2 \le$

$S+((I+S+4)^{(3^D-1)/2})^2+(I+S+4)^{(3^D-1)/2}*((I+S+4)^{(3^D-1)/2})^2$;

190

$$S+\text{Strexp}(I,S,D-1)^2+\text{Strexp}(I,S,D-1)*\text{Intexp}(I,S,D-1)^2 \leq$$
$$S+((I+S+4)^{(3^D-1)/2})^2 +((I+S+4)^{(3^D-1)/2})^3 ;$$
$$(I+S+4) \geq 1;$$

$$((I+S+4)^{(3^D-1)/2})^3 \geq S+((I+S+4)^{(3^D-1)/2})^2 ;$$

$$S+\text{Strexp}(I,S,D-1)^2+\text{Strexp}(I,S,D-1)*\text{Intexp}(I,S,D-1)^2 \leq$$
$$((I+S+4)^{(3^D-1)/2})^3 *(I+S+4);$$

$$S+\text{Strexp}(I,S,D-1)^2+\text{Strexp}(I,S,D-1)*\text{Intexp}(I,S,D-1)^2 \leq$$
$$(I+S+4)^{(3^{(D+1)}-3)/2}*(I+S+4);$$

$$S+\text{Strexp}(I,S,D-1)^2+\text{Strexp}(I,S,D-1)*\text{Intexp}(I,S,D-1)^2 \leq$$
$$(I+S+4)^{(3^{(D+1)}-1)/2-1}*(I+S+4);$$

$$S+\text{Strexp}(I,S,D-1)^2+\text{Strexp}(I,S,D-1)*\text{Intexp}(I,S,D-1)^2 \leq$$
$$(I+S+4)^{(3^{(D+1)}-1)/2};$$

return $(S+\text{Strexp}(I,S,D-1)^2+\text{Strexp}(I,S,D-1)*$
$$\text{Intexp}(I,S,D-1)^2)$$

fi   *assume for* Strexp;
end Strexp

6.6 EXERCISES

Section 6.1

(6-1) Write a function which finds the maximum of integers a,b. Write a procedure which finds the maximum of a and b returning the result in c. Compare the execution and implementation of these procedures. If you wanted to return the maximum and switch the values if necessary so that a<b, could you use a function (in PL/I, in Algol 60, in Pascal, in PL/CS, in the language of this monograph)?

(6-2) Notice that functions in some programming languages can be quite bizarre. Consider for instance

```
biz:    function (x,y) returns (integer)
        integer x,y;
        integer z external;
        integer w;   /* a local variable */
        y := x;
        x := z+w;
        z := 0;
        return (w)
        end biz
```

This function returns a random value totally unrelated to its inputs. Moreover it changes a variable, z, not even mentioned in the argument to biz. To top it all off, the arguments to biz are modified, randomly on each call.

Are any of these bizarre features permitted with the functions of this chapter? Are they permitted in FORTRAN? PL/I? Algol 60?

(6-3)   Read a programming textbook and compare the treatment of functions and procedures. What unusual properties of functions are allowed? Is a function described as a special type of procedure?

Section 6.2

(6-4)   In the body of the definition of function f, can the expression in *return* (exp) contain f? Can the conclude statement mention f? Can the first assumption mention f? Can any assumption mention f?

(6-5)   Given the function definition below, convert it to an equivalent procedure definition.

```
f:     function (x) returns (integer);
       integer x;
       assume x≥0;
       if even(x) then return (x/2)
                   else return (f(f(3x+1))) fi
       end f
```

(6-6)   In languages like Algol 60, the function identifier is used in the body of the function to name the value of the function. Thus, in place of *return* (exp) the phrase f := exp appears. Indicate how the BNF syntax changes to provide these Algol style function returns. We will see more serious ramifications of this syntax in (6-16).

Section 6.3

(6-7) What are the *apparent domains* and *actual domains* of the following functions: factorial, logarithm, tangent, exponentiation

(6-8) Consider the sets of states possible at all signif-icant positions of the following function definition when the initial set of states is $\{<s_1(b)=2, s_1(e)=-5, s_1(n)=4>,$
$<s_2(b)=2, s_2(e)=3, s_2(n)=4>\}$

    exp: *function* (b,e) *returns* (*integer*);
          integer b,e *readonly*;
          arbitrary integer n;   /* depth of recursion */
          assume e≥0 & e<n;
          assume ∀ *integer* x,y .
                  x≥0 & n-1>x => y>0 => exp(y,x)>0;
          if e=0 *then return* (1)
                  else return (b*exp(b,e-1)) *fi*
          end exp

(6-9) Consider the sets of states possible at the signif-icant positions of the programs of exercises (6-28) and (6-31) for some appropriate set of initial states.

(6-10) Compare the meaning of the following definitions in the alternative semantics of section 6.4 (called "assertive semantics").

    (a) f: *function* (x);
            integer x;
            assume x≥0;
            conclude **f**(x)≥0;
            return (f(x+1))
         end f

    (b) f: *function* (x);
            integer x;
            assume x≥0;
            conclude f(x)≥0;
            return (f(x))
         end f

(6-11) Write the meaning equations of Chapter IV for the commands with defined functions.

(6-12) One approach to partial functions (see [Scott 70], [Milner 76], [Manna 74]) is to introduce a special element into every domain and use it for the value of functions which would otherwise be undefined. For instance, add to the integers an element $\perp$, called *bottom*. Let

$\mathbf{Z} = \mathbf{Z} \cup \{\perp\}$. Now extend every partial function from

$f: \mathbf{Z}^n \to \mathbf{Z}$ to a total function $\hat{f}: \hat{\mathbf{Z}}^n \to \hat{\mathbf{Z}}$ by agreeing that $\hat{f}(x_1,\ldots,x_n) = \perp$ iff $f(x_1,\ldots,x_n)$ is un-defined. To render $\hat{f}$ total on $\hat{\mathbf{Z}}^n$, require that when any x_i is $\perp$, f has value $\perp$ (such functions are called

strict). Under certain conditions it is interesting to consider nonstrict functions, for instance a constant function $f(x) = c$ for all x might be extended so that $f(\perp) = c$.

(a) Show that the predicate calculus axioms are all valid when $\perp$ is added as a new constant.

(b) Show that the predicate calculus rules with defined recursive functions are valid for extended functions.

(c) Consider the additions to arithmetic axioms necessitated by the addition of $\perp$ as a new con-stant, e.g. what is $0+\perp$, $\perp+\perp$, etc.

(d) Show that the extended functions corresponding to the partial recursive functions over $\mathbb{N}$ are not computable.

(6-13) One approach to treating undefined expressions in assertions is to abandon conventional binary logic and regard such assertions as undefined. Atomic relations such as $x/0=x/0$ are undefined.

The expression A&B is true only if both A and B are, but the expression A∨B is true if either A or B is, regardless of whether the other is defined. This is a "parallel" type *or*. Implication can be regarded as true under the usual conditions plus those given by this table

A	A=>B	B
U	T	T
F	T	U

In all other cases, A=>B is undefined.

    (a)   Does this system satisfy the rules of Chapter II?

    (b)   If A=>B is considered true when A, B are both undefined, does the resulting system satisfy the rules of Chapter II?

(6-14) If we attempt to treat assertions containing undefined terms as undefined, then what do we make of arguments such as the following?

proof assume $0/0 = 1$;
   $0*1 = 0*2$ *by arith*;
   $\dfrac{0*1}{0} = \dfrac{0*2}{0}$ *by arith*;
   $0/0*1 = 0/0*2$ *by arith*;
   $1 = 2$ *by arith*
qed;

$$(0/0 = 1) \Rightarrow (1 = 2)$$

(6-15) Show that if we decide to treat assertions containing undefined expressions as syntactically "ill formed", then it is not decidable whether an assertion is "well-formed." What would be the status of the assertion

$$\forall \text{ integer } x,y \; . \; (x>0 \Rightarrow ((y*y)/x) \geq 0)?$$

Section 6.4

(6-16) Suppose the Algol 60 notation for function returns is used (see exercise (6-6)), how would it simplify the syntax of the definition of a completed set of procedures?

(6-17) Explain why each of the nine conditions on the definition of a completed set of procedures and functions is necessary.

(6-18)   If the programming language did not uniformly
initialize each new variable before use, then what would
be the meaning of the following function?

```
g:   function (x) returns (integer);
     integer x;
     integer y;
     assume x≥0;
     conclude y≥0;
     if y<0 then return (0);
          else return (y) fi
     end g
```

(6-19)   The function rule commonly proposed in *partial
correctness* systems (when translated to our notation) is

```
f:   function (x) returns (atype);
     btype x;
     assume a(x);
     conclude B(x,f(x));
     B(x,exp);        ⎫
     return (exp)     ⎬ before each return (exp)
     end f            ⎭                              A(y)
```

$$\frac{}{B(y,f(y))}$$

Why is this rule incorrect?   (See exercise (6-21) for the
answer.)

(6-20)   State the repeat until rule in a form that takes
into account defined functions.   (See the do until rule in
the appendix for an answer.)

(6-21)   Show that the following is a correct application of the commonly used unsound partial correctness
rule for functions.

```
bad:   function (x) returns (integer);
       integer x;
       assume x≥0;
       conclude false;
       while true do od;
       false;
       end f;
```

In a main program we could use bad as follows.

```
twin primes:  procedure (p);
              integer p readonly
              arbitrary integer x where x=p;
              assume p≥0;
              conclude prime(p) & prime(p+2) & p>x;
              p+1 > p by arith;
              false by function, bad (p+1);
              prime(p) & prime(p+1);
              return
end twin primes;
```

(6-22) The induction assumptions about recursive function f stated at the beginning of procedures and functions which call f, i.e., assumptions of the form

$$\forall \; atype \; \overline{u} \; . \; (A_f(\overline{u}, \; n_p-1) \; => \; B_f(f(\overline{u})))$$

are redundant. They can be deduced from the assertion made about f in its body, i.e. A_f, B_f are stated in the body of f. The PL/CV rules take advantage of this fact and do not force the user to state these hypotheses explicitly. What advantage is there to stating them? (Compare to the corresponding situation for procedures, exercise (5-27).)

(6-23) In logic and recursive function theory a recursive definition is called *primitive recursive* iff it has the form

$$f(0,\overline{x}) = g(\overline{x})$$
$$f(n+1,\overline{x}) = h(n,\overline{x},f(n,\overline{x})).$$

A direct analogue of this in our logic would be a recursion of the form

```
f:  function (x̄,n) returns (integer);
    ( f(x̄,n-1) is used exactly once in the body
    ( when n=0 there is no recursive call.
    end f
```

Show why all such recursions terminate (given that all commands in the body are well-defined).

(6-24)* Recursive definitions in this logic can be viewed as generalizations of the syntactic form of primitive recursion. The termination parameter (the logical variable of the arbitrary statement used to show termination) can be thought of as the variable n (the *induction variable*) of the primitive recursion. Can you rewrite the following function as a primitive recursion?

```
f:  function (x) returns (integer);
    integer x;
    arbitrary integer i where x≤i;
    if x=0 then return g(x+1);
          else
                y := f(x-1);
                z := f(x-3)²;
                return h(x,y,z)
    fi
    end f
```

(6-25) The following mutually recursive functions satisfy the criteria of a completed set of function definitions. Prove by induction that the functions are defined for all nonnegative integers, assuming that g_i, h_i are total.

$f_1(n_1, x_1) = $ if $n_1 = 0$ then $g_1(x_1)$
$$\text{else } h_1(f_1(n_1-1, g_1(x_1)), f_2(n_1-1, g_1(x_1)), f_3(n_1-1, g_1(x_1)))$$

$f_2(n_2, x_2) = $ if $n_2 = 0$ then $g_2(x_2)$
$$\text{else } h_2(f_1(n_2-1, g_2(x_2)), f_2(n_2-1, g_2(x_2)), f_3(n_2-1, g_2(x_2)))$$

$f_3(n_3, x_3) = $ if $n_3 = 0$ then $g_3(x_3)$
$$\text{else } h_3(f_1(n_3-1, g_2(x_3)), f_2(n_3-1, g_3(x_3)), f_3(n_3-1, g_3(x_3)))$$

Notice that the definitions are the same if n_1, n_2, n_3 are replaced by a single variable n. See exercise (6-26).

(6-26) Suppose the definition of a completed set of procedures is modified to allow separate n_f as the termination parameter in defined function f. This parameter
must be decreased on each recursive call. Show that any
termination proof for the modified procedures is also a
termination proof for the system with the same parameter
n in each procedure. So the added generality is specious.

(6-27) Convert the div procedure of ChapterV
to a function returning the value r, the remainder. Call
it rem(a,b). Prove that for f defined below,
f(a,b) = rem(a,b).

>   f: *function* (a,b) *returns* (*integer*);
>   *integer* a,b;
>   *assume* a≥0 & b>0;
>   *conclude* f(a,b) = rem(a,b);
>   *if* a<b *then return* (a);
>   *else return* (f(a-b,b))
>   *fi*
>   *end* f

(6-28) Complete the following argument

>   power: *function* (x,y) *returns* (*integer*);
>   *integer* x,y;
>   *assume* x≥0 & y≥0;
>   *conclude* f(x,0) = x^3;
>   *if* x=0 *then return* (y);
>   *else return* (f(x-1,(y+3*(x-1)*x+1))
>   *fi*
>   *end* power

(6-29)* Complete the argument that f given below is defined for all integers (by finding an appropriate T).

>   f: *function* (x) *returns* (*integer*);
>   *arbitrary integer* n;
>   *assume* x≥0 & T(n,x);
>   *conclude true* ;
>   *if* even(x) *then return* (x/2);
>   *else* n>0 & T(n-1,f(f(3x+1)))
>   *return* (f(f(3x+1)))
>   *fi*
>   *end* f

(6-30)   Write a function argument to take any word and replace repeated occurrences of any character (except the first) by *.

(6-31)   Complete the following argument.

f: *function* (x) *returns* (*integer*);
     integer x;
     assume x≥0;
     conclude f(x) = $(x^2+x)/2$;
     if x=0 *then return* (0)
               else return (x+f(x-1))
     fi
     end f

(6-32)   Given the equations

$$root(0) = 0$$
$$root(n+1) = \text{if } n+1 \neq (root(n)+1)^2 \text{ then } root(n)$$
$$\text{else } root(n)+1,$$

define an equivalent recursive function in the programming language and prove that it computes $[\sqrt{n}]$ where [x] is the greatest integer less than or equal to x.

(6-33)   *Pairing functions* map pairs of integers to single integers in such a way that the pairs can be recovered. (Such functions are used in set theory to show that the cardinality of the set of pairs of integers is the same as the cardinality of the set of integers.)
     Here is a set of pairing functions.

$$pair(x,y) = ((x+y)^2+3x+y)/2$$
first(z) = the least x such that
          ∃ *integer* ý *where* y≤z . pair(x,y) = z

second(z) = the least y such that
          ∃ *integer* x *where* x≤z . pair(x,y) = z

Write these functions in our programming language and prove that for x,y,z nonnegative

(a)   pair(first(z), second(z)) = z

(b)   first(pair(x,y)) = x

(c)   second(pair(x,y)) = y.

A geometric interpretation of "pair" is given by this diagram

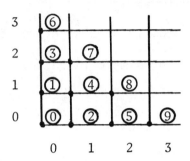

Numbers are paired by counting down the Cartesian constant sum diagonals.

(6-34) Another set of pairing functions is defined by the equation $pair(x,y) = (2^x*(2*y+1))-1$. Find expressions for "first", "second", the inverse functions. Prove the equations of (6-33) relating pair, first, second.

(6-35) Another interesting set of pairing functions arises from the sequences

<0,0> <0,1><1,0><1,1> <0,2><2,0><1,2><2,1><2,2>

<0,3><3,0><1,3><3,1><2,3><3,2><3,3> ... For the n-th group of numbers, we pair n with numbers up to n, first <0,n><n,0>, then <1,n><n,1> ... .
     We define the inverse pairing functions, *first*, *second* by mutual recursion as follows.

        first(0) = 0
        second(0) = 0

        first(n+1) = if first(n) < second(n) then second(n)
                     if first(n) > second(n) then second(n)+1
                     if first(n) = second(n) then 0

        second(n+1) = if first(n) ≠ second(n) then first(n)
                      if first(n) = second(n) then first(n)+1

We define the pairing function itself by:

        pair(a,b) = if a>b then a^2+2b+1
                    if a≤b then b^2+2a.

201

Prove that these three functions satisfy the properties of pairing functions.

(6-36) Consider two mutually recursive procedures cmd() and exp() to recognize the well-formed commands and expressions in the following simple language:

command → $f_1, f_2, \ldots$

(command ; command) | (command ∨ command)
(bexp ? command)

bexp → $b_1, b_2, \ldots$

(bexp & bexp) | (bexp ∨ bexp)
(b_2 ← command)

Suppose we have defined functions (over Σ^*, the string language) such that:

catom (x) iff x is an f_i

batom (x) iff x is a b_i

op(z) returns the operator in any of the compounds (x;y), (xvy), (x&y), (x?y) where x,y are strings. (It can simply match parentheses to do this.)

first(z) returns the component x in any of the binary forms listed above under op(z)

last(z) returns the component y in any of the binary forms listed above.

The procedures are defined as follows:

cmd: *function* (x) *returns* (*boolean*);
      string x;
      select
          when cantom (x) *return* (*true*);
          when op(x)=';'∨ op(x)='v'
              if cmd(first(x)) & cmd(last(x))
              then return (*true*) *else return* (*false*) *fi*
          when op(x)='?'
              if exp(first(x)) & cmd(last(x))
              then return (*true*) *else return* (*false*) *fi*
          otherwise return (*false*)
      od
      end cmd

```
exp:    function (x) returns (boolean);
        string x;
        select
           when batom(x) return (true)
           when op(x)='&' v op(x)='v'
                 if exp(first(x)) & exp(last(x))
                 then return (true) else return (false) fi
           when op(x)='←'
                 if batom(first(x)) & cmd(last(x))
                 then return (true) else  return (false) fi
           otherwise return (false)
        od
```

Show that this set of procedures is completed.

(6-37)   Notice that we can express partial correctness if we assume the existence of a termination predicate with the right properties.   The following argument shows that if f terminates, its value is 0.   Explain this argument.

```
f:   function (x) returns (integer);
     integer x;
     arbitrary integer n;
     assume x≥1 & T(n,x);
     conclude f(x) =0;
     assume V integer x'. (x'≥1 & T(n-1,x')) => f(x')=0;
     if x=1 then return (0)
               else
               if even(x)
               then assume T(n-1,x/2);
               f(x/2) = 0
               return (f(x/2))
               else
               assume T(n-1,f(3x+1));
               return (f(3x+1))
               fi
     fi
   end f
```

7

ARRAYS AND INPUT/OUTPUT

7.1 <u>INTRODUCTION</u>

Interesting computational problems frequently involve
processing a large collection of data with some structure.
The most common way to present such data in elementary
computing courses is an *array*. In its simplest form an
array is a finite sequence of values, called a *one
dimensional array*. [†]

Arrays are, of course, common in mathematics as well
where they usually appear as sequences or finite functions
or matrices. It is quite remarkable that arrays serve so
well to represent a myriad of abstract structures from
mathematics and nonnumerical data processing. In this
monograph we consider only an especially simple type of
array whose domain of indices is the set of n-tuples of
integers and whose range is one of the basic sets of
values (integers, strings or booleans), but even this
notion is adequate and natural for the data collections
occurring in elementary programming.

The concept of an array is so basic that most textbooks treat it earlier than procedures and functions.
So in this monograph, sections (7.1), (7.2), (7.3) can be
read immediately after any of Chapters IV, V or VI. However, such a primitive and widely used concept involves
a surprising number of subtle points and can be presented
from several different viewpoints. Our approach to
these points affects the very basis of the logic, the

[†] A *multi-dimensional array* can be thought of as a mapping
from some finite subset of n-tuples of indices into values,
i.e. $I^n \to$ Values, where I is a discrete ordered set of
indices and n is the dimension.

predicate calculus. So in some ways arrays are an advanced topic more clearly understood after procedures and functions. The reader can proceed as his interest dictates. Before we begin the technical presentation, we will discuss some of these viewpoints and subtleties.

An array has the properties of a finite function from $\mathbf{Z}^n \rightarrow$ Values; it can be evaluated at an index in its domain to produce a value in its range. But an array behaves differently than other functions in the logic. First, we want quantification over arrays but not over arbitrary functions. Second, the domain of an array is a decidable set specified in a very restricted manner. Third, arrays can be modified in ways not permitted for functions. In fact, an array behaves in these three ways somewhat like a new type of data object.

From one point of view then, the class of arrays is an addition to the purely logical part of the language. It is a special class of finite function and quantification over it leads us into the realm of weak second order logic. From the other point of view, an array is a new data type, a data type with structure. It is not an extension of the underlying logic only an application of it, and leads to an applied first order theory.

Our approach is to interpret arrays as finite functions, but to treat them syntactically differently from functions. No matter how we treat arrays, they lead to the following three essential complications of the logic:

(1) Array evaluations, such as a(i), might be undefined. So array evaluations appearing in expressions must be treated like function applications.

(2) Arrays need to appear as logical variables in statements such as *arbitrary array* a; and they appear in quantifiers, $\forall$ *integer array* a . P(a). A logic with such quantifiers is no longer first order if arrays are thought of as functions.

(3) The appearance of arrays complicates certain syntactic tests such as:
    (a) testing whether an assignment is simple, e.g.
        a(i) := a(j) is simple only if $i \neq j$.

> (b) testing whether parameters are being legally
> passed to a procedure, e.g. p(a(i),a(j)) will be
> illegal if i=j and one of the parameters is readwri
> This problem arises in PL/CV but not in the
> language of the monograph where array elements
> cannot be passed as parameters (the entire
> array must be passed as a parameter).

In order to systematically consider the additional
complexity caused by arrays, and to permit the reader to
introduce them at his discretion, we first present arrays
in the predicate calculus (and in number and string theory)
in (7.2). The important points in (7.2) are the new type
symbols, quantification over arrays and the semantics of
arrays. Next we introduce arrays in simple programs.
Here, in (7.3), the important point is array assignment
and the array modifier, *alt*(a,i,exp) used to describe
assignment. In (7.4) we consider arrays with procedures.
Finally in (7.5) we present a simple and tentative treatment of input output based on the idea that the input and
output files can be thought of as arrays of values.

7.2 ARRAYS IN THE PREDICATE CALCULUS
AND BASE THEORIES

syntax - expressions, assertions, arguments

Arrays first enter the syntax in two distinct ways.
They enter the class of ordinary expressions exactly as
functions do. So the new syntax for expressions includes:

exp → variable
      constant
      exp infix-operator exp
      function-symbol ({exp §,}$^+$)
      array-symbol ({exp §,}$^+$)
      (exp)

Second, an entirely new class of expressions is created
in which the variables and constants themselves are array
symbols and the operators and functions take arrays as well
as array values. The BNF productions are entirely like
the old. However, the type restrictions are different.

So to describe this class, and to complete the description of the ordinary expressions, we need to discuss the new *type symbols* and new *type restrictions* which we will do shortly.

The change in expressions affects every category of the grammar - boolean expression, assertion, proof-group, and argument. But it does not account for all the changes necessary to add arrays. They also enter the syntax in quantifiers and qualifiers. This entry can be accomplished with exactly two more changes, namely: the notion of a variable list must expand to allow type symbols for arrays, and a new primitive function is added specifying the upper and lower bounds of the array (as given by the type symbol). The new variable list syntax is

variable-list → {primitive-type idlist}*
primitive type → simple type | array type.

So to complete the syntactic changes needed when arrays are added, we need only examine the new type symbols and discuss the new primitive functions.

We need a new class of primitive type symbols to denote arrays. These have the form:

$$\text{simple type } array \ (\ \ell_1 : u_1, \ldots, \ell_n : u_n)$$

$$\text{simple type n } array^{\dagger}$$

where ℓ_i, u_i are integers.

For example, *string array*(1:2,2:5,3:7) is a primitive array type symbol

The form n *array* is like the PL/I notation $array(*,\overset{n}{\ldots},*)$. It tells us that the array has n dimensions. If we say simply *array*, we mean 1 *array*. We do not need to introduce primitive types in which the upper and lower bounds, u_i, ℓ_i, are permitted to be expressions. This simplifies the syntax of quantifiers (allowing us to preserve order independence in homogeneous blocks of quantifiers, see below). We do however allow

---

[†] In a more general theory these bounds can be elements of any index set.

the abbreviation array$(u_1,\ldots,u_n)$ where the lower bound
is assumed to be one. The precise syntax for new types
is:

> array type symbol → simple type symbol *array*
> ({integer [:integer]§,}+)
>
> → primitive type symbol [pos.integer]
> *array*

Now as in Chapter II, (2.3) we define compound type
symbols to be of the form

> primitive type ×...× primitive type
> primitive type ×...× primitive type → primitive type

where a primitive type is either a simple type (*integer,
string, boolean*) or an array type.

The association of a type symbol to each constant,
variable, function symbol and array symbol is described
by the following table:

symbol	*type description*
constant	simple type
array	array type
variable	simple type or array type
function	primitive type × ..× primitive type → simple type
infix operator	primitive type x primitive type → primitive type
predicate	primitive type ×...× primitive type

The type descriptions extend to expressions in the
natural way. If f is of type $\text{atype}_1 \times\ldots\times \text{atype}_n \to \text{btype}$
and $\exp_i$ is of type atype_i, then $f(\exp_1,\ldots,\exp_n)$ is of
type btype. If a is of array type btype n *array* and
$\exp_1,\ldots,\exp_n$ are of type *integer*, then $a(\exp_1,\ldots,\exp_n)$
is of type btype. An expression, assertion or argument in
the predicate calculus with arrays is *syntactically correct* if every subexpression may be assigned a type by the
rule above, and in every subassertion of the form
$R(\exp_1,\ldots,\exp_n)$ where R is of type $\text{atype}_1 \times\ldots\times \text{atype}_n$,
each $\exp_i$ is of type atype_i. Note that each array has

two possible array types, type *array*($\ell:u_1,\ldots,\ell_n:u_n$)
and type n *array*. Notice that variables can be of array
type and predicates, functions and operators can accept
arguments of type array as well as of simple type. Thus
for example a predicate like permutation (a,b) is possible where a and b are arrays. Likewise the equality
predicate extends to arrays, a=b. Also we may extend
various operators to arrays, such as a+b. In the main
language described here functions are not allowed to return
arrays as values. Array indices may also be allowed to
range over index sets other than subranges of the integers. The set of characters is a common choice for an
index set.

syntax - new primitive functions and predicates

We add new primitive functions and predicates to the
syntax. To describe their types we let "array" indicate any
array type (any dimension with values of any simple type).
The symbols are

lbound	of type	array x integer $\rightarrow$ integer
hbound	of type	array x integer $\rightarrow$ integer
dom	of type	array x integer$^+$.

Intuitively lbound(a,n) gives the lower bound of dimension n of array a, while hbound(a,n) gives the high
bound. The domain predicate is a derived notion, namely

$$\text{dom}(a,i) \text{ iff } \text{lbound}(a,1) \le i \le \text{hbound}(a,1)$$

or more generally

$$\text{dom}(a,i_1,\ldots,i_n) \text{ iff } \text{lbound}(a,1) \le i_1 \le \text{hbound}(a,1) \ \&$$

$$\ldots \text{lbound}(a,n) \le i_n \le \text{hbound}(a,n).$$

An immediate need for these boundary functions is seen
by contemplating quantifiers.

Had we allowed array types of the form *array*(1:n)
integer for variables n we would have changed the be-
havior of quantifiers. For example, $\forall$ *integer* n $\forall$ *integer*
array(1:n) a . P(a,n) should be different than

$$\forall \text{ } integer \text{ } array(1:n) \text{ } \forall \text{ } integer \text{ } n \text{ . } P(a,n).$$

However, it is important to be able to describe arrays
with variable dimensions. This can be done using primitive

209

functions *hbound* and *lbound*. If a has type
array($\ell_1:u_1,\ldots, \ell_n:u_n$) then hbound(a,i) = u_i and
lbound(a,i) = ℓ_i for i=1,...,n. If a has type n array,
then the bounds are not specified.

To write an assertion equivalent to

$$\forall \; integer \; n \; \forall \; integer \; n \; array \;\; a \; . \; P(a,n)$$

we write

$\forall \; integer \; n \; \forall \; integer \; array \; a \; where$ hbound(a,1)=n . P(a,n).

To achieve complete compatibility with our PL/I
subset we must loosen the notion of array type to allow
expressions for the bounds of indices of arrays which are
bad to definitions as long as all free variables in these
expressions are readonly parameters.

syntax - substitution and binding

The notions of variable binding and substitution for
free variables carry over verbatim from Chapter II, (2.3).
No new ideas are needed to handle arrays.

syntax - an example

Here is a simple example of an argument

($\forall \; integer$ i,j . $\exists \; boolean \; array$ b . (dom(b,i) & dom(b,j)
& (i$\neq$j => b(i)$\neq$b(j)))) =>

($\forall \; integer$ x,y. (($\forall \; boolean \; array$ a $where$ dom(a,x) &
dom(a,y) . a(x)=a(y)) => x=y))

proof assume $\forall \; integer$ i,j . $\exists \; boolean \; array$ b . (dom(b,i)
& dom(b,j) & (i$\neq$j => b(i)$\neq$b(j)))
proof arbitrary integer x,y;
$\exists \; boolean \; array$ b . (dom(b,x) & dom(b,y) & (x$\neq$y =>
b(x)$\neq$b(y))) *by* $\forall$E.
choose boolean array b_0 *where* (dom(b_0,x) & dom(b_0,y) &
(x$\neq$y => b_0(x)$\neq$$b_0$(y)));
dom(b_0,x) & dom(b_0,y);

proof;
assume ∀ *boolean array* a *where* dom(a,x) & dom(a,y) .
  a(x)=a(y);
$b_0(x) = b_0(y)$ *by* ∀E, b_0;

D: x=y ∨ x≠y;
    proof;
    assume x≠y;
    $b_0(x) \neq b_0(y)$;

    x=y
    qed;
  x=y *by cases,*D
qed;
(∀ *boolean array* a *where* dom(a,x) & dom(a,y) . a(x) = a(y))
=> x=y
qed;
∀ *integer* x,y . ((∀ *boolean array* a *where* dom(z,x) &
dom(a,y) . a(x)=a(y) => x=y))
qed;

Notice in this example we must assume the trivially
true hypothesis that for any pair of distinct integers
there is a boolean array separating them. This must be
assumed in any theory where we have no axioms for building
arrays. (A similar situation holds for pure second order
logic without comprehension axioms for building functions.)

semantics - models and states

As we said in the discussion of (7.1), arrays are
interpreted as finite functions from $\mathbf{Z}^n$ into values.
This decision is first reflected in the formal semantics
in our definition of *model*. We must now append to the
definition in Chapter II, (2.4) the following:

Definition: A *model* of the predicate calculus with arrays
assigns to the primitive type symbol
atype array($\ell_1:u_1,\ldots,\ell_n:u_n$) the set of amppings from
$[\ell_1,u_1] \times \ldots \times [\ell_n,u_n] \to \mathcal{M}(atype)$ where
$[\ell,u] = \{x| \ell \leq x \leq u\}$. Likewise
atype n array is mapped to the set of all functions
$[\ell_1,u_1] \times \ldots \times [\ell_n,u_n] \to \mathcal{M}(atype)$ for all sequences of indices
$\ell_i \leq u_i$. We can summarize this by equations of the form

$$\mathcal{M}(atype \; n \; array(\ell_1:u_1,\ldots,\ell_n:u_n)) =$$
$$[\ell_1,u_1] \times \ldots \times [\ell_n,u_n] \rightarrow \mathcal{M}(atype)$$

The meaning of compound type symbols, such as *integer array* x *integer* → *string*, is now given exactly as before.

We must distinguish two sets of basic values in the language.

Definition: Simple values = $\{x \mid x \in \mathcal{M}(simple \; type)\}$ and

Values = $\{x \mid x \in \mathcal{M}(primitive \; type)\}$.

This change in the set of values affects the definition of state in the appropriate way. Namely a state may now map array variables to array values. We recall the definition.

Definition: A *state* is any function s: Variables → Values.

States = $\{s \mid s$ a state$\}$.

semantics - expressions, assertions and arguments

The meaning of expresssions and assertions is quite routinely given following the method of Chapter II, (2.4). However there is one critical difference caused by the partial nature of array functions. Thus if a is an array of type *integer array*(n) and a(exp) appears in an expression, then a(exp) has a meaning only if

$1 \leq \mathcal{M}(s)(exp) \leq n$. We can reflect this in the formal semantics if we add a line (3b) in the definition of

$\mathcal{M}(s)(exp)$ in Chapter II, (2.4). Just as in Chapter VI, we adopt Keisler's conventions in which atomic assertions containing undefined expressions are false.

Definition:
(3b) If $< \mathcal{M}(s)(exp_1),\ldots,\mathcal{M}(s)(exp_n)>$ is in the domain of

a, $\mathcal{M}(s)(a(exp_1,\ldots,exp_n)) =$
$$\mathcal{M}(s)(a)(\mathcal{M}(s)(exp_1),\ldots,\mathcal{M}(s)(exp_n)).$$

We must then prefix every equation with the condition

"If $\mathcal{M}(s)(exp)$ is defined then..."

The meaning (with respect to model $\mathcal{M}$ and state s) of an assertion A containing an array reference a(exp) is built up from the meaning of atomic relations exactly as in Chapter II, (2.4). For atomic statements we modify equation (11) in (2.4) to read as:

(11) If $\mathcal{M}(s)(exp_i)$ is defined for i=1,...,n, then

$$<\mathcal{M},s> \models p(exp_1,...,exp_n) \text{ iff}$$

$\mathcal{M}(p)(\mathcal{M}(s)(exp_1),...,\mathcal{M}(s)(exp_n))$ = true. If the expression is not defined, then the atomic assertion is false.

semantics - added expressive power

Adding arrays whose indices range over finite subsets of the integers does not increase the expressive power of standard number theory because arrays can be coded as single integers (see [Kleene 52]), but adding arrays (as done here) to first order Peano arithmetic does increase the expressive power, with either of two reasonable semantic definitions of an array expression.

(1) Let D be the domain of some (standard or nonstandard) model of first order Peano arithmetic. We may add the array domain

A = {f| f:[ℓ,u] → D where [ℓ,u] is the standard (finite) part of D}, i.e. ℓ,u are standard.

In this case,

$$\forall \textit{ integer } x . \exists \textit{ integer array } a .$$
$$(hbound(a,1) - lbound(a,1)) = x$$

characterizes the standard models of the integers.

(2) Let D be as before. We may add the array domain A = {f| f:[ℓ,u] → D where ℓ,u∈D}. Now the assertion of (1) is true in all models, standard and nonstandard, but the following assertion categorizes the standard models, essentially by saying that no array index set may be put in a one-to-one correspondence with a proper subset of itself. So every number is finite.

$$\neg\exists \textit{ integer array } a.[(\forall \textit{ integer } i,j \textit{ where } i{\neq}j.a(i){\neq}a(j))$$
$$\& (\forall \textit{ integer } i \textit{ where } dom(a,i).dom(a,a(i)))$$
$$\& (\exists \textit{ integer } i \textit{ where } dom(a,i).$$
$$\forall \textit{ integer } j \textit{ where } dom(a,j).a(j){\neq}i)].$$

The above formula always holds in the extensions of (1).
The conjunction of the two formulas would characterize the
standard integers in either type of array semantics. In
analogy with (1), we could extend the domain D of a
model of any pure predicate calculus language by adding
$A = \{f \mid f:D' \to D$ where D' is a finite subset of $D\}$.
The result is a weak second order theory, and the set of
valid formulas is not enumerable. Adding
$A = \{f \mid f:D' \to D$ where $D' \subseteq D\}$ gives us unrestricted second
order logic, which is even more powerful.

proof rules

   We have tried to arrange the logic so that there is
a minimum change in the predicate calculus proof rules
when arrays are added. The only serious difficulties to
doing this are the undefined expressions. We must be
certain that our proof rules of Chapter II, (2.5) do not
allow introducing undefined expressions into an argument.
These can enter the logic only through substitution and
the equality axioms. Therefore we must examine these
axioms carefully. (Those of Chapter II will need modification.)
   We do not intend to provide a complete calculus for
arrays since, by the constructions of the last section, such
a calculus has a nonenumerable set of valid assertions.

   Only three rules allow us to introduce new terms:
∨ intro, all elimination, reflexity of equality. We must
in fact modify each of them.

(1)   or introduction

$$\frac{A_i, \; dom(a,t)}{A_1 \vee \ldots \vee A_i \vee \ldots \vee A_n}$$

for all a(t) occurring in
the new assertions

$$\frac{A_i, \; dom(a_1,t_1), \ldots, dom(a_m,t_m)}{A_1 \vee \ldots \vee A_i \vee \ldots \vee A_n}$$

$a_1(t_1), \ldots, a_m(t_m)$ include
all array expressions oc-
curring in A_j for $j \neq i$

(2)   all elimination

$$\frac{\forall \alpha \; B.A, \; dom(a_1,e_1),\ldots,dom(a_m,e_m)}{A(t_1/x_1,\ldots,t_n/x_n)}$$
for any $d_i(\ell_i)$ occurring in $t_1,\ldots,t_n$.

(3)

$$\frac{dom(a_1,e_1),\ldots,dom(a_m,e_m)}{exp=exp}$$
for any $d_i(\ell_i)$ occurring in $t_1,\ldots,t_n$.

(4)   declaration introduction

$$\frac{\ell_1 \leq u_1, \ldots, \ell_n \leq u_n}{[declare] \; atype \; array(\ell_1:u_1,\ldots,\ell_n:u_n) \; .b}$$

(5)   bound introduction (immediate)

$$\frac{[declare] \; atype \; array(\ell_1:u_1,\ldots,\ell_n:u_n) \; b}{lbound(b,i) = \ell_i, \; hbound(b,i) = u_i}$$
$$i=1,\ldots,n.$$

(6)   initial values (immediate)[†]

$$\frac{[declare] \; atype \; n \; array \; b, \; dom(b,i_1,\ldots,i_n)}{b(i_1,\ldots,i_n) = initial \; atype}$$

We also have the rule

$$\frac{[declare] \; atype \; x}{x = initial \; atype}$$

The initial types are *initial integer* = 0,
initial string = ⊘, *initial boolean* = true.

[†] This is a rule imposed by the PL/CS language. It is convenient for us, but may upset the asymptotic runtimes of some algorithms.

(7)   extensionality

$$lbound(a,1) = lbound(b,1),\ldots,lbound(a,n) = lbound(b,n),$$
$$hbound(a,1) = hbound(b,1),\ldots,hbound(a,n) = hbound(b,n),$$

$\forall$ *integer* $i_1,\ldots,i_n$ *where* $lbound(a,1){\le}i_1{\le}hbound(a,1)$

$$\&\ldots\& \; lbound(a,n){\le}i_n{\le}hbound(a,n).$$

$$a(i_1,\ldots,i_n) = b(i_1,\ldots,i_n)$$

$$a=b$$

(8)   comprehension

$\forall$ *integer* $i_1,\ldots,i_n$ *where* $\ell_1{\le}i_1{\le}u_1 \; \&\ldots\& \; \ell_n{\le}i_n{\le}u_n$.
$$\exists \; atype \; x \; . \; P$$

$\exists \; atype \; array(\ell_1{:}u_1,\ldots,\ell_n{:}u_n)a$.

$\forall$ *integer* $i_1,\ldots,i_n$ *where* $\ell_1{\le}i_1{\le}u_1 \; \&\ldots\& \; \ell_n{\le}i_n{\le}u_n$.
$$P(a(i_1,\ldots,i_n)/x)$$

example - one

    In section (7.3) we give two examples of programs to find the maximum value in an array.   One of them requires the following lemma about the predicate maximum defined as follows:

    define maximum (a,u,max) =
    $\forall$ *integer* j *where* $lbound(a,1){\le}j{\le}u \le hbound(a,1)$. $a(j){\le}max$.

/* max lemma1: $\forall$ *integer* array a.$\forall$ *integer* k,m_1,m_2 .

  $(maximum(a,k,m_1) \; \& \; m_1{\le}m_2 => maximum(a,k,m_2))$ */

proof arbitrary integer array a, *integer* k,m_1,m_2;

    proof assume $maximum(a,k,m_1) \; \& \; m_1{\le}m_2$;

        define $\ell = lbound(a,1)$;
        proof arbitrary integer j *where* $\ell{\le}j{\le}k$;
            $a(j) \le m_1$ *by* $\forall E$, $maximum(a,k,m_1)$;

            $a(j) \le m_2$ *by arith*, $m_1{\le}m_2$, $a(j){\le}m_1$
        qed
    qed;
        $maximum(a,k,m_1) \; \& \; m_1{\le}m_2 => maximum(a,k,m_2)$
qed;

We will not repeat the conclusion after the proof when it has been formally written as a comment at the beginning. (Note, in the PL/CV style the statement of the theorem comes first.)

```
/*  max lemma 2:  ∀ integer array a, integer k,n .
    maximum(a,k-1,m) & dom(a,k) & a(k)≤m => maximum(a,k,m); */
```

proof arbitrary integer array a, *integer* k,m;
    proof assume maximum(a,k-1,m) & a(k)≤m;
    define ℓ = lbound(a,1);
        proof arbitrary integer j *where* ℓ≤j≤k;
            j≤k-1 ∨ j=k *by arith*, j≤k;
            proof assume j≤k-1;
                a(j)≤m *by* ∀E, maximum(a,k-1,m);
            qed;
            proof assume j=k;
                a(j)≤m;
            qed;
            a(j)≤m *by* ∀E
    qed;   *qed*;
qed;   maximum(a,k-1,m) & a(k)≤m => maximum(a,k,m)
qed;

This type of proof about arrays is especially common and especially tedious. There are simple ways to avoid proving such trivialities, one of the most general is to formulate proof rules for first order logic with substitutions for free predicate variables. The general theorem is:

    (∀ *integer* j *where* m≤j≤n-1 . P) & P(n/j) =>
    ∀ *integer* j *where* m≤j≤n . P

In this case we substituted the predicate a(j)≤max for P. However, in this monograph we do not wish to treat these advanced forms of proof. The interested user will see them in future releases of PL/CV.

example - two

In (7.4) we will need various facts about permutations of arrays. We prove one of them here because it involves only logical and number theoretic concepts. It also illustrates the need for the array existence axiom (*array comprehension*).

First we define what it means for an array a to be a permutation of array b between m and n.

define permutes(p,a,b,m,n) = m≤n & dom(a,m) & dom(a,n)
  & dom(b,m) & dom(b,n) & lbound(p,1) = m & hbound(p,1) = n &
  ∀ *integer* i,j *where* dom(p,i) & dom(p,j) .
                  (dom(p,p(i)) & (p(i) = p(j) => i=j))
    ∀ *integer* k *where* dom(p,k) . b(p(k)) = a(k)
  [& ∀ *integer* k *where* dom(p,k) . ∃ *integer* i . p(i) = k];
define perm(a,b,m,n) = ∃ *integer* array p . permutes(p,a,b,m,n)

perm lemma 1: ∀ *integer array* a,b, *integer* m,n,k
    (m≤k<n & perm(a,b,m,k) & perm(a,b,k+1,n)) =>
    perm(a,b,m,n).
        proof arbitrary integer array a,b *integer* m,n,k
            where m≤k<n & perm(a,b,m,k) & perm(a,b,k+1,n);

/* Pick the two permutations assumed to exist under the */
/* conditions already assumed. */

    choose p_1 *where* permutes(p_1,a,b,m,k);

    choose p_2 *where* permutes(p_2,a,b,k+1,n);

/* Now we build the new permutation array on m,n by com-
    bining p_1,p_2 using array comprehension. The new array
    p is simply p_1 up to k and p_2 after k. We observe
    while building it that a is a permutation of b on the
    entire range m,n. */

    proof arbitrary integer t *where* m≤t≤n;

    /* consider the two subranges of m to n */
        t≤k ∨ k+1≤t *by arith*;
    /* m≤t≤k ∨ k+1≤t≤n; */

```
/* In the first subrange describe an integer satisfying
   the condition needed for p */
   proof assume m≤t≤k;   /* suppose t is in first range */
        dom(p₁,t);
        b(p₁(t)) = a(t) by VE, permutes(p₁,a,b,m,k), t;
        m≤t≤k => p₁(t) = p₁(t);
        proof assume k+1≤t≤n;
            t≤k;
            t≥k+1;
            false;
            p₁(t) = p₂(t)
        qed;
        k+1≤t≤n => p₁(t) = p₂(t);
        ∃ integer x . (b(x) = a(t) & m≤t≤k => x=p₁(t) &
                    k+1≤t≤n => x=p₂(t)) by ∃I, p₁(t)
   qed;
/* in the second subrange describe an integer satisfying
   the conditions needed for p */
   proof assume k+1≤t≤n; /* suppose t is in the second
                            subrange */
        dom(p₂,t);
        b(p₂(t)) = a(t) by VE, permutes(p₂,a,b,k+1,n), t;
        k+1≤t≤n => p₂(t) = p₂(t);
        proof assume m≤t≤k;
            t≤k;
            t≥k+1;
            false, by arith, t≤k, t≥k+1;
            p₂(t) = p₁(t)
        qed;
        m≤t≤k => p₂(t) = p₁(t);
        ∃ integer x . (b(x) = a(t) & m≤t≤k => x=p₁(t) &
                    k+1≤t≤n => x=p₂(t)) by ∃I,  p₂(t)
   qed;
   ∃ integer x . (b(x) = a(t) & m≤t≤k => x=p₁(t) &
               k+1≤t≤n => x=p₂(t)) by VE;
```

qed;
$\forall$ *integer* t *where* m≤t≤n . $\exists$ *integer* x . (b(x) = a(t) &
(m≤t≤k => x=p_1(t)) & (k+1≤t≤n => x=p_2(t)));

Now we apply the array existence axiom to conclude that
array p exists whose values satisfy the properties that
x does.

$\exists$ *integer array* p . (lbound(p,1) = m & hbound(p,1) = n &
  $\forall$ *integer* x *where* dom(p,x) . b(p(x)) = a(x) &
  m≤x≤k => p(x)=p_1(x) & k+1≤x≤n => p(x)=p_2(x))

  by array comprehension.
proof /* We must now show that p has the three properties needed in the definition of permutes. P1 says that
the bounds are correct. P2 says that p is a permutation.
It consists of subproperty SP1 saying that the range of p
is the same as its domain, and subproperty SP2 saying that
p is one to one (and subproperty SP3 saying it is onto).
Finally property P3 says that a is a permutation, by
p, of b. */

choose integer array p *where*
lbound(p,1) = m & hbound(p.1) = n &
$\forall$ *integer* x *where* dom(p,x) . b(p(x)) = a(x) &
m≤x≤k => p(x)=p_1(x) & k+1≤x≤n => p(x)=p_2(x);
P0: m≤n & dom(a,m) & dom(a,n) & dom(b,m) & dom(b,n);
P1: lbound(p,1) = m & hbound(p,1) = n;
P2: *proof arbitrary integer* i,j *where* dom(p,i) & dom(p,j);
     m≤i≤k ∨ k+1≤i≤n by arith;
     proof assume m≤i≤k;   *proof assume* k+1≤i≤n;
         dom(p_1,i);   dom(p_2,i);

         p(i) = p_1(i);   p(i) = p_2(i);

         dom(p_1,p(i));   dom(p_2,p_2(i));

         dom(p,p(i))   dom(p,p(i))
     qed;   *qed;*

SP1:   dom(p,p(i)) *by* VE;

```
/* Now we show property SP2 that p is one to one.  Again
   this is a case analysis. */
   proof assume p(i) = p(j);
      /* we analyze this equality by cases on where i,j
         appear in the domain of p */
         (i≤k v k+1≤i) & (j≤k v k+1≤j) by arith;
         (i≤k & j≤k) v (k+1≤i & k+1≤j) v
         (i≤k & k+1≤j) v (j≤k & k+1≤i) by arith;
```

$(\text{dom}(p_1,i) \; \& \; \text{dom}(p_1,j)) \; \vee \; (\text{dom}(p_2,i) \; \& \; \text{dom}(p_2,j)) \; \vee$

$(\text{dom}(p_1,i) \; \& \; \text{dom}(p_2,j)) \; \vee \; \text{dom}(p_1,j) \; \& \; \text{dom}(p_2,i);$

proof assume $\text{dom}(p_1,i) \; \& \; \text{dom}(p_1,j);$

$$p_1(i) = p_1(j);$$
$$p_1(i) = p_1(j) \Rightarrow i=j;$$
$$i=j;$$

qed;
proof assume $\text{dom}(p_2,i) \; \& \; \text{dom}(p_2,j);$

$$p_2(i) = p_2(j);$$
$$p_2(i) = p_2(j) \Rightarrow i=j;$$
$$i=j;$$

qed;
proof assume $\text{dom}(p_1,i) \; \& \; \text{dom}(p_2,j);$

$$p(i) = p_1(i);$$
$$p_1(i) \le k;$$
$$p(j) = p_2(j);$$
$$k+1 \le p_2(j);$$
$$p_1(i) = p_2(j);$$

false by arith, $p_1(i) \le k$, $k+1 \le p_2(j);$
$$i=j$$

qed;

  proof assume $\text{dom}(p_1,j)$ & $\text{dom}(p_2,i)$;

    $p_2(i) = p_1(j)$;

    $p_1(j) \leq k$;

    $p_2(i) = p_1(j)$;

    $k+1 \leq p_2(i)$;

    false by arith $p_1(j) \leq k$, $k+1 \leq p_2(i)$;

    $i=j$;

  qed;

  $i=j$ *by VE*;

 qed;

SP2: $p(i) = p(j) \Rightarrow i=j$;

qed;

$\forall$ *integer* i,j *where* $\text{dom}(p,i)$ & $\text{dom}(p,j)$.

 $(\text{dom}(p,p(i)))$ & $(p(i)=p(j) \Rightarrow i=j))$ *by* $\forall I$;

/* we now show that p is onto by cases. */
/* this part is optional as we discuss below. */

 proof arbitrary integer i *where* $\text{dom}(p,i)$;

  $i \leq k$ $\vee$ $k+1 \leq i$ *by arith*;

  proof assume $i \leq k$;

   $\text{dom}(p_1,i)$

    choose integer j *where* $p_1(j) = i$;

    $p(j) = p_1(j)$;

    $p(j) = i$;

   $\exists$ *integer* j . $p(j) = i$;

  qed;

  proof assume $k+1 \leq i$;

   $\text{dom}(p_2,i)$;

    choose integer j *where* $p_2(j) = i$;

    $p(j) = p_2(j)$;

    $p(j) = i$;

   $\exists$ *integer* j . $p(j) = i$

  qed;

 $\exists$ *integer* j . $p(j) = i$ *by VE*;

 qed; SP3: $\forall$ *integer* i *where* $\text{dom}(p,i)$. $\exists$ *integer* j .

    $p(j) = i$;

/* Now we establish the final property P3 of the permutation P */

   proof arbitrary integer k *where* dom(p,k);
      b(p(k)) = a(k) by ∀E, k; /* from definition of P */
  qed;
P3: ∀ *integer* k *where* dom(p,k) . b(p(k)) = a(k);
   permutes(p,a,b,m,n);
   perm(a,b,m,n) by ∃E;
qed;
   perm(a,b,m,n);
qed; /* end of perm lemma 1 */

Remarks: It is easy to show set theoretically that any
one-one maps from a finite set into itself must be onto.
Conversely, any function from a finite set onto itself
must be one-one. So we need only establish one of the
properties and derive the other. However, it is not easy
to derive one form the other in the absence of general
cardinality arguments for sets. Therefore a user may wish
to define permutations so that both properties are given
explicitly. If so we have shown how to prove each. In
future uses of permutations in part 7.3 we will prove
only the one to one property.

7.3 ARRAYS IN SIMPLE PROGRAMS

discussion

    Arrays are not a useful data structure in a language
until there are means for constructing new ones, either
from scratch or from given arrays. The predicate calculus
provided only array comprehension and the number theory
we have presented gives no additional explicit construction
methods for arrays.
    Iteration is an ideal mechanism for constructing
arrays or modifying them. Procedural languages like
FORTRAN, ALGOL and PL/I do their array construction almost
exclusively through iteration and assignment. But there
is no reason not to add various direct operators similar
to APL array operations, in fact there would be a con-
siderable advantage doing this. Our treatment of array
constructions will however follow the conventional procedural language approach.

Typically, an array can be built or modified in a loop containing assignments of the form

$$a(i) := exp.$$

As long as we are concerned only with making statements about the values in the array, i.e. about subscripted variables, it would appear we should use the existing assignment rule. For example, to set an array to a segment of **Z** we could write

```
ℓ := lbound(a,1);
u := hbound(a,1);
for i=ℓ to u do a(i) :=i od
∀ integer j where ℓ≤j≤u . a(j) = j;
```

The assertion could be proved by instantiating the ordinary assignment rule, in the form

$$\frac{P(exp/a(i))}{a(i) := exp} \qquad \text{i.e.} \qquad \frac{i=i}{a(i) := i}$$
$$\overline{P(a(i)).} \qquad\qquad\qquad \overline{a(i) = i}$$

But this rule is based on the conception of an array as a set of subscripted variables. That is not our view of an array. Moreover, that view runs into complications with such examples as the following. If a(1) = 1 and a(2) = 3 initially, we might make the following argument

$$2=2;$$
$$a(a(1)) := 2;$$
$$a(a(1)) = 2;$$

Note that [a(a(1)) = 2](2/a(a(1))) is 2=2, so the argument is an instance of the generalized assignment rule. Yet execution of a(a(1)) := 2 results in a(1) = 2 and a(2) = 3, so a(a(1)) = 3 finally, and the rule is unsound.

To achieve sound reasoning, we view the assignment a(i) := exp as an operation on the entire array. In proof rules, the assignment above acts as a shorthand for a := alt(a,i,exp)† The appropriate assignment rule should have the form

---

†We borrow the mnemonic alt for alter from [Dijkstra 76]. Before his book we were using the notation <a:i, exp>.

$$\frac{P(\text{alt}(a,i,\exp)/a)}{a := \text{alt}(a,i,\exp)}$$

$$P$$

alt may be defined by $\text{alt}(a,i,\exp)(j) = \begin{cases} \exp & \text{if } j=i \\ a(j) & \text{if } j \neq i. \end{cases}$
One might imagine other operations $F_1, F_2, \ldots$ on arrays,
and the general form of the assignment rule would be

$$\frac{P(F(a)/a)}{a := F(a)}$$

$$P$$

The only operators we will consider beyond assignment of constants (as a := 0) are a modifier to change
single values of the array and a function to exchange
values. These have proven to be very important primitive
notions. The reader could imagine a theory in which other
operators such as these are added:

right shift(a,n)   means to shift the elements n
                   positions to the right (wrapping
                   around to the start)
left shift(a,n)

The only addition we must make to the rules of
Chapter IV when adding arrays is a set of axioms for the
array function, *alt* and a set of conditions on each of the
other rules guaranteeing that expressions containing
arrays are well-defined. The latter change will be
nearly invisible because it belongs to the automatic
rules of the logic. However, we will see the need to
explicitly mention array domains in declarations.

syntax - modifiers

The most direct syntax for array modification in
simple programs is to allow a class of array operations,
$F_1, F_2, \ldots$ and expand the class of expressions in (7.2) to
include $F(a_1, \ldots, a_n)$ where a_i are of the appropriate type.

Among these operators F would be the modifier, $alt(a,i,exp)$ and the exchanger swap(a,i,j).† (We would in fact need the operators defined over the *union* of types of the form simple type array × integer × simple type for each simple type.)

Such a syntax is simple and elegant and is compatible with the notation in existing procedural languages. For our purposes, the new syntax requires only the addition of the special function symbols *altn* for n=1,2,...

function symbol → *altn*

The type of *altn* is (t n array × n_tuple × t) → t n array for t a simple type, i.e. the *union* of the types t n array × n_tuple × t. The type of $swap_n$ is

(t n array × n_tuple × n_tuple) → t n array. The syntax for assignment commands is exactly as before. But the conventions of existing procedural languages would prohibit the assignment a := $alt(b,i,exp)$. This is an unfortunate limitation which we will ignore in this monograph.

We abbreviate the assignment a := alt(a,i,exp) by the usual a(i) := exp. But this is purely a syntactic abbreviation.

The syntax for other commands is also not affected by the addition of arrays. Even the syntax of arguments requires no alteration. The reader should note however, that an argument containing assignments may also contain declarations. Recall the syntax from Chapter IV.

---

†The operation swap(a,i,j) can be defined in terms of alt as swap(a,i,j) = alt(alt(a,i,a(j)),j,a(i)). We will take this definition to be permanent for the rest of this chapter.

```
proof-group → [label:] proof
                      qualifier;
                      [declaration;]
                      argument
                      qed
```

The declaration of an array has the form

$$\text{btype n } array \text{ variable} \qquad \text{(as discussed in (7.2)).}$$

semantics - primitive concepts

The meaning of the array assignment command, a := F(b,...) is defined only when a and F(b,...) have the same type and when F(b,...) is well-defined. In particular alt(b,i,exp) can be undefined if exp is undefined or if i is not in *dom*(b).

The meaning of alt(a,i,exp) is an array whose value at i is the meaning of exp. Thus $\mathcal{M}(s)(\text{alt}(a,i,exp)) = b$ where if k=i then b(k) = $\mathcal{M}(s)(exp)$ and if k≠i and dom(a,k), then b(k)= $(\mathcal{M}(s)(a))(k)$. Notice that the domain of a and alt(a,i,exp) are the same as long as exp is defined and i is in the domain of a.

The meaning of the swap function can be defined terms of alt. Namely

$$\text{swap}(a,i,j) = \text{alt}(\text{alt}(a,i,a(j)),j,a(i)).$$

semantics - descriptive power

The addition of arrays to a pure simple programming language does increase its computational power as is shown in [Constable, Gries 72].

proof rules

Adding arrays to the logic of simple programs does not change the definition of accessibility. An array variable is treated like any other variable, so an assignment such as a := alt(a,i,exp) modifies the variable a and renders certain assertions containing a inaccessible.

The notion of proof changes only by the addition of new rules and new conditions on old rules. The new rules are listed first.

alt elimination

(1) for dimension 1

$$\frac{i=j, \; dom(a,j), \; exp \; defined}{alt(a,i,exp)(j) \; = \; exp} \qquad \frac{i \neq j, \; dom(a,j), \; exp \; defined}{alt(a,i,exp)(j) \; = \; a(j)}$$

for dimension n

$$\frac{i_1 = j_1, \ldots, i_n = j_n, \; dom(a, j_1, \ldots, j_n), \; exp \; defined}{altn(a, i_1, \ldots, i_n, exp)(j_1, \ldots, j_n) \; = \; exp}$$

$$\frac{i_1 \neq j_1 \; \vee \ldots \vee \; i_n \neq j_n, \; dom(a, j_1, \ldots, j_n)}{altn(a, i_1, \ldots, i_n, exp)(j_1, \ldots, j_n) \; = \; a(j_1, \ldots, j_n)}$$

(2) bound propagation (immediate)

$$\frac{exp \; defined, \; dom(a,i)}{\begin{array}{l} lbound(alt(a,i,exp),j) \; = \; lbound(a,j) \\ hbound(alt(a,i,exp),j) \; = \; hbound(a,j) \end{array}}$$

(3) domain propagation (immediate)

$$\frac{exp \; defined, \; dom(a,i)}{dom(alt(a,i,exp),j) \; <=> \; dom(a,j)}$$

The propagation axioms hold for each dimension n.

Just as in Chapter VI, we must add hypotheses to all rules which introduce new expressions. Specifically, the VI, VE, arithmetic, assignment, conditional, while and repeat rules must also have the hypotheses $dom(a, i_1, \ldots, i_n)$ for each array subexpression $a(i_1, \ldots, i_n)$ in any introduced expression. For example, the assignment rule appears as

228

$$P(exp/x), \ dom(a_1, i_1, \ldots, i_{n_1}), \ldots, dom(a_m, i_1, \ldots, i_{n_m})$$
$$x := exp$$

$$P$$

where the $a_k(i_1, \ldots, i_{n_k})$ include all array expressions in exp

(See the Appendix for rules with there restrictions.)

example one - finding maximum in an array, two methods.

```
amax:   procedure(a,max,m);

        /* this procedure finds the largest integer in
           array a */

        integer array a readonly;
        integer max, m;
        integer i;
        define maximum(a,u,max) =
        V integer j where lbound(a,1)≤j≤u . a(j)≤max;
        conclude maximum(a,hbound(a,1),max) & a(m) = max;
        m := lbound(a,1); i := lbound;
        max := a(m);
        a(m) = max;
        proof arbitrary integer j
                  where lbound(a,1)≤j≤lbound(a,1);
            j=m by arith, lbound(a,1)≤j≤lbound(a,1),
                     m = lbound(a,1);
            a(j) = max;
        qed;
        maximum(a,lbound(a,1),max);
        for k = lbound(a,1)+1 to hbound(a,1)
        do assume maximum(a,    ,max) & a(m) = max;
          k≤hbound(a,1);
          dom(a,k);
          if max < a(k) then
                      maximum(a,k-1,a(k)) by max lemma 1
                                 (a,k-1,a(k));
                      max := a(k); /* example 1, section
                                       7.2 */
                      m := k;
                      max := a(m)
                      a(k)≤max by arith, max=a(k) fi;
```

229

```
                maximum(a,k,max) by max lemma 2 (a,k-1,max);
                            else max≥a(k);
                            maximum(a,k,max) by
                                max lemma 2 (a,k-1,max)
            fi
            maximum(a,k,max) & a(m) = max
        od;
        maximum(a,hbound(a,1),max) & a(m) = max;
```

The maximum argument could be considerably simplified if we introduced a rule to directly establish $\forall$ *integer* i *where* dom(a,i) . a(i)≤max. The heart of the proof is the loop argument:

```
        for i = lbound(a,1) to hbound(a,1) do
            if max < a(i) then max := a(i);
                            a(i) ≤ max fi
            a(i) ≤ max
        od
        ∀ integer i where dom(a,i) . a(i)≤max.
```

This type of argument could be cast as a rule about predicates and loops. Formulating it precisely would require careful attention to the matter of substituting predicate names for free predicate variables. This is one of the most delicate parts of second order logic. We will not treat it in this monograph, but we expect the 1979 version of PL/CV to include such rules.

example two

A frequently needed property of swap is that it permutes arrays, i.e., if perm(a,b,m,n) then perm(swap(a,i,j),b,m,n) provided that i,j are in bounds. This basic fact will be used right away in the next example of a partitioning algorithm.

perm lemma 2:

$\forall$ *integer array* a,b . $\forall$ *integer* m,n,i,j *where*
  (dom(a,i) & dom(a,j) & dom(a,m) & dom(a,n) & m≤i≤n & m≤j≤n).
    perm(a,b,m,n) => perm(swap(a,i,j),b,m,n);
proof arbitrary integer array a,b, *integer* m,n,i,j
  where dom(a,i) & dom(a,j) & dom(a,m) & dom(a,n) & m≤i≤n &
  m≤j≤n;

/* claim: perm(a,b,m,n) => perm(swap(a,i,j),b,m,n) */

proof assume perm(a,b,m,n);

/* Our goal is to prove perm(swap(a,i,j),b,m,n). */
/* We first expand the definition of perm(a,b,m,n) */

∃ *integer array* p . permutes(p,a,b,m,n);
choose integer array p *where* permutes(p,a,b,m,n);

/* by definition p satisfies these conditions */

lbound(p,1) = m & hbound(p,1) = n &
∀ *integer* i,j *where* dom(p,i) & dom(p,j) .
(dom(p,p(i)) & (p(i)=p(j) => i=j)) &
∀ *integer* k *where* dom(p,k) . b(p(k)) = a(k);

/* We can choose the new permutation to be swap(p,i,j) */
/* because b(swap(p,i,j)(k)) = swap(a,i,j)(k). */
lcases: k=i ∨ k=j ∨ (k≠i & k≠j) *by arith*;

proof arbitrary integer k *where* dom(p,k);
    proof assume k=i;
        swap(a,i,j)(k) = a(j);
        swap(p,i,j)(k) = p(j);
        dom(p,j);   /* from m≤j≤n */
        b(p(j)) = a(j) *by* ∀E, j;
        b(swap(p,i,j)(k)) = swap(a,i,j)(k)
    qed;
    proof assume k=j;
        swap(a,i,j)(k) = a(i);
        swap(p,i,j)(k) = p(i);
        dom(p,i);   /* from m≤i≤n */
        b(p(i)) = a(i) *by* ∀E,i;
        b(swap(p,i,j)(k)) = swap(a,i,j)(k)
    qed;
    proof assume k≠i & k≠j;
        swap(a,i,j)(k) = a(k);
        swap(p,i,j)(k) = p(k);
        b(p(k)) = a(k) *by* ∀E,k;
        b(swap(p,i,j)(k)) = swap(a,i,j)(k)
    qed;
  b(swap(p,i,j)(k)) = swap(a,i,j)(k) *by* ∀E, lcases;
  qed;

```
/* We must now show that if p is a permutation, so is
   swap(p,i,j).  This is basic and could be done as a
   separate lemma in basic theory of permutations, but
   we show it here */
        dom(p,i) & dom(p,j);
        lbound(swap(p,i,j),1) = m;
        hbound(swap(p,i,j),1) = n;
proof arbitrary integer k,ℓ where dom(swap(p,i,j),k) &
                                       dom(swap(p,i,j),ℓ);
        proof assume k=i;
            swap(p,i,j)(k) = p(j);
            dom(p,p(j)) by VE,j;
            dom(swap(p,i,j),p(j));
            dom(swap(p,i,j),swap(p,i,j)(k))
        qed;
        proof assume k=j;
            swap(p,i,j)(k) = p(i);
            dom(p,p(i)) by VE,i;
            dom(swap(p,i,j),p(i));
            dom(swap(p,i,j),swap(p,i,j)(k))
        qed;
        proof assume k≠i & k≠j;
            swap(p,i,j)(k) = p(k);
            dom(p,k);
            dom(p,p(k)) by VE,k;
            dom(swap(p,i,j)(k),p(k));
            dom(swap(p,i,j)(k),swap(p,i,j)(k));
        qed;
        k=i ∨ k=j ∨ k≠i & k≠j;
        dom(swap(p,i,j),swap(p,i,j)(k)) by VE;
/* The above argument would be much shorter and more
   illuminating in set theory */
/* Finally we need to show that swap(p,i,j) is one-one.
   This is also a triviality. */
```

```
proof assume swap(p,i,j)(k) = swap(p,i,j)(ℓ);
     proof assume k=i;
          swap(p,i,j)(k) = p(j);
          proof assume ℓ=i;
               ℓ=k
          qed;
          proof assume ℓ=j;
               swap(p,i,j)(ℓ) = p(i);
               p(i) = p(j);
               p(i) = p(j) => i=j by ∀E i,j;
               i=j;
               ℓ=k
          qed;
          proof assume ℓ≠i & ℓ≠j;
               swap(p,i,j)(ℓ) = p(ℓ);
               p(ℓ) = p(j);
               p(ℓ) = p(j) => ℓ=j by ∀E, i,j;
               false;
               ℓ=k
          qed;
          ℓ=i ∨ ℓ=j ∨ ℓ≠i & ℓ≠j;
          ℓ=k by ∀E;
```

/*   The exact same argument is now repeated for j in
place of i. This can be treated in the formal system by
a proof macro which we will not discuss here. So all
the steps are left for the reader.   */

```
     proof assume k≠i & k≠j;
          swap(p,i,j)(k) = p(k);
          swap(p,i,j)(ℓ) = p(k);
          proof assume ℓ=i;
               swap(p,i,j)(ℓ) = p(j);
               p(j) = p(k);
               p(j) = p(k) => j=k by ∀E,j,k;
               j=k;
               false;
               ℓ=k
          qed;
```

233

```
        proof assume ℓ≠i & ℓ≠j;
            swap(p,i,j)(ℓ) = p(ℓ);
            p(ℓ) = p(k);
            p(ℓ) = p(k) => k=ℓ by ∀E,ℓ,k;
            k=ℓ
        qed;
        ℓ=i ∨ ℓ=j ∨ (ℓ≠i & ℓ≠j);
        k=ℓ by ∨E;
    qed;
```

/* We now know that swap(p,i,j) is one-one. We have
   found our new permutation. */

```
qed;
∀ integer k,ℓ where dom(swap(p,i,j),k) & dom(swap(p,i,j),ℓ).
 dom(swap(p,i,j),swap(p,i,j)(k) & swap(p,i,j)(k) =
 swap(p,i,j)(ℓ) => k=ℓ by ∀I;

    ∃ integer array q . (lbound(q,1) = m & hbound(q,1) = n &
    ∀ integer i,j where dom(q,i) & dom(q,j) .
            (dom(q,q(i)) & q(i) = q(j) => i=j &
        ∀ integer k where dom(p,k) . b(q(k)) = swap(a,i,j)(k))).
                by ∃I swap(p,i,j).
qed; /* proof that swap(a,i,j) is a permutation */
   perm(swap(a,i,j),b,m,n)
 qed  /* ends proof of claim */
 perm(a,b,m,n) => perm(swap(a,i,j),b,m,n)
qed  /* end lemma 2 */
```

Remark: Even though the formal proof of this fact about
permutations is tedious, we need only write it once. It
then becomes a permanent part of our theory of permutations.
For applications we only need the statement of the theorem
and an intuitive appreciation of it.

example three - a partitioning algorithm

The following is a simple algorithm to partition an
array a(m:n) into two parts, those elements less than or
equal to some pivot element, a(k), and those greater
than the pivot element. This procedure is crucial to
the recursive sorting algorithm, quicksort, presented in
(7.4).

The program looks very simple, especially given a few
explanatory remarks concerning it. Perhaps on the first
reading, you might think the algorithm is obviously
correct. However, even for such a simple algorithm, the
correctness argument is subtle. Every time a doubt is
raised, some serious reasoning is required to dispell it.
Before reading our asserted program you might want to
examine the program standing alone and ask certain questions
about it such as those we list after the program. In
order to facilitate this typical approach to a program, we
present the exact analysis and introduction to it that is
given in [Conway and Gries 75] p. 328. (We have taken
the liberty of using the programming language syntax of
this book rather than PL/C.)

Partition algorithm. This algorithm is given an array
segment a(ℓ:u) as input. It rearranges the values of the
array segment and stores an integer in variable k so that
the array looks like

a(ℓ)	a(k-1)	a(k)	a(k+1)	a(u)
$\leq$a(k)			>a(k)	

The value initially in a(ℓ) will end up in a(k); this is
used as the "pivot" value. The main loop has the invariant relation:

a(ℓ)	a(n)	a(k)	a(u)
a(ℓ)	unknown values	>a(ℓ)	

When the loop halts the array looks like

a(ℓ)	a(k)	a(n)	a(u)
$\leq$a(ℓ)		>a(ℓ)	

and we need only swap values of a(ℓ) and a(k) to yield
the desired result.

```
n := ℓ+1; k := u;
while (n≤k) do

/* decrease k or increase n, keeping relation invariant */

    if a(n) ≤ a(ℓ)
      then n := n+1
      else while (a(k) > a(ℓ)) do k := k-1 od;
           if n<k then a := swap(a,n,k);
                       n := n+1; k := k-1 fi
    fi
od;
a := swap(a,ℓ,k)
```

Questions concerning the program

Is it advisable to simplify the algorithm somewhat by unnesting the loops and writing for the first loop *while* a(n) ≤ a(ℓ) *do* n := n+1 *od*?

Could we leave out the assignment n := n+1 after the swap and still have a correct algorithm?

Is it really necessary to test n<k before the swap?

Is a(k) ≤ a(ℓ) when we leave the main loop? Is it necessary to know whether a(k) < a(ℓ) or a(ℓ) < a(k)?

Can the conclusion be established after the final swap using a simple substitution rule for subscripted variables rather than our array rules?

partition:

```
procedure(a,ℓ,u,k,b);
    integer array a;
    integer array b readonly;
    integer ℓ,u readonly;
    integer k;
    define permutes(p,a,b,m,n) =
            m≤n & dom(a,m) & dom(a,n) & dom(b,m) & dom(b,n) &
            lbound(p,1) = m & hbound(p,1) = n &
            ∀ integer i,j where dom(p,i) & dom(p,j) .
            (dom(p,p(i)) & (p(i) = p(j) => i=j))
            ∀ integer k where dom(p,k) . b(p(k)) = a(k);
```

```
define perm(a,b,m,n) = ∃ integer array p .
        permutes(p,a,b,m,n);
define same(a,b,m,n) = ∀ integer j where dom(a,j) &
        ¬(m≤j≤n) . a(j)=b(j);
assume perm(a,b,ℓ,u) & same(a,b,ℓ,u) &
        lbound(a,1)≤ℓ≤u≤hbound(a,1);
```

/* Partition a into two parts, lower, upper, such that
   indices in lower satisfy a(j) ≤ pivot and indices in
   upper satisfy pivot ≤ a(j). Pick pivot value (arbitrarily) as a(ℓ). After partitioning, put pivot in
   a(k) to permit a simple description */

```
conclude ℓ≤k≤u & ∀ integer i,j where (ℓ≤j≤k & k<i≤u) .
                a(j) ≤ a(k) & a(k) < a(i) &
                perm(a,b,ℓ,u) & same(a,b,ℓ,u);
define lower(n,p) = ∀ integer j where ℓ≤j<n . a(j) ≤ p;
define upper(n,p) = ∀ integer j where n<j≤u . p<a(j);
define dom(a,k) = lbound(a,1)≤k≤hbound(a,1);

n := ℓ+1  /* n is upper bound index of lower */
k := u    /* k is lower bound index of upper */
al := a(ℓ)  /* al is the pivot value */
```

first main step: ; /* attain lower(k+1,al) & upper(k+1,al)
which is a partition of a. Do this by increasing the
boundaries of lower and upper until they meet. Only
(u-ℓ)+1 steps are taken since each element of the array
is examined only once. */

```
define
main invariants = ℓ≤n≤k+1 & ℓ≤k≤u & lower(n,al)
                & upper(k,al) & perm(a,b,ℓ,u) &
                same(a,b,ℓ,u);
```

/* prove main invariants */

```
    n≤k+1 by arith, n=ℓ+1, ℓ≤u, u=k;
    proof arb integer i where ℓ≤i<n; i=ℓ by arith, ℓ≤i<ℓ+1;
                        a(ℓ) ≤ al qed;
    proof arb integer i where k<i≤u; false by arith, u<i≤u;
    qed; upper(k,al);
    main invariants;  /* by & introduction */
```

```
/* for the main loop termination, the value (u-ℓ)+1
   decreases */

   (u-ℓ)+1≥0 by arith, ℓ≤u;
   (u-ℓ) < (u-ℓ)+1 by arith;
   ∃ integer i . (i≥0 & k-n<i) by ∃I;
/* attain n=k+1 & lower(n,a1) & upper(k+1,a1) &
   perm(a,b,ℓ,u) */

   while (n≤k) do
           assume main_invariants;
           arbitrary integer i where k-n<i;
           ¬(k-n)<0 by arith, n≤k;   /* from loop conditions */
           /* examine next element of the array and determine
              in which partition it belongs */

           if (a(n)≤a1)
           then  /* we know a(n) belongs in lower */
                 lower(n+1,a1) by lemma_lower(a,n,a1,ℓ);
                 k-(n+1)<i-1 by arith, k-n<i;
                 n+1 ≤ k+1 by arith, n≤k;
                 n := n+1
           else  /* we know a(n) belongs in upper, try to find
                    an element that belongs to lower to ex-
                    change with it by expanding upper as far as
                    possible (decreasing k until a(k) ≤ a(ℓ),
                    which takes at most (k-ℓ)+1 steps */

                 /* establish termination for search */
                 (k-ℓ)+1≥0 by arith, ℓ≤k;
                 (k-ℓ) < (k-ℓ)+1 by arith;
                 ∃ integer i . (i≥0 & k-ℓ≤i) by ∃I;
     while (a(k)>a1) do
           assume ℓ≤k≤u & upper(k) & n≤k+1;
           arbitrary integer d where k-ℓ ≤ d;
           a(k)≠a(ℓ) => k≠ℓ;
           a(k)≠a(ℓ) by arith, a(k)>a1;
           ¬(k-ℓ)<0 by arith, ℓ≤k, k≠ℓ;
           upper(k-1,a1) by lemma_upper(a,k,a1,u);
           ℓ<k by arith, ℓ≤k, ℓ≠k;
           ℓ≤k-1 by arith, ℓ<k;

           /* show n≤k+1 is preserved since a(k)>a1 */
```

```
      proof assume a(k)>al;
            proof assume -(n≤k);
            a(k)≤al by ∀E, lower(n);
            qed
      qed
      a(k)>al => n≤k;
      n≤k;
      n≤(k-1)+1 by arith, n≤k;

      /* d decreases */
      (k-1)-ℓ <= d-1 by arith, k-ℓ≤d;
      k := k-1
   od;
   a(k)≤al & ℓ≤k≤u & upper(k) & n≤k+1;
   a(k)<a(n) by arith, a(k)≤al, a(k)>al;
/* attain main_invariants */
/* see whether upper and lower now overlap */

if (n<k)
   then  /* we know upper and lower are disjoint */
         /* a(n) belongs in upper, a(k) belongs in lower
            so swap values */

         proof arb integer i where ℓ≤j<n;
               j≠n by arith, j<n;
               j≠k by arith, j<n, n<k;
               swap(a,k,n)(j) = a(j);
               a(j) ≤ al by ∀E, lower(n)
         qed
         ∀ integer i where ℓ≤j<n . swap(a,k,n)(j) ≤ al;
         proof arb integer i where n<j≤u;
               j≠n by arith, n<j;
               j=k ∨ j≠k by arith;
               proof assume j=k; swap(a,k,n)(j) = a(n);
               al < a(n); al < swap(a,k,n)  qed;
               proof assume j≠k; swap(a,k,n(j) = a(j);
                     al < a(j) by ∀E, upper(k)  qed;
               swap(a,k,n)(j) > al by ∀E
         qed
         ∀ integer i where n<j≤u . al < swap(a,k,n)(j);
```

```
                perm(swap(a,k,n),b,ℓ,u) by perm_lemma 1
                    (a,b,k,n,ℓ,u);
                same(swap(a,k,n),b,ℓ,u) by same_lemma 1
                    (a,b,k,n,ℓ,n);
                a := swap(a,k,n);
                perm(a,k,ℓ,u) & same(a,b,ℓ,u);
                lower(n+1,a1) by lemma_lower(a,n,a1,ℓ);
                upper(k-1,a1) by lemma_upper(a,k,a1,u);
                (k-1)-(n+1) < i-1 by arith, k-n<i;
                k-1 ≤ u by arith, k≤u;
                ℓ≤k-1 by arith, ℓ≤n<k;
                n+1≥ℓ by arith, ℓ≤n;
                n+1≤k+1 by arith, n<k;
            n := n+1; k := k-1;
        else /* we know upper and lower overlap, thus a(n)
                 is already moved into upper.  We only need to
                 establish termination. */

                a(k)≠a(n) => k≠n;
                k<n by arith, k≤n, k≠n;
                k-n<0 by arith, k-n,-,u;
                0<n-k by arith, k<n,-,k;
                k-n<n-k by arith, k-n<0,0≤0,0<n-k;
                k-n<i-1 by arith, k-n<n-k, n-k<i
fi
od
 main_invariants & n>k & n≤k+1;
 n=k+1 by arith, n>k,n≤k+1;
 lower(k+1,a1) & upper(k+1,a1);

second_main_step:   /* make technical adjustments to attain
conclusion; put pivot in a(k), adjust bounds in lower
from <n to ≤n. */

proof arb integer j where ℓ≤j≤k;
        swap(a,k,ℓ)(k) = a1;
        proof assume j=k; swap(a,k,ℓ)(j) = a1 qed;
        proof assume j=ℓ; swap(a,k,ℓ)(j) = a(k);
            a(k) ≤ a(ℓ) by ∀E, lower(k+1,a1) qed
        proof assume j≠k & j≠ℓ;
            swap(a,k,ℓ)(j) = a(j);
            a(j) ≤ a1 by ∀E, lower(k+1,a1) qed
        j=k ∨ j=ℓ ∨ j≠k & j≠ℓ;
        swap(a,k,ℓ)(j) ≤ swap(a,k,ℓ)(k)
qed
∀ integer j where ℓ≤j≤k . swap(a,k,ℓ)(j) ≤ swap(a,k,ℓ)(k);
```

∀ *integer j where* k<j≤u . swap(a,k,ℓ)(k) < swap(a,k,ℓ)(j)
 by lemma (exercise for reader);

FL: ∀ *integer j where* ℓ≤j≤k . a(j) ≤ a(k);
FU; ∀ *integer i where* k<i≤u . a(k) < a(i);
     perm(swap(a,k,ℓ),b,ℓ,u) by perm_lemma 1(a,k,ℓ,ℓ,u);
     same(swap(a,k,ℓ),b,ℓ,u) by same_lemma 1(a,k,ℓ,ℓ,u);
     a := swap(a,k,ℓ);

/* establish final conclusion */

        proof arb integer i,j *where* (ℓ≤j≤k & k<i≤u);
            a(j) ≤ a(k) *by* ∀E,FL;
            a(k) < a(i) *by* ∀E,FU
        qed;
        ∀ *integer* i,j *where* (ℓ≤j≤k & k<i≤u) . (a(j) ≤ a(k)
                            & a(k) < a(i));

lemma lower:

procedure(a,n,al,ℓ);
    integer array a *readonly*;
    integer a,al,ℓ *readonly*;
    define lower(n,al) = ∀ *integer j where* ℓ≤j<n .
                                        a(j) ≤ al;
    assume lower(n,al) & a(n)≤al;
    conclude lower(n+1,al);
    proof arbitrary integer j *where* ℓ≤j<n+1;
        j<n ∨ j=n *by arith*, j<n+1;
        proof assume j<n;
            a(j)≤ al by ∀E, lower(n,al)   *qed*
        proof assume j=n;
            a(j)≤al   /* since a(n)≤al is given */ *qed*;
        a(j)≤al *by* ∀E;
    lower(n+1,al)
end lemma_lower;

lemma_upper:

procedure (a,k,ℓ,u);

The reader can fill in the dozen lines of proof by following the example of lemma_lower.

end lemma_upper;

same_lemma 1:

procedure (a,b,i,j,ℓ,u);
    integer array a,b *readonly*;
    integer i,j,ℓ,u *readonly*;

/* same, dom are externally defined */

assume same(a,b,ℓ,u);
      dom(a,ℓ) & dom(a,u);
       ℓ≤i≤u & ℓ≤j≤u;
conclude same(swap(a,i,j),ℓ,u);
proof arbitrary integer k *where* (dom(a,k) & ¬(ℓ≤k≤u));
            k≠i *by arith*, ℓ≤i≤u, & ¬(ℓ≤k≤u);
            k≠j *by arith*, ℓ≤j≤u, & ¬(ℓ≤k≤u);
            swap(a,i,j)(k) = a(k);
            a(k) = b(k) *by* ∀E, same(a,b,ℓ,u)
qed;
same(swap(a,i,j),b,ℓ,u)
end same_lemma 1

7.4 ARRAYS WITH PROCEDURES AND FUNCTIONS

In Algol-like languages, e.g. PL/I which prohibit functions from returning arrays, procedures are essential for computing with arrays. They are the only mechanism for constructing new operations on arrays.

Our treatment of procedures with arrays is rendered very elementary by imposing one restriction: *array elements* (*subscripted variables*) *cannot be passed as read-write parameters to a procedure.* With this restriction, the *rules for procedures are just as in Chapter V,* and the rule for functions is just as in Chapter VI (of course the restriction is irrelevant for functions).

In order to appreciate the value of this restriction, the reader can compare the simple procedure rule of Chapter V to the more complex rule of part VI of the PL/CV manual in the Appendix. In PL/CV, array elements can be readwrite actual parameters and provisos 1 and 3 of the PROCEDURE CALL rule are needed to provide a sound rule.

The difficulty caused by array elements as readwrite parameters is illustrated by this simple example.

p_0: *procedure* (x,y);
    integer x,y;
    arbitrary integer x.,y. *where* $x=x_0, y=y_0$;
    x := x+1;
    y := y+1;
    return
    end p_0

We can prove that for all distinct x,y, after the call, $x=x_0+1$ and $y=y_0+1$. In Chapter V, we have avoided the problem of what to conclude after calling $p_0(a,a)$ (the conclusions $a=a_0+1$ is wrong of course) by not allowing such a call. In the case of arrays the same restriction would disallow $p_0(a(i),a(j))$ when $i \neq j$. (Now this condition would be more difficult to check, requiring a proof.)

A more subtle problem occurs in a form unique to arrays. Consider the call $p(i,a(i))$. The normal substitution rule would allow us to wrongly conclude that $a(i) = y_0+1$.

example

The recursive sorting algorithm *quicksort* illustrates the use of arrays with recursive procedures. Quicksort calls the partitioning algorithm of section (7.3). Indeed, the partitioning is central to the algorithm. Moreover the proof uses several lemmas built up in other sections of the chapter. This is typical of mathematical development. The specialized arguments of program correctness are built on general lemmas and elementary theorems about their components.

A Programming Logic

quicksort:

procedure (a,m,n);

/* This procedure recursively sorts the integer array a
in the segment from m to n into increasing order by
partitioning a into two parts and sorting each part
separately. */

    integer array a;
    integer m,n;

/* perm and same are as defined the partition program */

    define sorted(a,m,n) = (dom(a,m) & dom(a,n)) &
        ∀ *integer* i,j *where* m≤i≤n & m≤j≤n .
         a(i)<a(j) => i<j;
    arbitrary integer array b, *integer* d *where* d≥0;
    assume perm(a,b,m,n) & same(a,b,m,n)
        & lbound(a,1)≤m≤n≤hbound(a,1)
        & n+1-m≤d;
    conclude same(a,b,m,n) & perm(a,b,m,n) & sorted(a,m,n);
    integer k;
    integer. array c_1,c_2;

/* same(a,b,m,n) and perm(a,b,m,n) are invariants of
the procedure as well as conclusions */

    if n≤m
    then   /* the segment m,n has zero or one elements and
            is by definition already sorted */
        perm(a,b,m,n) & same(a,b,m,n);
        proof arbitrary integer i,j *where* (m≤i≤n & m≤j≤n);
            n<m ∨ m=n;
            proof assume n<m;
                false *by arith,* m≤n, n<m *qed;*
            proof assume m=n;
                i=m *by arith,* m≤i≤n, m=n;
                j=m *by arith,* m≤j≤n, m=n;
                ¬(a(i)<a(j))
            qed;
            a(i)<a(j) => i<j *by* VE
        qed
        sorted(a,m,n);
        return
    fi

244

```
m<n;
if n = m+1
then  /* the segment m,n contains precisely two elements,
          a(m), a(n). */

      if a(m)<a(n) then  /* array segment is sorted  */
                  perm(a,b,m,n) & same(a,b,m,n);

                  /* prove that a is sorted */

                  proof arbitrary integer i,j where
                      (m≤i≤n & m≤j≤n);
                  i=m ∨ i=m+1 by arith, m≤i≤n, n=m+1;
                  j=m ∨ j=m+1 by arith, m≤j≤n, n=m+1;
                  proof assume a(i)<a(j);
                      proof assume i=m qed;
                      proof assume i=m+1;
                          j=m => false;
                          j=m+1 => false qed;
                      i=m by VE;
                      j=m+1 => j=m+1;
                      j=m => false;
                      j=m+1 by VE;
                      i<j
                  qed;
                  sorted(a,m,n);
                  return
                  else

                  /* establish invariants */

                  perm(swap(a,m,n),b,m,n) &
                      same(swap(a,m,n),b,m,n) by
                      perm_lemma(a,b,m,n);
                  sorted(swap(a,m,n),m,n) by
                      same_lemma(a,b,m,n);
                  a := swap(a,m,n);
                  return
      fi
```

```
    perm(a,b,m,n) & same(a,b,m,n);
    lbound(a,1)≤m & hbound(a,1)≥n;
    m+1<n;
    define split(a,k) = V integer i,j where (m≤i≤k & k<j≤n)
                          . (a(i)≤a(k) & a(k)<a(j)));
    call partition(a,m,n,k,b);
    m≤k≤n;
    split(a,k);  /* from partition procedure array a is
                      split into two parts by a(k) */
    perm(a,b,m,n) & same(a,b,m,n);  /* from partition
                                       procedure */
    k+1-m>0 by arith, m≤k;  /* arguments permit recursive
                                call */
    c₁ := a;  /* save values of a */

    perm(a,c₁,m,n) by perm_lemma 2:  (see note 3)

    perm(c₁,b,m,n) & same(c₁,b,m,n) & split(c₁,k);/*by eq-
                                                    uality*/
```

/* sort the lower partition of a */

```
    assume call quicksort(a,m,k-1) for quicksort;
    assume same(a,b,m,k-1) & same(a,c₁,m,k-1) for
     quicksort; /* induction hypothesis */
    assume perm(a,b,m,k-1) & perm(a,c₁,m,k-1) for
     quicksort; /* induction hypothesis */
    assume sorted(a,m,k-1) for quicksort;
```

/* we must prove split(a,k) by reference to c₁ */

```
    proof arbitrary integer i,j where m≤i≤k & k<j≤n;

        /* a subtle point of this program is that a(k)
           does not change on the call to quicksort; we
           use it here */

        ¬(m≤k≤k-1) by arith, k-1<k;
         a(k)=c₁(k) by VE, same(a,c₁,m,k-1);
        ¬(m≤j≤k-1) by arith, k<j;
         a(j)=c₁(j) by VE, same(a,c₁,m,k-1);
         a(k)<a(j);
```

```
        i≤k-1 ∨ i=k by arith, i≤k;
        proof assume i≤k-1;
              choose integer array p where
               permutes(p,a,c,m,k-1);
              a(i)=c₁(p(i)) by VE, permutes(p,a,c,m,k-1);

              p(i)≤k-1;
              c₁(p(i))≤c₁(k) by VE, split(c₁,k);

              a(i)≤a(k)
        qed;
        proof assume i=k;
              a(i)≤a(k);
        qed;
        a(i)≤a(k) by VE
   qed;
   split(a,k);
   c₂ := a;   /* same values of a */
   split(c₂,k);
/* establish the invariants */

   perm(a,b,m,n) by perm_lemma 3; (see note 2)
   same(a,b,m,n) by same_lemma 3; (see note 2)
   m+1-k>0 by arith, k≤n;

/* sort the upper partition of a */

   assume call quicksort(a,k+1,n) for quicksort;
   assume same(a,c₂,m,k) & same(a,b,m,k) for quicksort;

   assume perm(a,c₂,k+1,n) & perm(a,b,k+1,n) for quicksort;

   assume sorted(a,k+1,n) for quicksort;

/* we must prove sorted(a,m,n) by a case analysis on
   the distribution of indices over the partitions; both
   indices in the same partition or not in the same
   partition */

   proof arbitrary integer i,j where m≤i≤n & m≤j≤n;
         proof assume a(i)<a(j);

         /* goal: show i<j */

              j≤k ∨ k<j by arith;
              i≤k ∨ k<i by arith;
```

```
            /* case analysis on j */
                proof assume j≤k;
                    proof assume i≤k;   /* both indices in lower
                                            partition */
                        i<j by VE, sorted(a,m,k) qed;
                    proof assume k<i;   /* j in lower, i in
                                            upper which is con-
                                            tradictory */
                        k+1≤i;
                        choose integer array p where
                         permutes(p,a,c₂,k+1,n);
                        a(i)=c₂(p(i)) & k+1≤p(i)≤n;
                        a(j)=c₂(j) by VE,same(a,c₂,m,k);
                        c₂(j)<c₂(p(i)) by VE,split(c₂,k);
                        a(j)<a(i);
                        false by arith, a(i)<a(j), a(j)<a(i)
                        qed
                    i<j by VE
                qed
                proof assume k<j;   /* j in upper partition */
                    k+1≤j;
                    proof assume k<i;   /* i and j in upper
                                            partition */
                        k+1≤i; i<j by VE,sorted(a,k+1,n);
                    qed;
                    proof assume i≤k;   /* i in lower, j in
                                            upper */
                        i<j by arith, i≤k, k<j
                    qed
                    i<j by VE
                qed
        qed;
        sorted(a,m,n);
        perm(a,b,m,n) by perm_lemma 3; (see note 2)
        same(a,b,m,n) by same_lemma 3; (see note 2)
        return
  end quicksort
```

Note 1: The proof of perm(swap(a,m,n),b,m,n) is by our general lemma on permutations in (7.3); the proof of same(swap(a,m,n),b,m,n) follows an even simpler pattern and is a general lemma, not a fact specific to this program.

Note 2: The proof of perm(a,b,m,n) from perm(a,b,m,k-1) and same(a,b,m,k-1) is a general lemma not specific to this program. The problem was treated in exercise (7-12).

Note 3: The proof of (perm(a,b,m,n) & a=c) => perm(a,c,m,n) is a simple general fact about permutations covered in exercise (7-13).

Remarks: The proof of the quicksort program is almost unbearably tedious in this system. We must argue about properties of the program in ways that do not correspond to our intuitions. The difficulties stem from two sources, programming language limitations and proof rule limitations. For instance, the proof and its notation would be simpler if the programming language allowed sections of an array to be treated as a new array. We could then pass the sections a(m:k-1) and a(k+1:n) to quicksort and dispense with the predicate same and the arguments using it.

More fundamentally, the entire issue of proving that a is a permutation of its initial value should be treated in the extended programming logic ([Constable 77a,77b]) rather than in the asserted program logic of this monograph. Instead of proving that perm(a,b,m,n) is an invariant at each step, we could argue that certain classes of programs have the property that they do not add to or delete from an array but only permute it. We would then establish that partition and quicksort were programs of this class.

Such a logic has been developed and will eventually become part of our verification system. Explaining it will add more chapters to an already long account of elementary program verification. See CONCLUSION for further discussion of this matter.

A Programming Logic

7.5   INPUT AND OUTPUT

discussion

   We present here a very simple and tentative approach
to input and output. It is not intended to be a definition
treatment. Rather it allows the reader to prove the
correctness of very simple programs involving input and
output.
   We take the view that the input file is a *sequence*
of *simple values*. It is thus very similar to an array
(except that it may contain several distinct types). The
output file is also considered such a sequence. The
input file is *readonly* and the output file is "write
only." Obviously with such a simple view of input and
ourput, we do not consider the issue of formats.
   There are even in this simple approach some subtle
points. One concerns the domain of the input file. How
do we know when we have reached the end of the file?
For input from devices such as card readers or tapes this
is normally solved by an *end of file* marker, but input
from a user terminal is not treated in the same way. For
such inputs, it is not obvious how to handle the issue
of the proper termination of the program. In this monograph we will only treat the case in which the user provides
an explicit means of determining the end of file. But
we will not use the handy PL/I ON CONDITIONS for this
purpose. Instead the programmer must specify the file
size or designate the final value.
   Another subtle point is that assertions in the program
need global access to variables describing the position of
the reading head in the input file (called *in*) and the
writing head in the output file (called *out*). These
variables must be external variables to all procedures
(functions in PL/CS cannot perform input/output operations).

syntax

   We add to the class of expressions as follows.

            file functions   →   *input*
                                       output
            position predicates →   *in*
                                       out

The type of input and output is *integer* → (*integer*, *string*,*boolean*). The position predicates have type *integer* → *boolean*. Expressions are formed in the usual way. None of these constants are allowed among the boolean expressions (i.e. none are program constants).
We add the new commnads

$$\text{I/0 commands} \rightarrow read \; (\{\text{variable,subscripted variable}\}^+)$$
$$write \; (\{\text{variable,subscripted variable}\}^+)$$

semantics

Let $\mathbb{N} = \{1,2,3,\ldots\}$.

The meaning of a file function is a function (finite or infinite) from positive integers to values. Thus

$$\mathcal{M}(input) \; : \; \mathbb{N} \rightarrow \text{Values}$$
$$\mathcal{M}(output) \; : \; \mathbb{N} \rightarrow \text{Values}$$

The meaning of *in* and *out* are predicates on the integers (giving position in the file).

$$\mathcal{M}(in) \; : \; \mathbb{N} \rightarrow \text{Boolean}$$
$$\mathcal{M}(out) \; : \; \mathbb{N} \rightarrow \text{Boolean}$$

The read and write commands modify the state and the position predicates given the state, the input file and the position predicates. Since they must modify both the state and the position predicate, they have two components. The first component of the *read*(x) command (x a simple variable) produces a new state. The equation is:

$$(\;\mathcal{M}[\![\; read(x)\;]\!](s,input,in))\; state(y) =$$
$$\begin{cases} input(n) & \text{if } y=x \text{ and } n \text{ is the unique integer for which } in(n) \text{ is true and the type of } x \text{ matches the type of } input(n) \\ s(y) & \text{if } y \neq x \end{cases}$$

If the type of x and input(n) do not match, then the new value of x is arbitrary.
The second component produces a new position predicate as follows:

$$(\mathcal{M}[\![\; read \;]\!](s,input,in))\; predicate(y) =$$
$$\begin{cases} in(n-1) & \text{if } n-1 \geq 1 \\ false & \text{otherwise} \end{cases}$$

251

A Programming Logic

Note, the meaning of $read(x_1,\ldots,x_n)$ is the same as the meaning of $read(x_1);\ldots;read(x_n)$.

The first component of the meaning of the write com-cand produces a new state as follows:

$(\mathcal{M}\llbracket write(x) \rrbracket (s,output,out))$ state(n) =
$$\begin{cases} s(x) & \text{if } n \text{ is the unique integer such} \\ & \text{that } out(n) \\ output(n) & \text{otherwise} \end{cases}$$

The second component, which produces a new position predicate satisfies:

$(\mathcal{M}\llbracket write(x) \rrbracket (s,output,out))$ predicate(n) =
$$\begin{cases} out(n-1) & \text{if } n-1 \geq 1 \\ false & \text{otherwise} \end{cases}$$

The meaning of $write(x_1,\ldots,x_n)$ is the same as the meaning of $write(x_1);\ldots;write(x_n)$.

None of these equations apply when x or x_i is any array variable.

proof rules

The proof rules for read and write commands are quite simple, namely:

$$\frac{read(x_1,\ldots,x_p), \; in(n)}{x_1 = input(n) \& \ldots \& x_p = input(n+p-1) \; \& \; in(n+p)}$$

provided $x_1,\ldots,x_p$ are distinct simple variables.

$$\frac{write(x_1,\ldots,x_p), \; out(n)}{output(n) = x_1 \& \ldots \& output(n+p-1) = x_p \; \& \; out(n+p)}$$

(the x_i need not be distinct).

We also need a rule stating that $in(1)$ and $out(1)$ initially (before any read or write operations) in the main procedure

procedure
$in(1)$

procedure
$out(1)$

252

example

Here is a routine example showing how the input/output axioms are used. The program first reads an integer n and then reads a sequence of n integers. The output is the square of these integers. The type declarations of the variables are assumptions about the inputs which must be satisfied for the program to be correct. They have the status of input assumptions.

```
square:   procedure;
          integer x,n,i;
          conclude V integer i where 2≤i≤input(i) .
          output(i) = input(i)²;
          in(1);
          read(n);
          input(1) = n;
          out(1);
          write(n);
          output(1) = n;
          in(2) & out(2) & V integer k where 2≤k<2.
          output(k) = input(k)²;
          for j=2 to n do
              assume in=j & out=j & V integer j where
                  2≤k<j . output(k) = input(k)²;
              read(x);
              x = input(j);
              in(j+1);
              write(x²);
              x² = output(j);
              in(j+1);
              out(j+1);
              output(k) = input(k)²;
          od
          end square
```

7.6 EXERCISES

Section (7.1)

(7-1) Give examples from your programming experience showing the wide variety of structured data that can be represented as arrays, e.g. trees, graphs, character strings, chess boards, payroll accounts, personnel records, etc.

(7.2) Enumerate advantages and disadvantages of treating
arrays as new data objects rather than as finite functions.
Discuss how functions could also be viewed as new data
objects thereby giving a first order representation of
second order logic.

(7-3) Explore the idea (mentioned also in Chapter VI)
that an array (for simplicity a 1 array) is always a

total function $\mathbf{Z} \to$ Values. The domain of the array is
simply a computational property associated with the array.
We need to verify that dom(a,i) before a(i) can be used
in any command, but not before a(i) is used in an assertion. Thus a(i)= a(i) is always true. When an array is
declared and initialized, its values outside the initial
domain are arbitrary (in PL/C, PL/CS, PL/CV they are 0
for integer arrays, blank for string arrays and '1'B for
bit arrays.)

Section 7.2

(7-4) Parse each of these expressions and if possible assign
the appropriate types to them given the initial type information. Some expressions, such as a(x), are type incorrect.

    dcl integer 2 array a,b,c
    dcl boolean array e,f,g

    e(a(x,y),c(a(x,y),z))
    h(e(x),b(x,y))
    e(x) & f(y)
    k(a,x,y)
    a(k(a,x,y),z)

(7-5) Which of the following are legal type symbols.

    boolean array(1:3,2:7)
    integer array(3,2:0)
    boolean array array(1:2,1:5)
    string array(3,5)
    string array
    integer 2 array
    boolean 2 array(3:5,7:9)
    integer array(n:m)
    integer m array

(7-6) Which of these assertions is valid according to the
semantics of (7.2)?

∀ *integer* n .∀ *boolean array*(10) a . (a(n) = *true* ∨
a(n) = *false*)

∀ *integer* n *where* 1≤n≤10 .∀ *boolean array*(10) a .
(a(n) = *true* ∨ a(n) = *false*)

∀ *integer array* a . ∀ *integer* n . a(n) = a(n)

∀ *integer array*(10)a . ∀ *integer* n . a(n)=a(n) =>
1≤n≤10

∀ *integer array* a . ∃ *integer* ℓ,u .∀ *integer* j .
(a(j)=a(j) <=> ℓ≤j≤u)

(7-7) Show how to use array quantification to express
the fact that a set is finite. Can you think of a way to
say this in the predicate calculus of Chapter II.?

(7-8) Prove the following valid formulas.

∀ *integer* n *where* 1≤n≤10 . ∀ *boolean array*(10) a .
(a(n) = *true* ∨ a(n) = *false*)

¬∃ *integer array* a . ∀ *integer* n . a(n)=0

(7-9) One might want to consider initializing arrays
when they are declared, as in

dcl integer array(1:7) a *where* a := 5.

One is tempted to try initializations such as

dcl integer array(1:7) a *where* a(2)=5 &
∀ *integer* j *where* 1≤j≤7 & j≠2 . a(j)=0.

What are the dangers of such initializations?

Section 7.3

(7-10) Can you formulate conditions under which the rule

$$\frac{P(exp/x)}{a(i) := exp}$$

$$P(a(i)/x)$$

is valid? That is, when can array values be treated as
subscripted variables?

(7-11) Show that same(a,b,m,n) and (m≤i≤n & m≤j≤n) imply same (swap(a,i,j)b,m,ṅ).

(7-12) Show that perm(a,b,ℓ,k) and n≤hbound(a,1) & same(a,b,ℓ,k) imply perm(a,b,ℓ,n).

(7-13) Show that perm(a,b,ℓ,u) & b=c implies perm(a,c,ℓ,u).

(7-14) Show that perm(a,b,ℓ,u) <=> perm(b,a,ℓ,u).

(7-15) Show that perm(a,b,ℓ,u) and perm(b,c,ℓ,u) imply perm(a,c,ℓ,u).

(7-16) Prove

$$n<m => perm(a,b,m,n).$$

(7-17) Suppose integer arrays a(1:n) and b(1:m) are sorted in ascending order. Sort them into a combined array c(1:n+m).

(7-18) Write an argument for the problem of finding the first index of an array such that a(i)>n for some given n.

(7-19) Write an argument for the problem of putting the componentwise maximum of integer arrays a and b into a i.e. a(i) = max(a(i),b(i)).

(7-20) Write an argument to show how to take a sequence of inputs of the form <name,integer> and use them to update the bank accounts of a data base, stored as a sequence <name,integer>. The input integer is to be added to the account integer (the balance), if the balance becomes negative, then the name should be listed in a file of delinquent accounts.

(7-21) Here is a program to search for the value true in a boolean array. Try to prove it correct. What is the error in the program?

```
search:   procedure(b,i);
          dcl boolean array b readonly;
          dcl integer u,i;
          u := hbound(b,1);
          while (i≤u & ¬b(i)) do i=i+1 od
      end
```

The claim is that if i=u+1 then b(i) contains no true value.

(7-22) Write an argument to reverse the order of an array. Prove it is correct. (Compare this to a recursive version used in part VI of the Appendix.)

(7-23) The *median* value in an array of integers, a(1:n), is that value such that half the values are greater and half are less. Write an argument to compute the median. (Note, there is a very sophisticated linear time algorithm for this problem, see [Aho,Hopcroft,Ullman 74].)

(7-24) Write an argument to compute in array c the product of two n×n integer matrices a,b. Thus

$$c(i,k) = \sum_{j=1}^{n} a(i,j)*b(j,k).$$

(7-25) Suppose we have an array a(1:n) which contains only the values 1,2,3. Suppose we want to sort it using only swap(a,i,j). Write a program that does this correctly. (A variant of this problem is called the Dutch national flag problem when the values are the colors red, white, and blue.)

(7-26) Develop an argument for the *line justifier* program (discussed in "An Illustration of Current Ideas on the Derivation of Correctness Proofs and Correct Programs," *IEEE Trans. on Software Engineering*, vol SE-2,4, Dec. 1976, 238-244 by David Gries). The line justifier must insert blanks between the words on a line so that the last character of the last word appears in the rightmost column. Moreover, the number of blanks between different pairs of words should differ by at most one. For example,

```
        justifyingƀlinesƀby
        insertingƀextraƀblanksƀis
```

becomes

```
        justifyingƀƀƀƀlinesƀƀƀƀƀby
        insertingƀƀextraƀblanksƀis
```

In order to make the text look uniform, the extra blanks are inserted in an alternating manner. Say on odd(even) lines more blanks are inserted toward the right(left) of the line.

We want an algorithm which takes the column numbers where the words begin in the unjustified line and produces numbers where they begin on the justified line.

(7-27) Develop an argument for listing the first n prime numbers based on the method of the Sieve of Eratosthenes. The following program should do the computation.

```
        sieve: procedure;
        integer x, square,i,k,lim;
        integer array p,v;
        boolean prim;
        p(1) := 2; x := 1; lim := 1; square := 4;
        for i=1 to n do
           repeat
             x := x+2;
             if square≤x
                then v(lim) := square;
                     lim := lim+1;
                     square := p(lim)*p(lim) fi;
             k := 2; prim := true;
             while (prim & k<lim) do
                if v(k)<x
                   then v̇(k) := v(k)+p(k);
                        if x≠v(k) then prim := true
                                  else prim := false fi fi od
           until prim;
         p(i) := x;
        end sieve
```

(7-28)   Show that the following program solves the Dutch
national flag sorting problem of exercise (7-25).

```
nl := 1; fu := 1; lu := n
dutch:  while (fu≤lu) do
        if a(fu) = 1
        then swap(a,nl,fu);
             fu := fu+1;
             nl := nl+1
        else if a(fu) = 2 then fu = fu+1
                          else swap(a,fu,lu);
                               lu := lu-1
                fi
            fi
        od
```

Section 7.4

(7-29)   Since swap is a basic array function it is
interesting to observe how it behaves with respect to a
more conventional swap procedure. Here is the outline of
such a procedure which the reader can expand to an argument.

```
exchange:  procedure(a,i,j);
           dcl integer array a;
           dcl integer i,j,t;
           arbitrary integer array b;
           assume dom(a,i) & dom(a,j) & a=b;
           conclude a = swap(b,i,j);
           t := a(i);
           a := alt(a,i,a(j));
           a := alt(a,j,t)
end exchange
```

(7-30)   If we consider a procedure call as a concurrent
assignment a,b,c := p(a,b,c,x) (as in exercise (5-)   ),
then how should we interpret a(i) := p(a,x), given that
a(i) := exp is only an abbreviation?

(7-31) If subscripted variables were allowed as read-write parameters, how would we avoid the following problem.

```
p:   procedure(x,y);
     assume x=x₀,y=y₀;
     conclude x=x₀+y₀ & y=x₀-y₀;
     x := x+y;
     y := x-y*2;
     return
     end p
```

Given p above, suppose in a main program, i=j and we call p, *call* p(a(i),a(j)). What can we conclude? (See PL/CV procedure rule for an answer.)

(7-32) Searching is a basic programming problem and binary search is one of the most basic techniques for efficient searching. Here is the outline of a binary search argument. The reader should fill in the missing details. The integer division function, div, from Chapter VI is used.

```
search:   procedure(a,x,message,location);
          dcl string array a readonly;
          dcl string x,message;
          dcl integer location,m,n;
```

/* The procedure accepts an ordered array of strings a and a key string x. It searches a for x and returns a message indicating whether x was found and a location where it was found. */

```
define ordered(b) =
V integer i,j where dom(b,i) & dom(b,j)
          b(i)<b(j) => i<j;
define exist =
∃ integer i where dom(a,i) . a(i)=x
define exist(m,n) =
∃ integer i where m≤i≤n . a(i)=x
define found = message='found' & a(location)=x
```

```
assume ordered(a);
conclude exist <=> message='found' &
                  a(location)=x;
ℓ := lbound(a,1);
u := hbound(a,1);
ℓ≤u;
if a(ℓ) = x then message := 'found';
                  location := ℓ;
                  return fi;
if a(u) = x then message := 'found';
                  location := u;
                  return fi;
a(ℓ)≠x & a(u)≠x;
exist => exist(ℓ+1,u-1);
while true do
      arbitrary integer i where u-ℓ<i & ℓ≤u
      -(u-ℓ)< 0;
m := ℓ+div(u-ℓ,2);
n=ℓ => u≤ℓ+1 & ⌐∃ integer i . ℓ<i<u;
if m=ℓ then message := 'not found';
                  location := m;
                  message ≠ 'found';
                  a(location) ≠ x;
                  exist <=> found;
                  return fi
if a(m) = x then message := 'found';
                  location := m;
                  exist <=> found;
                  return fi
a(m) ≠ x;
if x<a(m) then
                  exist => exist(ℓ+1,m-1);
                  u := m;
                  u-ℓ < i-1
                  else x>a(m);
                  exist => exist(m+1,u-1);
                  ℓ := m;
                  u-ℓ < i-1;
                  fi
od
end search
```

A Programming Logic

Section 7.5

(7-33) Write an argument to generate the first n terms
of the Fibonacci sequence, $0,1,1,2,3,5,8, \ldots$ where
$F_{n+2} = F_{n+1} + F_n$.

(7-34) Write an argument to generate the partial sums
of $\sum_{i=1}^{n} i^2$.

(7-35) Consider the following game played by two players
A and B on a rectangular grid of points of any size.

$$
\begin{matrix}
\cdot & \cdot & \cdot & \cdot & \cdot \\
\cdot & \cdot & \cdot & \cdot & \cdot \\
\cdot & \cdot & \cdot & \cdot & \cdot
\end{matrix}
$$

Player A can draw horizontal or **vertical** solid lines
connecting two adjacent dots. He tries to form a
closed figure, as in:

Player B draws dotted horizontal or vertical lines
connecting two adjacent dots. He tries to prevent A from
closing his lines.
    Player B has a simple winning strategy easily ex-
pressed as an invariant of the main playing loop where
the program is player B.

>   *while* there is another move *do*
>   read player A's move
>   generate B's move
>   *end*

Find this invariant and give an argument showing that B
can always win.

See [Conway, Gries 75] p. 331-332 for a further description of the problem.

CONCLUSION

The reader who shares our belief in the value and feasibility of this enterprise will have imagined a plethora of new features, rules and extensions which would improve the utility of the system. These fall into several distinct categories.

(1) Broaden the assertion language to include real numbers, set theory, and functions of higher type.

(2) Build a well organized library of useful theorems and definitions.

(3) Increase the power of the automatic reasoning performed by the proof checker.

(4) Broaden the programming language component, perhaps by including more of PL/I or perhaps by moving to a richer language.

(5) Develop a more general logic of arguments which include commands but are not themselves asserted programs.

(6) Develop a general facility for extending the logic by adding new definitions, axioms and lemmas for special areas of application.

We are examining many of these issues at Cornell. There are interesting ways to combine automatic arithmetic with the immediate rules, and there are interesting ways to permit limited automatic reasoning with quantifiers, but there are serious limitations to extending the automatic rules very far (see [Krafft 78]). Furthermore, we do not judge these rules to be the major weakness of the system.

We are considering carefully the problems of a computational set theory and we are building a library of basic facts and theorems. But there is no effort underway to consider a theory of real numbers or floating point numbers.

We are considering carefully the question of proof rules for a more general class of arguments which allow commands but are not themselves asserted programs. These arguments are well suited to naturally expressing the type of informal program correctness found in [Knuth 68, Aho, Hopcroft, Ullman 74]. The thesis of John Privitera [78] and the paper [Constable 77] consider some of the theoretical issues arising in such logics. When this *extended logic* has been carefully analyzed and tested on paper, then we will consider implementing it as an extension to PL/CV.

APPENDIX

PL/CV2 PROGRAM VERIFIER

REFERENCE MANUAL

Robert L. Constable

Scott D. Johnson

This section of the reference manual is included with the permission of the authors and the Cornell University Computer Science Department.

PREFACE

PL/CV is a logic for reasoning about programs as well as an experimental program verification system. As a logic it offers a foundation for rigorous program development and for informal or formal correctness proofs. PL/CV has been used successfully at Cornell to teach the elements of program verification and modern programming methodology to sophomores as well as graduate students.

As a formal logic, PL/CV is a tool for investigating the theory of programming. It has been studied in that capacity as part of a larger programming logic [1].

The PL/CV Proof Checker provides an elementary but highly flexible basis for program verification. This aspect of the system is experimental. For some problems even the basic system is ideal, for others it is unbearably cumbersome. But users are able to build within PL/CV their own specialized program verification theories. The Proof Checker is fast enough and the rules are simple enough that interested computing groups with limited resources can develop their own experimental theories. We at Cornell have begun such work and will issue periodic progress reports through our Computer Science Technical Report series (see references).

A Programming Logic

OUTLINE

PREFACE

I   INTRODUCTION

Composition of PL/CV system
Purpose of PL/CV system
Plan of the manual

II   THE PREDICATE CALCULUS

§2.1 INTRODUCTION
   1. Arguments
   2. Overview

§2.2 SYNTAX
   0. Conventions
   1. Expressions
       (i) integer expressions   (ii) string ex-
       pressions   (iii) boolean expressions
   2. Assertions
       (i) propositional structure   (ii) quantifiers
   3. Arguments
       (i) proof group   (ii) qualifier   (iii) state-
       ments   (iv) justifications   (v.) declarations
       (vi) arguments   (vii) examples
   4. Type restrictions
       (i) types of basic operators and relators
       (ii) binding occurrences, bound variables
       (iii) types of expressions   (iv) type
       correctness   (v) examples

§2.3 SUBSTITUTIONS
   1. Discussion
       (i) free and bound variables   (ii) substi-
       tution operator   (iii) examples
   2. Capture problem
   3. Macro substitutions

266

ADDENDA
(FINE POINTS not included in the monograph.)

I   INTRODUCTION

The PL/CV system consists of a programming language
and a formal logic. The *programs* are a subset of PL/CS
and can be executed by the PL/CS Compiler. (PL/CS is a
PL/I dialect and is largely upward compatible with PL/C
and PL/I, see [4] for a detailed description.) Formal
arguments in the logic express reasoning about integers,
strings and PL/CS commands. These arguments can be checked
for correctness by the PL/CV Proof Checker. The system
taken as a whole supports a style of formal program verification.

The PL/CV system was designed for elementary instruction in verification oriented programming and in certain
mathematical aspects of programming and computer science -
in particular the application of formal logic to the study
of a program's structure and behavior. PL/CV is part of
a larger logical system which is primarily a research
tool in the investigation of theories of programming.
This aspect is discussed in [1].

This Reference Manual and User's Guide is a brief
account of the PL/CV logical system. It is written for a
reader familiar with the basic elements of mathematical
logic and computer programming at the sophomore level. A
more complete introduction is provided by the monograph,
A Programming Logic, by R.L. Constable and M.J. O'Donnell.
The programming language PL/CS is introduced in *A Primer
on Disciplined Programming* by R.W. Conway.

271

II THE PREDICATE CALCULUS

§2.1 INTRODUCTION

1. Arguments are distinguished from ordinary discourse
by their logical structure. An abstract description of
arguments involves only this structure. The simplest
language adequate for the expression of the abstract logical reasoning found in most mathematical arguments is the
predicate calculus. The PL/CV logic is based on this
predicate calculus.

This section of the manual describes a PL/CV version
of the predicate calculus. The language of the calculus
allows the programmer to express properties of the PL/I
data types, integers, character strings and boolean values.
However, in the predicate calculus he can only deduce the
purely logical facts about these data types, e.g. that
x>0 & y>0 => x>0 but not that x>1 => x>0. (These logical
facts should be contrasted with those of III, the number
theory.) Moreover, he can only write arguments specifically in terms of these data types. So for example, he
cannot use the language of set theory since sets are not
PL/I data types. [†]

2. Overview

The programmer can regard the predicate calculus as
an extension of the set of PL/I boolean expressions
(relations) obtained by adding the *connectives* => (arrow
for implication) and <=> (double arrow for equivalence)
to &,|,¬ and by adding logical operators on boolean ex-
pressions called *quantifiers*. The *existential quantifier*
begins with the keyword SOME (logicians usually begin it
with ∃). The universal quantifier begins with the key
word ALL (logicians usually begin it with ∀).

[†] This particular limitation is sometimes very painful, and
future versions of the PL/CV system should have the set
data type in the assertion language.

§2.2   <u>SYNTAX</u>

0.   <u>Conventions</u>

The syntax of the predicate calculus presents in order
the grammatical categories: *expressions, assertions* and
arguments.

Note: The syntax is specified in two closely related
forms, *syntax charts* and BNF equations.   The forms are not
equivalent in every detail.   For instance, more information
may be presented in the BNF, as in the case of the category
assertions where the BNF shows the right associativity
of =>.

In the BNF syntax, square brackets, [ ], are used to
indicate an optional phrase.   Braces, { }, indicate a group
of words or phrases to be repeated the number of times
given by a superscript; $\{a_1,\ldots,a_n\}^+$ denotes the set of
all finite nonempty strings of a_1 to a_n; $\{a_1,\ldots,a_n\}^*$ is
similar but includes the empty string as well; $\{a_1,\ldots,a_n\}$
abbreviates $\{a_1,\ldots,a_n\}^1$, that is, one of the elements
a_i is chosen.   In the BNF equations, when symbols such as
commas, braces, asterisks, etc. are part of the language being
defined (e.g. terminal characters of the grammar), they are
underlined as in <u>*</u>, <u>,</u>, <u>}</u>, etc. (except for underscore
itself, _, and except when no confusion is likely).

1.   <u>Expressions</u>

Informally, an expression is either a constant, a
variable, or a function application (including arrays as
functions) either of type integer, string or boolean.
The functions are denoted by the ordinary infix operators
+,-,*,**,|| and identifiers.

A Programming Logic

expression

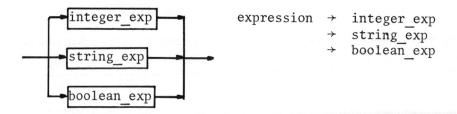

expression → integer_exp
→ string_exp
→ boolean_exp

(i) integer expressions

integer_exp

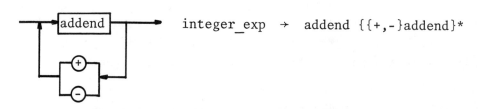

integer_exp → addend {{+,-}addend}*

addend

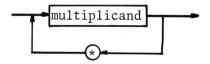

addend → multiplicand {* multiplicand}*

multiplicand

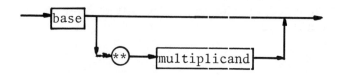

multiplicand → base [** multiplicand]

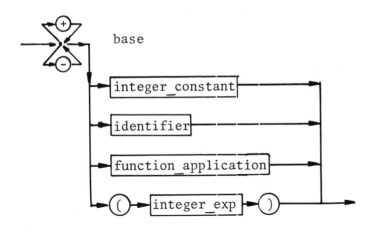

base

```
base  →  {+,-}* integer_constant
      →  {+,-}* identifier
      →  {+,-}* function_application
      →  {+,-}* (integer_exp)
```

integer_constant

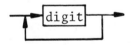

$$\text{integer\_constant} \rightarrow \{\text{digit}\}^{+}$$

identifier

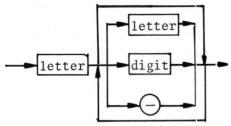

identifier → letter {letter,digit,_}*

function_application

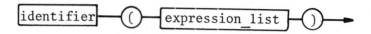

function_application → identifier (expression {,
                                 expression}*)

expression_list

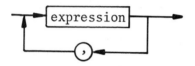

expression_list → expression {, expression}*

A digit is one of the decimal numerals 0,1,2,...,9.
A letter is one of the 26 capital letters of the English
alphabet. Note, unlike PL/C, an identifier cannot contain
any special symbols. Moreover, there is a list of
reserved words which may not be used as identifiers. The
list includes, PL/C reserved words:

ALLOCATE, BEGIN, BY, CALL, CHECK, CLOSE, DECLARE, DCL,
DELETE, DO, ELSE, END, ENTRY, EXIT, FLOW, FORMAT, FREE,
GET, GO, GOTO, IF, LEAVE, NO, NOCHECK, NOFLOW, ON, OPEN,
PROCEDURE, PROC, PUT, READ, RETURN, REVERT,
REWRITE, SELECT, SIGNAL, STOP, THEN, TO, UNTIL,
WHILE, WRITE.

PL/CS reserved words;

ALL, ASSERT, BIT, CHAR, CHARACTER, DATA, DATAEND, EDIT,
ENDFILE, EXT, EXTERNAL, FIXED, FLOAT, FOR, INIT, INITIAL,
LIST, MAIN, OTHERWISE, READONLY, RETURNS, SKIP, SOME,
STATIC, WHEN, VAR, VARYING.

PL/CV reserved word: CHOOSE

Examples of integer expressions

+x*+y--z**+2, 2**z+3, (LENGTH(x)+y)*2+z, A(I)+A(J),
1+2, +1--2, x**y**-z, 1+++2.

(ii)   string expression

string_exp

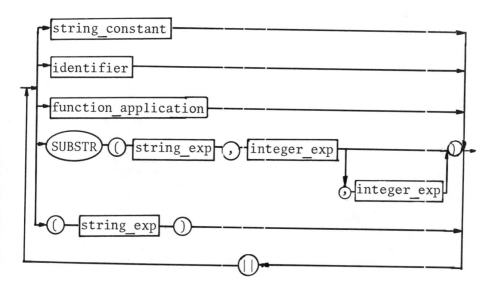

```
string_ exp  →  concatenand {|| concatenand}*
concatenand  →  string_constant
             →  identifier
             →  function_application
             →  SUBSTR(string_exp, integer_exp
                      [, integer_exp])
             →  (string_exp)
```

string_constant

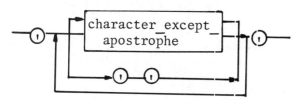

```
string_constant  →  '{character_except_apostrophe, ''}*'
```

character_except_apostrophe is the set of all PL/I characters except apostrophe. The set of all characters in
their correct lexicographic order is:

ɓ . < (+ | & $ *) ; ¬ - / , % _ > ? : # @ ' = "
ABCDEFGHIJKLMNOPQRSTUVWXYZ0123456789

(The symbol ɓ denotes a blank.)

Examples of string expressions.

SUBSTR(X,I+J,2), X||SUBSTR(X,1), X||Y||Z

(iii) boolean expression

      Boolean expressions evaluate to *true* ('1'B) or
false ('0'B). They are built up using the operators &
(and), | (or), ¬ (not) from constants, variables, boolean
function evaluations and simple relations, such as x<y.

boolean_exp

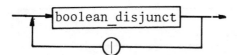

boolean_exp → boolean_disjunct {| boolean_disjunct}*

boolean_disjunct

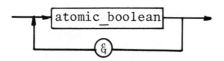

boolean_disjunct → atomic_boolean {& atomic_boolean}*

atomic_boolean

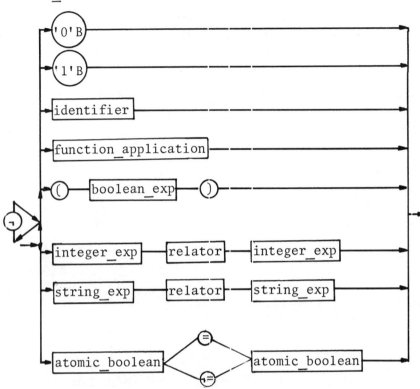

atomic_boolean → {¬}* '0'B
            → {¬}* '1'B
            → {¬}* identifier
            → {¬}* function_application
            → {¬}* (boolean_exp)
            → integer_exp relator integer_exp
            → string_exp relator string_exp
            → atomic_boolean {=,¬=} atomic_boolean

relator

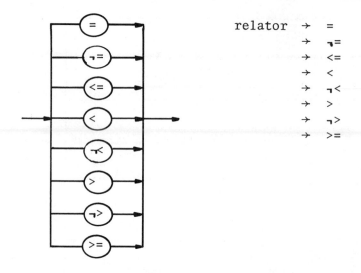

relator → =
        → ¬=
        → <=
        → <
        → ¬<
        → >
        → ¬>
        → >=

Examples: X|Y, A(I)&B(I), ¬A(I)|X&Y,
            '0'B&X, X+Y<Z | X+Y>W,
            X=Y & F('0'B),

Note, $\exp_1 \neg < \exp_2$ is treated as $\neg(\exp_1 < \exp_2)$, $\exp_1 \neg = \exp_2$ is treated as $\neg(\exp_1 = \exp_2)$. This will be clear from the proof rules.

2. Assertions

Assertions are the formal equivalent of declarative sentences. They are built with &,|,¬,=>,<=>, and quantifiers starting from atomic relations. A quantified assertion begins with a quantifier, either *existential*, SOME, or *universal* ALL.

(i) propositional structure

assertion (also see ADDENDA)

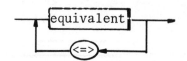

assertion → equivalent {<=> equivalent}*

Note, A<=>B<=>C means A<=>B & B<=>C.

equivalent

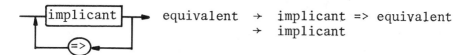

equivalent → implicant => equivalent
          → implicant

implicant

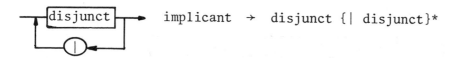

implicant → disjunct {| disjunct}*

disjunct

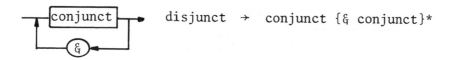

disjunct → conjunct {& conjunct}*

conjunct

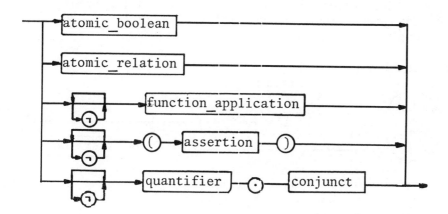

```
conjunct  →  atomic_boolean
          →  atomic_relation
          →  {¬}* function_application
          →  {¬}* (assertion)
          →  {¬}* quantifier . conjunct
```

Note, the assertion following the period after a quantifier is called the *scope* of the quantifier.

Function applications are in this case allowed to be applications of definitions.

atomic_relation

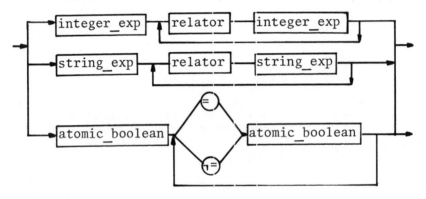

Note, the identifiers in integer expressions and string expressions are allowed to be definitions or labels of assertions.

(ii) quantifier

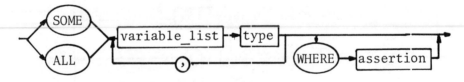

```
quantifier  →  {SOME,ALL} variable_list type
               {, variable_list type}*
               [WHERE assertion]
```

variable_list

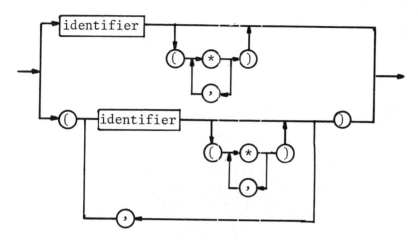

```
variable_list  →  variable
               →  (variable {, variable}*)
variable  →  identifier[(*{,*}*)]
```

type

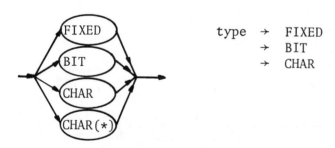

```
type  →  FIXED
      →  BIT
      →  CHAR
```

Examples of atomic relations

X¬=Y, X¬<Y
1<2, 2<=X<=4, X+1<=3<=F(X),
1<2<3<4, SUBSTR(X,1)<=Y<=SUBSTR(Y,3),

Examples of quantifiers

SOME X FIXED
SOME Y BIT WHERE Y <=> Z
ALL(X,Y) CHAR,
ALL(X) CHAR WHERE LENGTH(X)=1

A Programming Logic

Examples of assertions

ALL X FIXED . X=0 => 1=0, ALL X CHAR . LENGTH(X) >=0
SOME X FIXED . SOME Y FIXED . X>Y,
ALL X FIXED . SOME Y FIXED . X<Y,
ALL A(*) BIT . ALL I FIXED . A(I) = '0'B | A(I) = '1'B
ALL A(*) BIT . ALL I FIXED . (A(I) & A(I+1) => A(I))

3. Arguments

An argument is a sequence of assertions with certain
internal logical structure made manifest in justifications
for these assertions. An argument may also contain definitions of predicates (define statements) and of variables
(choose statements). A basic building unit for an argument is a proof-group which encapsulates an argument into
a single unit which may be used to justify assertions. The
details of this section are not needed until §4.

(i) proof group

proof_group

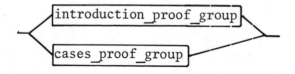

introduction_proof_group

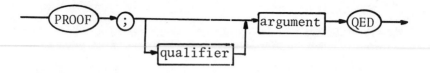

cases_proof_group

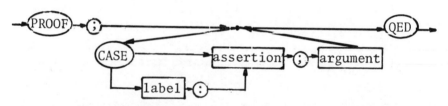

proof_group → introduction_proof_group
              → cases_proof_group

introduction_proof_group → PROOF; [qualifier] argument
                                           QED

cases_proof_group → PROOF; {CASE[label:] assertion ;
                                   argument}* QED

Note, the scope of the qualifier to a proof group is the
set of assertions and statements between PROOF and its
matching QED.

(ii) qualifier

qualifier

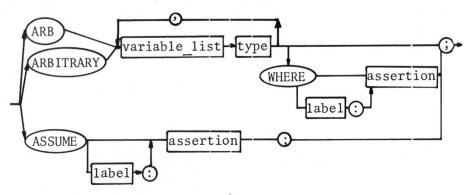

qualifiers → {ARB,ARBITRARY} variable_list type {, var-
                       iable_list type} [WHERE [label:] assertion];
             → ASSUME [label:] assertion;

(iii) statements

statement

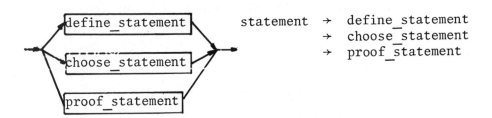

statement → define_statement
              → choose_statement
              → proof_statement

define_statement

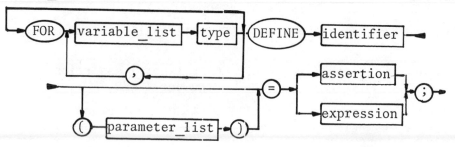

parameter_list

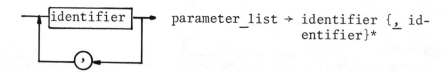

parameter_list → identifier {, id-
entifier}*

define_statement → [FOR variable_list type {, variable_
list type}*]
DEFINE identifier[(identifier {,
identifier}*)] = {assertion,expres-
sion};

choose_statement

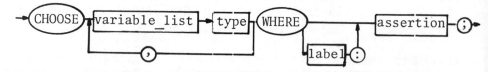

choose_statement → CHOOSE variable_list type {, variable_
list} WHERE [label:] assertion;

proof_statement

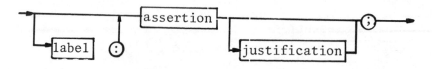

286

proof_statement → [label:] assertion [justification];

(iv) justifications

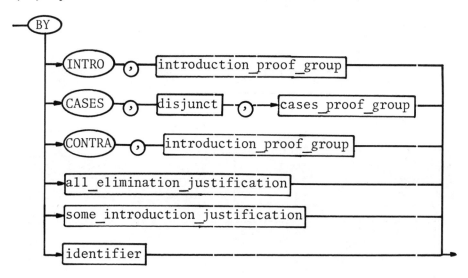

justification →   BY INTRO, introduction_proof_group
                   BY CASES, disjunct, cases_proof_group
                   BY CONTRA, introduction_proof_group

                   BY all_elimination_justification.
                   BY some_introduction_justification

(v) declarations

declaration

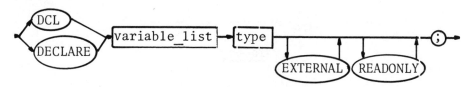

declaration →   {DCL,DECLARE} variable_list type [EXTERNAL]
                 [READONLY];

(vi)   arguments

argument

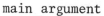

argument → {statement}*

main_argument

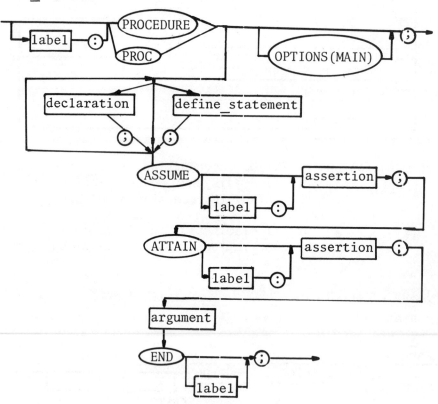

```
main_argument  →  [label:] {PROC, PROCEDURE} [OPTIONS(MAIN)];
                            {define_statement, declaration}*
                            ASSUME [label:] assertion;
                            ATTAIN [label:] assertion;
                            argument
                            END [label];
```

Note 1: In order that main_arguments can be processed as
PL/CS, (PL/C or PL/I) programs, all non-PL/CS (PL/C or
PL/I) statements are *shielded* by special comment delimiters,
/*/ and */.

(This feature is useful only when the argument includes
commands, as in Part IV.)

Examples of proof groups and justified assertions.

```
PROOF; ASSUME L:ALL X FIXED . X=0;
       1=0 BY ALLEL, L;
QED;
PROOF; ARBITRARY (A(*),X,Y) FIXED WHERE X=Y;
       A(X)=A(Y);
QED;
```

Here is an example of a main argument except for the
justifications which are provided by the rules in §4.
This is indeed a valid argument. It will be fully explained in §4. For now it is merely a piece of correct
syntax.

```
GOV: PROC;
/*/   DCL (G,ITH,NYC) BIT;                         */
/*/   ASSUME (G => (ITH|NYC))&¬NYC;                */
/*/   ATTAIN ¬ITH => ¬G;                           */
/*/      ¬ITH => ¬G BY INTRO,                      */
/*/      PROOF; ASSUME ¬ITH;                       */
/*/      ¬G BY PROOF; ASSUME G;                    */
/*/      '0'B BY CASES, ITH|NYC                    */
/*/         PROOF;                                 */
/*/         CASE ITH;                              */
/*/            ¬ITH;                               */
/*/         CASE NYC;                              */
/*/            ¬NYC;                               */
/*/         QED;                                   */
/*/      QED;                                      */
/*/      QED;                                      */
END GOV;
```

A Programming Logic

4. Type restrictions

The words FIXED, CHAR and BIT are PL/CV simple type symbols. They describe the intended range of expressions of their type. To insure that each expression has associated with it a unique type, we require that every syntactic object generated by the BNF productions or syntax charts given above also satisfy certain syntactic *type restrictions* stated here.

To describe the type of any expression, we must first assign to each constant, function symbol, predicate symbol, infix operator and infix relator a type symbol. Some of these are *compound type* symbols. Then in an assertion or main argument, we must assign to each variable a type description. Given these initial type descriptions, the type of any type correct expression can be determined. (Note, some forms of type correctness can only be checked inside assertions or main arguments.) To describe these assignments, we let *array* denote any of the function types

FIXED {× FIXED}*→ FIXED	FIXED *array*
FIXED {× FIXED}*→ BIT	BIT *array*
FIXED {× FIXED}*→ CHAR	CHAR *array*

(i) The initial assignments are:

symbol	*type description*

constants

0, 1, 2,...	FIXED
'A', 'B', 'C',...	CHAR
'1'B, '0'B	BIT

infix operators

+,-,*	FIXED × FIXED → FIXED
**	FIXED × FIXED → FIXED
||	CHAR × CHAR → CHAR
&,|,=>,<=>	BIT × BIT → BIT
¬	BIT → BIT

basic functions

LENGTH	CHAR → FIXED
LBOUND, HBOUND	*array* × FIXED → FIXED
SUBSTR	CHAR × FIXED [× FIXED] → CHAR

290

relators

=,¬=	FIXED × FIXED → BIT
	CHAR × CHAR → BIT
	BIT × BIT → BIT
<,<=,>,>=,¬<,¬>	FIXED × FIXED → BIT
	CHAR × CHAR → BIT

(ii)   In order to extend the type descriptions to expressions, we need the notion of free and bound variables. The type of the binding occurrences of a bound variable in an assertion gives its type. The type of variables free in an argument is determined only inside main arguments by the declaration of the variable.

Definition: An occurrence of a variable x of the form SOME x or ALL x is a *binding occurrence* (also included are all the variants of this, such as SOME x(*), SOME(...,x,...), etc.). An occurrence of x within an assertion R of the form ALL(...x...) type symbol.P or SOME(...x...) type symbol.P (or any of the variants such as ALL(x(*,*)) type symbol WHERE assertion.P) is called a *bound* occurrence of x. Any other occurrence is *free*.
    Recalling that the *scope* of a quantifier is the assertion following it (delimited by the period), we say that a bound variable occurring in a subassertion Q is *bound by* the binding occurrence of that variable in the quantifier of smallest scope containing Q. We say that the variable has this scope, i.e. the scope of a bound variable is the scope of its binding operator. We also say that the quantifier containing the binding occurrence *binds* the variable. Thus, in SOME Y CHAR . SOME X FIXED . LENGTH(Y)=X & LENGTH(X||Y)>LENGTH(Y); the occurrence of X in LENGTH(Y)=X is bound by the X in SOME X FIXED, but the occurrence of X in the rest is free.
    The *type* of a *binding occurrence* of a variable is the type of the quantifier containing it. (The type of a quantifier is the unique type symbol occurring in it.) The *type of a bound variable* is the type of the quantifier which binds it. The type of a variable free in an assertion is not explicitly determined by the assertion itself.
    We now examine the similar notions of free and bound variables in arguments.

A Programming Logic

Definition: An occurrence of a variable x of the form
ARBITRARY...x... or CHOOSE...x... or FOR...x or DEFINE x
or x: (i.e. x as a label) is called a binding occurrence
of x. (As before, we include also the variants of this
such as ARB x, ARB...x(*), etc.) An occurrence of x
within a subargument qualified by a qualifier containing
a binding occurrence of x or containing a choose statement
or define statement or label which binds x is called
bound. All variables in an argument which are neither
bound in this way nor bound in assertions are called
free in that argument.

A bound variable is bound by the qualifier or choose
statement or define statement or label in the argument of
smallest scope containing it. Except in the case of
variables bound by labels, this scope is called the scope
of the variable and of the binding occurrence of the
variable. For label names, the scope is the segment of
the innermost argument from the occurrence of the label
to the end of the argument. The type of a bound variable
is determined by the type of its binding occurrence except in the case of a label (whose type is always BIT).

The *type of a variable* free in a main argument is
the type of its occurrence in the declaration for that
argument.

(iii) Type descriptions are extended to expressions in
the usual way. For instance, if f is of type $atype_1 \times ... \times$
$atype_n \to btype$ (where the $atype_i$ are simple types or
array types, and $btype$ is a simple type), and exp_i are of
type $atype_i$ respectively, then $f(exp_1,...,exp_n)$ is of
type $btype$. If p is a predicate of type $atype_1 \times ... \times$
$atype_n$, then $p(exp_1,...,exp_n)$ is of type BIT. If □ is an
infix operator of type $atype_1 \times atype_2 \to btype$, then
$exp_1 \; □ \; exp_2$ is of type $btype$. If ⊥ is a relator of type
$atype_1 \times atype_2$, then $exp_1 \perp exp_2$ is of type BIT.

(iv) An expression is *type correct* if and only if it
(and consequently every subexpression) is assigned a
unique type by these rules. An *argument* is *type correct*
if and only if each expression occurring in it has a
unique type.

292

Examples

(2+3)**7<5 is of type BIT, each side of the relation is of type FIXED.

(2&3)+1 < '1'B is not type correct because 2&3 cannot be assigned a type.

2+1 < '1'B is not type correct because no relator compares FIXED and BIT, thus no type can be assigned.

X+Y < Z is neither type correct nor type incorrect until we know the types of X,Y,Z.

Notice X&Y = Z can only be type correct if X,Y,Z are all BIT, but X=Y can be correct either if all are BIT or all are FIXED.

A(X+Y,1)=5 is neither correct nor incorrect.   It depends on A.   But A(X&Y,1)+A(5,1) is type incorrect.

The declaration DCL A(1:7) FIXED creates an array of type FIXED → FIXED.   DCL A(1:7, 2:5) CHAR creates an array of type FIXED × FIXED → CHAR.

In SOME(X,Y,Z) BIT . X|Y&Z = X the expressions Y&Z and X|Y&Z and X are all of type BIT.   In the sample argument about the Governor of New York, all variables are free variables of type BIT.

§2.3 SUBSTITUTIONS

1. Substitutions of expressions for variables in assertions and arguments is critical to the description of rules for writing correct arguments. Variables play essentially two different roles in assertions and arguments. In ALL X FIXED . X**2 >= 0 the variable X is simply part of the quantifier serving to relate that quantifier to the assertion on which it operates.   In this role it is similar to x in $\int_0^1 x^2 \, dx$. Such variable occurrences are *bound*.
In the assertion X**3+27=0 the variable X purports to name an integer with a certain property. It should make sense to *SUBSTITUTE* for this X other names for integers. Such variable occurrences are *free*.

Definition: If P is an assertion, then P(exp/x) is the assertion obtained by replacing every free occurrence of x in P by the expression exp. $P(exp_1/x_1, \ldots, exp_n/x_n)$ is the result of simultaneously substituting exp_i for every free occurrence of x_i. $P(exp_1/x_1)(exp_2/x_2) \ldots$ (exp_n/x_n) indicates consecutive substitutions starting with exp_1 for x_1.

Examples:

Let P be X>Y. Then P(X+Y/X, X+1/Y) is X+Y>X+1 and P(X+Y/X)(X+1/Y) is X+(X+1)>X+1.

2. The intuitive meaning of substitution is that P(exp/x) says about exp the same thing that P said about x. But this intuition can fail because of the dual use of variables as names and as place markers. For example, if we let P(X) be

SOME Y FIXED . Y>X,

then P(X) is saying there is some integer larger than X, which should be true for all X. If we substitute Y for X we have the absurdity:

SOME Y FIXED . Y>Y.

The problem is that the expression Y changes meaning when it is substituted. We say that Y has been *captured* by the quantifier SOME Y FIXED. Therefore, we put the following restrictions on substitution that prevents capture.

Definition: Expression exp is *free for x in P* if and only if no free occurrence of a variable in exp becomes bound in P(exp/x).
    Hereafter we assume that an expression is free for the variable for which it is being substituted. We can arrange to have any expression free in P if we first re-name any binding occurrences of variables that occur also in the expression. We will always be explicit about such renaming.

3. Macro substitutions

Definitions which are introduced by define statements
are treated as programming language macros. That is, the
body of the definition replaces the defined term syntactically where ever it appears. Furthermore, parameters of
such definitions are also replaced syntactically before
substitution of the body.[†] See FINE POINTS for discussion
of scopes of free variables in the macro body.

§2.4   PROOF RULES

1. An argument is essentially a sequence of assertions
which compels rational agreement to its conclusion. This
agreement is based on prior acceptance of certain rules
for using assertions. These rules describe how to add new
assertions to an argument provided certain assertions are
already present. In PL/CV these rules can be classified
into two types, INTRODUCTION and ELIMINATION, depending
on whether the new assertion is formed by *introducing* a
logical symbol to connect existing assertions or is formed
by *eliminating* a logical symbol to disconnect parts from
an existing assertion.[††]

2. The format for presenting the predicate calculus rules
is to show how new assertions can be brought into an
argument on the basis of assertions already present in
the argument. The presentation of most rules obeys the
following scheme:

$$\frac{A_1, A_2, \ldots, A_n}{C \quad BY \quad \text{justification}}$$

[†]This in Algol terms, amounts to calling the definition
by name. Also this means that external variables of such
definitions have static scope, i.e. they receive their
value at the point where the definition is given.

[††]Logical systems organized in this way are called
natural deduction systems. The PL/CV logic is modeled
after the system of Dag Prawitz, [9].

which is an abbreviation for: If $A_1, A_2, \ldots, A_n$, called the
hypotheses, are assertions that are accessible from the
point in the argument where we wish to write assertion C
(or are immediate from accessible assertions), then C may
be added to the argument by writing C BY justification.
The justification serves to identify the rule being
applied, making it easier to see the logical structure
of the proof and easier to confirm the correctness of the
proof mechanically.   The exact form of a justification is
specified with each rule that requires one.

Note, some rules require no explicit justification.   In
this case the rule format is

$$\frac{A_1, \ldots, A_n}{C}$$

Some rules require as hypotheses an entire subargument in the form of a proof group.   This proof group is
included in the justification so that the rule has the
form

C BY justification

and the justification contains PROOF;...;QED.   In conventional natural deduction systems this type of rule is
called a *deduction rule* and is written with the proof-
group as a hypotheses,

PROOF;

.

.

.

$$\frac{\text{QED;}}{\text{C.}}$$

Some steps of reasoning in an argument, such as the
introduction of X>0 & Y>=0 from X>0 and Y>=0, are so
obvious that they can be performed automatically without
writing anything down in the argument.   Conclusions drawn
by such steps are *immediate*.   However, in order to describe
these steps, we must know exactly what rules are being
applied automatically.   Therefore in the list of rules
given below there will occur some for which no justification is provided.   In place of a syntactic form for
justification, the phrase *immediate* appears.   The manner in

which these immediate rules are applied is described in the definition of proof.

3. Enumeration of rules

DECLARATION INTRODUCTION   (immediate)

$$\frac{lower_1 <= upper_1, \ldots, lower_n <= upper_n}{DCL\ A(lower_1: upper_1, \ldots, lower_n: upper_n)}$$

If $lower_i = 1$ it (and the separating colon) may be omited from the conclusion.

ARRAY BOUNDS INTRODUCTION   (immediate)

$$\frac{DCL\ A(lower_1: upper_1, \ldots, lower_n: upper_n)}{LBOUND(A,i) = lower_i,\ HBOUND(A,i) = upper_i}$$

Note if i is not between 1 and n, no conclusion can be drawn from the declaration. When these functions are used in commands they must be well-defined (see IV).

BOUNDS AXIOM   (immediate)

$$\frac{A\ as\ variable\ of\ array\ type}{LBOUND(A,i) <= HBOUND(A,i)}$$

INITIAL VALUES   (immediate)

$$\frac{DCL\ A[(lower_1: upper_1, \ldots, lower_n: upper_n)]}{[ALL\ (I_1, \ldots, I_n)\ FIXED\ .]\ A[(I_1, \ldots, I_n)] = 0}$$

Note, this axiom is valid for PL/CS and PL/C only. It is useful to the user who wishes to think of arrays as infinite objects.

INTRODUCTION	ELIMINATION
AND (immediate)	AND (immediate)
$$\frac{A_1,\ldots,A_n}{A_1 \& \ldots \& A_n}$$	$$\frac{A_1 \& A_2 \& \ldots \& A_n}{A_i}$$
OR (immediate)	OR $A_1 \mid \ldots \mid A_n$
$$\frac{A_i}{A_1 \mid \ldots \mid A_i \mid \ldots \mid A_n}$$	Q BY CASES, $A_1 \mid \ldots \mid A_n$,
	PROOF;
	CASE A_1;
	argument
	Q;
	.
	.
	.
	CASE A_n;
	argument
	Q;.
	QED;
IMPLICATION	IMPLICATION (immediate)
A => B BY INTRO,	A => B, A
PROOF;	
[ASSUME A;]	$$\frac{}{B}$$
.	
.	
B	
QED;	

Note, it is allowable but
not necessary to write
ASSUME A, so the state-
ment is bracketed.

INTRODUCTION	ELIMINATION
EQUIVALENCE (immediate)	EQUIVALENCE (immediate)

EQUIVALENCE (immediate)

$$\frac{A \Rightarrow B, \quad B \Rightarrow A}{A \Leftrightarrow B}$$

EQUIVALENCE (immediate)

$$\frac{A \Leftrightarrow B}{A \Rightarrow B} \qquad \frac{A \Leftrightarrow B}{B \Rightarrow A}$$

NOT

¬A BY INTRO,
   PROOF;
    [ASSUME A;]
      .
      .
      .
    '0'B;
   QED;

NOT (immediate)

$$\frac{A, \quad \neg A}{\text{'0'B}}$$

FALSE (immediate)

$$\frac{A, \quad \neg A}{\text{'0'B}}$$

FALSE (immediate)

$$\frac{\text{'0'B}}{A}$$

ALL

ALL$(x_1,\ldots,x_n)$ type
  [WHERE Q].P
BY INTRO,
  PROOF;
[ARB $x_1,\ldots,x_n$ type
  [WHERE Q];]
  .
  .
  .
P;
QED;

See FINE POINTS for the rule with mixed type quantifiers.

ALL

$$\frac{[Q(\exp_1/x_1,\ldots,\exp_n/x_n)] \quad \text{ALL}(x_1,\ldots,x_n) \text{ type} \quad [\text{WHERE } Q].P}{P(\exp_1/x_1,\ldots,\exp_n/x_n)}$$

BY ALLEL, ALL$(x_1,\ldots,x_n)$
  type [WHERE Q].P,$\exp_1,\ldots,$
                $\exp_n$;

See FINE POINTS for an extended all elimination rule.

299

INTRODUCTION	ELIMINATION
SOME	SOME

INTRODUCTION — SOME

$$\frac{P(\exp_1/x_1,\ldots,\exp_n/x_n)}{\text{SOME}(x_1,\ldots,x_n)\ \text{type.P}}$$

BY SOMIN, $\exp_1,\ldots,\exp_n$

See FINE POINTS for the bounded quantifier version.

ELIMINATION — SOME

$$\frac{\text{SOME}(x_1,\ldots,x_n)\ \text{type.P}}{\text{CHOOSE}(y_1,\ldots,y_n)\ \text{type}}$$

WHERE P

Provided y_i are new. See FINE POINTS for the bounded quantifier version.

The above rules are all called *constructive*. The final rule is not and is not permitted in constructive proofs.

CLASSICAL CONTRADICTION RULE

```
    A BY CONTRADICTION,
       PROOF;
       [ASSUME ¬A;]
           .
           .
           .
       '0'B
       QED;
```

end of enumeration of rules.

4. The rules marked immediate in the above table are called *immediate rules of inference*. (The introduction rules: AND, OR, EQUIVALENCE and FALSE, the elimination rules: AND, IMPLICATION, EQUIVALENCE, FALSE). In addition the following special cases of implication introduction are immediate. [†]

$$\frac{\neg A}{A => B} \qquad \frac{B}{A => B} \qquad \frac{A}{\neg A => B}$$

[†] In classical logic, where A => B is equivalent to ¬A|B, these are instances of OR introduction, which is immediate.

Given a set of assertions S, we say assertion B is
immediate from S if and only if

(1)   B is in S or
(2) $A_1, \ldots, A_n$ are immediate from S and B follows

from them by an immediate rule of inference.

5.   In an argument without proof-groups, an assertion may
be inferred if it follows from lexically previous lines
of the proof by a rule of inference.[†] However, in arguments with block structure the availabilty of previous
assertions as hypotheses depends on their relative positions.   For example, consider

```
((A => B) & A|B) => B BY INTRO,
PROOF;
ASSUME (A => B) & A|B;
B BY CASES, A|B;
PROOF;
   CASE A;
    B;
   QED;
QED;
```

At this point, although B is a previous line in the argument, we cannot assert B because it occurs inside a
proof block.
      A similar "scope problem" arises with qualifiers.
For example, the following argument is fallacious.

```
(P(X) => Q(X)) => ALL X FIXED WHERE P(X).Q(X) BY INTRO,
  PROOF;
  /# assume P(X) => Q(X) #/
  ALL X FIXED WHERE P(X).Q(X) BY INTRO,
      PROOF; ARBITRARY X FIXED WHERE P(X);
      Q(X) /# by implication elimination #/
      /# this step is erroneous because X has a #/
      /# different meaning inside the proof-group #/
      /# than outside, e.g. suppose X=2 is added to the
         antecedent #/  QED;
  QED;
```

[†]The *lexical order* of assertions in an argument is the
linear order in which they appear.   Proofs in PL/CV are
one dimensional linear sequences (rather than trees).

To eliminate these scope errors, we must say precisely when an assertion at one point p in a proof is accessible from another point q.

Definition: A predicate calculus *proof block* is a proof group. (In part IV a proof block achieves a more general status.)

Definition: An occurrence of an assertion A at position p with variables $x_1, \ldots, x_n$ free in A is *accessible* from a position q in a Predicate Calculus argument if and only if

    (0)   q does not occur in the justification of this occurrence of A, and

    (1)   A at p occurs lexically before q, and

    (2)   any proof block containing p also contains q, and

    (3)   A is the same at p and q, that is the variables x_i have the same scope at p and q. (Thus if q is in the scope of any binding occurrence of an x_i, then so is p.)

Definition: A *proof* is an argument in which every assertion is either an assumption or follows from accessible lines, immediate assertions and proof groups by a rule of inference.

Note: We can simplify the definitions of proof and accessibility somewhat if we think of writing the justification lexically before the line being justified. Then we do not need line (0) of accessibility, and it is easier to think of a proof in linear order (no assertion is justified by lines occurring lexically beyond it).

6. Undefined and well-defined expressions

The PL/CV2 Proof Checker is based on a semantics which assigns meaning to assertions containing undefined expressions. For example,

```
EX: PROC;
    DCL A(5) FIXED;
/*/ A(6) = A(6); */
    END EX;
```

is a valid argument even though A(6) is an undefined expression (since 6 is not in the domain of A). The details of this semantics are discussed in *A Programming Logic*.[†]

An alternative semantics for assertions containing undefined expressions is discussed in *A Programming Logic*. It may appear more natural, so we mention it for the user who wants his arguments to remain consistent with the alternative semantics.

An expression, exp, is said to be *well-defined* if and only if all array indices are in the domain of the array. (In general after part VI we must insist that all defined functions are applied only to elements of their domains.) An atomic assertion involving expressions is valid only if all expressions are well-defined and the assertion is true for their values. This approach introduces the anomaly that A(6) = A(6) can be false and A(6) ¬= A(6) can be false as well (as they are in the EX example). (Note ¬(A(6) = A(6)) and ¬(A(6) ¬= A(6)) are both true.)

To conform to this semantics, one must change the all elimination rule to:

ALL ELIMINATION

$$[Q(\exp_1/x_1, \ldots, \exp_n/x_n)]$$

$$ALL(x_1, \ldots, x_n) \text{ type } [WHERE\ Q].P$$

$$\{\exp_i \text{ are well-defined}\}$$

$$P(\exp_1/x_1, \ldots, \exp_n/x_n) \text{ BY ALL, } ALL(x_1, \ldots, x_n) \text{ type}$$
$$[WHERE\ Q].P;$$

As new rules are introduced, we will discuss any changes needed to make them conform to the alternative semantics

---

[†] An assertion P involving an array A is valid if and only if it is valid for all possible extensions of the actual declared array to an array defined on a larger domain.

7. An example

```
GOV:PROCEDURE;
/* If the Governor of New York is from Ithaca, or        */
/* New York City, and Mr. Jones is not from New York     */
/* City, then show that if he is not form Ithaca,        */
/* then he is not governor.
   DCL (G,ITH,NYC) BIT;
/*/ ASSUME (G => (ITH|NYC)) & ¬NYC;                       */
/*/ ATTAIN ¬ITH => ¬G;                                    */
/*  Begin the proof                                       */
/*/ ¬ITH => ¬G BY INTRO;                                  */
/*/ PROOF; ASSUME ¬ITH;                                   */
/*/   ¬G BY INTRO,                                        */
/*/     PROOF;                                            */
/*/     '0'B BY CASES,                                    */
/*/         PROOF;                                        */
/*/         CASE ITH;                                     */
/*/              ¬ITH;                                    */
/*/         CASE NYC;                                     */
/*/              ¬NYC;                                    */
/*/         QED;                                          */
/*/     QED;                                              */
/*/   QED;                                                */
/*/ END GOV;
```

Note: G is Mr. Jones is Governor of New York
        ITH is Mr. Jones is from Ithaca
        NYC is Mr. Jones is from New York City

§2.5 EQUALITY

1. Until rules are provided for the relational operators, =, ¬=, <, <=, etc., we can deduce only facts about them which would be true of any binary relator. Thus we can prove ALL X FIXED . X=X => 0=0 but not ALL X FIXED . X=X. Since equality is such a primitive concept, regardless of the type of the objects, rules for the equality relator, =, are usually given as part of the underlying logic. Thus

we treat equality here rather than in part III.[†]

2. Equality rules

The specific equality rules are:

REFLEXIVITY	TRANSITIVITY
$exp = exp$	$exp_1 = exp_2, \ exp_2 = exp_3$ $$\overline{\qquad exp_1 = exp_3 \qquad}$$
SYMMETRY $$\frac{exp_1 = exp_2}{exp_2 = exp_1}$$	SUBSTITUTION $$\frac{t_1 = t_2, \ A(t_1/x)}{A(t_2/x)}$$

The equality relation on boolean expressions is equivalent to <=>, i.e. $bexp_1$ = $bexp_2$ iff $bexp_1$ <=> $bexp_2$.
Thus the equality axioms provide a more powerful treatment of <=>.

3. Immediate consequence of equality

Ideally the equality rules would all be immediate. However, at the moment they are not implemented this way because we cannot fully integrate them with the other immediate rules. But they are immediate to this extent: say that A is an *immediate consequence of equality* from a set of assertions S if and only if AεS or A follows by the equality rules from immediate consequences of equality from S. Then at any point of an argument we can introduce a consequence of equality from accessible and immediate assertions. (Somewhat more can be immediately inferred as we describe in FINE POINTS.)

[†]Equality behaves well in PL/I only on *integers* and *booleans*, so it might be more appropriate to treat it with the data types rather than with the logic. However, our proof rules for it are best treated as part of the immediate predicate calculus rules.

A Programming Logic

4. Array equality

One special axiom is needed for array equality.[†] Let $DOM(A,i_1,\ldots,i_n)$ mean

$LBOUND(A,1) \leq i_1 \leq HBOUND(A,1)$ &...&

$\quad LBOUND(A,n) \leq i_n \leq HBOUND(A,n)$.

ARRAY EXTENSIONALITY

D: $LBOUND(A,i_j) = LBOUND(B,i_j)$, $HBOUND(A,i_j) = HBOUND(B,i_j)$,
$\quad 1 \leq j \leq n$

V: $ALL(i_1,\ldots,i_n)$ FIXED $A(i_1,\ldots,i_n) = B(i_1,\ldots,i_n)$

$$A=B \text{ BY EXT, D, V}$$

Note, we also have from the equality axioms that $\quad A=B$

$$A(I)=B(I).$$

5. In the restricted predicate calculus rules we must write the reflexivity rule as:

REFLEXIVITY

{exp well-defined}

$\quad exp = exp$

§2.6 EXAMPLES

Here is a variety of carefully chosen examples to illustrate the development of basic logical facts in the PL/CV predicate calculus with equality. Arguments are used rather than main arguments in order to avoid writing comment delimiters and procedure headings. Certain fine points are introduced in these examples. They are covered in detail in FINE POINTS.

[†]See FINE POINTS for a stronger form of this axiom.

1. (A=>B) => ¬B => ¬A BY INTRO,
          PROOF;
          ¬B => ¬A BY INTRO,
              PROOF;
              ¬A BY INTRO,
                  PROOF;
                      ASSUME A;
                              B;   /# immediate from A => B, A #/
                          ¬B;   /# assumed in ¬B => ¬A Block #/
                      '0'B;
              QED;
          QED;
      QED;

This argument can be compressed using the feature that the
argument inside a proof block may be eliminated when it
consists entirely of immediate assertions. The keyword
INTRO is left to indicate what happened. This results
in:

      (A=>B) => ¬B => ¬A BY INTRO,
      PROOF;
      ¬B => ¬A BY INTRO,
          PROOF;
          ¬A BY INTRO;
          QED;
      QED;

The proof can be further collapsed to:

   (A => B) => (¬B => ¬A) BY INTRO, INTRO, INTRO;

The converse, (¬B => ¬A) => (A => B) requires the classical
rule CONTRADICTION.

2. A & (B|C) => A&B|A&C BY CASES, B|C,
    PROOF;
    CASE B;
        A&B;
    CASE C;
        A&C;
    QED;

    {This compresses to:

    A&(B|C) => A&B|A&C BY CASES, B|C;}

    The converse, A&B|A&C => A&(B|C), is also true.

Exercise.   Notice that with the CONTRADICTION you can
            prove:
                    (A|B => C) => (A => C)|(B => C).

            Can you prove the other direction?

3. ALL X FIXED . (A(X) => B(X) =>
    SOME X FIXED . (A(X) => B(X))
    BY INTRO,
        PROOF;
            ASSUME H: ALL X FIXED . (A(X) => B(X));
            A(0) => B(0) BY ALLEL, H;
            SOME X FIXED . (A(X) => B(X))
            BY SOMIN, 0;
        QED;

4.   SOME X FIXED . (A(X) => C) => (ALL X FIXED . A(X) => C)
        BY INTRO,
        PROOF;
        ASSUME SOME X FIXED . (A(X) => C);
        CHOOSE X0 FIXED WHERE A(X0) => C;
        ALL X FIXED . A(X) => C BY INTRO,
         PROOF; ASSUME H: ALL X FIXED . A(X);
         A(X0) BY ALLEL, H, X0;
         C;
         QED;
        QED;

5.   SOME X FIXED . ¬A(X) => ¬ALL X FIXED . A(X)
     BY INTRO,
     PROOF;
        CHOOSE X0 FIXED WHERE ¬A(X0);
        ¬ALL X FIXED . A(X)
            BY INTRO,
               PROOF;
               ASSUME A1:ALL X FIXED . A(X);
               A(X0) BY ALLEL, A1, X0;
               '0'B;
               QED;
        QED;

The converse of this requires CONTRADICTION.

Exercise.   Show ALL X FIXED . A(X) => ¬SOME X FIXED . A(X);
Note, the converse requires classical reasoning.

6.   Here is a compressed example of a proof of A|¬A using
the contradiction rule.   Expand this to a full proof.

        A|¬A BY CONTRADICTION,
           PROOF;
              ¬A BY INTRO;
           QED;

7.   Use the method of the last proof to establish
¬(B|C) => ¬B&¬C.   Is the converse true?

8. (ALL X FIXED . P(X) => C) => SOME X FIXED . (P(X) => C)
    BY INTRO, CONTRA,
    PROOF;
      ALL X FIXED . P(X) BY INTRO, CONTRA,
      PROOF;
        P(X) => C;
        SOME X FIXED . (P(X) => C) BY SOMIN, X;
      QED;
      SOME X FIXED . (P(X) => C) BY SOMIN, 0;
    QED;

9. Here is an expansion of example 8.

    (ALL X FIXED . P(X) => C => SOME X FIXED . (P(X) => C)
    BY INTRO,
    PROOF;
      SOME X FIXED . (P(X) => C) BY CONTRA,
      PROOF;
      ASSUME ¬SOME X FIXED . (P(X) => C);
      ALL X FIXED . P(X) BY INTRO,
      PROOF; ARBITRARY X FIXED;
        P(X) BY CONTRA,
        PROOF; ASSUME ¬P(X);
          P(X) => C
          SOME X FIXED . (P(X) => C) BY SOMIN, X;
          '0'B;
        QED;
      QED;
      C;
      P(0) => C;
      SOME X FIXED . (P(X) => C) BY SOMIN, 0;
      QED;
    QED;

III   INTEGERS AND STRINGS

§3.1   INTRODUCTION

To reason about the basic data types of integers, strings and booleans we need axioms and rules of inference for their constants, operations and relations. Elementary arithmetic arguments are requisite to reasoning about programs. Termination proofs and computational complexity analyses of almost any algorithm involve properties of integers. Fortunately, this indispensable theory has been thoroughly studied and we can draw upon the labors of others to frame the PL/CV theory of integers. This theory, to be described below, is very powerful and useful, but provides only the first steps toward a convenient workaday theory.

The string theory offered in this version of PL/CV is extremely primitive. Strings must be regarded as arrays of single characters. No special theory is provided beyond the theory of equality and arrays already discussed.

The theory of booleans, the remaining basic type to discuss, is already provided by the propositional logic.

§3.2   ARITHMETIC RULES

1.   Ordinary axioms of number theory

There is one main rule of arithmetic in PL/CV called *Arithmetic*. To explain it we need to classify the ordinary axioms of number theory as follows:

(0)   Constant arithmetic
$$1+1 = 2$$
$$2+1 = 3$$
$$3+1 = 4$$

　　　．

　　　．

(1) Ring axioms and the definition of minus, -. For all
     integers x,y,z

(i)   x+y=y+x   commutativity
        x*y=y*x

(ii)   (x+y)+z=x+(y+z)   associativity
        (x*y)*z=x*(y*z)

(iii)   x*(y+z)=x*y+x*z   distributivity

(iv)   x+0=x   additive identity

(v)   x*1=x   multiplicative identity

(vi)   x+(-x)=0   additive inverse

(vii)   x-y=x+(-y)   subtraction

(2) Discrete linear order. For all integers x,y,z.

(i)   ¬(x<x)   irreflexivity

(ii)   x<y ∨ y<x ∨ x=y   trichotomy

(iii)   x<y & y<z => x<z   transitivity

(iv)   ¬(x<y<x+1)   discreteness

(3) Definitions of order relations and inequality. For
     all integers x,y,z. [†]

(i)   x≤y <=> x<y ∨ x=y

(ii)   x>y <=> y<x

(iii)   x≥y <=> x>y ∨ x=y

(4) Monotonicity of + and *. For all integers w,x,y,z.

(i)   x≥y & z≥w => x+z≥y+w   monotonicity of +

        If z,w are constants, this is called an instance of
        trivial monotonicity.

(ii)   x≥y & z≤w => x-z≥y-w   monotonicity of -

        If z and w are constants, this is called an instance
        of *trivial monotonicity*.

[†]See FINE POINTS for a diccussion of how PL/CV actually processes x≥y, x>y. It provides slightly more power since the
parser translates x≥y into y≤x and x>y into y<x.

(iii)   x≥0 & y≥z => x*y≥x*z   monotonicity of *

(iv)   x>0 & x*y≥x*z => y≥z   cancellation (factoring)

2.   Variants of basic axioms

To make the proof system more powerful, many variants of the above axioms are incorporated into the arithmetic proof rule. These variants, modulo the ring axioms, are. given in the following tables, in which each entry contains the conclusion from the hypotheses corresponding to its row and column.

Addition

	z>w	z≥w	z=w	z≠w
x>y	x+z≥y+w+2	x+z≥y+w+1	x+z≥y+w+1 & x+w≥y+z+1	———
x≥y	x+z≥y+w+1	x+z≥y+w	x+z≥y+w & x+w≥y+z	———
x=y	x+z≥y+w+1 & y=z≥x+w+1	x+z≥y+w & y+z≥x+w	x+z=y+w & x+w=y+z	x+z≠y+w & x+w≠y+z
x≠y	———	———	x+z≠y+w & x+w≠y+z	———

Subtraction

	z>w	z≥w	z=w	z≠w
x>y	x-w≥y-z+2	x-w≥y-z+1	x-w≥y-z+1 & x-z≥y-w+1	———
x≥y	x-w≥y-z+1	x-w≥y-z	x-w≥y-z & x-z≥y-w	———
x=y	x-w≥y-z+1 & y-w≥x-z+1	x-w≥y-z & y-w≥x-z	x-w=y-z & y-w=x-z	x-w≠y-z & x=z≠y-w
x≠y	———	———	x-w≠y-z & x-z≠y-w	———

Multiplication (using xy for x*y)

	y≥z	y>z	y=z	y≠z
x>0	xy≥xz	xy>xz	xy=xz	.xy≠xz
x≥0	xy≥xz	xy≥xz	xy=xz	───── ─
x=0	xy=xz & xy=0	xy=xz & xy=0	xy=xz & xy=0	xy=xz & xy=0
x≤0	xy≤xz	xy≤xz	xy=xz	───────── -
x<0	xy≤xz	xy<xz	xy=xz	xy≠xz
x≠0	─────	xy≠xz	xy=xz	xy≠xz

Cancellation (factoring using xy for x*y)

	xy>xz	xy≥xz	xy=xz	xy≠xz
x>0	y>z	y≥z	y=z	y≠z
x<0	y<z	y≤z	y=z	y≠z
x≠0	y≠z	───	y=z	y≠z

3. The arithmetic proof rule ARITH

Definition: A *trivial* application of monotonicity is an application of a monotonicity axiom for addition, with one of the hypotheses given in the form

$$a \rho b$$

where a, b are integer constants, and ρ is any infix arithmetic relational operator. Any other application of a monotonicity axiom will be called *nontrivial*.

Intuitively, a trivial application of monotonicity corresponds to adding constants to both sides of a relation, in a meaningful way. Thus we can conclude x+3≠y+4 from x=y, but from x≠y we cannot make any conclusion about x+3 and y+4, since x≠y does not preclude any of the 3

314

possibilities x+3>y+4, x+3=y+4, x+3<y+4. These two cases
are, respectively, an example and a non-example of a trivial
application of monotonicity.

The proof system is designed so that whenever the
arithmetic proof rule ARITH is invoked, any necessary applications of the arithmetic axioms, *other than nontrivial
application of monotonicity,* will be supplied automatically.
Only nontrivial applications of monotonicity need be
specified explicitly.

All arithmetic steps in PL/CV arguments have the
following restricted form. First, all inferences involve
only *quantifier free* arithmetic relations, i.e. of the form
$[\neg]t_1 < t_2$, $[\neg]t_1 \leq t_2$, $[\neg]t_1 > t_2$, $[\neg]t_1 = t_2$, $[\neg]t_1 \geq t_2$, $[\neg]t_1 \neq t_2$
for t_i expressions. Second, each step involves drawing a
conclusion in the form of a disjunction of arithmetic
relations, $C_1 | C_2 | \ldots | C_m$ from a finite set of arithmetic
relations $H_1, \ldots, H_n$. (When m=0 the disjunct is regarded
as '0'B, i.e. *false.*) We write $H_1, \ldots, H_n \vdash_{RA} C_1 | C_2 | \ldots | C_m$
if and only if the conclusion can be deduced from the hypo-
theses using the rules of the propositional calculus, restricted
equality rules, plus the rules in classes 1,2,3 and trivial
monotonicity. We call this a restricted arithmetic (RA)
inference. Such an inference, which may be very complex,
can be written in PL/CV as a single step justified in the
form:

Rule 1:   C BY ARITH, $H_1, \ldots, H_n$;
C is a disjunction, $C_1 | C_2 | \ldots | C_m$.

The second type of inference allowed is a single
application of nontrivial monotonicity, specified precisely
in the justification, followed by an application of restricted
arithmetic inference. The justification has one of these
three forms:

Rule 2,3: Addition/Subtraction
            C BY ARITH, $\{{}^{rel}_{exp}\}$, $\{{}^+_-\}$, $\{{}^{rel}_{exp}\}$, $\{,rel\}*$

The second relation is added to/subtracted from the first
relation, yielding a relation according to the table of
axioms. If exp is used, it means the trivial relation

exp=exp.

Rule 4: Multiplication

$$C \text{ BY ARITH, } rel_1, *, \{^{rel_2}_{integer}\}, \{,rel\}*$$

Here rel_2 gives the sign of the multiplier exp, i.e. of
the form exp ρ 0 where ρ is any arithmetic relational
operator. If integer is used instead, then the integer is
the multiplier, with obvious sign.

rel_1 gives the relation to be multiplied by the multiplier

on both sides.

Rule 5: Cancellation (factoring)

$$C \text{ BY ARITH, } rel_1, /, \{^{rel_2}_{integer}\}, \{rel\}*$$

Here rel_2 or integer refers to the factor to be factored

out of the relation given by rel_1. Conventions are as for

multipliction. As in all rules, labels may be used in
place of relations. See FINE POINTS for more detail.

4. <u>Examples</u>

Here are isolated examples of PL/CV arithmetic reasoning.

1.   X+2>0 BY ARITH, X>0;

2.   X*X>0 BY ARITH, X>0, *, X>0;

3.   (A-B)+B <= I-1 BY ARITH, A+B <= I, -, B >= 1;

4.   A<B BY ARITH, A <= B, A¬=B

5.   A+2<A+3 BY ARITH, A;

6.   A+B >= 2 BY ARITH, A >= 1, +, B >= 1;

7.   2 <= X|X<0 BY ARITH, X<X*X, /, X¬ = 0;

8.   Z>0 BY ARITH, Z>W, W>0;

9.   X*Z>Y*Z BY ARITH, X>Y, *, Z>0;

10. X*Z>W*Y BY ARITH, Z>W, *, Y>0, X*Z>Y*Z;

11. 3*X+Y >= 2*Z-1 BY ARITH, X+Y>Z,+, 2*X >= Z;

12. X=Y|Y=Z|Z=X BY ARITH, X-1 <= Y <= X+1, X-1 <= Z,
     Z <= X+1, Y-1 <= Z, Z <= Y+1;

§3.3 SPECIAL FUNCTIONS

1. The functions /, **, ABS, MAX, MIN, MOD, and SIGN are
basic number theoretic functions built into PL/I. But
they are not treated by the proof rule ARITH. Since even
informal reasoning about these functions is not always
immediate, it is not unfitting for them to be given
special treatment. Axioms are given for each function
from which its basic properties can be derived.

2. <u>Enumeration of axioms</u>

1. ABSOLUTE VALUE

    ABS: ALL X FIXED . ((X<=0 => ABS(X)=-X) & (X>=0 =>
                          ABS(X)=X)) & X=0 => ABS(X) = 0

2. SIGN

    SIGN: ALL X FIXED . (X<0 <=> SIGN(X)=-1) &
                         (X=0 <=> SIGN(X)=0) &
                         (X>0 <=> SIGN(X)=1)

3. DIVISION

    Note, when division appears in commands, it must be the
    outermost operator, i.e. it *cannot appear in subexpres-
    sions*. This restriction is needed because PL/I
    division is not ordinary integer division; instead of
    truncating the fractional part of a real number divi-
    sion, it retains the fraction. Thus 2/3 is .666666
    rather than 0.

DIVISION: $(A>=0 \And B\neg=0 \Rightarrow A = B*(A/B)+MOD(A,B)) \And$

$(A<=0 \And B\neg=0 \Rightarrow A = B*(A/B)-MOD(A,B)) \And$

ALL (Q,R) FIXED . (

$A>=0 \And B\neg=0 \Rightarrow ((A = B*Q+R \And 0<=R<ABS(B))$
$\Rightarrow (Q = A/B \And R = MOD(A,B)))$

$A<=0 \And \neg B=0 \Rightarrow ((A = B*Q-R \And 0<=R<ABS(B))$
$\Rightarrow (Q = A/B \And R = MOD(A,B)))) \And$

$(A>0 \And 0<B<=A \Rightarrow A/B>0) \And$
$(A<0 \And A<=B<0 \Rightarrow A/B>0) \And$
$(A>0 \And -A<=B<0 \Rightarrow A/B<0) \And$
$(A<0 \And 0<B<=A \Rightarrow A/B<0) \And$
$(A=0 \And B\neg=0 \Rightarrow A/B=0) \And$
$(A\neg=0 \And 0<ABS(A) < ABS(B) \Rightarrow A/B=0)$

4. MODULUS

MOD: ALL (Q,R) FIXED .
$((A = B*Q+R \And 0<=R<ABS(B)) \Rightarrow R = MOD(A,B)) \And$

SOME Q FIXED . $(A = B*Q+MOD(A/B)) \And$
$0<=MOD(A,B) < ABS(B)$

5. EXPONENTIATION

    EXP: ALL (B,E) FIXED.
        ABS(B)>=1 => B**0 = 1) &
        ABS(B)>=1&E>=1 => (B**E = B*(B**E-1) &
                       (B**E)/B = B**E-1)

6. BINARY MAXIMUM

    MAX: ALL (A,B) FIXED . (MAX(A,B)>=A & MAX(A,B)>=B &
                       (MAX(A,B)=A | MAX(A,B)=B))

7. BINARY MINIMUM

    MIN: ALL (A,B) FIXED . (MIN(A,B)<=A & MIN(A,B)<=B &
                       (MIN(A,B=A | MIN(A,B)=B))

3. Applying the axioms

    For convenience these axioms can all be applied in a simple format. The rule name can be used as the label of the axiom for all elimanation. (This will be the format for user defined functions in part VI.)

    ABS(2) = 2   BY FUNCTION, ABS(2);
    SIGN(-1) = -1 BY FUNCTION, SIGN(-1);
    5*X/5 = X   BY FUNCTION, DIVISION(5*X,5)

§3.4   INDUCTION

PL/CV provides a simple form of induction so that the arithmetic rules include Peano arithmetic (see Kleene [7]).

INDUCTION

        P(K/N);
        ALL N FIXED WHERE $\{{}^{N<=K}_{N>=K}\}$. P by induction,

        PROOF; [ARBITRARY N FIXED WHERE $\{{}^{N<=K}_{N>=K}\}$ & P;]
                  :
                  :
           $\{{}^{P(N-1/N)}_{P(N+1/N)}\}$
        QED;

The braces show two possible forms, increasing and decreasing induction.
    The rule is used in the long example of the next
section.

§3.5   <u>EXAMPLE</u>


```
/# EXTENDED EXAMPLE OF PL/CV ARITHMETIC AND PREDICATE   #/
/# CALCULUS:   PROOF THAT THERE IS NO LARGEST PRIME      #/

FOR (D, A) FIXED DEFINE DIV(D, A) = SOME M FIXED . M*D = A;

FOR P FIXED DEFINE NO_DIVISORS(P) = ALL D FIXED WHERE D>1
 & DIV(C,P) . D=P;
FOR P FIXED DEFINE PRIME(P) = P>1 & NO_DIVISORS(P);

LEMMA L:
/# FOR D>1, A>1, IF D DIVIDES A THEN D<=A   #/
ALL (D,A) FIXED WHERE D>1 & A>1 . (DIV(D,A) => D<=A)
 BY INTRO, INTRO,
PROOF;
     CHOOSE M FIXED WHERE M*D=A;
     M<=0 | M>=1 BY ARITH;
     D>=0 BY ARITH, D>1;

     D<=A BY CASES, M<=0 | M>=1,
     PROOF;
     CASE M<=0;
          M*D<=0 BY ARITH, M<=0,   *, D>=0;;
          '0'B BY ARITH, 1 < A = M*D <= 0;
     CASE M>=1;
          M*D>=D BY ARITH, M>=1, *, D>=0;;
          A = M*D >=D;
     QED;
QED;
```

LEMMA_T:
/# TRANSITIVITY OF DIVIDES #/
ALL (A, B, C) FIXED . (DIV(A,B) & DIV(B, C) => DIV(A, C))
BY INTRO,
PROOF;
    CHOOSE M1 FIXED WHERE M1*A = B;
    CHOOSE M2 FIXED WHERE M2*B = C;
    M2*(M1*A) = C; /# BY SUBSTITUTION #/
    (M2*M1)*A = C; /# BY ASSOCIATIVITY OF * #/
    DIV(A,C) BY SOMIN, M2*M1;
QED;

LEMMA_P:
/# EVERY INTEGER GREATER THAN ONE HAS A PRIME DIVISOR. #/
ALL A FIXED WHERE A>1 . SOME P FIXED WHERE PRIME(P) .
DIV(P, A) BY INTRO,
PROOF;
    FOR N FIXED DEFINE IH(N) =
        ALL K FIXED WHERE 1<K<=N .
                SOME PD FIXED WHERE PRIME(PD) .
                DIV(PD, K);

    IH(1) BY INTRO; PROOF; '0'B BY ARITH, 1<K<=1; QED;

    STRONG: ALL N FIXED WHERE N>=1 . IH(N) BY INDUCTION,
    PROOF;
        ARB N FIXED WHERE N>=1 & IH(N);
        IH(N+1) BY INTRO,
        PROOF;
        ARB K FIXED WHERE 1<K<=N+1;

        EXIST_DIV:
        SOME PD FIXED WHERE PRIME(PD) . DIV(PD,K)
        BY CONTRADICTION,
        PROOF;
            ASSUME ¬EXIST_DIV;

            ¬PRIME(K) BY INTRO;
            PROOF;
                ASSUME PRIME(K);
                /# SINCE K DIVIDES ITSELF, IT HAS A
                    PRIME DIVISOR #/

```
                        1*K = K BY ARITH;
                        DIV(K,K) BY SOMIN, 1;
                        EXIST_DIV BY SOMIN, K;
                        ¬EXIST_DIV;  /# ASSUMED #/
                  QED;

                  NO_DIVISORS(K) BY INTRO,
                  PROOF;
                        /# SHOW THE ONLY PROPER DIVISOR OF K IS
                           K ITSELF #/

                        ARB D FIXED WHERE D>1 & DIV(D,K);
                        D<=K BY ALLEL, LEMMA_L, D, K;
                        D=K | D<=N BY ARITH, D<=K<=N+1;

                        D = K BY CASES, D=K|D<=N,
                        PROOF;
                        CASE D<=N;
                              SOME PD FIXED WHERE PRIME(PD) .
                              DIV(PD,D)
                                    BY ALLEL, IH(N), D;
                              CHOOSE PD FIXED
                                    WHERE PRIME(PD) & DIV(PD,D);
                              DIV(PD,K) BY ALLEL, LEMMA_T,
                                    PD, D, K;
                              EXIST_DIV BY SOMIN, PD;
                              ¬EXIST_DIV;  /# ASSUMED #/
                        QED;
                  QED;
            QED;
            QED;
      QED;

      /# APPLY THE RESULTS OF THE INDUCTION TO THE ARBITRARY
         VARIABLE A #/
      A>=1 BY ARITH, A>1;
      A>=A BY ARITH;
      IH(A) BY ALLEL, STRONG, A;
      SOME PD FIXED WHERE PRIME(PD) . DIV(PD,A)
      BY ALLEL, IH(A), A;
QED;
```

```
/# EXISTENCE OF FACTORIAL FUNCTION #/
/# THE PROPERTIES GIVEN DO NOT COMPLETELY CHARACTERIZE  #/
/# THE FACTORIAL FUNCTION -- ONLY THE PROPERTIES NEEDED #/
/# ARE GIVEN                                            #/
FOR X FIXED DEFINE FAC(X) =
    SOME F FIXED WHERE F>=X . ALL D FIXED WHERE 1<D<=X .
    DIV(D, F);

ALL D FIXED WHERE 1<D<=1 . DIV(D, 1) BY INTRO,
PROOF;

    '0'B BY ARITH, 1<D<=1;

QED;


1 >= 1 BY ARITH;
FAC(1) BY SOMIN, 1;

ALL X FIXED WHERE X>=1 . FAC(X) BY INDUCTION,
PROOF;
    CHOOSE F FIXED WHERE F>=X,
                        ALLDIV: ALL D FIXED WHERE 1<D<=X .
                        DIV(D, F);

    ALL D FIXED WHERE 1<D<=X+1 . DIV(D, F*(X+1)) BY INTRO,
    PROOF;
        C:  D<=X | D = X+1 BY ARITH, D<=X+1;
        DIV(D, F*(X+1)) BY CASES, C;
        PROOF;
        CASE D<=X;
            DIV(D, F) BY ALLEL, ALL_DIV, D;
            DIV(F, (X+1)*F) BY SOMIN, X+1;
            DIV(D, (X+1)*F) BY ALLEL, LEMMA_T, D, F,
                (X+1)*F;
        CASE D = X+1;
            DIV(X+1, F*(X+1)) BY SOMIN, F;
        QED;
    QED;

    X+1 >= 0 BY ARITH, X>=1;
    F   >= 1 BY ARITH, F>=X>=1;
    F*(X+1) >= X+1 BY ARITH, F>=1, *, X+1>=0;

    SOME FF FIXED WHERE FF>=X+1 . ALL D FIXED WHERE
    1<D<=X+1 . DIV(D,FF) BY SOMIN, F*(X+1);
QED;
```

```
/# THERE IS NO LARGEST PRIME #/
¬ SOME MP FIXED WHERE PRIME(MP) . ALL LP FIXED WHERE
PRIME(LP) . LP <= MP
BY INTRO, PROOF;
     CHOOSE MP FIXED WHERE PRIME(MP), MAX:  ALL LP WHERE
     PRIME(LP) . LP <= MP;

     MP >= 1 BY ARITH, MP>1;
     SOME F FIXED . FAC(MP) BY ALLEL, ALL X FIXED WHERE
     X>=1 . FAC(X), MP;
     CHOOSE F FIXED WHERE F >= MP,
            ALLDIV:  ALL D FIXED WHERE 1<D<=MP . DIV(D, F);

     /# F IS SOME MULTIPLE OF MP FACTORIAL #/

     F+1 > 1 BY ARITH, F>= MP>1;
     NO_DIVISORS(F+1) BY INTRO,
     PROOF;
          ARB D FIXED WHERE D>1 & DIV(D, F+1);
          D <= F+1 BY ALLEL, LEMMA_L, D, F+1;
          D<=F | D=F+1 BY ARITH, D<=F+1;

          D=F+1 BY CASES, D<=F | D = F+1,
          PROOF; CASE D<=F;
               SOME P FIXED WHERE PRIME(P) . DIV(P,D)
                 BY ALLEL, LEMMA_P,D;
               CHOOSE P FIXED WHERE PRIME(P) & DIV(P,D)
               P <= MP BY ALLEL, MAX, P;
               DIV(P, F) BY ALLEL, ALLDIV, P;
               DIV(P, F+1) BY ALLEL, LEMMA_T, P, D, F+1;

               /# THE ABOVE TWO LINES, WITH P>1, LEAD  #/
               /# TO A CONTRADICTION                   #/
               CHOOSE M FIXED WHERE E:  M*P = F;
               CHOOSE M1 FIXED WHERE E1: M1*P = F+1;
               EQ_1:  (M1 - M) * P = 1 BY ARITH, E1, -, E;

               C:  M1-M<=0 | M1-M>0 BY ARITH;
               '0'B BY CASES, C,
               PROOF;
               CASE M1-M <= 0;
                    P>=0 BY ARITH, P>1;
                    '0'B BY ARITH, (M1-M)<=0, *, P>=0,EQ_1;
               CASE M1-M > 0;
                    '0'B BY ARITH, P>1, *, (M1-M)>0, EQ_1;
               QED;
          QED;
```

324

```
    QED;
    PRIME(F+1);

    /# PRIME(F+1) CONTRADICTS THE ASSUMPTION THAT MP   #/
    /# IS THE LARGEST PRIME #/
    F+1 <= MP BY ALLEL, MAX, F+1;
    '0'B BY ARITH, F+1<=MP, F>=MP;
QED;
```

IV SIMPLE PROGRAMS

§4.1 INTRODUCTION

PL/I is an Algol-like programming language organized
around the concept of a command acting on a state through
variables. To reason about these commands, they must be
allowed in arguments. Their free use in arguments creates
a logic far more expressive than the predicate calculus.
This richness of expression is paid for by added complexity
in the proof rules.

The logic of commands described in this section is the
heart of the PL/CV asserted program logic. There are three
new ideas which must be mastered. First, commands introduce new types of binding, new block structure and with
gotos, a nonlinear order among statements. The added complexity appears in 4.3. Second, proof rule formats must
now display information about positions of the hypotheses
and conclusion in the program, especially concerning their
lexical order. This added complexity appears in the presentation of rules in 4.1. Third, commands are allowed
as part of the purely logical structure of a program, as
inside proof-groups. These commands are not meant to be
executed. To indicate this fact, they are shielded (from
the compiler) just as assertions are. Special rules for
shielding commands must be stated.

§4.2 SYNTAX

1. Shielding

(i) To insure that PL/CV programs are compatible with
dialects of PL/I, all PL/CV assertions occurring in programs are enclosed in special PL/I comment delimiters,
/*/ and */. Therefore a main PL/CV argument is actually
a program which will compile under either the PL/I, PL/C
or PL/CS compiler depending on which commands are used
(e.g. PL/C release 7 does not include DO UNTIL, LEAVE,

SELECT, whereas PL/I does not include READONLY, etc.)

(ii) Commands are, of course, essential in the part of the argument which we intend to execute, the *program*. But they may also be valuable in the purely logical part of the argument; for instance, to construct an object exclusively for the sake of the proof or to preserve relationships among the logical variables and various program variables, whose values may be changing. These commands, which we do not intend to execute, must be shielded. But since = is both the equality and assignment symbol, /*/ A=0; */, is ambiguous. Is it the *assertion* "A equals 0" or the *command* "A gets 0?" The command is written as /*: A=0; */, resolving the ambiguity but necessitating two kinds of left-hand shielding delimiters, /*/ and /*:.·

(iii) To be more precise about shielding, we define the notion of program, program variable, logic variable, and shielding.

Definition: Given a PL/CV main argument, the associated *program* is the sequence of statements not enclosed in comment delimiters. All variables and statements in the program are called *program variables* and *program statements* respectively. Any token enclosed in the special comments which begin /*/ or /*: and end */ is called *shielded*. Any variable declared in shielded declarations is called an *auxiliary variable*. Any shielded command is called an *auxiliary command*. A variable not appearing in a declaration is *logical*.

Note 1: Ordinary Pl/I comments may not be used inside PL/CV shielded text because the */ will prematurely close the shield, e.g. /*/ DCL (A(*) /* PERMUTATION ARRAY */, B) */. To include a comment inside shielded text, use the delimiters /#, #/, as in /*/ DCL (A(*) /# PERMUTATION ARRAY #/, B) */.

Note 2: Real comments /*...*/ cannot cross a card boundary in PL/CS.

(iv) To describe the shielding rules in the syntax below, the following definitions are useful. Let T be a piece of an argument.

> T is completely shielded iff every token in T is shielded.

> T is completely unshielded iff no token in T is shielded.

> T is partially shielded iff there is at least one shielded and one unshielded token.

2. Grammar of commands

Note, "stmt" is used throughout to abbreviate "statement" and "boolean" or "bexp" are sometimes used to abbreviate "boolean_exp".

(i) general categories
command

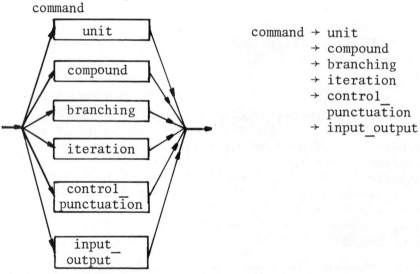

command → unit
→ compound
→ branching
→ iteration
→ control_
   punctuation
→ input_output

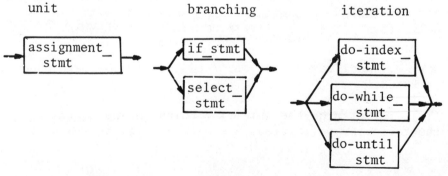

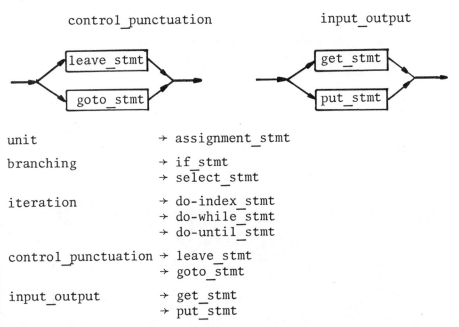

control_punctuation   input_output

unit   → assignment_stmt

branching   → if_stmt
                        → select_stmt

iteration   → do-index_stmt
                        → do-while_stmt
                        → do-until_stmt

control_punctuation → leave_stmt
                        → goto_stmt

input_output   → get_stmt
                        → put_stmt

Note: In all categories, the ATTAIN statements must be shielded.

proof_stmt

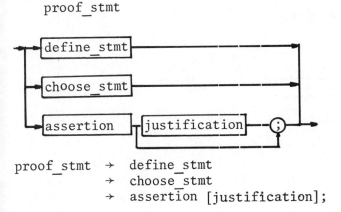

proof_stmt →   define_stmt
            →   choose_stmt
            →   assertion [justification];

A Programming Logic

stmt

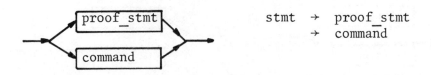

stmt → proof_stmt
→ command

(ii)   unit commands

assignment_stmt

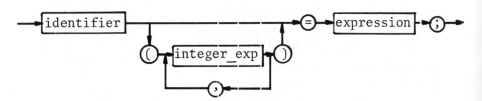

assignment_stmt →
   identifier [(integer_exp {, integer_exp}*)] = expression ;

Assignments must be completely shielded or unshielded. The left side of a shielded assignment may not contain a variable declared in an unshielded declaration

(iii) compound commands

compound

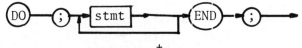

compound → DO;{stmt}⁺END;

330

(iv)   branching commands

if_stmt

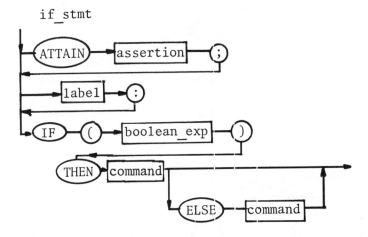

if_stmt →   [ATTAIN assertion ;] IF (boolean_exp) THEN stmt
             [ELSE command]

Note: In order to use conditional or select in proofs
they must be preceded by the ATTAIN statement.

select_stmt

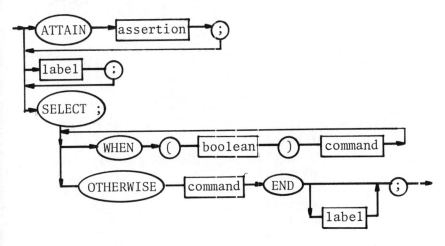

A Programming Logic

```
select_stmt  →  [ATTAIN assertion ;]
                [label : ] SELECT;
                          {WHEN (boolean_exp) command}⁺
                          OTHERWISE command END [label];
```

Note: As with the if_stmt, selected parts may be shielded.
See FINE POINTS for details. Also note, the select_stmt
is not compatible with PL/C7.

(v)   iteration commands

    do-index_stmt

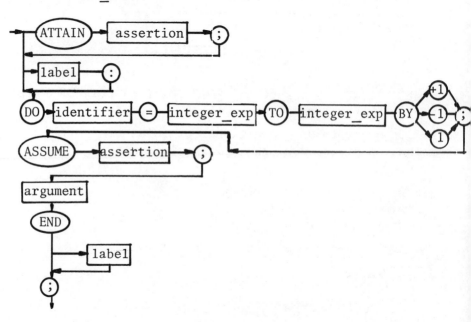

```
do-index_stmt  →  [ATTAIN assertion ;]
                  [label :]
                  DO identifier = integer_exp TO integer_exp
                   BY {+1,1,-1};
                  ASSUME assertion ;
                  argument
                  END [label] ;
```

do-while_stmt

```
do-while_stmt  →  [ATTAIN assertion;]
                  [label:]
                  DO WHILE (boolean_exp);
                     ASSUME assertion;
                     {proof_stmt}*
                  {ARBITRARY,ARB}identifier
                     FIXED WHERE assertion;
                     {proof_stmt}*
                     argument
                  END [label];
```

333

do-until_stmt

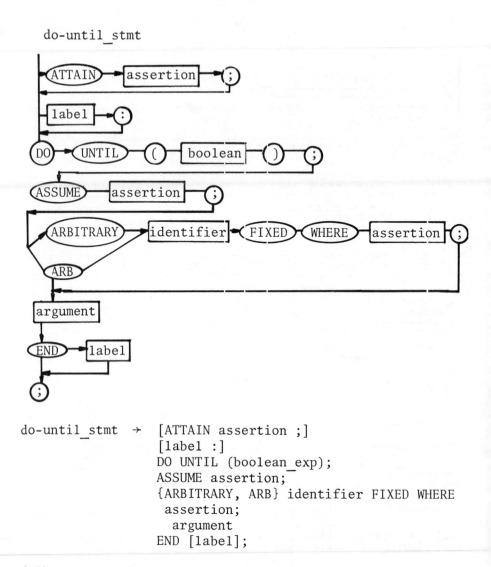

do-until_stmt →   [ATTAIN assertion ;]
                   [label :]
                   DO UNTIL (boolean_exp);
                   ASSUME assertion;
                   {ARBITRARY, ARB} identifier FIXED WHERE
                    assertion;
                      argument
                   END [label];

(vi) punctuation

goto_stmt   leave_stmt

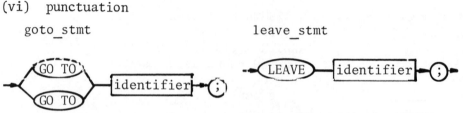

Note: Gotos cannot exit a proof-group. The labeled statement must lie lexically beyond the goto itself, but not
inside any block not containing the goto itself.
    We do not provide syntax for input-output statements
since we have no rules for them in this version of the system.

§4.3   SUBSTITUTIONS

1.   Discussion

    Program variables have free occurrences in arguments
just as logical variables have free occurrences in assertions.
For example, in the one line program Y=X+1, X is a free
varaible and Y is bound. We do not need the concept of
substitution for free program variables at this point, but
the concept of a bound program variable is useful in
describing the proof rules, so we define it here.

2.
Definition: Any of the following occurrences of a variable
x are binding occurrences (the first six were defined in
II §2.4.(ii))

    1.   SOME...x   ALL...x

    2.   ARBITRARY...x (or ARB...x)

    3.   CHOOSE...x

    4.   FOR...x

    5.   DEFINE x

    6.   x: (as a label of an assertion)

    7. DO x= ...

    8.   x=exp (in an assignment)

A nonbinding occurrence of the variable x in an argument
A is said to be *bound in A* (*tightly bound in A*) if and
only if any of the following hold:

    1.   The occurrence is in a subassertion P within the
         assertion

              ALL...x... .P or SOME...x... .P

335

A Programming Logic

2. A is qualified by ARBITRARY...x or ARB...x
    or the occurrence is in a subargument B within an
    argument qualified by ARBITRARY...x or ARB...x.

3. A contains the statement CHOOSE...x or the occur-
    rence is in a subargument B containing CHOOSE...x.

4. The occurrence is within the assertion or expres-
    sion following = in FOR...x DEFINE...= .

5. A contains DEFINE x or the occurrence is within a
    subargument B containing the definition DEFINE x.

6. The occurrence is lexically below the label
    x: on an assertion in A or in a subargument B of A.

7. The occurrence is within the do-index loop DO
    $x=exp_1$ to exp_2...END.

8. The occurence is in an assertion or command L of
    A for which there is an assignment x=exp on
    some execution path (on *every* execution path)
    from the beginning of A to L.

Remark. A bound variable which is not tightly bound is
called *loosely bound*. Such variables arise when one
execution path finds x and another does not.
For instance x is loosely bound in

            IF X>0 THEN X=5;
                    ELSE Y=7;
        /*/ X-1≥0   */

It would be tightly bound if Y=7 were replaced by X=7.
    The next definition tells exactly which binding oc-
currence of x finds which other occurrences of x. Intuitively, a variable is bound by each binding occurrence
which might affect its meaning.

Definition: Every free or loosely bound occurrence of
a variable x in argument segments α,β,γ is bound by the
binding occurrence of x in

1. ALL...x α;   SOME...x α;

2. ARBITRARY...x α QED;

3. CHOOSE...x α QED;

4. FOR...x DEFINE α;

5. FOR...DEFINE x α QED;

6. x: assertion α QED;

7. DO x=exp_1 TO exp_2 α END;

8. (a) x=exp; α or

   (b) IF bexp THEN... x=exp α ELSE DO: ...END; β or

   (c) DO index = exp_1 TO exp_2 BY exp_3; α; x=exp; β END; γ

   (d) DO WHILE bexp α x=exp β END; γ or

   (e) DO UNTIL bexp α x=exp β END; γ

For instance in line 1, α is any well formed part of an assertion up to the first semi-colon. So in ALL N FIXED WHERE N>0 . F(N) = 0 the occurrences of N in N>0 and F(N) = 0 are bound by ALL N. In line 8, clause (a) means that after x=exp any free or loosely bound occurrence of x in the rest of the argument is bound by this assignment. Thus in X=0; IF Y>0 THEN X=2; ELSE Y=2; P(X) the loosely bound occurrence of x in IF Y>0 THEN X=2; ELSE Y=2; P(X) is bound by X=0. Assignments x=exp inside loops bind all free or loosely bound occurrence of x in the body.

All other occurrences of x in A are *free* in A.

§4.4   PROOF RULES

1.   Rule formats

Proof rules for commands require a more complex format than those for the predicate claculus. The rule must show relative lexicographic order of hypotheses. This is done by making vertical order significant, e.g. if hypothesis H_i occurs vertically above hypothesis H_j then H_i must occur lexically before H_j in the argument (unless there is an explicit remark to the contrary). Some rules must show even more about the relative position of hypotheses and conclusion; this is done by including segments of commands such as conditionals and loops to indicate context. In the case of the loop introduction rules, the loop body is a hypothesis to the introduction of the entire loop (which, of course, contains the body); so sometimes the conclusion

337

A Programming Logic

must be specified in words.

In all rules, certain hypotheses need only be implicitly known, that is they may be immediate from other assertions appearing previously. Such hypotheses are enclosed in braces.

In some cases, special provisos must be stated to indicate accessibility relationships among hypotheses and conclusions. Subject to these conditions and the syntactic rules, the hypotheses of any rule can be separated by other commands and assertions *provided that for positions not separated by ellipses (...), the first is accessible to the second.*

2. Well-defined expressions

For each rule involving the evaluation of an expression which may contain defined functions (in this section arrays are the only such functions), and for each occurrence of a defined function application, there must be an hypothesis guaranteeing that the function application is defined.[†] The programming languages PL/C or PL/CS guarantee that any variable uninitialized by the programmer is initialized by the compiler, so an expression is undefined only if array indices are out of bounds.

An expression exp is *well-defined* if and only if every array application occurring in it is defined. Thus an expression is well-defined if for each array A in it and for each $A(exp_1,...,exp_n)$ the assertion $LBOUND(A,i) <= exp_i <= HBOUND(A,i)$ is true.

In the proof rules, the phrase "exp is well-defined" will mean the conjunction of all assertions that each array application in exp is defined. For example, the expression

$$(A(2,X)+Z) * B(A(X,Y))$$

is well-defined means

$LBOUND(A,1) <= 2 <= HBOUND(A,1)$ & $LBOUND(A,2) <= X <= HBOUND(A,2)$ &

$LBOUND(A,1) <= X <= HBOUND(A,1)$ & $LBOUND(A,2) <= Y <=$

[†]When any partial infix operators, such as division, are allowed, then we require also that its arguments are in its domain, e.g. non-zero.

HBOUND(A,2) &

LBOUND(B,1) <= A(X,Y) <= HBOUND(B,1).

3. Accessibility

(i) In order for an assertion A at position p to be accessible in an argument at position q, it must mean the same thing at q and p, and it must be visible from q. Commands may cause an assertion A to become inaccessible after the command by changing the meaning of free variables in A. For instance,

1. /*/ Y>0 */
2. /*/ X>2 */
3. /*: X=-3 */
4. /*/ X*Y>2*Y BY ARITH, X>2,*,Y>0 ; */

Line 4 is false because the command at 3 changed the meaning of X. The same thing can happen even though the command lies beyond the assertion, as in this illustration:

1. /*/ X>0; */
2.   DO WHILE Y>0;
3.   Y=Y-1;
4. /*/ X>0; */
5. /*: X=X-1; */
6.   END;

The assertion X>0 at line 4 may be false although no command changes X in the *lexical segment* from 1 to 4.

(ii) In order for an assertion A at position p to be accessible in an argument at position q, it must be the case that any way of getting to position q passes through position p. Here is an example where this fails:

1. GOTO L;
2. /*/ X>0; */
           .
           .
           .

3. L: ;

4. /*/ Y>0; */

5. /*/ X+Y>0 BY ARITH, X>0,+,Y>0; */

(iii) For the purpose of determining accessibility, we use
a generalization of the concept of an execution path.
This generalization affords a fast check of accessibility.
     First we examine the apparently *possible* execution
paths. To define these, ignore the actual values of any
boolean and consider execution for both possible values.
Replace any unconditional goto, GOTO L, by IF _____ THEN
GOTO L ELSE ; and consider both possible paths. (Thus
the goto will be ignored in one case.) We say that execution paths determined this way are *execution paths in the
general sense.*

Definition: A position p in an argument *dominates* position
q if and only if every execution path in the general sense
from start to q must pass through p. (This is a generalization of lexical order.)

Definition: A *proof-block* is either a proof-group, or a
THEN clause or an ELSE clause or a WHEN clause or a WHILE
loop or an UNTIL loop or a DO-index loop.

Let $A(x,\ldots,x)$ indicate that $x_1,\ldots,x_n$ are all the variables free in A.

Definition: An occurrence of an assertion $A(x_1,\ldots,x_n)$
at position p in an argument with commands is *accessible*
from position q if and only if:

(0) q does not occur in a proof block used as justi-
     fication for the occurrence of $A(x_1,\ldots,x_n)$ at p,

(1) position p *dominates* position q, and

(2) any proof-block containing p also contains q
     (say, p is *visible from* q), and

(3) $A(x_1,\ldots,x_n)$ is the same at q and p that is:

     (a) x_i have the same scope at p as at q.

     (b) no x_i is changed on any execution path (in
          the general sense) from p to q.

Note: Using the concept of a bound variable of an argument, we can simplify (3) to case (a) since x_i=exp is a
binding of x_i which changes its scope.

4. Proofs

Definition: A *proof* in the language of PL/CV programs is
an argument in which every occurrence of an assertion at
a position p is either an assumption or follows from accessible lines and immediate assertions by a rule of inference.

Note, logical variables CANNOT be modified by commands.
They are *readonly*. (See FINE POINTS for a relaxation of
this condition and the definition of proof.)

5. Enumeration of command rules

(1)   ASSIGNMENT INTRODUCTION (immediate)

{exp is well-defined}   If x is an array, exp must
———————————————   have the same domain as x.
      x=exp

{exp, t_1,...,t_n are well-defined}
{<t_1,...,t_n> is in the domain of A}
————————————————————————————
   $A(t_1,...,t_n)$ = exp

(2)   ASSIGNMENT ELIMINATION (immediate)

P(exp/x)   A=C   C a constant
x=exp   ————————————————————
————   ALL $(I_1,...,I_n)$ FIXED .
  P $A(I_1...,I_n)$ = C

(3)   ARRAY ASSIGNMENT ELIMINATION

$\hat{A}$=A, $\hat{t}_1$=t_1,...,$\hat{t}_n$=t_n, $\hat{exp}$=exp
  $A(t_1,...,t_n)$ = exp
———————————————————————— $\hat{t}_i$, $\hat{exp}$, $\hat{A}$ cannot contain A
$A(\hat{t}_1,...,\hat{t}_n)$ = $\hat{exp}$ &
ALL$(I_1,...,I_n)$ FIXED WHERE $\neg(I_1$=$\hat{t}_1$&...&I_n=$\hat{t}_n)$.
  $\hat{A}(I_1,...,I_n)$ = $A(I_1,...,I_n)$

341

(4) CONDITIONAL INTRODUCTION (immediate)

{bexp is well-defined}

IF(bexp)THEN ... [ELSE...]

The content of the branches must be filled in by other introduction rules.

(5) SELECT INTRODUCTION (immediate)

{all $bexp_i$ are well-defined}

[label :] SELECT;
    WHEN $(bexp_1)$ ...
       .
       .
       .
    WHEN $(bexp_n)$ ...
    OTHERWISE ... END [label];

(6) BOOLEAN EXPRESSION INTRODUCTION (immediate)

conditional

    IF (bexp) THEN ... [ELSE ...]

    IF (bexp) THEN bexp ... [ELSE ¬bexp ...]

select

    SELECT;
      .
      .
      .
      WHEN $(bexp_i)$ ...
      .
      .
      .
    OTHERWISE ... END;

    WHEN $(bexp_i)$ DO; $¬bexp_1 \& ... \& ¬bexp_{i-1} \&$
      . $bexp_i$ ... END;
      .
      .
    OTHERWISE DO; $¬bexp_1 \& ... \& ¬bexp_n$ ... END;
             END;

The above rules describe which boolean expressions can be introduced as assertions at which points inside conditional and select statements governed by these boolean expressions.

(7) CONDITIONAL ELIMINATION

```
{bexp is well-defined}
ATTAIN E;
IF (bexp) THEN [DO;] ... E ; [END;]
         ELSE [DO;] ... E ; [END;]
```
_____

                E

```
{bexp is well-defined}
¬bexp => E
ATTAIN E;
IF (bexp) THEN [DO;] ... E ; [END;]
```
_____

                E

(8) SELECT ELIMINATION

```
{bexp_i are well-defined}

ATTAIN E;
SELECT;
  WHEN bexp_1 [DO;] ... E ; [END;]
    .
    .
    .
  WHEN bexp_n [DO;] ... E ; [END;]
  OTHERWISE [DO;] ... E ; [END;]
END;
```
_____

                E

These rules describe which boolean expressions can be introduced as assertions at which points inside conditional and select statements governed by these boolean expressions.

(9)   DO-INDEX INTRODUCTION (immediate)

{the expressions lower, upper are well-defined}

DO index = lower TO upper BY {+1,1,-1}; ...END;

(10) DO-INDEX BOUNDS INTRODUCTION (immediate)

```
DO index = lower TO upper          DO index = upper TO lower
BY {+1,1};                         BY -1;
lower <= index <= upper;           upper >= index >= lower;
    .                                  .
    .                                  .
    .                                  .
END;                               END;
```

(11) DO-INDEX ELIMINATION

upward form

```
              P(lower/i);
              [ATTAIN E ;] [lower > upper => E ;]
                 DO index = lower TO upper BY {+1,1};
                    ASSUME P(index/i);

                       .
                       .
                       .

                    index ¬= upper => P(index +1/i);
                    index = upper => E;
              END
```

E

Note 1: P(upper +1/i) is the default for E if the attain statement is missing, in which case the last two hypotheses are replaced by P(index +1/i).

Note 2: Index and all variables in upper and lower are readonly inside the do block.

Note 3: E may not depend on index, which has an arbitrary value upon exit from the block.

downward form

        P(upper/i), {lower, upper well-defined}
        [ATTAIN E;] [lower > upper => E ;]
        DO index = upper TO lower BY-1;
             ASSUME P(index/i);

                .
                .
                .
             index ¬= lower => P(index-1/i);
             index = lower => E;
        END;
──

        E

Note 1: If ATTAIN E is missing, the default is P(lower-1/i)
in which case the two final assertions are replaced by
P(index-1/i).

Note 2: Index and all variables in upper and lower are
readonly inside the do block.

Note 3: E may not depend on index which has an undefined
value upon exit from the block.

(12) DO WHILE INTRODUCTION

        {bexp is well-defined}, SOME n FIXED . (n>=0 & T);
        DO WHILE (bexp);
        ARBITRARY n FIXED WHERE T;
        ¬T(0/n);
                .
                .
                .
        body
                .
                .
                .
             T(n-1/n); {bexp and all expressions in T are
                        well-defined}
        END;

The loop itself is the conclusion. The rule is used to
justify introducing loops into a proof. They can only be
introduced if they terminate.

(13)   DO WHILE BOOLEAN INTRODUCTION (immediate)

DO WHILE (bexp);

.

.

.

END;

_____

DO WHILE (bexp);
   ASSUME P;
   bexp;

.

.

.

END;

This rule indicates where the boolean expression governing the loop can be introduced into a loop body, after ASSUME.

(14)   DO WHILE ELIMINATION

[ATTAIN E;], P[& ($\neg$bexp => E)] & {bexp is well-defined}
DO WHILE (bexp);
   ASSUME P[& ($\neg$bexp => E & {bexp is well-defined}

.

.

.

body

.

.

.

{P[& ($\neg$bexp => E)];}
{bexp is well-defined}
END;

_____

E

See FINE POINTS for a liberalization of the invariant concerning bexp as well-defined.

Note 2:   If the exit condition E is missing, the default is P & $\neg$bexp, in which case $\neg$bexp => E is not necessary.

Note 3:   If ATTAIN E is present, then $\neg$bexp => E must be part of the invariant P.   See FINE POINTS for a liberalization of this requirement.

(15) DO UNTIL INTRODUCTION

      SOME i FIXED . i>=0 & T;
      DO UNTIL (bexp);
         ARBITRARY i FIXED WHERE T;
         ¬T(0)
           .
           .
           .
         body
           .
           .
           .
         {bexp is well-defined}
         T(i-1/i)
      END

The loop itself is the conclusion.

(16) DO UNTIL ELIMINATION

      P,
      ATTAIN E;
      DO UNTIL (bexp);
         ASSUME P;
           .
           .
           .
         body
           .
           .
           .
         bexp => E;
         ¬bexp => P;
      END

Note 1: The attain statement is necessary for the until loop.

(17)   CONTROL PUNCTUATION

GOTO label;	LEAVE label;
A	A

This rule permits the introduction of an arbitrary assertion
A immediately after (accessible to) GOTO and LEAVE.

(18)   LABEL

A			
A ATTAIN A;		E̵ E	
GOTO L, L:		LEAVE L, L:	

L:	END L;
A	E

Provided A is accessible to each occurrence of GOTO L
or LEAVE L, E is the exit condition of the loop labeled L.

§4.5   EXAMPLES

Here are some selected examples of arguments with
commands. There are examples of program correctness
proofs.

1.   "largest" example

/* This is a procedure fragment */

/* Find largest element in an integer array */
    DCL A(10) FIXED; /* READONLY */
    DCL (M,I,J)FIXED;

/*/ ATTAIN ALL I FIXED WHERE 1<=I<=10.   M>= A(I) & SOME J
    FIXED WHERE 1<=J<=10 . M = A(J);

    M=A(1);

/*/ SOME K FIXED. M=A(K) BY SOMIN, 1; */

/*/ ALL K FIXED WHERE 1<=K<2 . M>=A(I) BY INTRO, PROOF;
    K=1 BY ARITH, 1<≠K<2; M>=A(1) BY ARITH, M=A(1); QED;
    DO I=2 TO 10 BY 1;

348

```
/*/ ASSUME ASM: ALL K FIXED WHERE 1<=K<I. M>=A(K) & SOME
            SOME K FIXED WHERE 1<=K<=10 . M+A(K); */

/*/ I>=1 BY ARITH, I>=2; */

/*/ ATTAIN ALL K FIXED WHERE 1<=K<I+1 . M>=A(K) & SOME K
      FIXED WHERE 1<=K<=10 M=A(K); */

    IF M<A(I)
    THEN DO;
        M=A(I);
/*/     SOME K FIXED WHERE 1<=K<=10 . M=A(K) BY SOMIN, I;
        ALL K FIXED WHERE 1<=K<I+1. M>=A(I)
        BY INTRO,
          PROOF;
          ARBITRARY K FIXED WHERE 1<=K<I+1;
          K<I | K=I BY ARITH, K<I+1;
          M>=A(K) BY CASES, K<I | K=I,
            PROOF;
            CASE K<I;
            M>=A(K) BY ALLEL, ASM, K;
            CASE K=I;
            M=A(K);
            M>=A(K) BY ARITH, M=A(K);
            QED;
          QED;  */
    ELSE DO;
/*/     M>=M(I) BY ARITH, ￢(M<A(I));

        ALL K FIXED WHERE 1<=K<I+1. M>=A(I)
        BY INTRO,
          PROOF;
          ARBITRARY K FIXED WHERE 1<=K<I+1;
            K<I | K=I BY ARITH, K<I+1;
            M>=A(K) BY CASES, 1<=K<I | K=I,
              PROOF;
              CASE K<I;
              M>=A(K) BY ALLEL, ASM,  ;
              CASE K=I;
              M>=A(I) BY ARITH, ￢(M<A(I));
              M>=A(K);
              QED;
          QED;  */
    END;
END;
/*/ ALL K FIXED WHERE 1<=K<10+1 . M>A(K)   */
```

2.
```
DIVIDE:  PROCEDURE (A,B,Q,R);
DCL (A,B) FIXED READONLY;
DCL (Q,R) FIXED;

/*/ ASSUME A>=0, B>0;
    ATTAIN A = B*Q+R, 0<=R<B;   */

/* COUNT IN Q THE NUMBER OF TIMES B CAN BE SUBTRACTED
   FROM A   */

/*/ R = B*0+R BY ARITH;
    R<=R BY ARITH;   */

R=A;
Q=0;

/*/ SOME I FIXED . (I>=0 & R<=I) BY SOMIN, R;   */

DO WHILE (R-B>=0);

   /*/ ASSUME A = B*Q+R, R>=0;   */
       ARB I FIXED WHERE R<=I;
       -(R<=0) BY ARITH, R-B>=0,+,B>0;
       A = B*(Q+1) + (R-B) BY ARITH, A = B*Q+R;
       R-B<=I-1 BY ARITH, R<=I,-,B>0;   */
       R = R-B;
       Q = Q+1;
END;

/*/ R<B BY ARITH, ¬(R-B>=0),+,B;   */
END DIVIDE;
```

V PROCEDURES

§5.1 INTRODUCTION

Procedures are as important to proofs as they are to programs. They serve like lemmas in conventional proofs, decomposing the argument into logically separate pieces which may be analyzed and structured independently. They are most useful when parameterized to apply at several different steps of the argument. Adapting them to a particular step usually involves substituting expressions for the parameters. These parameters are program variables as well as logical variables. Thus, the notion of substitution for program variables is critical to the use of procedures. It is a subtle notion requiring even more care than the already delicate matter of substitution of expressions for (logical) variables (discussed in II §3). The fact that we treat only external procedures without static external variables helps keep the presentation of rules simple.

Procedures are especially useful if they can be recursive. However, proofs involving recursive procedures require careful attention because they involve patterns of inductive argument far more intricate than the already error prone simple inductions of part IV and of ordinary number theory.

§5.2 SYNTAX

1. In addition to the components of ordinary PL/CS procedures, PL/CV procedures may have auxiliary (shielded) parameters and logical information in the heading.

procedure-def → label: PROCEDURE[(parameter_list)]
 [RECURSIVE];

This portion
is called the
heading.

 {declaration, define_statement}*
 ASSUME [label:] assertion;
 ATTAIN [label:] assertion;
 [ARBITRARY n FIXED WHERE T;]
 argument
 END [label];

Note: The attribute RECURSIVE is needed on recursive procedures only for compatibility with PL/I.

2. We add to the old categories as follows:

procedure_call_stmt → CALL identifier[(expression_list)];

unit → procedure_call_statement

control_punctuation → return_statement

 return_statement → RETURN;

 expression_list → expression {, expression}*

Note: Actual parameters corresponding to shielded formal
parameters must be shielded.

§5.3 SUBSTITUTION

1. We extend an analysis of substitution for free variables to the case of variables occurring in commands.

Definition: Among the *binding occurrences* of a variable
x enumerated in II.2.4(ii) and IV.3.2 is now included
case 9, occurrence of x as a readwrite parameter to a
procedure call (said to be *binding call*), i.e.

 9. CALL p(...x...) where the formal parameter corresponding to x is readwrite.

An occurrence of a variable is said to be *bound in* an argument A iff the conditions of the definition in IV.3.2 hold or

9. The occurrence is in an assertion or command L of A (or of a subargument of A) for which there is *some* execution path from the beginning of A to L containing a binding call, CALL p(...x...).

Definition: If $A(x_1,\ldots,x_n)$ is an argument with free variables $x_1,\ldots,x_n$, then expression t_i is *free for* x_i provided x_i does not occur in the scope of any operators containing binding occurrence of variables in t_i, i.e. no variable of t_i is captured when t_i is substituted for x_i.

For example, in the two line argument

```
/*: Y=X+1 */
/*: Z=Y*Z */
```

the expression Y+2 is free for X but not for Y or Z.

2. In order to describe substitution for bound variables, we use the notation A(y//x) to mean that y is substituted for *every* occurrence of x, bound and unbound, in the argument A. Thus for the argument

```
/*: Y=X+Y;                    */
/*/ ALL X FIXED . X≠Z;        */
/*/ IF X<0 THEN Y=2; ELSE Y=X; */
```

The operator Y//X results in

```
/*: Y=Y+Y;                    */
/*/ ALL Y FIXED . Y≠Z;        */
/*/ IF Y<0 THEN Y=2; ELSE Y=Y; */
```

Notice that when Y is substituted for X in the ELSE clause, it is "captured" by the binding occurrence of Y at the assignment Y=X+Y.

Definition: Say that y is *free for bound x in A* if and only if in A(y//x) no variable occurrence in A acquires a new binding in A(y//x).

In the above example, Y is not free for X since at the occurrence of X in the ELSE Y=X phrase, the occurrence of X acquires a new binding in A(y//x), it is bound by

353

Y=Y+Y.

The notation is extended in the obvious way to treat $A(y_1//x_1,\ldots,y_n//x_n)$. These notions will be useful in describing the rules for parameter substitution in PL/CV.

§5.4   PROOF RULES

1. In describing the proof rules it will be convenient to have this definition.

Definition: The *apparent domain* of a procedure is the cartesian product of the types of the parameters in order of appearance. The *(real) domain* is the subset of the apparent domain on which the procedure halts. The *assumed domain* is the subset of the apparent domain which satisfies the input assumption.

The proof rules must guarantee that the assumed domain is a subset of the real domain.

2.   Enumeration of rules

A procedure definition can be introduced when we know that its body is a correct argument from the input assumption. The following rule says this. (The tokens PROOF, QED are enclosed in <> to indicate that they are not actually present.)

NONRECURSIVE PROCEDURE INTRODUCTION

```
        <PROOF;>
           ASSUME A;
           argument

              where B before each
              RETURN
              '0'B
        <QED;>
```

```
        p: PROCEDURE (parameter_list);
           {declaration, definition}*
           ASSUME A;
           ATTAIN B;
           ARBITRARY n FIXED WHERE T;
           argument
           END p;
```

354

RECURSIVE PROCEDURES INTRODUCTION

A set of mutually recursive procedures can be introduced if and only if they each terminate on their assumed domains.[†] An argument involving these procedures can be (simultaneously) introduced if it is a correct induction argument. Namely:

p: PROCEDURE $(\overline{v}, \overline{w})$ [RECURSIVE];
   $\overline{v}$ READONLY;
   $\overline{w}$ READWRITE;
   $\overline{x}$ EXTERNAL;
   ASSUME IN_p $(\overline{v}, \overline{w}, \overline{x})$
   [ARBITRARY n FIXED WHERE $T_p(n, \overline{v}, \overline{w}, x);$]
   ATTAIN OUT_p;
   $\neg T(0);$
    .
    .
    .

   $\left. \begin{array}{l} T_q(n, \overline{t}, \overline{u}, \overline{x}) \\ IN_q(\overline{t}, \overline{u}, \overline{x}) \\ CALL\ q\ (\overline{t}, \overline{u}); \end{array} \right\}$ for each call of a procedure q in the set.

    .
    .
    .

   OUT_p $(\overline{v}, \overline{w}, \overline{x});$
   before each RETURN;
    .
    .
    .

   END p;

The conclusion is the set of procedures itself and the mutually recursive argument.

The arbitrary statement is needed only for recursive procedures.

The $\overline{x}_p$ is the subset of the external variables used in p.

[†] These are the completed procedures of *A programming Logic*.

PROCEDURE CALL(PROCEDURE ELIMINATION)

```
p: PROCEDURE (v̄,w̄);
       v̄          READONLY;
       w̄     /* READWRITE */;
       x̄          EXTERNAL;
       ASSUME IN_p;
       ARBITRARY n FIXED WHERE T_p(n);
       ATTAIN OUT_p;
       .
       .
       .
       OUT_p;     }    for each return    SOME m FIXED.(m>=0 &
       RETURN;    }    in the body            T_p(m,t̄,ū,x̄)
       .                                      IN_p(t̄,ū,x̄)
       .
       .
       END ;
```

$$\text{CALL } p(\bar{t},\bar{u});$$

$$\text{OUT}_p(\bar{t}/\bar{v},\ \hat{u}/\bar{w},\ \bar{x});$$

provided 1. If ū consists entirely of simple variables,
             then û=ū. But if an array element
             $a(\exp_1,\ldots,\exp_n)$ occurs in u, then in û
             that element is replaced by $a(\hat{\exp}_1,\ldots,\hat{\exp}_n)$
             as described in ARRAY ACCESSIBILITY.

2. No variable of ū,x̄ occurs in t̄.

3. All variables in ū,x̄ are distinct.

This means that if $a(\exp_1,\ldots,\exp_n)$ and $a(\exp'_1,\ldots,\exp'_n)$
appear as parameters in t̄,ū or x̄ and if the proviso
requires that these variables be distinct, then there must
be a hypothesis that $\neg(\exp_1=\exp'_1 \ \&\ldots\&\ \exp_n=\exp'_n)$

These provisos are simple sufficient ways to guarantee
that no capture of variables occurs in the substitution.
They are not always necessary. See FINE POINTS for other
less stringent guarantees.

When array elements are passed to a procedure as in CALLp(A(I); A(J), I, J) we would like to conclude by general accessibility conditions that A(K) for K$\neq$I, K$\neq$J are not changed. The current version of the implemented system does not allow this generality, but as a temporary measure it allows the user to easily deduce it using the following accessibility axiom. ARRAY ACCESSIBILITY

for each list of (m) occurrences of an array A of dimension n as a readwrite parameter

$$IN_p(\ldots A(e_1),\ldots,A(e_m)\ldots),\hat{A}=A,\ \hat{e}_1=e_1,\ldots,\hat{e}_m=e_m$$
$$CALL\ p(\ldots A(e_1),\ldots,A(e_m)\ldots)$$

$$OUT_p(\ldots A(\hat{e}_1),\ldots,A(\hat{e}_m)\ldots)\ \&$$
$$ALL\ (i_1,\ldots,i_n)\ FIXED\ WHERE$$
$$"\neg(i_1,\ldots,i_n) = \hat{e}_1"\ \&\ldots\&$$
$$"\neg(i_1,\ldots,i_n) = \hat{e}_m"\ .$$
$$A(i_1,\ldots,i_n) = \hat{A}(i_1,\ldots,i_n)$$

where e_j is a list of n expressions, say $exp_{j1},\ldots,exp_{jn}$.
The phrase

$$"\neg(i_1,\ldots,i_n) = \hat{e}_j"\ \text{abbreviates}\ \neg(i_1=\hat{exp}_{j1}\&\ldots\&i_n=\hat{exp}_{jn}).$$

For completeness we also need the RETURN RULE

$$\frac{RETURN}{A}$$

which allows any conclusion at a position from which RETURN is accessible.

3. Proofs

The definition of proof is as in IV.4 except that the definition of accessibility must now be additionally restricted to include the changes to the concept of bound variable introduced in §5.3.

357

§5.5 <u>EXAMPLES</u>

```
DSWAP:  PROCEDURE(X,Y,I,J /*/, X0,Y0,I0,J0 */);
        DCL (X,Y,I,J) FIXED;
  /*/   DCL (X0,Y0,I0,J0) FIXED;   */
  /*/   ASSUME X=X0 & Y=Y0 & I=I0 & J=J0;  */
  /*/   ATTAIN Y=X0 & X=Y0 & J=I0 & I=J0;  */
        DCL(T1,T2) FIXED;
        T1=X;
         X=Y;
  /*/    X=Y0;  */
        Y=T1;
        T2=I;
         I=J;
  /*/    I=J0;  */
        J=T2;
  /*/    X=Y0 & Y=X0 & I=J0 & J=I0  */
        END DSWAP;
```

Now let us use this double swap in a main program.

```
TEST:   PROC OPTIONS(MAIN);
        DCL (A(3) I,J) FIXED;
  /*/   DCL (B(3), AI, AJ, I0, J0) FIXED      */
        A(1)=1; A(2)=2; A(3)=3;
        I=2; J=3;
  /*:   B=A;                                  */
  /*:   AI=A(I);                              */
  /*:   AJ=A(J);                              */
  /*/   AI=B(I) & AJ=B(J)                     */
  /*:   I0=I;                                 */
  /*:   J0=J;                                 */
  /*/   I0=2 & J0=3;                          */
        CALL DSWAP(A(I), A(J), I, J /*/, AI, AJ, I0, J0 */);
  /*/   A(I0)=AJ & A(J0)=AI & I=J0 & J=I0;
  /*/ HYP:  ALL K FIXED WHERE K ¬=I0 & K ¬=J0 . A(K)=B(K);
  /*/   1 ¬=2 BY ARITH;                       */
  /*/   1 ¬=3 BY ARITH;                       */
  /*/   A(1)=B(1) BY ALLEL, HYP, 1;           */
  /*/   A(J)=AJ & A(I)=AI;                    */
  /*/   A(J)=B(J) & A(I)=B(I);                */
        END TEST;
```

```
ASSIGN:   PROCEDURE(A,B);
          DCL A FIXED;
          DCL B FIXED READONLY;
    /*/ ASSUME B>=0; */
    /*/ ATTAIN A=B; */
          DCL BB FIXED;
          A=0;
          BB=B;
    /*/ BB < BB+1 BY ARITH; */
    /*/ BB+1 >= 0 BY ARITH, BB >= 0; */
    /*/ SOME D FIXED WHERE D>=0 . BB<D BY SOMIN, BB+1; */
          CALL INCR (A,BB /*/, 0, (b) */);
    /*/ A=B BY ARITH, A = 0+B; */
          RETURN;
END ASSIGN;

INCR:    PROCEDURE(A,B /*/,AA,BB */)
          DCL (A,B) FIXED;
   /*: DCL (AA,BB) FIXED READONLY; */
   /*/ ASSUME B>=0, AA=A, BB=B; */
   /*/ ARB D FIXED WHERE B<D; */
   /*/ ATTAIN A = AA+BB, B=0; */
   /*/ ¬(B<0) BY ARITH, B>=0;
   /*/ ATTAIN A = AA+BB, B=0;
          IF B¬=0
          THEN DO;
              /*/ B-1 >= 0 BY ARITH, B>=0, B¬=0; */
              /*/ B-1 < D-1 BY ARITH, B<D; */
                  A = A+1;
                  B = B-1;
                  CALL INCR (A,B /*/, AA+1, BB-1 */);
              /*/ A = AA+BB BY ARITH, A = (AA+1)+(BB-1); */
                  END;
          ELSE DO;
              /*/ B=0 BY ARITH, ¬(B¬=0); */
              /*/ A = A+0 BY ARITH, A = AA; */
                  END;
          RETURN;
END INCR;
```

REVERSE:

PROCEDURE (A,L,U /*/,
    DCL A(*) FIXED;
    DCL (L,U) FIXED READONLY;
/*: DCL B(*) FIXED;
    DCL C(LBOUND(A,1): HBOUND(A,1)) FIXED;   */

    ASSUME A=B & LBOUND(A,1)<=L&U<=HBOUND(A,1);
    ATTAIN INNER: ALL I FIXED WHERE 0<=I<=U-L. A(L+I) =
               B(U-I),
        OUTER: ALL I FIXED WHERE (LBOUND(A,1)<=I<L|U<I<=
               HBOUND(A,1). A(I) = B(I);
/*   ACHIEVE THE REVERSAL OF A BETWEEN L AND U BY
    EXCHANGING A(L), A(U) AND REVERSING A FROM L+1 TO U-1 */
/*/   ARBITRARY D FIXED WHERE U-L+1<D;
    ¬(U-L+1<0) BY ARITH, L<=U+1,-,L; */
/*/   ATTAIN INNER & OUTER; */
    IF (U<=L)
        THEN DO;
    /* ATTAIN INNER: SINCE U<=L, I=0, RESULT IS DIRECT */
    /*/ ALL I FIXED WHERE 0<=I<U-L. A(L+1) = B(U-I)
        BY INTRO;
        PROOF;
        ARBITRARY I FIXED WHERE 0<=I<=U-L;
            U-L<=0 BY ARITH, U<=L,-,L;
            U-L=0 BY ARITH, 0<=I<=U-L<=0;
            I=0 BY ARITH, 0<=I<=U-L<=0;
            L+0=L BY ARITH;
            U-0=L BY ARITH, U-L=0,+,L;
            A(L+1)=(AU-I); /# BY SUBST, I=0 #/
        QED;
    /* ATTAIN OUTER: NO CHANGE TO A, RESULT IMMEDIATE. */
    /*/ OUTER BY INTRO; */
END;

ELSE DO; L<U BY ARITH, ¬(U<=L);
       /* INITIAL INFORMATION FOR SWAP */
           /* ARRAY SUBSCRIPTS IN BOUNDS */
              L<HBOUND(A,1) BY ARITH, L<U, U<=HBOUND(A,1);
              LBOUND(A,1)<=U BY ARITH, L<U, LBOUND(A,1)<=L;*/

```
     /* SUBSTITUTIONS ARE FREE - NO ALIASING */
     /*/ L ¬=U BY ARITH, L<U;   */

        CALL SWAP(A(L), A(U), /*/, B(L), B(U)  */)
     /* CONCLUSIONS OF SWAP LEMMA  */
     /*/ C1: A(U)=B(L) & A(L)=B(U)  */
     /*/ C2: ALL J FIXED WHERE J ¬=L & J ¬=U. A(J)=B(J)  */
 /*   INITIAL INFORMATION FOR REVERSE   */
     /* INPUT CONDITION SATISFIED */
     /*/ L+1<=(U-1)+1 BY ARITH, L<U; */

     /* DEPTH PARAMETER SATISIFIES INPUT ASSUMPTION TO
        REVERSE */
     /*/ (U-1)-(L+1)+1 < D-1 BY ARITH, U-L+1<D,-,1; */
     /* CURRENT VALUES OF A NAMED                */
     /*: C=A;                                    */
     /*/ C(U)=B(L) & C(L)=B(U);                  */
     /* RELATE B AND C  */
 /*/ CB: ALL J FIXED WHERE J ¬=L & J ¬=U. C(J)=B(J)  */

CALL REVERSE (A,L+1,U-1,/*/,C       */);
  /*  INDUCTION HYPOTHESES  */
 /*/  IND1: ALL J FIXED WHERE 0<=J<=(U-1)-(L+1).
          A(L+1+J)=C(U-1-J);  */
 /*/  IND2: ALL K FIXED WHERE (LBOUND(A,1)<=K<L+1|U-1<K<
          HBOUND(A,1)). A(K)=C(K);  */
  /* CONCLUSIONS FROM INDUCTION HYPOTHESIS  */
 /*/  ALL J FIXED WHERE (LBOUND(A,1)<=J<L|U<J<HBOUND(A,1)).
      A(J)=B(J);
      BY INTRO,
          A(J)=B(J) BY CASES,  LBOUND(A,1)<=J<L|U<J<=
                               HBOUND(A,1)
          PROOF;
          CASE LBOUND(A,1)<=J<L;
              J<L+1 BY ARITH, J<L;
              A(J)=C(J) BY ALLEL, IND2,J;
              J ¬=L by ARITH, J<L;
              J ¬=U BY ARITH, J<L<U;
              C(J)=B(J) BY ALLEL, CB,J;
          CASE U<J<=HBOUND(A,1);
              U-1<J BY ARITH, U<J;
              A(J)=C(J) BY ALLEL, IND2,J;
              J ¬=U BY ARITH, U<J;
              J ¬=L BY ARITH, L<U<J;
              C(J)=B(J) BY ALLEL, CB,J;
      QED;
```

361

```
/#   CONCLUDE INNER  #/
          ALL I FIXED WHERE 0<=I<=U-L. A(L+1)=B(U-I)
          BY INTRO, PROOF;
          /#   CONSIDER THE CASES I=0, 1<=I<=(U-L)-1,
               I=U-L                                           #/
          /#   CASE 1<=I<=(U-L)-1 IS TREATED AS
               0<=I<=(U-1)-(L+1)                               #/
          /#   THE CASES MUST BE TREATED INDIRECTLY BE-
               CAUSE OF LIMITATIONS OF ARITHMETIC RULES    #/


     DI:  I=0|I>0 BY ARITH, I>=0;
          A(L+I)=B(U-I) BY CASES, DI;
          PROOF;
               CASE I=0;  /# FIRST MAIN CASE #/
                         L<L+1 BY ARITH;
                         A(L)=C(L) BY ALLEL, IND2,L;
                         A(L)=B(U);  /# SUBSTITUTION IN
                                          C(L)=B(U) #/
                         A(L+0)=B(U-0) BY ARITH, A(L)=B(U)
               CASE I>0;

                         DUL:  I<U-L|I=U-L BY ARITH,
                               I<=U-L;
                         A(L+I)=B(U-I) BY CASES, DUL
                         PROOF;
                              CASE I<U-L; /# SECOND MAIN
                                             . CASE      #/
                                             /# 1<=I<=(U-L)-1,
                                             /# USE INDUCT- #/
                                             /# ION HYP     #/
                                   /# TRANSFORM INTERVAL TO   #/
                                   /# MATCH INDUCTION FORMULA #/
                                   0<=I-1 BY ARITH, 1<=I;
                                   I-1<=(U-1)-(L-1) BY ARITH
                                                   I<(U-L);
                                   0<=I-1<=(U-1)-(L-1);
                         X: A(L+1-(I-1))=C(U-1-(I-1)) BY ALLEL, ID1,I-1;
                            A(L+I)=C(U-I) BY ARITH, X;
                            L<U-I BY ARITH, I<U-L,+,L-I
                            U-I ¬=L BY ARITH, L<U-I;
                            U-I ¬=U BY ARITH, U=U,-,I>0;
                            C(U-I)=B(U-I) BY ALLEL, CB, U-I;
```

```
          CASE I=U-L;   /# THIRD MAIN CASE  #/
                L+(U-L)=U BY ARITH;
                U-(U-L)=L BY ARITH;
                L+I=U & U-I=L;
                C(L+I)=B(U-I)  /# BY SUB IN C(U)=B(L)  #/
                U-1<U BY ARITH;
                A(U)=C(U) BY ALLEL, IND2,U;
                A(L+I)=C(L+I);
          QED;
       QED;                                      */
   END;
   RETURN;
END REVERSE;
```

VI   FUNCTIONS

§6.1   INTRODUCTION

Rules for introducing recursive and nonrecursive function definitions are nearly identical to the corresponding rules for recursive and nonrecursive procedures. However, since functions play an entirely different role in the logic than do assignments and their generalization to procedures, the rules for using defined functions have an entirely different character than the rules for using procedures. The first difference is that functions affect the most basic level of the logic, the predicate calculus. Secondly, all arguments to functions (including external variables) are readonly, so the intricate problem of substitution for bound variables does not arise. Thirdly, defined functions occur in every type of expression, so their use complicates every rule which mentions expressions, that is every rule except the goto and label rules.

§6.2   SYNTAX

```
      f:   PROCEDURE(parameter_list) RETURNS(type)
           [RECURSIVE];
           {declaration, define_statement}*
           ASSUME assertion;
           [ARBITRARY variable FIXED WHERE assertion;]
heading    ATTAIN assertion;
           {proof_stmt}*
           {declaration}*
           argument
           END f;
```

Note 1: f is any label. It is the function name. The attain statement may involve f itself.

Note 2: A function argument in PL/CS may not involve procedure calls or input/output statements. This is to guarantee that function evaluations produce no side effects.

Note 3:   External variables must be readonly.

§6.3   PROOF RULES

In order to introduce a set of mutually recursive function definitions, we must know that each halts on its assumed domain.   This is demonstrated almost exactly as in the case of procedures.

RECURSIVE FUNCTION INTRODUCTION

> f: PROCEDURE $(\overline{v})$;
>
> > v   READONLY;
>
> > $\overline{x}$ EXTERNAL;
> > ASSUME $IN_f(\overline{v},\overline{x})$;
> > ARB D FIXED WHERE $T_f(D,\overline{v},\overline{x})$
> > ATTAIN $OUT_f(\overline{v},\overline{x};\ f(\overline{v}))$);
> > $\neg T_f(0,\overline{v},\overline{x})$;
> >
> > .
> > .
> > .
> >
> > $\left\{ \begin{array}{l} T_g(D\text{-}1,\ \overline{u},\overline{x}),\ IN_g(\overline{u},\overline{x}) \\[6pt] \text{before any occurrence} \\ \text{of } g(\overline{u}) \text{ for any } g \text{ in} \\ \text{the set of mutually} \\ \text{recursive definitions} \end{array} \right.$ $\left\{ \begin{array}{l} OUT_f(\overline{v},\overline{x},exp) \text{ before} \\[6pt] \text{each occurrence of} \\ RETURN(exp) \end{array} \right.$
> >
> > .
> > .
> > .
> >
> > '0'B
> > END f;

Note, not all externals need be mentioned in IN_f, IN_g.

A function definition in PL/CV comprises an algorithm and a lemma bout the defined function.   This lemma has the form

$$IN_f(\overline{v},\overline{x})\ \&\ T_f(d,\overline{v},\overline{x}) \Rightarrow OUT_f(\overline{v},\overline{x},f(\overline{v}))$$

where $\overline{v}$ can be considered universally quantified (and $\overline{x}$ are parameters of the definition). The lemma is proved by a form of induction, so we call it the *recursive function induction* rule. The invocation rule is simple called *function lemma invocation.*

FUNCTION LEMMA INVOCATION

f: PROCEDURE $(\overline{v})$ RETURNS(atype);

    v READONLY;

    x READONLY EXTERNAL;
ASSUME $IN_f(\overline{v},\overline{x})$;

ARBITRARY d FIXED WHERE $T_f(d,\overline{v},\overline{x})$;

ATTAIN $OUT_f(\overline{v},\overline{x},f(\overline{v}))$;

      .   SOME m FIXED.m>=0&$T_f(\overline{m},\overline{u},\overline{x})$;
      . $IN_f(\overline{u/v},\overline{x})$
      .

    END f

$OUT_f(\overline{u},\overline{x},f(\overline{u}))$ BY FUNCTION, f(u);

For completeness we also need the rule

RETURN RULE

$$\frac{RETURN(exp)}{A}$$

EXAMPLES

Here is an example of a recursively defined exponential function.

```
REXP:   PROCEDURE(V,E) RETURNS(FIXED) RECURSIVE;
    DCL (B,E) FIXED;  /*/ READONLY */
/*/ ASSUME E>=0, B>0; */
/*/ ARBITRARY N FIXED WHERE E<N */
/*/ ATTAIN REXP(B,E) = B**E */
    ¬(E<0) BY ARITH, E>=0;
/*/ ATTAIN REXP(B,E) = B**E */
IF (E=0)
    THEN DO;
/*/       B**0 = 1 BY FUNCTION, EXP(B,0); */
          RETURN(1);
          END;
    ELSE DO;
/*/       E>0 BY ARITH, E¬=0, E>=0; */
/*/       E-1 < N-1 BY ARITH, E<N; */
          B**E = B*(B**(E-1)) BY FUNCTION, EXP(B,E);
          REXP(B,E-1) = B**(E-1) BY FUNCTION, REXP(B,E-1);
          RETURN(B*REXP(B,E-1));
          END;
END EXP;
```

Correspondingly, a LOG function may be defined

```
LOG:   PROCEDURE (B,N) RETURNS (FIXED) RECURSIVE;
DCL (B,N) FIXED;
/*/ ASSUME B>1, N>0; */
/*/ ATTAIN B**LOG(B,N)<=N, LOG(B,N)>=0, B**(LOG(B,N)+1)>N; */
/*/ ARBITRARY D FIXED WHERE N<=D; */
/*/ ¬(N<=0) BY ARITH, N>0; */
/*/ ATTAIN '0'B; */
    IF (N<B)
    THEN DO;
          /*/ B**0 = 1 BY FUNCTION, EXP(B,0); */
          /*/ 1<=N BY ARITH, N>0; */
          /*/ 0>=0 BY ARITH; */
          /*/ B**(0+1) = B*B**0 BY FUNCTION, EXP(B,0); */
          /*/ B*1 > N BY ARITH, N<B; */
          RETURN(0);
          END;
    ELSE DO;
```

```
/*/ B>0 BY ARITH, B>1;  */
/*/ DEFINE R = MOD(N,B);  */
/*/ 0<=R<=ABS(B) BY FUNCTION, MOD(N,B);  */
/*/ ABS(B) = B BY FUNCTION, B>0;  */
/*/ (N/B)*B+R = N BY FUNCTION, DIVIDE(N,B);
/*/ N>=B;  */
/*/ N>0; */
/*/ B>0; */
/*/ N/B>0 BY FUNCTION, DIVIDE (N,B); */
/*/ B/B > 0 BY FUNCTION, SIGN;  */

/* PROVE TERMINATION */
/*/ S1:  N/B < (N/B)*B BY ARITH, 1<B, *, N/B>0; */
/*/ S2:  (N/B)*B <= N BY ARITH, (N/B)*B+R = N, -,
            R>=0; */
/*/ N/B <= D-1 BY ARITH, S1, S2, N<=D; */

/* PROVE FIRST ATTAIN */
/*/ T0:  LOG(B,N/B) >=0 BY FUNCTION, LOG(B,N/B); */
/*/ T1:  B**(LOG(B,N/B)+1) = B*B**LOG(B,N/B) */
/*/          BY FUNCTION, EXP(B, LOG(B,N/B)); */
/*/ T2:  B**LOG(B,N/B) <= N/B BY FUNCTION,
            LOG(B,N/B); */
/*/ T3:  B*B**LOG(B,N/B) <= (N/B)*B BY ARITH,
            T2, *, B>0; *; */
/*/ B**(LOG(B,N/B)+1) <= N BY ARITH, T1, T3, S2; */

/* PROVE SECOND ATTAIN */
/*/ LOG(B,N/B)+1 >=0 BY ARITH, T0; */

/* PROVE THIRD ATTAIN */
/*/ U1: B**(LOG(B,N/B)+1+1) = B*B**(LOG(B,N/B)+1) */
/*/          BY FUNCTION, EXP(B, LOG(B,N/B)+1); */
/*/ U2: B**(LOG(B,N/B)+1) > N/B BY FUNCTION,
            LOG(B,N/B); */
/*/ U3: B**(LOG(B,N/B)+1) >= N/B+1 BY ARITH, U2; */
/*/ U4: B*B**(LOG(B,N/B)+1) >= (N/B)*B+B BY ARITH,
            U3, *, B>0; */
/*/ U5: (N/B*B+B > N BY ARITH, B>R, +, (N/B)*B =
            (N/B)*B, N=(n/B)*B+R; */
/*/ B**(LOG(B,N/B)+1+1) > N BY ARITH, U1, U4, U5; */
RETURN(LOG(B,N/B)+1); */
END;
END LOG;
```

ADDENDA

When large software systems are new, even the basic
parts may be dynamic. For this first public issue of the
manual we have provided this section to list the latest
minor additions and corrections which can not be easily
encorporated into the main text. The changes are listed
by part and section.

Part II

§2.2
   2. Assertion

An assertion list is

assertion_list → [label:] assertion {, [label:2 assertion}*

Assertion lists can be used anywhere in the grammar that
[label:] assertion appears. Thus for example these forms
are permitted:

   ASSUME assertion_list
   CHOOSE variable_list type WHERE assertion_list

§2.4

The justification BY INTRO, $\exp_1, \ldots, \exp_n$ is allowed
for existential introduction as well as the phrase
BY SOMIN, $\exp_1, \ldots, \exp_n$.

Part III

§3.2

Consequences of the associativity and commutativity
rules for the arithmetic operators +, * as well as the
boolean operators &, v are immediate from formulas actually
appearing in the proof. However, the immediate propositional rules and the immediate equality rules cannot be applied to these consequences until they are written in the
proof.

REFERENCES

Aho, Alfred V. and Jeffrey D. Ullman, *The Theory of Parsing, Translation and Compiling*, Vol. I: *Parsing*, Prentice-Hall, Englewood Cliff, N.J., 1972.

Aho, Alfred V., John E. Hopcroft, and Jeffrey D. Ullman, *The Design and Analysis of Computer Algorithms*, Addison-Wesley, Reading, Mass., 1974.

Aiello, L., M, Aiello, and R.W. Weyhrauch, PASCAL in LCF: Semantics and examples of proof, *Theoretical Computer Science*, 5, 2, Oct. 77, 135-178.

Anderson, John M. and Henry W. Johnstone, *Natural Deduction*, Wadsworth Publishing Co., Belmont, Ca., 1962.

Ashcroft, E.A. and W.W. Wadge, Lucid - A Formal System for Writing and Proving Programs, *SIAM J. on Computing*, 5,3, Sept. 1976, 336-354.

Ashcroft, E.A., M. Clint, and C.A.R. Hoare, Remarks on Program proving: jumps and functions, *Acta Informatica*, Vol. 6, 1976, 317.

Backus, John W., Programming Language Semantics and Closed Applicative Languages, *Proceedings of the ACM Symposium on Principles of Programming Languages*, ACM, 1973, 71-86.

Banachowski, L., A. Kreczmar, G. Mirkowska, H. Rasiowa, and A. Salwicki, *An Introduction to Algorithmic Logic*, Banach Center Publications, Vol. 2, Warsaw, 1977.

Bishop, Errett, *Foundations of Constructive Analysis*, McGraw Hill, New York, 1967.

Boyer, R.S. and J.S. Moore, Proving theorems about LISP functions, *JACM*, Vol. 22, 1, Jan, 1975, 129-144.

Burstall, R.M., Proving properties of programs by structural induction, *Computing* J. Vol. 12, 1, 1969, 41-48.

Burstall, R.M., Program Proving as Hand Simulation with a Little Induction, *Information Processing 1974, IFIP* North-Holland, Amsterdam, 1974, 308-312.

Brady, J.M., *The Theory of Computer Science, A Programming Approach*, Chapman and Hall, London, (John Wiley & Sons, Inc., N.Y.), 1977.

Cardoza, E., R. Lipton, and A.R. Meyer, Exponential-Space Complete Problems for Petri Nets and Commutative Semi-groups, *Proceedings of the Eighth Annual ACM Symposium on the Theory of Computing*, ACM, New York, May, 1976.

Cartwright, Robert S., User defined data types as an aid to verifying Lisp programs, *Proceedings of Third International Conference on Automata, Programming Languages*, Edinburgh Press, Edinburgh, 1976, 228-256.

Cartwright, Robert and Derek C. Oppen, Unrestricted procedure calls in Hoare's logic, *Conference Record of the Fifth Annual ACM Symposium on Principles of Programming Languages*, ACM, 1978, 131-140.

Chan, Tat-Hung, An Algorithm for Checking PL/CV Arithmetic Inferences, Technical Report 77-326, Computer Science Department, Cornell University, 1978.

Chang, C.C. and H.J. Keisler, *Model Theory*, North-Holland, Amsterdam, 1973.

Cherniavsky, John C., Function Iteration Logics and Flowchart Schemata, *Computing*, 14, 1975, 285-314.

Cherniavsky, John C. and Robert L. Constable, Representing
Program Schemes in Logic, *Proceedings Thirteenth Annual
Symposium on Switching and Automata Theory*, College Park,
Maryland, Oct. 1972, 27-39.

Church, Alonzo, *Introduction to Mathematical Logic*, Vol. I,
Princeton University Press, Princeton, 1956.

Clint, M. and C.A.R. Hoare, Program Proving: Jumps and
Functions, *Acta Informatica* 1, 1972, 214-224.

Constable, Robert L., On the Theory of Programming Logics,
*Proceedings of the Ninth Annual ACM Symposium on
Theory of Computing*, ACM, May, 1977, 269-285.

Constable Robert L., A Constructive Programming Logic,
Information Processing 77, North-Holland, New York,
1977, 733-738.

Constable, Robert L. and James E. Donahue, An elementary
formal semantics for the programming language PL/CS,
Cornell Computer Science Department, Technical Report
76-271, March 1976.

Constable, Robert L. and David Gries, On Classes of Program
Schemata, *SIAM J. on Computing*, 1, 1, March 1972, 66-118.

Conway, Richard W., *A Primer on Disciplined Programming
Using PL/I, PL/CS and PL/CT*, Winthrop, Cambridge, Mass.,
1978.

Conway, Richard W. and Robert L. Constable, PL/CS a Disciplined Subset of PL/C, Technical Report 76-273, Cornell University, Computer Science Department, 1976.

Conway Richard W. and David Gries, *An Introduction to
Programming, A Structured Approach Using PL/I and PL/C-7*,
Second Edition, Winthrop, Cambridge, Mass., 1975.

Cook, Stephen A., Soundness and Completeness of an Axiom System for Program Verification, *SIAM J. on Computing*, 7,1, Feb. 1978, 70-90.

Cooper, David C., Programs for Mechanical Program Verification, *Machine Intelligence 6*, B. Meltzer, D. Michie, [ed], American Elsevier, New York, 1971, 43-59.

Corcoran, John, William Frank, and Michael Maloney, String Theory, *Journal of Symbolic Logic*, 39,4, Dec. 1974, 625-637.

Dahl, O.J., E.W. Dijkstra, and C.A.R. Hoare, *Structured Programming*, Academic Press, New York, 1972.

deBakker, J.W., *Recursive Procedures*, Mathematical Center, Amsterdam, 1971.

deBakker, J.W. and W.P. deRoever, A Calculus for recursive program schemes, *Automatia, Languages and Programming*, M.Nivat [ed.], North-Holland, Amsterdam, 1973, 167-196.

deBruijn, N.G., The mathematical language AUTOMATH, its usage and, some of its extensions, *Symposium on Automatic Demonstration Lecture Notes in Math*, Vol. 125, Springer-Verlag, New York, 29-61, 1970.

Dijkstra, E.W., A Constructive Approach to the Problem of Progran Correctness, *BIT*, 8,3, 1968, 174-186.

Dijkstra, E.W., *A Discipline of Programming*, Prentice-Hall, Englewood Cliffs, N.J., 1976.

Donahue, James E., *Complementary Definitions of Programming Language Semantics Lecture,Notes in Computer Science 42*, Springer -Verlag,New York, 1976, 172pp. (also Ph.D. thesis University of Toronto, 1975).

Dummett, Michael, *Elements of Intuitionism*, Clarendon Press, Oxford, 1977.

Enderton, Herbert B., *A Mathematical Introduction to Logic*, Academic Press, New York, 1972.

Engeler, E. *Formal Languages: Automata and Structures*, Markham, Chicago, 1968.

Elspas, B, K. Levitt, R. Waldinger, and A. Waksman, An Assessment of Techniques for Proving Program Correctness, *Computing Surveys*, 4,2, June 1972, 97-147.

Fischer, M.J. and Richard Ladner, Propositional Modal Logic of Programs, *Proceedings Ninth Annual ACM Sumposium on Theory of Computing*, ACM, May 1977, 286-294.

Fitting, Melvin C., *Intuitionistic Logic Model Theory and Forcing*, North-Holland, Amsterdam, 1969.

Floyd, Robert W., Assigning meaning to programs, *Proceedings of Symposia in Applied Mathematics*, Vol. XIX, American Math. Soc., Providence, 1967, 19-32.

Gentzen, Gerhard, Investigations into logical deductions, in *The Collected Works of Gerhard Gentzen*, M.E. Szabo [ed.], North-Holland, Amsterdam, 1969, 68-128. Original in Untersuchungen uber das logische Schliessen *Math. Zeitschrift* 39, 1935, 176-210, 405-431.

Gödel, Kurt, On Formally Undecidable Propositions of *Principia Mathematica* and Related Systems, *From Frege to Gödel*, J. van Heijenoort [ed.], Harvard University Press, Cambridge, 1967, 596-616. (Original published in 1931).

Goldstine, H.H. and John von Neumann, Planning and coding of problems for an electronic computing instrument, *John von Neumann Collected Works*, Part 2, Vols. 1-3, A.H. Taub [ed.], Pergamon, New York, 1963. (Original published in 1947.)

Good, D.I., Ralph L. London, and W.W. Bledsoe, An Interactive Program Verifier, *IEEE Transactions on Software Eng.*, Vol. SE-I, March 1975, 59-67.

Good, D.I. and L.C. Ragland, Nucleus - A Language of Provable Programs, *Program Test Methods* W. Hetzel [ed.], Prentice-Hall, Englewood Cliffs, N.J., 1973.

Gordon, M., R. Milner, and C. Wadsworth, Edinburgh LCF internal report CSR-11-77, Department of Computer Science, University of Edinburgh, Sept. 1977.

Greibach, S., *Theory of Program Structures: Schemes, Semantics, Verification, Lecture Notes in Computer Science*, Vol. 36, Springer-Verlag, New York, 1975.

Gries, David, *Compiler Construction for Digital Computers*, John Wiley & Sons, New York, 1971.

Gries, David, The Multiple Assignment Statement, *IEEE Transactions on Software Eng.*, Vol. SE-4, 2, March 1978, 89-93.

Harel, David, A.R. Meyer, and V. Pratt, Computability and Completeness in Logics of Programs, *Proceedings Ninth Annual ACM Symposiun on Theory of Computing*, ACM, May, 1977, 261-268.

Harel, David, Amir Pnueli, and J. Stavi, A Complete Axiomatic System for Proving Deductions about Recursive Programs, *Proceedings Ninth Annual ACM Symposium on Theory of Computing*, ACM, May, 1977, 249-260.

Hartmanis, Juris, Relations between Diagonalization, Proof Systems, and Complexity Gaps, Technical Report 77-312, Computer Science Department, Cornell University, 1977 (to appear in *Theoretical Computer Science*).

Hilbert, David and P. Bernays, *Grundlagen der Mathematik* I, (2nd edition), Springer-Verlag, 1968, (first edition 1934).

Hoare, C.A.R., Quicksort, *Computing J.*, 5,1, 1962, 10-15.

Hoare, C.A.R., An Axiomatic Basis for Computer Programming, *Comm. ACM* 12, Oct. 1969, 576-581.

Hoare, C.A.R. Procedures and Parameters, an Axiomatic Approach, *Symposium on Semantics of Algorithmic Languages*, E. Engeler [ed.], *Lecture Notes in Math* No. 188, Springer-Verlag, New York, 1971, 102-116.

375

Hoare, C.A.R. and P.E. Lauer, Consistent and Complementary Formal Theories of the Semantics of Programming Languages, *Acta Informatica*, 3, 2, 1974, 135-154.

Hoare, C.A.R. and Niklaus Wirth, An Axiomatic Definition of the Programming Language Pascal, *Acta Informatica* 2, 1973, 333-355.

Hopcroft, John E. and Jeffrey D. Ullman, *Formal Languages and their Relation to Automata*, Addison-Wesley, Reading, Mass., 1969.

Igarashi, Shigeru, Ralph L. London, and David C. Luckham, Automatic Program Verification I: A Logical Basis and its Implementation, *Acta Informatica* 4, 1975, 145-182.

Iverson, K., *Algebra: An Algorithmic Approach*, Addison-Wesley, Menlo Park, Ca., 1975.

Jensen, Kathleen and Niklaus Wirth, *PASCAL User Manual and Report* (second edition), Springer-Verlag, Berlin, 1975.

Keisler, H. Jerome, *Elementary Calculus*, Prindle, Weber & Schmidt, Inc., Boston, Mass., 1976.

Kernighan, Brian W. and P.J. Plauger, *Software Tools*, Addison-Wesley Publishing Co., Reading, Mass., 1976.

King, James C., Symbolic Execution and Program Testing, *Comm. ACM*, 19, 7, July 1976, 385-394.

King, James C. and R.W. Floyd, An intepretation oriented theorem prover over the integers, *Proceedings Second Annual ACM Symposium on Computing Theory*, ACM, 1970, 169-179.

Kleene, S.C., *Introduction to Metamathematics*, D. Van Nostrand, Princeton, 1952.

Knuth, D., *The Art of Computer Programming*, Vol. I, Addison-Wesley, Reading, Mass., 1968.

Knuth, D.E., Structured Programming with go to Statements, *ACM Computing Surveys*, 6, 4, Dec. 1974, 261-302.

Kozen, Dexter C., *Complexity of Finitely Presented Algebras*, Ph.D. Thesis, Cornell University, Computer Science Department, 1977.

Krafft, Dean B., The Assertion Table system for the PL/CV2 Program Verifier, Technical Report 78-337, Computer Science Department, Cornell University, 1978.

Kreisel, G., A survey of proof theory II, *Proceedings of the Second Scandinavian Logic Symposium*, J.E. Fenstad [ed.], North-Holland, Amsterdam, 1971, 109-170.

Kröger, F., Logical rules for natural reasoning about programs, *Automata, Languages and Programming*, S. Michaelson, R. Milner [ed.], Edinburgh Press, Edinburgh, 1976, 87-98.

Lampson, B.W., J.J. Horning, R.L. London, J.G. Mitchell, and G.J. Popek, Report on the programming language Euclid, *SIGPLAN Notices*, 12, 2, 1977.

Linger, R.C., H.D. Mills, and B.I. Witt, *Structured Programming Theory and Practice*, Addison-Wesley, Reading, Mass., (to appear) (IBM, Addison-Wesley preliminary version, 1977).

London, R.L., Bibliography of Proving the Correctness of Computer Programs, *Machine Intelligence* 5, Edinburgh University Press, Edinburgh, 1970, 569-580.

Luckham, David C., Program Verification and Verification Oriented Programming, *Information Processing* 77, B. Gilchrist [ed.], IFIP, North-Holland, Amsterdam, 1977, 783-794.

Luckham, D.C., M.R. Park, and M.S. Paterson, On Formalized Computer Programs, *JCSS*, 4, 1970, 220-249.

Luckham, David C. and Norihisa Suzuki, Automatic Program Verification V: verification-oriented proof rules for arrays, records and pointers, Report No. STAN-CS-76-549, Computer Science Department, Stanford University, March 1976.

Manna, Zohar, *Mathematical Theory of Computation*, Mc-Graw Hill, New York, 1974.

Manna, Zohar and A. Pnueli, Formalization of properties of functional programs, *JACM*, 17, 3, July 1970, 555-569.

Manna, Zohar, and R.J. Waldinger, *Studies in Automatic Programming Logic*, North-Holland, Amsterdam, 1977.

Manna, Zohar and Richard Waldinger, The Logic of Computer Programming Report NO. STAN-CS-77-611, Computer Science Deaprtment, Stanford University, Aug. 1977.

Matiyasevich, Y.V., Diophantine representation of recursively enumerable predicates, *Proceedings of the Seoncd Scandinavian Logic Symposium*, J.E. Fenstad [ed.], North-Holland, Amsterdam, 1970, 171-178.

McCarthy, J., Recursive Functions of Symbolic Expressions and Their Computation by Machine, Part I, *Communications ACM*, 3, April 1960, 184-195.

McCarthy, John, A Basis for a Mathematical Theory of Computation, *Computer Programming and Formal Systems*, P. Braffort and D. Hirschberg [ed.], North-Holland, Amsterdam, 1963, 33-70.

Mills, Harlan D., Top-down programming in large systems, *Debugging Techiques in Large Systems*, R. Rustin [ed.], Prentice-Hall, Englewood Cliffs, N.J., 1971, 41-55.

Milne, Robert and Christopher Strachey, *A Theory of Programming Language Semantics parts a and b*, Chapman and Hall, London (John Wiley & Sons Inc., New York), 1976.

Milner, Robin, Implementation and applications of Scott's Logic for Computable Functions, *Proceedings ACM Conference on Proving Assertions about Programs*, Las Cruces, New Mexico, ACM, 1972, 1-6.

Milner, R., L. Morris and M. Newey, A Logic for Computable Functions with Reflexive and Polymorphic Types LCF Report No. 1, Department of Computer Science, University of Edinburgh, Jan. 1975.

Morris, J.H. Jr. and B. Wegbreit, Subgoal induction, *Comm. ACM*, 20, 4, April 1977, 209-222.

Musser, David R., A Proof Rule for Functions, ISI/RR-77-62, Information Sciences Institute, 1977.

Myhill, John, Constructive Set Theory, *The Journal of Symbolic Logic*, 40, 3, Sept. 1975, 347-382.

Naur, P., Proof of Algorithms by General Snapshots, *BIT* 6, 4, 1966, 310-316.

O'Donnell, Michael J., *Computing in Systems Described by Equations, Lecture Notes in Computer Science*, 58, Springer-Verlag, Berlin, 1977.

Ore, Oystein, *Number Theory and its History*, McGraw-Hill, New York, 1948.

Park, David, Fixed Point Induction and Proofs of Program Properties, *Machine Intelligence 5*, American Elsevier, New York, 1969, 59-78.

Peter, Roza, *Recursive Functions* (2nd edition), Academic Press, New York, 1967.

Pratt, Terrence W., *Programming Languages: Design and Implementation*, Prentice-Hall, Englewood Cliffs, N.J., 1975.

Pratt, Vaughan R., Semantical Considerations on Floyd-Hoare Logic, *Proceedings of Seventeenth Annual Symposium on Foundations of Computer Science*, ACM, Oct. 1976, 109-121.

Prawitz, D., *Natural Deduction*, Almqvist & Wiksell, Stockholm, 1965.

Prawitz, Dag, Ideas and results in proof theory, *Proceedings of the Second Scandinavian Logic Symposium*, J.E. Fenstad [ed.], North-Holland, Amsterdam, 1970, 235-308.

Privitera, John, *On the Proof Theory of Programming Logics*, Ph.D. thesis, Cornell University, Computer Science Department, 1978.

Quine, Willard Van Orman, *Methods of Logic* (revised edition), Holt, Rinehart and Winston, New York, 1961.

Rasiowa, Helena, *Algorithmic Logic*, Institute of Computer Scince Polish Academy of Science, Warsaw, 1977.

Sierpinski, W., *Cardinal and Ordinal Numbers*, Warsaw, 1965.

Schwartz, J.T., Correct-Program Technology, Courant Computer Science Report #12, Courant Institute of Math. Sciences, New York University, Sept. 1977.

Scott, Dana, Existence and description in formal logic, *Bertrand Russell Philosopher of the Century*, R. Schoenman [ed.], George Allen & Univin Ltd., 1967, 181-200.

Scott, Dana, Outline of a Mathematical Theory of Computation, *Proceedings Fourth Annual Princeton Conference on Information Sciences & Systems*, Princeton, 1970, 169-176.

Scott, Dana, Data Types as Lattices, *SIAM Jouranl on Computing*, 5, 3, Sept. 1976.

Scott, Dana and Christopher Strachey, Toward a Mathematical Semantics for Computer Languages, *Proceedings of the Symposium on Computers and Automata*, Polytech Institute of Brooklyn, New York, 1971, 19-46.

Smullyan, R.M., *First-Order Logic*, Springer-Verlag, New York, 1968.

Stanat, Donald F. and David F. McAllister, *Discrete Mathematics in Computer Science*, Prentice-Hall, Inc., Englewood Cliffs, N.J., 1977.

Stoy, Joseph E., *Denotational Semantics: The Scott-Strachey Approach to Programming Language Theory*, The M.I.T. Press, Cambridge, 1977.

Szabo, M.E., *The Collected Papers of Gerhard Gentzen*, North-Holland, Amsterdam, 1969.

Tarski, A., The semantic conception of truth and the foundations of semantics, *Philos and Phenom. Res.*, 4, 1944, 341-376.

Troelstra, A.S., *Metamathematical Investigation of Intuitionistic Arithmetic and Analysis, Lecture Notes in Math*, Vol. 344, Springer-Verlag, New York, 1973.

Turing, A.M. On checking a large routine, in Report of a Conference on High-Speed Automatic Calculating Machines, University Math. Lab., Cambridge, 1949, 67-69.

Vuillemin, Jean, Correct and Optimal Implementation of Recursion in a Simple Programming Language, *Proceedings of the Fifth ACM Symposium on Theory of Computing*, ACM, 1973, 239-244.

Wegbreit, Ben, Constructive Methods in Program Verification, *IEEE Transactions on Software Engineering* SE-3, 3, May 1977, 193-209.

Weyhrauch, Richard W., A Users Manual for FOL Report No. STAN-CS-77-432, Computer Science Department, Stanford University, July 1977.

Wirth, Niklaus, *Systematic Programming: An Introduction*, Prentice-Hall, Inc., Englewood Cliffs, 1973.

Yeh, Raymond T., *Current Trends in Programming Methodology*, Vol. I, *Software Specification and Design*, Vol. II, *Program Validation*, Prentice-Hall, Englewood Cliffs, N.J., 1977.

INDEX